GLOBAL PERSPECTIVES ON E-COMMERCE TAXATION LAW

Markets and the Law

Series Editor:
Geraint Howells
Lancaster University, UK

Series Advisory Board:
Stefan Grundmann – Humboldt University of Berlin, Germany
Hans Micklitz – Bamberg University, Germany
James P. Nehf – Indiana University, USA
Iain Ramsay – York University, Canada
Charles Rickett – University of Queensland, Australia
Reiner Schulze – Münster University, Germany
Jules Stuyck – Katholieke Universiteit Leuven, Belgium
Stephen Weatherill – University of Oxford, UK
Thomas Wilhelmsson – University of Helsinki, Finland

Markets and the Law is concerned with the way the law interacts with the market through regulation, self-regulation and the impact of private law regimes. It looks at the impact of regional and international organizations (e.g. EC and WTO) and many of the works adopt a comparative approach and/or appeal to an international audience. Examples of subjects covered include trade laws, intellectual property, sales law, insurance, consumer law, banking, financial markets, labour law, environmental law and social regulation affecting the market as well as competition law. The series includes texts covering a broad area, monographs on focused issues, and collections of essays dealing with particular themes.

Other titles in the series

The Intersection of Rights and Regulation
New Directions in Sociolegal Scholarship
Edited by Bronwen Morgan
ISBN 978-0-7546-4982-3

The Yearbook of Consumer Law 2007
Edited by Geraint Howells, Annette Nordhausen, Deborah Parry
and Christian Twigg-Flesner
ISBN 978-0-7546-4733-1

Consumer Protection in the Age of the 'Information Economy'
Edited by Jane K. Winn
ISBN 978-0-7546-4709-6

Global Perspectives on
E-Commerce Taxation Law

SUBHAJIT BASU
Queen's University Belfast, UK

Routledge
Taylor & Francis Group

LONDON AND NEW YORK

First published 2007 by Ashgate Publishing

Published 2016 by Routledge
2 Park Square, Milton Park, Abingdon, Oxfordshire OX14 4RN
711 Third Avenue, New York, NY 10017, USA

First issued in paperback 2016

Routledge is an imprint of the Taylor & Francis Group, an informa business

British Library Cataloguing in Publication Data
Basu, Subhajit
   Global perspectives on e-commerce taxation law. - (Markets
   and the law)
   1. Electronic commerce - Taxation - Law and legislation
   2. Internet industry - Taxation - Law and legislation
   I. Title
   343'.0558538433

Library of Congress Cataloging-in-Publication Data
Basu, Subhajit, 1973-
   Global perspectives on E-commerce taxation law / by Subhajit Basu.
      p. cm. -- (Markets and the law)
   Includes bibliographical references and index.
   ISBN 978-0-7546-4731-7
   1. Electronic commerce--Taxation--Law and legislation. 2. Electronic commerce--
Taxation--Law and legislation--United States. I. Title.

   K4487.E43B37 2007
   343.04--dc22

                                                                    2007002013

ISBN 13: 978-1-138-24707-9 (pbk)
ISBN 13: 978-0-7546-4731-7 (hbk)

Contents

List of Figures and Tables

Preface

Taxation of e-commerce is a major concern for international agencies and tax authorities worldwide. In its most advanced form, e-commerce allows unidentified purchasers to pay obscure vendors in 'electronic cash' for products that are often goods, services and licences all rolled into one. A payee may be no more than a computer that can take up 'residence' anywhere; national boundaries are of no consequence whatsoever. The current debate over taxation of e-commerce has, to some extent, been little more than a rehash of a similarly inconclusive scholarly and legislative debate that raged over mail-order sales during the 1980s. However, in the case of e-commerce, the added question is how to reconcile national fiscal boundaries with the borderless world of the internet.

The concept of taxation involves jurisdiction: we see this from the '*Boston Tea Party Rebellion*' in which tea was taxed as it physically landed on American shores, to sophisticated concepts in international taxation. A government's authority to tax had always been based on territory and jurisdiction. These systems now face a serious challenge from the development of e-commerce. The trade in goods and services over the internet has fundamentally altered the accepted boundaries and conventions. Some of the concepts underlying the principles of international consensus on taxation were always flawed, but those flaws have become much more apparent with the advent of e-commerce. E-commerce makes the concepts of permanent establishment (to determine location of manufacture), point of sale (for the application of relevant tax rates), income classification (based on source of income), product classification (for preferred tax rates), etc. difficult to apply. Within the borderless world of the internet, e-commerce effectively obliterates any footprints leading to the buyers' and sellers' locations. Governments are already losing millions in tax revenue through the penetration of e-commerce within their jurisdictions and their tax authorities are finding it increasingly difficult to stem this haemorrhage.

While examining the impact of e-commerce on taxation, there is always the danger of jumping to a conclusion without adequately understanding the nature of the problem raised by the rules that evolved before the dawn of the internet or e-commerce. Hence, the purpose of this book is directed at answering two questions: who will bear the tax and compliance burden? How will the resulting taxes be collected? It includes a glimpse at the innovations in the fields of technology and taxation that are in the offing and represents a preview of the e-commerce dynamic. It is the very existence and character of this dynamic that makes advancement on these questions so important and mandates a solution which is neither a patchwork of calibration nor a reengineering that is too tightly structured, but has the flexibility necessary to accommodate the ever-changing face of e-commerce. The argument presented shows that international e-commerce taxation is a real problem rather than a conceptual problem. In the text, I have tried to include both direct taxation and indirect taxation by detailing the principles of taxation surrounding them in an even-handed manner. However, in some areas more emphasis has been put on consumption taxation, particularly in Chapter 7 while dealing with the loss of revenue and in Chapter 10 where a possible mechanism for a solution is suggested.

The book begins by thoroughly describing and analyzing how the basic concepts and principles of international taxation are affected by e-commerce. It also presents general facts that are intended to give some overall sense of the e-commerce phenomena. The information describes both the current status of e-commerce as well as projections for its growth. The book covers a wide array of activities such as discussions on the basic principles that govern direct and indirect taxes, a concise explanation of how and what happens when e-commerce is conducted, examination of the ways in which businesses are using the new technology in conducting their everyday activities, discussion of the application of existing tax principles to e-commerce, exploration of questions and problems raised by applying tax rules that evolved before e-commerce, and observations and suggestions for a variety of approaches to international tax problems resulting from e-commerce and the associated benefits and problems. Since the implications of e-commerce vary from industry to industry, it focuses on the broader issues and presents the arguments for and against taxation of e-commerce. The book also presents a synthesis of the conclusions reached by the various commentators and selected economic and technological developments that give a fuller dimension to the issues but also raise the level of complexity of the issue of tax collection proposals ranging from the traditional vendor collection method to models employing third parties. The discussion and observations are focused on basic rules and policy choices;[1] no specific course of action from the direct taxation point of view is advocated. The most important feature of my argument is presented in the last chapter where I present a proposal of how to achieve in practice an online collection and compliance mechanism for e-commerce by an effective utilization of the technology that created the internet and then e-commerce, based on the principle that a system should be simple and transparent, capable of capturing the overwhelming majority of appropriate revenues, and easy to implement. Trade, whether conducted via the medium of the internet or any other, is (very simply) trade. Therefore, the taxation of it is a legal issue not a technological one. However, if the technology makes it impossible to extract tax, society has a problem. In my view the technology has the capacity to provide a solution.

---

1   Representative national laws are only discussed at applicable points.

Acknowledgements

I am greatly indebted to all those, too many to name individually, too extensive to fully acknowledge, who, in various ways, contributed towards the successful realization of this book. Nevertheless, an attempt needs to be made. This book would not have been completed without the continued guidance and inspiration of Philip Leith. I would like to gratefully acknowledge the support of John Morrison, Kirean McEvoy and Sally Wheeller. I would like to express my sincere gratitude to Richard Jones for his invaluable advice as the work progressed, which provided me with much needed confidence, and Scott Taylor, whose arguments in various venues advanced my learning and understanding of the project.

I am particularly indebted to Caroline Woods, Physiotherapist at Queen's PEC, for her treatment to overcome my shoulder and back pain; without her help it would have been nearly impossible to finish this book. I must also thank all my friends and my colleagues at Queen's for their generous and helpful advice.

It is the love of my parents that has inspired me to write this book; I thank my father for being an inspiration, my mother, my elder brother, my sister-in-law and my nephew for their support and encouragement; I wouldn't be in the position of writing this book without them. Finally, I thank my wife Baishakhi for her love and for being there during the time of pain and difficulties.

This book is dedicated to the memory of my grandfather,
Basanta Kumar Basu

Chapter 1

Internet and E-Commerce

Introduction

The relationships between taxation and technological developments have always been interactive, dynamic and complex. Law-making can be slow and tedious but technology often proceeds at breakneck speed. What are the implications of this apparent temporal gap between technological innovation and legal change? On the downside, the gap in time promotes legal uncertainty where affected parties cannot fully understand their legal rights and obligations.

> On the upside, the gap in time would seem to permit more analysis and sober thought prior to policy implementation. Moreover, the unpredictable nature of technological developments suggests that, in many circumstances, legal reform may not be suitable, at least not until the implications of the technological changes can be better understood.[1]

The internet represents the greatest technological revolution since the industrial revolution of the nineteenth and twentieth centuries. The advancement of technology has always aided international business. This first, introductory chapter will provide an insight into the technology that created the internet and other electronic networks. The second part of the chapter will provide a background discussion of the issues relating to e-commerce and its influence on taxation. It will cover e-commerce issues like growth and benefit of e-commerce, direct and indirect e-commerce and security issues. In terms of taxation, this section will analyze the models of internet economy and their impact on e-commerce and the key reasons why e-commerce raises the tax issue. In this chapter, instead of dealing with these issues with respect to the particular provisions they challenge, I approach them on the basis of their technological features. This will be a more useful means for the categorization of these issues and will help to identify potential solutions that must be tailored for the technology.

1.1 Digital Challenge to Taxation: Importance of 'Getting It Right'

> We are in the midst (or perhaps only at the beginning) of a revolution in the technology of commerce that will have important but perhaps largely unknown ramifications for the ability to levy and collect taxes. Radical improvements in our ability to store, process, and communicate information are changing the way products are packaged and delivered.

---

1 Cockfield (2004c) Toward a Law and Technology Theory Canadian Association of Law Teachers Annual Meeting, June 2, 2004, Law Forum Panel on 'What is Legal Knowledge?' University of Winnipeg.

Understanding these technological developments and their ramifications is necessary if we are to be successful in designing the tax policies and institutional arrangements needed to cope with them. As is often the case, it is useful to look back, to prior revolutions in information technology, to understand the future and the nature of the problems to be faced. Several times in the past, as now, developments in the technology of storage, processing, and communication of information have led to changes in modes of commerce in information and thus in the feasibility of various forms of taxation.[2]

The concept of taxation is co-related to jurisdiction. From the '*Boston Tea Party Rebellion*' in which tea was taxed as it physically landed on American shores, to sophisticated concepts in international taxation, a government's authority to tax has always been based on territory and jurisdiction. These systems now face a serious challenge from the development of e-commerce; the trade in goods and services over the internet has fundamentally altered accepted boundaries and conventions.[3] The definition of a 'tax' is thus far from straightforward, even if conventional taxes are considered. However, in many countries, in addition to legally imposed taxes, there are also arbitrary and irregular tax-like levies imposed by the authorities. These are a part of a larger phenomenon of the necessity to make extra payments when interacting with government officials in many countries, particularly at the local level and at lower levels of bureaucracy. These also form a part of the burden of taxation and have socio-economic consequences. In most countries, conventionally defined legal taxes and levies constitute a significant proportion of the Gross Domestic Product (GDP), and finance a major part of government expenditure. It is therefore essential that these systems be designed to achieve the appropriate trade-offs among revenue generation, allocation efficiency, equity, and administration and compliance costs.

Taxation is not simply a matter of efficient economic management and functional governance but serves to define, enable and constrain the historical meaning of the state and the possibility of society.[4] However, the emergence of international and possibly global dimensions of taxation is a far more recent phenomenon. 'As this implies, the institutional practices of taxation have been subject to continuous if not constant renegotiation throughout their history in response to the changing forms and functions of the societies they help to constitute.'[5] Much argument about the internet proceeds as if the problem were new and thousands of years of political and legal thought simply irrelevant in the light of the internet's uniqueness. Some commentators have argued that this notion is manifestly false: many of the questions that apply to the internet today arose in similar form during the popularization of other technologies such as modern shipping, aviation and telecommunications (to name

---

2 McLure (1997) 'Taxation of Electronic Commerce: Economic Objectives, Technological Constraints, and Tax Laws', *Tax Law Review*, Symposium on Taxation and Electronic Commerce.

3 Basu (2003) 'Relevance of E-Commerce for Taxation: an Overview', *Global Jurist Topics*: Vol. 3: No. 3, Article 2, http://www.bepress.com/gj/topics/vol3/iss3/art2.

4 Cameron (2006) Turning Point? The Volatile Geographies of Taxation, *Antipode* 38 (2), 236-258. doi: 10.1111/j.1467-8330.2006.00578.x.

5 Cameron (2006) Turning Point? The Volatile Geographies of Taxation, *Antipode* 38 (2), 236-258. doi: 10.1111/j.1467-8330.2006.00578.x.

only a few). The answers that human societies forged to those questions then can help us answer analogous questions today. Yet recognizing that the internet lays on a historical continuum of transformative technologies leads us to ask two interrelated questions that merit attention before delving into others: What characteristics mark the internet as a novel and genuinely disruptive technology? What about the new challenges the internet poses? I have probably managed to answer the first question here in this chapter. In response to the second, taxation is an area where the internet and e-commerce have raised grave concerns. Five or ten years ago, it was fashionable in academic circles to make dire predictions about what the internet would do to the nation state. Nothing less than the very survival of the state seemed to be in question.[6] Today, probably in embarrassment at this former misjudgment, it is fashionable to doubt that cross-border e-commerce is of any consequence to the state's main source of revenue, taxation. The truth, of course, lies somewhere between these two extremes of thought. The internet is neither fatal nor irrelevant for the nation state; it is one important factor in its continuous transformation.

Understanding the implications of the fiscal consequence of the e-commerce revolution is also a very difficult task, for reasons similar to those given above, not least the rate of change. First, there is this sheer increase in the magnitude of cross-border transactions. By significantly reducing the transaction costs of communicating and selling without regard to geographic boundaries or the size of the company, the internet permits companies that were once confined to local markets to sell goods, services and information internationally.[7] While tax authorities worldwide could fine-tune their existing catalogue or distance sales rules for indirect e-commerce, direct e-commerce makes tax evasion easy and bears low risk. Second, the digitization of information, the conversion of text, sound, images, video and other content into a series of ones and zeroes that can be transmitted electronically creates difficulties in defining the source, origin and destination of both production and consumption.[8] Third, the technical features of internet transactions create enormous problems for taxing authorities in establishing audit trails, in verifying parties to transactions, in obtaining documentation and in fixing convenient taxing points.[9] The nature of the internet is that it is uncontrolled[10] and anonymous. This weak link between activities carried out on the internet and the identity of the physical parties does not allow for accurate identification of the legal entity associated with an internet site or e-mail address. As the technology stands, internet addresses do not need to be permanent, nor do they automatically allow locating either the server or the legal entity behind it. Although domain names in internet addresses (internet addresses are URLs, that is 'uniform resource

---

6   Goldsmith and Wu (2006) *Who Controls the Internet? Illusions of a Borderless World* (Oxford University Press).

7   Neubig and Poddar (2000) 'Blurred Tax Boundaries: The Economy's Implications for Tax Policy', *Tax Notes*, August 28, 2000, pp. 1153, 1158.

8   Neubig and Poddar (2000) 'Blurred Tax Boundaries: The Economy's Implications for Tax Policy', *Tax Notes*, August 28, 2000, pp. 1153, 1158.

9   Owens (1997) 'The Tax Man Cometh to Cyberspace', paper presented at the Harvard Law School International Tax Program Symposium on Multi-jurisdictional Taxation of Electronic Commerce, April 5, 1997, p. 10.

10 Although there are different views on this.

locators') can state the location, domain names are not binding and are not always used. Similarly, e-mail addresses start to follow a certain structure but, again, there is no regulation that must be followed. By eliminating the need for intermediaries, particularly financial intermediaries on which governments have traditionally relied to facilitate tax compliance through reporting obligations, the internet enhances the danger of increased tax avoidance and evasion. 'From a tax compliance and administration perspective it is also problematic that the web address is not tied to a certain geographical location. This would further accumulate with the growth of m-commerce, whereby mobile communication using Wireless Application Protocols (WAPs) or other techniques that make distant communication possible are applied.'[11]

The basic question is how e-commerce interacts with traditional principles of taxation. While some authors debate that e-commerce has not transformed the fundamentals of taxation, others argue that there is a need for dramatic change.[12] Those favouring a tax assert that the introduction of an e-commerce tax would do irreparable harm to the growth of e-commerce as consumers will return to high street shops. However, this perception is not accepted without argument. Their opponents cite concerns of lower state government revenues due to increasing e-commerce sales, the resulting decrease in public good provision and issues regarding equity. The concern is for potential revenue loss and the uncertainties created for tax authorities. A provocative and interesting thought is submitted by Krever, who states that 'a more sober study will reveal that in many respects much of the hyperbole about e-commerce and tax is just that and in the overall scheme of things the impact of e-commerce on tax systems may be limited'.[13] Li[14] has also commented that there is nothing absolutely new under the sun. Governments and tax authorities continue to struggle with the same old problems such as determining what is the appropriate nexus that permits the exertion of tax jurisdiction over cross-border sales. Nevertheless, Li[15] maintains that the current international tax regime does not properly address the many vexing challenges faced by tax authorities and multinational firms today. These challenges include increasing regional and global trade and capital market integration and the movement toward more service-oriented economic activities for many countries. Cockfield[16] categorized tax commentators trading in this broader discourse as 'Doubting Thomases', 'Purists', and 'Pragmatists'.

Concerns have been expressed that e-commerce could result in the erosion of tax bases. Consumption taxes are levied on the principle of taxation at the place of

---

11 Westberg (2002) Cross-border Taxation of E-Commerce, IBFD p. 4.

12 Westberg (2002) Cross-border Taxation of E-Commerce, IBFD p. 53.

13 Krever (2000) 'Electronic Commerce and Taxation- A Summary of Emerging Issues', *Asia-Pacific Tax Bulletin*, at p. 151.

14 Li (2003) International Taxation in the Age of Electronic Commerce: A Comparative Study (Toronto: Canadian Tax Foundation, 2003)

15 Li (2003) International Taxation in the Age of Electronic Commerce: A Comparative Study (Toronto: Canadian Tax Foundation, 2003).

16 Cockfield (2004a) 'Formulary Taxation Versus the Arm's Length Principle: The Battle Among Doubting Thomases, Purists, and Pragmatists, *Canadian Tax Journal* Vol. 52, pp. 114-123.

consumption and according to rates set in individual countries or in individual states in the case of federal nations. E-commerce, however, has the potential to undermine the application of domestic and national tax rules. Tax planning for an e-business differs from tax planning for a traditional bricks and mortar company. Historically, the generation of income depended on the physical presence of assets and activities. This physical presence, or permanent establishment (PE), generally determined which jurisdiction had the primary right to tax the income generated. Because of the growth of electronic commerce, new e-business models (including digital market places, online cataloguess, virtual communities, subscription-based information services, online auctions and portals) have emerged. Each allows taxpayers to conduct business and generate income in a country with little or no physical presence in that country. The separation of assets and activities from the source of the income represents a significant departure from historic business models. This change creates new tax planning challenges and opportunities.

In this book I will examine several issues relevant to the current e-commerce tax debate in relation to direct and indirect taxation. The questions for this are derived from three broad questions: what should be taxed? Who should be entitled to tax? How should tax operate for e-commerce? The main concern is how to enforce taxes in the digital environment. Some attention is given to the problems of the application of traditional concepts to new phenomena. But there is hardly anyone who questions the concepts or the fundamental principles of tax law. The problems that I have outlined in the book are of three kinds: enforcement problems, application problems, and principal problems.

The enforcement problems are obvious. These are the problems that have been most thoroughly analyzed. They are also the problems most urgently needing a solution. The application problems have also been recognized and received their due share of attention. The principal problems, those concerning the fundamental principles and assumptions of tax law, have not been thoroughly analyzed. In fact, they are not recognized as problems. I have tried to show that these problems are more alarming than the problems of enforcement and the problems of application but that they tend to be overshadowed by these more easily grasped problems. This conservative approach may be justified from the point of view that one should not jump to conclusions. In the long run, however, it will not be tenable. The strain on traditional tax concepts will eventually result in the breakdown of the tax system. If we do not address the fundamental questions, but wait and see, we may wake up one day and find that the tax system has been so alienated from the economic and technological reality, that applying the rules is not just hard but downright impossible. The tax system will lose its legitimacy, which will benefit nobody. Such a breakdown could be avoided if the problems are recognized as problems and included in discussions among legislators. The questions that should be addressed include: can information be a relevant category in tax law? If so, how can it be defined in a way that is adequate from a legal, as well as an economic, and technological perspective? Should traditional taxation principles be abandoned? Should the tax system of the future be developed at a national or an international level? In what ways is the design of tax law dependent on other areas of law?

There is no doubt that any solutions that will be pursued will be constructed on compromises needed to maintain the revenue yield without placing unrealistic compliance burdens on the new businesses whose concern is understandably with markets, growth and profit and not with paying taxes. It is therefore immediately evident that it is crucial for the online entrepreneur to be aware of and fully understand all the implications of such means of taxation. In the light of this, legislators are increasingly concerned about their responsibility to bring forward, as quickly as possible, solutions to solve the problems introduced by e-commerce. Without workable rules, there will be a stronger incentive, particularly for smaller businesses, simply to ignore indirect tax requirements. 'It is already the case that no consumption tax can be enforced and collected 100 percent or anything like it – the variable is always the relative size and competitive distortion caused by choosing to trade in the black economy.'[17]

Obviously, if a country wants a competitive taxation regime and a decent level of social services then it needs a taxation base to sustain it. To stay competitive the weight must be kept off direct tax – income tax and company tax – and the indirect tax base must carry the burden of funding social services. A narrow base indirect tax cannot do it. To re-weight the tax system out of indirect tax and, by definition, into direct tax is a reverse direction. With the competitive challenges we face we cannot afford errors. Narrowing our indirect tax base, and its consequence of higher direct taxes, could do us great damage.[18] The changes that technology and communication have brought mean that bad decision-making is more evident and reactions to it faster and more severe. The advantage is greater than ever, the benefits can be greater than before, but the margins for error are much smaller.

The political implications of globalization on taxation as discussed before are even more far-reaching, particularly since the history of the state is inseparable from the history of taxation. The modern state, defined by the principle of exclusive sovereignty over a bounded territory was born out of the fiscal crisis of medieval European feudalism, which by the fourteenth and fifteenth centuries was increasingly incapable of raising sufficient revenues to support the mounting expenses of warfare.[19] The modern state was able to survive because it made fiscal sense: it was a form of political organization that was particularly well suited to taxing wealth and commerce. Now, the development of technology and the rise of international e-commerce are undermining the efficiency of the state as a taxing entity. It points to a continuing shift of taxation authority away from the exclusive domain of states and towards international forums and institutions, which are likely to play an increasingly important role in the design and perhaps the administration of

---

17 Jenkins (2000) 'The Application of VAT to E-Commerce', Ernst and Young.

18 The Hon. Peter Costello MP, Treasurer to The Sydney Institute, Commonwealth of Australia, 'Challenges and Benefits Of Globalisation', Wednesday, 25 July 2001, The Commonwealth Treasurer - Speeches - Challenges And Benefits Of Globalisation (25-07-2001).htm.

19 Paris (2001) 'Global Taxation and the Transformation of the State', *Department of Political Science, University of Colorado at Boulder, Paper presented at the 2001 Annual Convention of the American Political science association, San Francisco, August 30–September 2, 2001.*

tax policy. E-commerce creates a most suitable context in which the core theories, principles, rules and policies of international taxation can be examined, challenged and reconsidered. Briefly, the above argument rests on the following premises:

- that international e-commerce will continue to grow (as I have discussed before);
- that the spread of e-commerce will cause more challenges to existing systems of taxation;
- the national governments will ultimately demand taxation of digital commerce;
- to develop effective tax collection mechanisms will require utilization of technology and will require extensive international coordination.

E-commerce is a classic case of economic and technological change which forces us to consider how overlapping sources of national and transnational law can be shaped to cope with the challenge of rapid and unpredictable market developments. Taxation of e-commerce, then, is fascinating in its own right from the global perspective but, on a broader scale, it offers an intriguing case of limitations and possibilities for moulding an effective tax administrative regime involving national and transnational, public and private, which is designed to regulate but not damage the growth of e-commerce. It has been noted that the Chinese word for crisis combines the characters for 'danger' and 'opportunity'.[20] If the internet and e-commerce are threatening a crisis for global tax administration because of the dangers they create for existing tax regimes, they have created opportunities as well. Some of the long-standing problems in taxing cross-border income flows will require new forms of international fiscal cooperation and an inevitable reduction in national fiscal sovereignty. Internally, the concept of individual privacy may be severely tested as governments struggle to maintain their revenues in the face of new pressures to expand the underground economy, with its concomitant tax evasion. When it comes to the implications of e-commerce for taxation, we may perhaps be at the end of the beginning, but we are still a long way from the end. An interesting irony of e-commerce, in fact, is that both consumption and income taxation seem to be equally threatened.[21]

1.2   Evolution of the Internet

Interaction between people from different societies is today best personified by the internet – a tool that allows many more people to influence and be influenced by countless other individuals. It transcends national borders and engenders a supra-territorial effect. 'Technologies diffuse rapidly in the modern global economy.

---

20 *LaShawn A. v. Kelly*, 887 F. Supp. 297, 317 (D.D.C. 1995) <www.renewlife.org/faqs/faq_10.htm>. As cited in Hellerstein (2001) 'Electronic Commerce And The Challenge For Tax Administration' Paper presented to the *United Nations Ad Hoc Group of Experts on International Cooperation in Tax Matters in Geneva, Switzerland*, on September 12, 2001.

21 Bird (2003) Taxing Electronic Commerce: A Revolution in the Making, *C.D. Howe Institute Commentary*, No. 187.

Certainly, the diffusion of the technologies that make up the Internet occurred with great rapidity over the past two decades.'[22] Hence, the first question is what is the internet? There are many possible ways to answer this question. From the early 1960s, the United States Department of Defence funded research into interconnection of computers through the Advance Research Project Agency. The first computer network, known as APANET, was conceived and created in 1969 with four nodes by connecting computers using satellite and radio transmission technology. This became known as the internet project.[23] One of the main aims of the internet project was to create a computer network which would enable communication to continue even if a part of the network was unavailable, lost or even destroyed.

The internet was perceived as a medium of communication; however it developed as a 'complex technological system consisting of a body of protocol agreements that permit individuals to use resident software (or middleware) to send and retrieve text, information, and images in a distributed physical network by digital signals'.[24] The term 'internet' is best defined by the United States' Federal Networking Council as follows:

> Internet refers to global information system that
> - is logically linked together by globally unique address space based on the Internet Protocol (IP).
> - is able to support communications using the Transmission Control Protocol/ Internet Protocol suite.
> - provides, uses or makes accessible, either publicly or privately, high level services layered on the communications and related infrastructure described herein.[25]

The internet is a complex technological system because it relies on several essential subsystems: the physical infrastructure, terminals and servers, and software and technical agreements. The distributed network consists of the communication backbone, the local access points, and local network and packet switches and terminals which include a stand alone computer.[26] 'This physical infrastructure ensures interconnection so that people with appropriate equipment can be connected to a common network. The physical infrastructure, however, does not guarantee interoperability or the ability of people with different types of equipment to communicate.'[27] The interconnection of the various devices and computational facilities is made possible with the use of a set of communication standards, procedures and formats.[28]

---

22 Kogut (2003) *The Global Internet Economy*, The MIT Press, Cambridge, p. 1.

23 Kitchin (1998) *Cyberspace: The World in Wires*, John Wiley and Sons, Chichester, p. 30.

24 Kogut (2003) *The Global Internet Economy*, The MIT Press, Cambridge, p. 2.

25 October 24, 1995, Resolution of the US Federal Networking Council.

26 Kogut (2003) *The Global Internet Economy*, The MIT Press, Cambridge, p. 9.

27 Kogut (2003) *The Global Internet Economy*, The MIT Press, Cambridge, p. 12.

28 Kahn and Cerf (2004) 'What Is The Internet (And What Makes It Work)' in *Open Architecture as Communications Policy Preserving: Internet Freedom in The Broadband Era* editor Mark N Cooper, p. 18.

The procedures by which computers communicate with each other are called 'protocols' that allow people using different machines to communicate and govern the transmission of a signal over a distributed network. While this infrastructure is steadily evolving to include new capabilities, the protocols initially used by the Internet are called the 'TCP/IP' protocols, named after the two protocols that formed the principal basis for Internet operation.[29]

'TCP/IP is a compilation of rules that guarantee interoperability.'[30] The most important feature of TCP/IP is that it defines a packet switching network, in which data is broken up into standardized packets that are sent along multiple paths to be reassembled at the destination.

Interconnecting computers is an inherently digital problem. Computers process and exchange digital information, meaning that they use a discrete mathematical 'binary' or 'two-valued' language of 1s and 0s. For communication purposes, such information is mapped into continuous electrical or optical waveforms. The use of digital signalling allows accurate regeneration and reliable recovery of the underlying bits. For digital communications, packet switching is a better choice because it is far better suited to the typical 'burst' communication style of computers. Computers that communicate typically send out brief but intense bursts of data and then remain silent for a while before sending out the next burst. These bursts are communicated as packets which are very much like electronic postcards. The special computers that perform this forwarding function are called variously 'packet switches' or 'routers'. A router can potentially connect to any number of different LANs, WANs or WAN backbones. Together these routers and the communication links between them form the underpinnings of the internet. The internet protocol manages the addressing system by recognizing individual network nodes and providing information to route packages in the network. The internet protocol operates closely with an addressing system called domain names. Whenever a new network connects to the internet it is assigned a unique set of IP addresses. Each computer attached to the internet has a unique numeric representation, depending upon the network operator which might be a 'static' or permanent IP address or 'dynamic'. The internet protocol is responsible for the maintenance of privacy and the secure transmission of data. In essence, the internet is architecture although many people confuse it with its implementation. From the engineering perspective the internet consists of several technological layers.

When the Internet is looked at as architecture, it manifests two different abstractions. One abstraction deals with communications connectivity, packet delivery and a variety of end-end communication services and the other abstraction deals with the Internet as an information system, independent of its underlying communications infrastructure, which allows creation, storage and access to a wide range of information resources, including digital objects and related services at various levels of abstraction.[31]

---

29 Kahn and Cerf (2004) 'What Is The Internet (And What Makes It Work)' in *Open Architecture as Communications Policy Preserving: Internet Freedom in The Broadband Era* editor Mark N Cooper, p. 18.

30 Kogut (2003) *The Global Internet Economy*, The MIT Press, Cambridge, p. 13.

31 Kahn and Cerf (2004) 'What Is The Internet (And What Makes It Work)' in *Open Architecture as Communications Policy Preserving: Internet Freedom in The Broadband Era* editor Mark N Cooper, p. 18.

Since its inception, the internet has experienced phenomenal growth.[32] It is the view of many in the internet community, like Lawrence Lessig, that the phenomenal growth of the internet rests fundamentally on its design principles.

The evolution of the internet was based on two technologies and a research dream. The technologies were packet switching and computer technology which, in turn, drew upon the underlying technologies of digital communications and semiconductors. The research dream was to share information and computational resources. But that is simply the technical side of the story. However, the internet is not simply the product of technological solutions. Success and failure of the internet is intertwined with decisions made by governments, companies and consumers. 'For example, the distributed network could consist of fiber optic lines owned by Telephone Company and leased to an Internet Service Provider (ISP). Who provides the ISP service is not a technological question.'[33] These ISPs might be the telephone company, owners of the backbone or companies that specialize in these services. The internet as a concept did not arise out of the commercial sector. It is somewhat stunning to realize that even as late as 1990, there were very few who understood the potential to create interoperability among computers.[34]

In 1986, the National Science Foundation (NSF) which funded the internet infrastructure created NSFNET, which replaced ARPANET 1988 as the backbone of the internet. In 1991, for the first time, NSF relaxed its ban on commercial applications. The most significant technical innovation that happened was undoubtedly the introduction of the World Wide Web (WWW) in 1992.[35] In essence, the development of WWW is a triumph of form over function. 'In retrospect, protocol and standard needed to operate the web seem so obvious that it is a wonder that they were not invented all at once from the very beginning.'[36] The advent of browsers such as Netscape Navigator and Microsoft Internet Explorer served as the complete transformation of the internet from a text-based network to what has been described as a 'multimedia tapestry of full-colour information'.[37] Business, sensing the opportunity, began a mad rush to establish a 'presence' on the web.[38] Websites

---

32 The estimated number of internet users has grown from approximately 26 million in December 1995 to approximately 972 million in November 2005, which is about 15.2% of the world population. The growth rate of world internet usage between 2000 and 2005 has been 169.5%, while the continent of Africa has seen growth of 429.8%.

33 Kogut (2003) *The Global Internet Economy*, The MIT Press, Cambridge, p. 10.

34 Kogut (2003) *The Global Internet Economy*, The MIT Press, Cambridge, p. 15.

35 It was Timothy Berners-Lee of the European Particle Physics Laboratory (known as CERN, a collective of European high-energy physics researchers) who used a system known as hypertext to create links between files. The protocol simplified the writing of addresses, automatically searched the internet for the address indicated and automatically called up the document for viewing. By the end of 1990, the first piece of Web software was developed with the ability to view, edit and send hypertext documents through the internet. The Web was born.

36 Kogut (2003) *The Global Internet Economy*, The MIT Press, Cambridge, p. 14.

37 International Telecommunications Union (1999) *Challenges to the Network: Internet for Development*, ITU, Geneva.

38 To the user, a website is a series of 'pages' of information maintained by the operator of a participating computer or computer network, and contributed to by a vast number of content

may contain purely textual information; however the development of interfaces like CGI and Java has now made it possible to incorporate highly dynamic and interactive information. The fact that a web page can be constructed from material in many places also complicates questions as to where things happen. Physical and logical locations do not necessarily match. What appears to be a single website may in fact be distributed around servers all over the world as it is possible to assemble a web page from different locations around the world. This has obvious implications for the law to be applied and to jurisdiction.[39]

Much of the internet is self-regulated, for instance, by the World Wide Web Consortium (W3C), a United States-European Union consortium of private and public organizations, and the similarly constituted Internet Engineering Task Force (IETF) and the Internet Corporation for Assigned Names and Numbers (ICANN), still with minimal direct government interference.

> The Internet today is a widespread information infrastructure, the initial prototype of what is often called the National (or Global or Galactic) Information Infrastructure. Its history is complex and involves many aspects - technological, organizational, and community. And its influence reaches not only to the technical fields of computer communications but throughout society as we move toward increasing use of online tools.[40]

The internet provides direct communication and anonymous communication, permitting consumers and purchasers to conduct transactions in private. The flexibility, the low cost of maintaining a website, the ability to quickly disseminate information and the instantaneous communication to a large population of consumers, makes the internet an ideal environment for business transactions. 'One of the many progenies derived from the use of the Internet in everyday life is the development of electronic commerce. Unlike the evolution of the telephone for doing business, the Internet allows businesses to have more access to more customers in a shorter amount of

---

providers, including individuals, groups, corporations and governments. Web pages are also known as hypertext documents, because they have been constructed using the computer language known as HyperText Mark-up Language (HTML). Hypertext is a defining feature of the internet, in which a user can begin one document and easily find related documents stored on the same computer or on other computers connected to the internet, if a word or concept is linked. The system by which the transfer occurs is known as the Hyper Text Transport Protocol. Hyperlinks take two forms, 'linking' and 'framing'. In ordinary linking, an internet user, upon following the hyperlink, is transported to a new web page, which can be 'shallow' if the user is transported to the homepage of the website, or can be 'deep linking' if the user is taken to some other page on the website. Framing on the other hand involves the inclusion of a hyperlink on a web page which, when followed, causes another party's web content to be displayed within a 'frame' on the original web page. See Comer (2000) *The Internet Book* (3rd Edition), Prentice Hall, London, pp. 207–22.

39 Todd (2005) E-Commerce Law, Cavendish, London at p. 9.

40 Leiner, Cerf, Clark, Kahn, Kleinrock, Lynch, Postel, Roberts, Roberts and Wolff, 'A Brief History of the Internet,' http://www.isoc.org/internet/history/brief.shtml last visited on 2005-08-26.

time.'[41] However, the widespread adoption of electronic commerce by businesses and consumers raises a number of questions, from the technical to the policy-related.

1.3   Internet Service Provider (ISP)

From the engineering perspective, as mentioned before, the internet consists of several technological layers. These technological layers have experienced dramatic increases in functionality, with technological progress in one layer driving the complementary engine of change in other layers.[42] The Internet Infrastructure Layer consists of the telecommunications companies, internet service providers (ISPs), internet backbone carriers, 'last mile' access companies and manufacturers of end-user networking equipment all of which are a prerequisite for the web and the proliferation of e-commerce. The basic architecture of the internet was made to be so simple and undemanding that it could work with most communication services.[43] As the technology stands today, access to the internet is achieved through the assignment of an IP address, which, in simple terms, directs the computer to a signal source connected to other computers. By dialling a person will call the server of another computer which will then be able to route the call to other internet nodes until finally the signal from the home computer is directed to (but also from) a remote computer anywhere else in the world. This network of nodes was what gave the internet its reputation of being a worldwide web connecting millions of computers to each other. The inevitable first 'port of call' for a person to connect to the internet is through the servers of an ISP. An ISP provides 'access to global information networks'. An ISP provides a private user with an IP address to call to gain access to the web. The access services provided by ISPs can be regarded as the other side of the coin of e-commerce, since companies would be unable to sell their products if nobody was able to connect through to their servers. ISPs may be grouped into three basic categories: (i) backbone providers; (ii) regional providers; and (iii) local providers.[44]

The best example of a backbone provider is a telecommunication company that, in addition to providing physical infrastructure for the internet with its cables and wires (thus allowing the physical connection among network users), also provides the logical infrastructure that makes it possible for customers to transmit and receive information on that physical network. It is not necessary, however, to hire a backbone provider in order to be connected to the internet. Regional networks can provide the link between local organizations and the backbone providers. While

---

41 Ferrette (2000) E-Commerce And International Political Economics: The Legal And Political Ramifications Of The Internet On World Economies, ILSA Journal of International and Comparative Law.

42 Kogut, (2003) *The Global Internet Economy*, The MIT Press, Cambridge, p 9.

43 Kahn and Cerf (2004) 'What Is The Internet (And What Makes It Work)' in *Open Architecture as Communications Policy Preserving: Internet Freedom in The Broadband Era* editor Mark N Cooper, p. 18.

44 Abrams and Doernberg (1997) 'How Electronic Commerce Works', *State Tax Notes*, Volume: 13, (July 14, 1997) at p. 1583.

a regional network operates within a limited geographic area, data sent over a regional network could still reach any computer anywhere in the world that would be connected to the internet. This could occur because the regional network had purchased services offered by a backbone provider (that is, by interconnecting with one or more backbone providers at one or more central locations) so that information could flow from the regional network to the backbone provider and then from the backbone provider perhaps to another regional carrier across the world that would be the ISP for the intended recipient. Local ISPs provide internet access within a city or limited geographical area. A local ISP subleases circuits from national or regional ISPs, adding its own support and application services. When a company decides to maintain its website, it has to contact an ISP to establish a connection to the internet. The company may choose to maintain its website on its own server or on the server of the ISP. Once the company has set up a server with an internet protocol address (IP), its website can be accessed by customers through any ISP. All the customers have to do is type the address of the enterprise (for example, http://www.acorp.com).

Suppose a country 'A' resident, A Corp., is a retailer selling a wide variety of goods and services. A Corp. is contemplating entering the market for country 'B' customers. A Corp. plans to have no offices, warehouses, factories or other facilities in country B. No employees of A Corp. would work in country B. However, residents of country B would be able to purchase goods from A Corp. by logging on to A Corp.'s website on the internet. To establish an internet presence, A Corp. arranges with an ISP ('Just connect Corp.') to establish a connection to the internet. A Corp. might maintain its website on its own server or arrange for space on a server maintained by 'Just connect Corp.' or by a third party that has an arrangement with an ISP. A Corp. might arrange to locate the web server in country A, in country B or in any other country or the server could regularly be moved from jurisdiction to jurisdiction. Once A Corp. has set up a server with an IP address, A Corp. customers may choose any ISP because all ISPs would provide access to all IP addresses on the internet. Having gained access, the customers would be free to select A Corp.'s internet address (for example, http://www.acorp.com), thereby accessing A Corp.'s website.

In order to surf the internet a user uses a web browser such as Netscape Communication's Navigator or Microsoft Internet Explorer. Once the browser is opened and a user enters an internet address, a four-part process begins: connection, request, response and disconnection. It starts with the web browser reading the address entered by the user and it tries to establish a connection with the website through a specific server. Once the connection is established, a user could request the server to retrieve some information that would be displayed to the user or to accept information such as add a customer's mailing address to the server's database. Once the connection is made and the user's request for an action had been transmitted to the server, the browser waits for a response. After the response had been sent, the server normally disconnects from the client and the document requested and displayed to the client is temporarily stored in the random access memory (RAM) of the user's computer. The document would not be stored in any permanent fashion on the hard drive of the user's computer unless the user decides to save it. When the user turns off his computer, the document is lost unless he has saved it. An interesting characteristic of the internet is that the server can easily be moved from place to place. There is no central control since the nature of the system is such that it has no physical location. Users of the internet have no control and, in general, no idea of the path travelled by the information they seek or publish. In practice, it makes no difference whether the information or digital token sought to be transmitted are within one jurisdiction or between several, as the internet pays little or no regard to national boundaries.[45]

1.4   E-Commerce: Doing Business Over the Internet

1.4.1   Definition of E-Commerce

Any discussions relating to e-commerce normally begin with the pronouncement that it represents a fundamental and revolutionary development in communications that is likely to dramatically change the way business is conducted.[46] 'The term "e-commerce' has only been in existence since about 1994. Economist and capital market analysts use the term loosely to describe anything from the amount of sales generated by an online bookstore to explanations regarding the fluctuations in the global market.'[47] Although, some consensus regarding its definition, novelty, advantages and disadvantages, ramifications, and even its very existence do exist, they fail to clearly define the term 'e-commerce'. Many of the disparities in the predicted growth of e-commerce are due to the fact that there is no universally accepted definition of e-commerce.[48] Much of it is because the internet market place and its participants are so numerous and their intricate relationships are evolving so rapidly. Different institutions use the term e-commerce to describe different things. However, consideration of two brief definitions raises some basic issues. Thus it has been said:[49]

> Electronic commerce is a broad concept that covers any commercial transaction that is effected via electronic means and would include such means as facsimile, telex, EDI, Internet and telephone. For the purposes of this report the term is limited to those trade and commercial transactions involving computer-to-computer communications whether utilising an open or closed network.[50]

---

45 Owens (1997b) 'The Tax Man Cometh to Cyberspace', paper presented at the Harvard Law School International Tax Program Symposium on Multi-jurisdictional Taxation of Electronic Commerce, at p. 1837.

46 Pinto (2002) *E-Commerce and Source Based Income Taxation*, Doctoral Series, Volume 6, International Bureau of Fiscal Documentation, Academic Council at p. 1.

47 Ferrette (2000) E-Commerce And International Political Economics: The Legal And Political Ramifications Of The Internet On World Economies, 7 *ILSA Journal of International and Comparative Law*, p. 15.

48 Pinto (2002) E-Commerce and Source Based Income Taxation, Doctoral Series, Volume 6, International Bureau of Fiscal Documentation, Academic Council, at p. 1.

49 Rowland and Macdonald (2005) *Information and Technology Law,* Cavendish, at p. 241.

50 Report of the Electronic Expert Group to the Attorney General (Australia), 'Electronic Commerce: Building the Legal Framework', 1998, available at <www.law.gov.au/aghome/advisory/ecag/single.htm>.

It has also been said:[51]

> Electronic commerce could be said to comprise commercial transactions, whether between private individuals or commercial entities, which take place in or over electronic networks. The matters dealt with in the transactions could be intangibles, data products, or tangible goods. The only important factor is that the communication transactions take place over an electronic medium.[52]

The above two definitions of e-commerce 'raise issues in relation to the form of communication, the subject matter of the transactions and contracting parties'.[53] The first definition emphasizes computer to computer transactions and it portrays e-commerce as commercial activity carried out by electronic means. The second definition includes the subject matter of electronic contracts. However, e-commerce does not simply provide new means of making contracts. In some circumstances it also provide a new method of performance.[54] A more general definition given by Wigand suggests:

> E-commerce is seamless application of information and communication technology from its point of origin to its endpoint along the entire value chain of business processes conducted electronically and designed to enable the accomplishment of a business goal. These processes may be partial or complete and may encompass business to business as well as business to consumer and consumer to business transactions.[55]

This definition introduces the value chain, an important point as e-commerce technologies can be applied in transactions between manufacturer and supplier, manufacturer and retailer and/or retailer/service supplier and consumer. The definition is, however, possibly a little too all-embracing; one is tempted to think of an order processing system of the EDP era as an e-commerce system with 'partial' e-commerce processing.[56]

During the early consumer development of the web, when most information was unencrypted and e-commerce was relatively crude, competing visions co-existed. The largely unpredicted growth of e-commerce raised international security, trade and cultural issues. A survey of business views on the definition of e-commerce conducted on behalf of Statistics Canada distinguishes between e-commerce and e-

---

51 Rowland and Macdonald (2005) *Information and Technology Law,* Cavendish, at p. 241.

52 Davies (1998) *Computer Program Claims,* EIPR at p. 429

53 Rowland and Macdonald (2005) *Information and Technology Law,* Cavendish, at p. 241.

54 Rowland and Macdonald (2005) *Information and Technology Law,* Cavendish, at p. 241.

55 Wigand (1997), 'Electronic Commerce: Definition, Theory and Context', *The Information Society,* Vol. 13, pp. 1–16.

56 However, one of the best ways of understanding e-commerce is to consider the elements of its infrastructure (technological infrastructure to create an internet marketplace, process infrastructure to connect the internet marketplace to the traditional marketplace and 'infrastructure' of protocols, laws and regulations), as I have disscussed below.

business. According to the findings of the survey 'the notion of transactions, computer-mediation, channels and trigger events were found to be key concepts in defining e-commerce'.[57] The various definitions of e-commerce given above suggest that e-commerce can be defined both in the narrow and broader sense. In brief, the broader term encompasses e-commerce business activity and the narrower definition covers e-commerce transactions only. Various definitions given by the same organization have also changed over time. This points to the fact that an e-commerce definition is dynamic and varies with the objective one wants to measure. It is also important to note that e-commerce is more than a technology; it is a business model built around the application of information and communication technologies to any aspect of the value chain for products and services.

1.4.2   E-commerce: The Elements

Who owns the internet? The most straightforward answer is that no one does. There is no single body which controls all activities on the internet. It simply exists and is virtually impossible to 'switch off'. The internet comprises three layers. First, it exists as 'physical' infrastructure – as a data network 'managed' at a high level by international bodies and at a day-to-day level by various public bodies and corporations whose networks it uses. Second, it exists as a 'service' infrastructure provided by ISPs who offer access to the internet. Third, it exists at the level of users. At the 'physical level', the networks within different countries are funded and managed according to national policies. Links between countries are managed by agreements between telecommunication providers. There are a number of different bodies responsible for the management of the internet. At the highest level, there are a number of organizations responsible for the technical and engineering aspects of the internet, such as the internet Engineering Task Force (IETF) and the Internet Research Task Force. The internet is the first global institution that has no government. This is one of the internet's greatest strengths and one of its weaknesses. Ownership is distributed between countries and their governments, corporations, universities and the major telecommunications utilities. A corporation, firm or an individual owns each individual computer attached to the internet. Large telecommunications utilities such as British Telecom own a large percentage of the physical wires and routers over which data are transferred.

At the 'service level', it includes hardware and software tools that provide an interface with the various network options and to the customer premises equipment (CPE), or terminal equipment, which is a generic term for privately owned communications equipment that is attached to the network. At this level as far as the user is concerned, the bodies responsible for managing the internet are the ISPs. ISPs own the majority of the servers on which information is hosted and are also responsible for ensuring that individuals and companies have access to the internet under the terms of the agreement signed between the parties. ISPs are self-regulating. They are subject to the laws of the jurisdiction in which they are based. It is the

---

57 Statistics Canada (1999), *A Reality Check to Defining E-Commerce*, a report prepared by CGI for Statistics Canada.

ISPs which represent the public face of the internet for most users. They are the connectors between the second 'service level' and that of the 'third level' of user (or e-commerce). Theoretically, it is the 'third level' of the internet which raises the most complex legal challenges.

The information content transferred over the network consists of text, numbers, pictures, audio and video. However, the network does not differentiate between content as everything is digital, that is, combinations of ones and zeros. Once content has been created and stored on a server, vehicles, or messaging and information distribution methods, carry that content across the network. The messaging vehicle is called middleware software that is located between the web servers and the end-user applications and masks the peculiarities of the environment. Messaging and information distribution also includes translators that interpret and transform data formats. Messaging vehicles provide ways for communicating non-formatted (unstructured) as well as formatted (structured) data. Unstructured messaging vehicles include fax and electronic mail (e-mail). Structured document messaging consists of the automated interchange of standardized and approved messages between computer applications. Purchase orders, shipping notices and invoices are examples of structured document messaging. For the purposes of e-commerce, existing messaging mechanisms must provide reliable, unalterable message delivery that is not subject to repudiation, to be able to acknowledge and give proof of delivery when required.

Three quite separate trends (business document exchange, logistics management and global networking) came together to provide the infrastructure and technology for e-commerce. Further, a combination of regulatory reform and technological innovation enabled the growth of e-commerce. The technological innovations associated with e-commerce have also had an influence at different levels. For example, consider Amazon.com, which has transformed the market structure for bookselling. The drivers of value for consumers may not be the reduced prices and wide selection of books that it offers in the market. Instead, it is the technology-assisted ability to quickly search a large database for specific kinds of books and to receive recommendations on books that are similar to those which they wish to purchase. Such 'recommendation technologies' in e-commerce, as well as a broad spectrum of other technological innovations, are based on computer software and systems, and telecommunication and hardware technologies. Thus, there are things that become possible in e-commerce that are not normally associated with the bricks and mortar world of traditional business. Any regulatory framework must be aware of the various competing interests present in an analysis of the process of e-commerce. E-commerce from a communications perspective is the delivery of information, products/services, or payments via telephone lines, computer networks or any other means. From a business process perspective, it is the application of technology toward the automation of business transactions and workflows. From a service perspective, e-commerce is a tool that addresses the desire of firms, consumers and management to cut service costs while improving the quality of goods and increasing the speed of service delivery which provides the capability of buying and selling products and information on the internet and other online services. From a production process point of view, e-commerce converts digital inputs into value-added outputs through a set of intermediaries. For example, in the case of online trading, production processes can add value by including more value-added processing (such as trend analysis) on the raw information (stock quotes) supplied to customers.

Broadly speaking, e-commerce emphasizes an improvement of the execution of business transactions over various networks. These improvements may result in effective performance (better quality, greater customer satisfaction, better corporate decision-making), greater economic efficiency (lower costs), more rapid exchange of information between parties (high speed, accelerated or real-time interaction). Hence, what exactly is a transaction? Transactions are exchanges that occur when one economic entity sells a product or service to another entity. A transaction takes place when a product or service is transferred across a technologically separable interface that links a consumer (client) with a producer (server). When buyer/seller transactions occur in the electronic market place, information is accessed, absorbed, arranged and sold in different ways. To manage these transactions, e-commerce also incorporates transaction management, which organizes, routes, processes and tracks transactions.[58] E-commerce also includes consumers making electronic payments and fund transfers. Hence, the combined effect of the economic forces, customer interaction forces and technology-driven digital convergence are fuelling interest in e-commerce. The context of this discussion showed e-commerce was born out of technology, its growth and working process is fuelled by technology, and its elements are part of that same technology; hence it is conceivable that all these forces would have to be taken into account when consideration is given on development of any tax collection mechanism.

1.4.3   E-commerce: The Components

The growth potential of e-commerce rests on three main components: the services, the infrastructure and the legal. These components combine and interact at the time of any e-commerce activity. For the development of its physical infrastructure, e-commerce relies on a variety of technologies, the development of which is proceeding at breakneck speed (for example, interconnectivity among telecommunications, cable, satellite, or other internet 'backbone'; ISPs to connect market participants to that backbone; and end-user devices such as PCs, TVs or mobile telephones). The service component of e-commerce is responsible for making sure that commercial transactions can actually take place and provides the viable means for committing to such transactions, such as providing means for making payment over the internet possible (through credit, debit or Smart cards or through online currencies). It also makes possible the distribution and delivery (whether online or physical) of those

---

58 Based on the extent to which the Internet is utilized in the course of a transaction, e-commerce can be 'indirect e-commerce' and 'direct e-commerce'. Indirect e-commerce involves transaction where the customers use the selection, ordering and payment process (electronic cash) of the retail stores or the mail order firms who use this medium for selling, marketing and advertising, but the delivery of product or service takes place by traditional process. The goods and services, in digitized form, acquired directly from the internet, is referred to as 'direct e-commerce'.

products purchased over the internet to the consumer. The legal component affects the conduct of those businesses engaging in and influenced by e-commerce, as well as the relationships between businesses, consumers and government. Examples include technical communications and interconnectivity standards; the legality and modality of digital signatures, certification and encryption; and disclosure, privacy and content regulations.

The detail of each of the components and their regulation depends on the requirements of the perspective. The boundaries of the components would accordingly vary to accommodate the scale of need of a perspective. The importance of infrastructure is more for the communication and business process perspective. Similarly, the legal regulations that provide certainty of electronic contract, privacy, consumer protection and taxation would be of much importance for the services perceptive.

1.4.4   Process of E-commerce

The process of e-commerce, in general, involves a multiplicity of transactions. It involves a large number of chains to complete the cycle of transactions. While it may not be possible to identify all the elements of e-commerce, it is possible to divide the three broad stages into which almost all types of e-commerce fit: first, the pre-purchase stage including advertising and information seeking; second, the purchase stage, including purchase and payment; and third, the delivery stage. In principle, all types of products could be advertised and purchased over electronic networks. The potential for electronic delivery, however, would be more limited. It would require that a final product could be presented as digitalized information and transmitted electronically. Many services could be supplied as digitalized information, including financial transactions or legal advice. Some information and entertainment products typically characterized as goods, such as books, software, music and videos embody digitalized information that could also be supplied electronically over the internet. All three aspects or stages of e-commerce defined here may have certain tax policy implications.

For the moment, most purchases of tangible goods are of uniformly generic products with no value-added service. The biggest sellers on the internet, for example, are books, music CDs and pornography. The retailer of a book or CD provides no service on top of selling the product, which is often sealed, and the contents do not vary from retailer to retailer. One reason consumers purchase over the internet in these cases rather than from a local retailer is because the internet supplier has a larger catalogue range and stocks titles not kept by a local smaller retailer. Because internet suppliers make large bulk purchases and generally operate from non-prime locations, their costs are often much lower than those faced by local suppliers. This often provides e-commerce sellers with a price advantage over local retailers. In all respects, apart from the means of viewing available stock and placing an order, internet orders of tangible goods are similar to conventional catalogue mail orders. The ability to provide instantaneous details of available stock, price, shipping time and so forth makes the internet store more attractive than the mail-order catalogue store.

The second element of e-commerce is the use of electronic media to provide services from a distant location. However, the use of electronic media to transmit information is far from a new development. Since the development of the telegram in the last century, electronic media has been used to conduct commerce. There is no inherent difference between purchasing advice provided over the internet and purchasing advice provided by telegram or its successors, telephone and fax. Until recently, it was the high price of communicating outside a person's jurisdiction that prevented service providers from regularly servicing clients in other jurisdictions. The plummeting price of communication has virtually eliminated the distance barrier to service provision and the choice between acquiring services from a local provider or using an offshore provider who will deliver the service electronically will turn on other factors such as the cost and quality of the actual service and, in some cases, taxes. The third element of e-commerce comprises the conversion of graphics (still and video), text or sound into digital form and delivery of a digital version of analogue information or the sale of a purely digital product such as a computer program. The customer who purchases a digital product uses his or her own equipment (computer, MP3 player, and so on) to reconstruct into analogue form documents, graphics, videos, text or music (in the case of converted information) or to process directly purely digital information (in the case of software).

1.4.5   Trends in the Growth of E-Commerce

Internet and e-commerce are growing so fast that forecasters regularly underestimate how many users will be online and how much revenue will be generated by e-commerce. Metcalf's law states that the utility of a network increases exponentially as each new user joins. It is a relatively simple concept that has been known since the first humans joined a community. Some of the greatest benefits of belonging to a group arise as a direct result of just belonging to that group. If millions of computers are connected together into a network, all of a sudden a utility is created. It establishes a standard simply because of the volume of the users. This concept is known as 'critical mass' and it is what companies are trying to achieve when they start an online business or migrate their existing business over to the world of e-commerce. Figure 1.1 illustrates that a distinction needs to be drawn between situations that a country might wish to know about:

- the readiness of its people, businesses, infrastructure and its economy generally to undertake e-commerce activities – this is likely to be of interest to countries in the early stages of e-commerce maturity or activity;
- the intensity with which information and communication technologies are utilized within a country and the extent to which electronic commerce activities are undertaken – this is likely to be of interest to countries where e-commerce is becoming much more prevalent; and
- the impact of e-commerce on national economies and business activities being carried out in those countries – this is likely to be of interest in countries where e-commerce activities are very well developed.

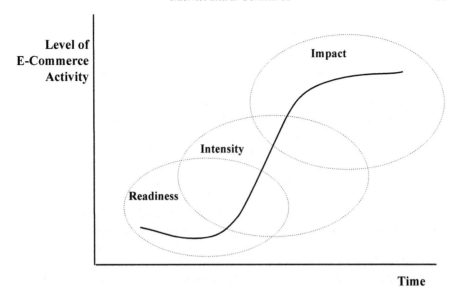

Figure 1.1   S-Curve: Level of E-Commerce Activity
*Source: Industry Canada, presented at the OECD Workshop on Defining and Measuring
E-Commerce (April 1999)[59]*

To measure the growth of e-commerce, each country or economy would first want
to reflect on what kind of e-commerce data they want to measure, depending on the
stage of development their country has achieved in the area of e-commerce. Some
countries (in particular, developing countries) may be at an early stage, while others
may already be very active users of e-commerce and the internet. A good model
for identifying these needs of e-commerce data users has been proposed by Canada
(Figure 1.1) and is generally considered a good starting point for statistical work on
e-commerce. As shown, there is a fair degree of overlap between the various stages
of maturity of e-commerce and the growth of e-commerce.

At the end of 2003, nearly 676 million people (or 11.8 per cent of the total population
of the world) had access to the internet. This represents an increase of 49.5 million
people or 7.8 per cent compared with the figures at the end of 2002. Developing
countries account for more than 36 per cent of all the internet users in the world and
their share in the internet population of the world grew by nearly 50 per cent between
2000 and 2003. However, internet users in the developing world are concentrated
in a handful of countries: China, the Republic of Korea, India, Brazil and Mexico
account for 61.52 per cent of them. Almost 75 per cent of the growth in the number
of internet users in the world occurred in the developing world. In spite of rapid rates
of improvement in the penetration ratios of developing countries, these remain ten
times lower than the average of the developed world.[60] A comparative analysis of the

59 Teltscher (2001) Measuring Electronic Commerce in Developing Countries,
UNCTAD's *Electronic Commerce and Development* Report 2001.

60 UNCTAD (2004), *E-commerce and Development Report, 2004*. United Nations
Conference on Trade and Development, UNCTD Secretariat, New York and Geneva.

data from the Organization for Economic Cooperation and Development (OECD) countries for 2000–2001 indicates that the share of internet users buying online was highest in the Nordic countries, the UK and the US, where 38 per cent of users had made purchases online; it was lowest in Mexico, where fewer than 0.6 per cent had done so. The Census Bureau of the Department of Commerce announced that the estimate of US retail e-commerce sales for the first quarter of 2006 was US$25.2 billion, an increase of 7 per cent from the fourth quarter of 2005.[61] The number of internet hosts worldwide grew by 35.8 per cent between January 2003 and January 2004, reaching a total of over 233 million, which represents a doubling of the growth rate in 2002. In terms of number of websites, as of June 2004 there were over 51,635,284 websites worldwide, 26.13 per cent more than a year before. The number of websites using the secure sockets layer protocol (SSL), which supports secure transactions, grew by 56.7 per cent between April 2003 and April 2004, reaching 300,000.[62] Online marketing and advertising firm Leadpile has claimed that it expects the next generation of internet users to push e-commerce sales over US$1 trillion by 2012.

The impact of e-commerce on developing countries is at present mainly in the international trade sector. Studies indicate that over the past few years, the import and export industries have grown significantly and, therefore, the impact of e-commerce will be quite significant. E-commerce will also have a significant impact on the services sector as this is not only the fastest growing sector of today but is also going to be the sector with the greatest potential for offering digitized services and transactions in the years to come. E-commerce penetration, however, varies from region to region. The Asia Pacific region has been ahead of others. It has added approximately 50 million internet users every year. Africa witnessed a 30 per cent growth in internet subscribers during 2001. The entire African continent has 1.3 million internet users. Most key African cities are 'Internet-enabled', with high data traffic. The markets of these regions, however, have low e-commerce activity, which may be due to the poor infrastructure. In Latin American countries such as Argentina, Brazil, Chile and Mexico e-commerce is confined to a few items such as automobiles. While these countries have significant growth in internet connectivity, this is mainly used for e-mail and information gathering. Online transactions in other commodities or services are low. The USA and Europe have the highest internet penetration and e-commerce activity. The share of online transactions in total sales is growing rapidly in all these regions. Most firms expect business-to-business (B2B) transactions to grow very quickly. A study by Forrester Research shows that B2B e-commerce activity accounted for business worth US$2,160 billion and this will rise to US$ 8,823 billion by 2005.

E-commerce is profoundly changing consumer behaviour. Instead of buying things from the usual market of bricks and mortar businesses, many consumers now behave differently. A survey of e-commerce in the USA indicated that 20 per cent

---

61 UNCTAD (2003), *E-commerce and Development Report 2003*, United Nations, New York.

62 UNCTAD (2004), *E-commerce and Development Report, 2004*. United Nations Conference on Trade and Development, UNCTD Secretariat, New York and Geneva.

of the customers going to 'Sears' department store in the US to buy an electrical appliance, for example, will have researched their purchase online.[63] Three-quarters of Americans start shopping for new cars online, even though most of them end up buying from traditional dealers. A study by Forrester shows that half the consumers in Europe who have an internet connection buy products offline after having investigated prices and other details online. In Italy and Spain, for instance, people are twice as likely to buy offline as online, after researching on the internet. But in Britain and Germany, the numbers are evenly split. Forrester says that people begin to shop online for simple, predictable products such as DVDs and then graduate to more complex items. Travel makes up the biggest chunk of business-to-consumer (B2C) e-commerce, accounting for about one-third of online consumer spending. According to the PhoCus Wright Consumer Travel Trends Survey nearly two-thirds of the travellers who had booked their tickets online were happy to buy personal travel tickets either from online agencies or directly from the websites of travel firms and often used both for different parts of the same trip.[64] The vast majority of customers consulted at least one online travel agency and the website of one supplier before purchasing anything online. Many more people did investigate their travel options online but then booked offline.

1.4.6   Electronic Money

> The money screamed across the wires, its provenance fading in a maze of electronic transfers, which shifted it, hid it, broke it up into manageable wads which would be withdrawn and redeposited elsewhere, obliterating the trail.[65]

The success and future of e-commerce is interwoven with the development of electronic payment systems. Electronic financial transaction systems have been distinguished according to whether they involve the transfer of account balances, incorporate electronic cheques, utilize secure value counters or are token-based.[66] The first two are in essence systems involving only electronically-communicated instructions about the transfer or payment of funds.[67] The latter two categories more closely approximate what we might term 'electronic money',[68] which is the

---

63 'A Perfect Market: A Survey of E-commerce', *The Economist*, 15 May 2004, pp. 3–16.

64 'A Perfect Market: A Survey of E-commerce', *The Economist*, 15 May 2004, pp. 3–16.

65 Davis (1995) *Nest of Vipers* (Orion mass market paperback). This book is a banking thriller.

66 Furche and Wrightson (1996), *Computer Money: A Systematic Overview of Payment Systems*, Heidelberg: Dpunk, at pp. 25–33.

67 Lee and Longe-Akindemowo (1998) Regulatory Issues in Electronic Money: A Legal-Economics Analysis, University of Wollongong Department of Economics, Working Paper Series.

68 Electronic money or e-money has been described as 'an electronic surrogate for coins and bank notes'. Currently, there is no formally adopted international terminology with respect to electronic money.

focus of this section. However, before electronic payments are widely accepted, several issues must be addressed.[69] A user making an electronic payment expects privacy and security particularly with respect to electronic cash payments. There are four different types of electronic payment: electronic cash, smart card, electronic cheques and credit cards.[70]

The question is what is the effect of elecronic money on e-commece for the purpose of taxation? Just as electronic money systems differ in their technical features, they also differ to the extent to which they create legal issues for tax returns.[71] Parallel with the evolution of secure credit-based systems which have credit card institutions as intermediaries and therefore create an audit trail, we are witnessing the development of anonymous electronic cash transaction systems.[72] Electronic money involves tokens of value expressed in digital form, in the same sense that casino chips are a token of value, expressed by providers of e-commerce as solutions for businesses.There are several different forms of electronic cash that can be used to pay for transactions. For transaction verification, the most important distinction is whether or not the transactions are fully accounted for by the issuer.

Electronic payment systems can be distingusighed in part based on whether they are accounted or unaccounted systems. In an accounted system, the electronic money issuer maintains a complete or partial audit trail of transactions and can identify the person to whom the electronic money is issued as well as the people and businesses receiving the electronic money as it flows thorough the economy. In an unaccounted system, however, electronic money passes through the economy anonymously and without an audit trail, operating exactly like paper money.[73] As with traditional forms of cash, it is generally believed that these systems will be of significance in the purchase of consumer items and in other areas such as entertainment and gambling. To the extent that the traditional cash economy creates the possibility of tax avoidance and evasion, unaccounted electronic cash can be seen as proposing similar threats to taxation revenue. Advantages and disadvantages exist for both systems. However, some commentators think that most electronic money systems

---

69 Electronic payment methods include access payment instruments and electronic money instruments.

70 Doernberg and Hinnekens (1999)Electronic Commerce and International Taxation Kluwer Law International, p. 92.

71 Depending on the type of system used, electronic money can cause various obstacles in terms of compliance and it has an advantage or a disadvantage for tax collection.

72 The use of digital or electronic cash in e-commerce transactions could lead to difficulties for Revenue auditors. Revenue auditors have traditionally had to grapple with the lack of controls associated with the cash economy. The increasing sophistication of business transactions and the development of a variety of payment methods have meant that cash payments have become a diminishing feature of business transactions.

73 The electronic money poses a serious threat to a tax evasion potential comparative to that created by paper money. This raises the issue of whether the evasion potential is manageable and what must be done to manage it. It is possible that the techniques that have been developed over time to combat tax evasion using paper money may not be workable to combat evasion through electronic money. Electronic money has made it easy to deposit unreported income in a bank or other financial institution in a fraction of time.

will be accountable because customers and vendors will want that protection. This might not be true for transactions like internet gambling and other entertainment services, where anonymity is valued higher than security.[74]

1.4.7   E-Commerce: Security

The major barrier to e-commerce today is the lack of security. It is essential to have the technological means to provide authentication, identification, accountability and liability in electronic transactions. All participants, from all perspectives, must have a confident reliance on user identities, while holding each party liable to perform their role in the transaction. Consequently, such technologies are needed which bolster consumer confidence in the reliability of the relationship, the identity of the participants and the veracity of the materials being exchanged. Concern could only be addressed through a combination of technology and legal rules. Accordingly, all three components should integrate and interact in order to develop a sustainable policy for tax collection and enforcement. E-commerce will not reach its full potential until customers perceive that the risks of doing business electronically have been reduced to an acceptable level. Confidentiality, authentication, integrity and non-repudiation are the four most important ingredients required for trust in e-commerce transactions. The objective is to develop an interrelated system where all these concerns are simultaneously addressed with relative simplicity.

In view of the available technology, it seems proper that 'digital certificates' together with the 'Certifying Authority' (CA) can provide the much-needed assurances. Digital signatures can be used to provide the necessary authentication, integrity and non-repudiation. PKI uses public/private-key pairs – two mathematically related keys. Typically, one of these keys is made public, by posting it on the internet, for example, while the other remains private. Public-key cryptography works in such a way that a message encrypted with the public key can only be decrypted with the private key and, conversely, a message signed with a private key can be verified with the public key. A subscriber first obtains a public/private key pair (generated by the subscriber or for the subscriber as a service). The subscriber then goes through a registration process by submitting their public key to a Certification Authority or a Registration Authority (RA), which acts as an agent for the CA. The CA or RA verifies the identity of the subscriber in accordance with the CA's established business practices (that may be contained in a Certification Practice Statement) and then issues a digital certificate. The certificate includes the subscriber's public key and identity information, and is digitally signed by the CA, which binds the subscriber's identity to that public key. The CA also manages the subscriber's digital certificate through the certificate life cycle (meaning, from registration through revocation or expiration). In some circumstances, it remains important to manage digital certificates even after expiry or revocation so that digital signatures on

---

74 Also it can not be denied that electronic money and the internet have substantially increased opportunities to open bank accounts abroad, with relative ease and safety, and to transmit money anonymously. Such accounts are, of course, providing opportunities for tax evasion in the home state by taking harbor in zero tax states.

stored documents held past the revocation or expiry period can be validated later. A transaction submitted by a customer to an online merchant via the internet can be encrypted with the merchant's public key and therefore can only be decrypted by that merchant using the merchant's private key ensuring a level of confidentiality. Confidentiality can also be achieved using Secure Socket Layer (SSL), Secure/Multipurpose Internet Mail Extensions (S/MIME), and other protocols, such as Secure Electronic Transaction (SET).

The following example illustrates how a digital signature is generated and the verification process for a reversible asymmetric cryptographic algorithm (such as RSA). Suppose a customer wishes to send a digitally signed message to a seller. The customer would have to run the message through a hash function (that is, a mathematical function that converts a message into a fixed length block of data, the hash, in a fashion such that the hash uniquely reflects the message – in effect, it is the message's 'fingerprint'). The customer then would transform the hash using the algorithm and the customer's private key to create the digital signature, which would be appended to the message. A header would also be appended to the message, indicating the seller's e-mail address, the sender's e-mail address and other information such as the time the message is being sent. The message header, the message itself and the digital signature would then be sent to the merchant. The customer can optionally send his or her public key certificate to the merchant in the message itself. The e-mail software usually does all of this in such a way that the process is transparent to the user.

To determine whether the message came from the customer (meaning, authentication) and to determine whether the message has not been modified (meaning, integrity), the seller validates the digital signature. To do so, the merchant must obtain the customer's public key certificate. If the customer did not send his or her public key certificate as part of the message, the seller would typically obtain the customer's public key certificate from an online repository (maintained by the CA or another party acting as the agent of the CA, or any other source even if unrelated to the CA). The seller then would validate that the customer's digital certificate (containing the customer's public key) was signed by a recognized CA to ensure that the binding between the public key and the customer represented in the certificate has not been altered. Next, the seller would extract the public key from the certificate and use that public key to transform the digital signature to reveal the original hash. The seller would then run the message as received through the same hash function to create a hash of the received message. To verify the digital signature, the seller would compare these two hashes. If they match, then the digital signature validates and the seller would know that the message came from the customer and that it had not been modified from the time the signature was made. Digital signatures can also be used to provide a basis for non-repudiation (meaning that the signer cannot readily deny having signed the message).

In order for these technologies to enable parties to securely conduct e-commerce, one important question must be answered. How would we know in the digital world that an individual's public key actually belongs to that individual? A digital certificate, which is an electronic document containing information about an individual and his or her public key, is the answer. This document is digitally signed by a trusted organization referred to as a Certification Authority (CA). The basic premise is that the CA is vouching for the link between an individual's identity and his or her public key. The CA provides a level of assurance that the public key contained in the certificate does indeed belong to the entity named in the certificate. The digital signature placed on the public key certificate by the CA provides the cryptographic binding between the entity's public key, the entity's name, and other information in the certificate, such as a validity period. For a relying party to determine whether a legitimate CA issued the certificate, the relying party must verify the issuing CA's signature on the certificate. The public keys of many common Root CAs (as later defined) are pre-loaded into standard web browser software (for example, Netscape Navigator or Microsoft Internet Explorer). This allows the relying party to verify the issuing CA's signature using the CA's public key to determine whether a trusted CA issued the certificate.

The purpose of a CA is to manage the certificate life cycle, which includes generation and issuance, distribution, renewal and re-key, revocation, and suspension of certificates. The CA frequently delegates the initial registration of subscribers to Registration Authorities (RAs) which act as agents for the CA. In some cases, the CA may perform registration functions directly. The CA is also responsible for providing certificate status information though the issuance of Certificate Revocation Lists (CRLs) and/or the maintenance of an online status checking mechanism. Typically, the CA posts the certificates and CRLs that it has issued to a repository (such as an online directory), which is accessible to relying parties. A Registration Authority (RA) is an entity that is responsible for the identification and authentication of subscribers, but does not sign or issue certificates. The above discussion is significant not least, because it has an important bearing on certain compliance advantage strategies but also it is fundamental to the proposal discussed in the final chapter of this book.

Chapter 2

International Taxation: Direct Taxation

Introduction

'Tax is often regarded as being about numbers. Tax law is about words. It is an odd thing that many lawyers and legal academics seem worried about studying tax, because they are worried about numbers.'[1] But what requires to be understood is that tax is also about interpreting and applying the laws that impose taxes. This is because every tax problem is a problem about statutory interpretation and application. The purpose of this chapter is to survey the principles of international direct taxation, which generally refers to the tax treatment of cross-national transactions. Since each nation has its own tax rules and the rules of one nation are rarely perfectly meshed with those of another, it is possible that income may well be taxed more than once (referred to as double taxation) or that it will go untaxed by any jurisdiction. To prevent this in principal, two methods of taxation have been distinguished for direct taxes: the territorial (or source) system of taxation and the worldwide (or residence) system; in terms of tax policy principles both residence- and source-based taxation can be justified. Double taxation is also guarded through an extensive network of bilateral and multilateral tax treaties, which attempt to allocate income earned to the source and to the residence according to 'permanent establishment' (PE). This chapter will discuss issues of source-based and residence-based taxation, the tax treaty concept of PE, transfer pricing and treaty characterization issues.

2.1   The Direct Tax System

Taxation is a fundamental function of the government. In a sense, it defines the state. There are a wide variety of taxes that the average citizen pays, often without being aware that the government is receiving the money, and it is difficult for most people to identify all the tax money they pay to government.[2] A direct tax is conventionally defined as a tax which is levied on the person who bears the burden. The theory of tax incidence suggests that it is likely to be a rare occurrence for the taxpayer to bear the full burden, but the conventional classification of direct taxation uses only superficial tax. Thus, income tax is classified as a direct tax because it is levied on the person who receives the income, although in fact he may pass at least part of the burden to others. The personal income tax is not, however, the only tax levied

---

1   Morse and Williams (2004) *Davis: Principle of Tax Law*, (London: Sweet and Maxwell) Fifth Edition, p. 21.

2   Peters (1991) The Politics of Taxation: A Comparative Perspective, (Blackwell: Cambridge).

on incomes. Corporations also have incomes and governments in all nations extract some revenue from that source.

In most industrialized nations personal income tax is the largest single source of revenue. The tax averages almost one-third of all tax revenues in all OECD countries.[3] Although the personal income tax is administrated somewhat differently in different countries, there are some common features. The first is that income tends to be defined very broadly so that it is difficult for anyone living in a country and earning a reasonable amount of income to escape paying some income tax. A second common feature of personal income tax is that it is a progressive tax and finally, although governments do have the legal right to tax any form of income, in most tax systems all the sources of income and all types of expenditure are not treated the same.

On the other hand corporations, as legal persons, also pay a tax on their income or profits. Sometimes it is viewed that this tax is generally a politically easier tax to adopt or increase. However, a number of economists have always been puzzled by the idea of a corporate income tax which 'does not quite fit into the conventional classification of taxes. They have been accustomed to thinking of a dichotomy between direct taxes on individuals ... and indirect taxes on merchandise ... The corporate tax fits into neither of these categories'.[4] The main justification for collecting corporate income tax has been a practical one: since most money earned and spent is channelled through corporations, there is a strong administrative convenience in collecting revenues from corporations rather than individuals. However, despite the political and administrative appeal, revenue generated from corporation tax is much less than one might expect. The reasons for the decline in importance of corporate tax revenues are complex; globalization certainly plays a role. They include both tax competition among host countries and the increased possibilities for tax avoidance that flow from international operations. Hines, for example, concludes that there is 'ample evidence' of the sensitivity of foreign direct investment of tax treatment and aggressive tax avoidance behaviour by multinational corporations.[5]

International taxation is one of the most important but least studied topics in all of tax; indeed, it may be one of the most undeservedly ignored topics in all of law.[6] One of the reasons the topic is so important in the real world and yet so little loved by scholars is that international tax law is both excruciatingly complex and fundamentally arbitrary. One of the principal reasons for this irrationality is simple: there is as yet no consensus as to how the tax base represented by the world

---

3   Peters (1991) The Politics of Taxation: A Comparative Perspective, (Blackwell: Cambridge).

4   Colm (1955), Essays in Public Finance and Fiscal Policy, Oxford University Press.

5   Hines (1999) 'Lessons from Behavioural Responses to International Taxation, National Tax Journal, 52(2): 305-322 as cited in Kobrin J. Stephen (2001) 'Territoriality and Governance of Cyberspace', Journal of International Business Studies, Vol. 32, No 4, pp. 687-704.

6   Lebovitz and Seto (2001) 'The Fundamental Problem of International Taxation', 23 Loyola of Los Angeles International and Comparative Law Review 4 p. 529.

economy should be shared among the world's roughly 200 nations. Currently, for the most part, each government decides unilaterally what portion of that base to claim. As a result, some parts of the world economy are taxed once, some twice, some many times and some not at all. Much of the theory on international taxation that has been developed over the years to address the above issues presupposes that there are, broadly speaking, no undue difficulties in identifying the economic activities from which the taxable income is derived, ascertaining the location where such activities are carried out and verifying the primary residence of the parties to which the income accrues. This presupposition, which forms the basis on which the boundaries of most national tax jurisdictions have traditionally been drawn, has become much less tenable today with the ever-increasing dominance in international commerce exerted by multinationals with highly integrated operations and the ease and speed with which financial capital can move from country to country.[7] While business is already truly global, the world's tax regimes are still largely parochial and uncoordinated. As a result, tax considerations routinely drive the structuring of international businesses and transactions.

In spite of the magnitude and complexities of international trade and commerce, and in spite of the diversities of domestic income tax regimes, the tax rules that apply to international transactions are surprisingly similar in most countries. Furthermore, they rest upon the use of a relatively small number of concepts: (1) the choice of specific principles (for example, residence- and source-based taxation) for governing the tax treatments of both domestic source income accruing to non-residents and foreign-source income accruing to residents; (2) the use of the concept of PE in establishing the economic nexus required to assert jurisdiction to tax business profits; (3) the economic effects of these principles (for example, their impacts on the worldwide allocation of investments and savings); (4) the application of alternative methods (for example, tax credits or exemptions) for effecting (juridical) double-taxation relief; (5) the formulation of appropriate provisions (for example, inter-company transfer pricing rules for multinationals) for the effective implementation of the chosen tax regime; and (6) the negotiation of bilateral (and sometimes multilateral) tax treaties to alleviate the undesirable effects of non-harmonized tax policies among countries.[8]

Some commentators have suggested that it is nothing short of a miracle that a consensus emerged among developed countries in the post-war period about the use of these concepts in guiding the allocation of worldwide income among the OECD countries. Other, more cynical commentators have argued that this apparent OECD consensus was really a Washington consensus and that the concepts largely served the self-interest of large capital-exporting countries. But whatever the political forces that accounted for and shaped the concepts, over the years they have come under increasing critical scrutiny in the light of the internationalization of most markets,

---

7   Zee (1998) 'Taxation of Financial Capital in a Globalized Environment: The Role of Withholding Taxes,' *National Tax Journal*, Volume 51 no. 3 (September 1998) pp. 587–599.

8   Zee (1998) 'Taxation of Financial Capital in a Globalized Environment: The Role of Withholding Taxes', *National Tax Journal*, Volume 51 no. 3 (September 1998) pp. 587–599.

changing technologies, aggressive tax planning and concerns over the equitable allocation of worldwide income among capital-exporting and capital-importing countries.

2.2   Determining Taxing Rights

The modern state system permitted territorialization of politics, the division of the globe's surface into mutually exclusive, geographically defined jurisdictions enclosed by discrete and meaningful borders.[9] The principle of sovereign territoriality provides autonomy and ultimate law-making and law, enforcing authority to states within their geographic borders and over their geographic borders and over their citizens abroad; applying law and regulations to non-citizens outside of one's borders violates the idea of mutually exclusive geography which underlies the modern state system.[10]

States have the sovereign right to charge and collect taxes related to their territories. The term 'fiscal sovereignty' implies a system of taxation based on territorial jurisdiction and geographic autonomy.[11] Accordingly,

> territorially-based economic governance is vectorial in that it assumes that all events, transactions and business entities can be located unambiguously in terms of fixed two dimensional geographic coordinates. It assumes that regardless of how international the world economy might be, one can determine where a transaction takes place and thus whose law, regulation or taxation applies.[12]

As the tax systems of most countries were developed when international trade and capital movements were limited,[13] historically countries adopted unilateral rules to deal with the relatively few incidences of cross-border transactions.[14] However, the hallmark of a global economy is greater mobility of economic transactions and economic agents. Internationalization of production or more precisely globalization has made, particularly with respect to the level of taxation, mix of taxes, design of particular taxes, the manner of their administration and compliance, the collection of taxes by territorial sovereigns more difficult. The cross national differences in taxation gave rise to four problems. In particular, governments became worried about competitiveness, tax evasion and avoidance, tax competition and the transnationalization of the tax base. Policy makers in an increasing number of countries have become alarmed by

---

9   Anderson (1986) The modernity of States, in James Anderson, (ed) The Rise of Modern State, Atlantic Highlands, NJ: Humanities Press International Inc.

10 Kobrin (2001) 'Territoriality and Governance of Cyberspace', Journal of International Business Studeis, Vol. 32, No 4, pp. 687–704.

11 Kobrin (2001) 'Territoriality and Governance of Cyberspace', Journal of International Business Studeis, Vol. 32, No 4, pp. 687–704.

12 Kobrin (2001) 'Territoriality and Governance of Cyberspace', Journal of International Business Studies, Vol. 32, No 4, pp. 687–704.

13 Tanzi (1996) *Globalization, Tax Competition and the Future of Tax Systems*, International Monetary Fund, Working Paper (Washington DC).

14 Yu, 'E-Commerce Relevance of Source and Residence Rules', <www.raymondyu. net/pub/papers/ecom_sr.pdf>.

the responsiveness of the domestic income tax base to international differences in tax policy, thus limiting their degree of freedom in setting domestic income tax rates and in mobilizing revenue.

This has forced the countries to exhibit much greater awareness of and sensitivity to the tax changes being undertaken by their trading partners and competitors, reducing autonomy concerning their tax policies. In other words, to some extent this notion of a 'natural nexus' between tax base and a particular territory has become a fiction.[15] Camaron has argued that 'the concept of sovereignty, by claiming to place many aspects of tax matters firmly within the domestic jurisdiction of a sovereign state, creates a dense ideological smokescreen',[16] the rhetoric of absolute fiscal sovereignty serves only to mask the degree to which the nature and articulation of fiscal geography is the subject of intense debate.[17] Hence, the primary purpose of international tax law has been, from its inception, to resolve problems arising from the fact that taxable corporations and individuals conduct their business across international boundaries and thus occupy more than one fiscal jurisdiction.[18] Tax rules were set up to govern economic activity that dealt with cross-border transactions. However, these were developed to assign tax jurisdiction to a specific geographic space. In order to determine which sovereign should enjoy the primary right to tax cross-border activity, tax rules ask questions like 'where does the transaction take place?', 'where is the company based?', 'where does income arise?'[19]

In general, for practical administrative and enforcement reasons, a country only asserts taxing authority over persons or property that are sufficiently connected with it to enable it to impose authority over the person or property. This is primarily based on the personal status of that person, such as residence, domicile or citizenship where individuals are concerned; for corporations, where it is incorporated or effectively managed. It typically includes the right to tax the worldwide income of the person involved.[20] 'In addition a state may base its jurisdiction to tax on the source of the income being situated within the territory of that state.'[21] However, for corporate income the primary problems of compliance and administration arise from the need to determine the geographic source of corporate income. Because of the economic interaction between activities occurring in various jurisdictions, it is

---

15 Genschel (2005) Globalization and the transformation of the tax state, European Review, Vol. 13, Supp. No. 1, pp. 53–71.

16 Cameron (2006) Turning Point? The Volatile Geographies of Taxation, Antipode 38 (2), 236-258.

17 Cameron (2006) Turning Point? The Volatile Geographies of Taxation, Antipode 38 (2), 236-258.

18 Picciotto (1992) International Business Taxation: A Study in the Internationalization of Business Regulation, (London: Weidenfeld and Nicoloson).

19 Cockfield (2002) The Law and Economics of Digital Taxation: Challenges to Traditional Tax Laws and Principles, *Bulletin for International Fiscal Documentation*, Vol. 56, p. 606.

20 Doernberg and Hinnekens (1999)Electronic Commerce and International Taxation Kluwer Law International, p. 11.

21 Doernberg and Hinnekens (1999) Electronic Commerce and International Taxation Kluwer Law International, p. 11.

generally impossible to isolate precisely the source of income of a corporation doing business in two or more jurisdictions. Rather, it is common to use a formula to divide the income of a corporation among the jurisdictions where it operates.[22]

No multilateral convention restricts a state's right to raise certain revenue from its own territory, although the international trading agreements forbid discriminatory taxation of imported goods and services as well as refunds of certain taxes related to export.[23] However, international tax laws were developed from the early twentieth century both to prevent incidence of double taxation and to ensure that the taxing state is able to protect its fiscal revenues. National tax laws define scope in respect of taxes. Persons with domestic activities in excess of a certain national threshold are liable for taxation within the jurisdiction.[24] Following the rise of the service sector and the development of 'traditional' intangible goods such as patents, trademarks or copyrights, tax rules have been modified to take into account the difficulties associated with determining the geographic connection between producers of these traditional intangible goods and consumers of the rights associated with these goods.[25]

There are two competing theories that have consistently influenced the reasoning regarding a country's right to taxation – the benefit theory and the sacrifice theory.[26]

> Under the benefit theory, a jurisdiction's right to tax rests on the totality of benefits and state services provided to taxpayers that interact with a country. Under the sacrifice theory, taxes are viewed as a sacrifice owed to a country due to the higher moral value of community purposes over individual aims.[27]

However, Vogel has argued that only benefit theory seems acceptable today.[28] The benefit principle assigns the primary right to tax active business income to source jurisdictions and the primary right to tax passive income to residence jurisdictions.

2.3 Source-Based and Residence-Based Taxation Principles

The most fundamental tax principle underlying tax systems of countries is establishing when and on what basis taxation should arise and when a country should cede jurisdiction to another country in respect to cross-border transactions. The former is often referred to as 'jurisdiction to tax', but it may also be said to encompass

---

22 McLure (1999): *The Tax Assignment Problem: Conceptual and Administrative Considerations in Achieving Subnational Fiscal Autonomy*. World Bank: Washington.

23 General Agreement on Tariffs and Trade 1947 (WTO 1986), Part II, Article III, General Agreement on Trade in Services (WTO 1994), Part II, Article II.

24 Westberg (2002) Cross-border Taxation of E-Commerce, IBFD p. 91.

25 Avi-Yonah and Slemrod (2001) (How) 'Should Trade Agreements Deal with Income Tax Issues?' University of Michigan, Working Paper #01-008.

26 Pinto (2002) E-Commerce and Source Based Income Taxation, IBFD p. 17.

27 Pinto (2002) E-Commerce and Source Based Income Taxation, IBFD p. 17.

28 Vogel (1998) Worldwide vs Source Taxation of Income- A Review and Re-evaluation of Arguments (Part III) 11 Intertax pp. 394–395 as cited in Pinto (2002) E-Commerce and Source Based Income Taxation, IBFD p. 18.

the latter. When tax laws are enacted by governments, the determination of who is liable to pay tax and in what circumstance forms the basis for jurisdiction to tax. As governments are generally able to enact whatever laws they wish, they could impose any number of bases for jurisdiction to tax, such as physical presence at a certain point in the calendar year, citizenship or some other seemingly arbitrary criteria. It is not difficult to see that where two countries do not use the same basis for jurisdiction to tax, the possibility exists that a person may fall within both tax jurisdictions. To some extent, such a situation can generally be avoided if different countries use more or less consistent bases for jurisdiction to tax or adopt standards in treaties for organizing the allocation of tax base. This has in fact occurred. In other words, the unrestricted exercise of the right to impose and collect taxes is rather limited if the resulting rules cannot be enforced outside the regulating state's own territory. Thus, most countries exercise their jurisdiction to tax by reference to factors that assume a sufficient connection between the relevant country and the taxable person and/or the taxable income.

There are two universally recognized and widely practised national entitlements to tax income: one to the country of residence of the income recipient and one to the country of the source of the income. The economic consequence of the interaction of these entitlements differs in settings of conflict and cooperation. In case of taxation according to the residence principle, the absolute, worldwide ability to pay is considered by the country of residence. This approach is based on the idea that a taxable entity can generally have only one single ability to pay. In contrast, in case of taxation according to the source principle, the ability to pay is split up into a domestic and a foreign part, that is, in the ability to pay in the country of residence and the one in the source country. This concept rests upon the notion that the taxable entity's ability to pay differs depending on the different economic conditions existing in different jurisdictions.[29]

The debate regarding source-based taxation versus residence-based taxation concerns the extent of the ties between people who own, control and manage an enterprise, versus, the location where most business employees, property and activities are situated.[30] The economists disentangled the idea of *situs* (or residence) from the idea of origin. *Situs* is a physical location where the business transaction takes place. Origin (source) is the specific place where income is produced. Direct taxation becomes complicated in an interdependent world as some countries adopt the residence principle, others the source principle or, as is most frequent, a combination of the two. Understanding residence and source as the two primary bases for tax jurisdiction is therefore essential to one's ability to appreciate the difficulties and peculiarities specific to international taxation.[31]

---

29 Schäfer and Spengel (2002) *ICT and International Corporate Taxation: Tax Attributes And Scope of Taxation* Centre For European Economic Research (ZEW) and University of Mannheim.

30 Mukherji (2002) Governing the taxation of digitized trade, Technical Report Working Paper no.2002/05, ASARC, RSPAS, ANU.

31 Begun (2004) 'The scope and Focus of Jinyan Li's Book', *Canadian Tax Journal*, Vol 52, No 1 pp. 109–113.

2.3.1   Source-Based Taxation Principles

A source-based approach (sometimes referred to as a territorial approach) entitles the 'source' country to tax the income of non-residents that is earned within its borders. These are economic activities and capital interests that are substantively connected with that state.[32] A typical example includes real property income and income from economic activities carried on through a commercial or industrial establishment or through an agency. With regard to income from intangible property, the taxing right of the source state, if any, is generally considered to be restricted to a low-rate gross-basis (withholding) tax.[33] Many countries, use 'territorial' systems because they tax only income from sources within their territories, relying even more heavily on sourcing to define the boundaries of their tax systems. Unfortunately, there is inadequate consensus with respect to sourcing rules.[34]

Source-based taxation owes its origin to four economists commissioned by the League of Nations in 1921 to evolve general principles for reducing the incidence of double taxation.[35] They explained that origin is: 'the place where wealth is produced, that is, the community of economic life which makes possible the yield of the acquisition of the wealth. This yield or acquisition is due, however, not only to a particular thing but to the human relations which may help in creating them.'[36] This entitlement to tax at source is the bedrock of most international tax treaties, which recognize as a fundamental entitlement the right of a jurisdiction to tax all income arising within its borders. This permits a country to share in the gains of foreign-owned factors of production operating within its borders, gains that are generated in cooperation with its own inputs, whether they are natural resources, an educated or low-cost workforce or proximity to a market.

The taxation at source of income earned domestically by non-residents preserves inter-nation equity, by giving the country in which resources and other rents are earned the first 'nibble', and, at the same time, the foreign tax credit extended to non-residents by their own government eliminates double taxation of their foreign source income, in effect preserving the residence principle despite taxation at source of non-residents. Source taxation also accords with the widely accepted principle of taxing individuals who receive benefits from public expenditures (the benefit principle of taxation). Both efficiency and common concepts of fairness dictate that those who benefit from government should help to pay for it.

In exercising this tax entitlement, the source country requires an *in rem* or impersonal form of taxation, since a personal form of income taxation is not appropriate for a situation in which only part of the taxpayer's global income is to

---

32 Doernberg and Hinnekens (1999)*Electronic Commerce and International Taxation*, Kluwer Law International.

33 Doernberg and Hinnekens (1999)*Electronic Commerce and International Taxation*, Kluwer Law International, p. 15.

34 Ault (1997) Comparative Income Taxation: A Structural Analysis pp. 431–458.

35 Forst (1997), 'The Continuing Vitality of Source-Based Taxation in the Electronic Age,' *Tax Notes International* 15, 8, pp. 1455–73.

36 Forst (1997), 'The Continuing Vitality of Source-Based Taxation in the Electronic Age,' *Tax Notes International* 15, 8, pp. 1455–73.

be taxed and the taxing authority's entitlement extends only to income earned within its own borders.[37] Source taxation of income is therefore appropriately implemented by a corporate income tax, a payroll tax (in the case of labour income), withholding taxes or an income-type, value-added tax based on the origin principle. The source country has two primary instruments for exercising its entitlement to tax income accruing to non-residents. One is its definition of source, which determines its share of the tax base, and the other is the tax rate that it applies to that share of the base. In the absence of international treaty rules, each source country will tend to choose policy options to serve its own interests with respect to each aspect.[38]

Corporations resident in one country and investing in another usually derive income not only from operations in that one source country but also from other source countries, including the residence country. Consequently, each source country has to determine what share of the worldwide profits of the multinational corporation it can claim for tax purposes. The current international practice of assigning profits to source countries by means of unilateral separate accounting is proving to be increasingly arbitrary as international business operations become more intertwined, with shared costs and overheads and other interdependencies.[39] Variability in accounting rules adds a further complication. In the absence of international agreements each source country will adopt accounting rules and permit transfer pricing that assign to it as large a share of the base as possible. On the other hand, a pure source-based taxation, also enables investors, especially multinational corporations, to play countries off against each other to obtain the lowest source-based tax rate. This type of tax competition already exists for active business income. But the problem would get much worse if source-based taxation were extended to passive income as well, since financial flows are extremely mobile. In that case it is doubtful whether any investment income would be subject to tax anywhere. In addition, the problems of determining the source of income and of combating abusive transfer pricing would become much more acute.

2.3.2   Residence-Based Taxation Principles

Taxation based on residence is partly grounded on the benefit principle, which means that the taxation should occur in the jurisdiction where the taxpayer benefits from the social welfare, infrastructure and other governmental activities paid from the revenue.[40] Under a residence-based system, a country asserts jurisdiction to tax the worldwide income of its residents, regardless of source, this includes dividends,

---

37 Musgrave (2006) 'Combining Fiscal Sovereignty and Coordination *National Taxation In A Globalizing World*', The New Public Finance: Responding to Global Challenges, OUP (NY).

38 Musgrave (2006) 'Combining Fiscal Sovereignty and Coordination *National Taxation In A Globalizing World*', The New Public Finance: Responding to Global Challenges, OUP.

39 Bird and JMintz (2003) 'Sharing the International Tax Base in a Changing World.' In Sijbern Cnossen and Hans Werner Sinn, eds., *Public* Finance and Public Policy in the New Century, Cambridge, Mass.: MIT Press.

40 Westberg (2002) Cross-border Taxation of E-Commerce, IBFD p. 93.

interest, royalty and capital gains that are not directly related to property in another state.[41] In the case of a company, this is usually the place where the company is 'incorporated, registered', or has its 'place of central management and control'.[42] [43] Under 'place of incorporation' a company is considered a resident if it is incorporated within the country in question. Companies incorporated outside the country are considered to be non-residents. Adopting the place of incorporation of a company as a test for determining the corporate residence has the advantage of being a bright-line rule that is easily understood and furthermore enjoys the advantages of certainty and requires minimal cost for compliance and administration.[44]

On the other hand, the test is artificial and formalistic as such, residency can be changed by simply changing the country of incorporation. Further, the 'place of incorporation' test does not require a business to maintain an economic presence within the country; the simple act of filing articles of incorporation will suffice to fulfil the residency requirement. Whilst clearly the 'place of incorporation' of a company provides certainty for corporate taxpayers, it has been described as arbitrary and unrelated to economic reality. It is principally due to these reasons that the OECD Model Convention[45] rejected the place of incorporation as a tie-breaker test for the purposes of determining corporate residence under the OECD Convention.[46]

The 'place of central management and control' test normally involves looking to the location of a company's head office, corporate seat or in the place where the board of directors meet. The test looks to where the 'heart' of a company is located or where the company 'really keeps house and does business', and because it takes into account various factors in making this determination, it is less artificial than the place of incorporation test.[47] Furthermore, it is less vulnerable to manipulation than the place of incorporation test because it is usually a more difficult practical matter to move the location of the management of a company as compared with relocating its place of incorporation. The case of *De Beers Consolidated Mines Ltd v Howe* [1906] AC 455, which dealt with '*central management and control*', demonstrates the importance of the board of directors of the foreign subsidiary carrying out their duties properly in order that the foreign subsidiary be treated as a resident of the

---

41 The OECD Model Convention, Arts 10–13.

42 Avi-Yonah (1996) 'The Structure of International Taxation: A Proposal for Simplification', 74 Tax Law Review, pp. 1301, 1303–06.

43 Some countries, such as United States, adopt a place of incorporation test, while countries including Australia and United Kingdom adopt central management and control test as part of their domestic tests for determining the residence of companies.

44 Pinto (2005) 'A New Three-Tire Proposal for Determining Corporate Residence Based Principally on Individual Residence', Asia-Pacific Tax Bulletin, IBFD January/February, p. 15.

45 Para. 22 of the Commentary to Art. 4 of the OECD Model Convention

46 Pinto (2005) 'A New Three-Tire Proposal for Determining Corporate Residence Based Principally on Individual Residence', Asia-Pacific Tax Bulletin, IBFD January/February, p. 15.

47 Pinto (2005) 'A New Three-Tire Proposal for Determining Corporate Residence Based Principally on Individual Residence', Asia-Pacific Tax Bulletin, IBFD January/February, p. 15.

country where the board meets.[48] This general rule is, however, subject to a number of exceptions. According to Pinto (2005):

> the courts have determined residence under this test where actual business operations occur, notwithstanding that directors may meet in another place.[49] In other cases, the courts have decided that despite operations being conducted abroad, a company may be considered a resident of the domestic country if a managing director exercises complete management and control over the business operations from the domestic jurisdiction.[50]

The place of management test, however, is not a single concept. Article 4(3) of the OECD Model Convention uses the place of effective management as a tie-breaker rule in cases of corporate dual residency. Adopting the place of effective management as a test for corporate residence is based on the concern that exclusive taxation may otherwise reside with a country in which a company is incorporated, while the entire business of the company, including its management, may be controlled from outside that country. It was this concern that led to the adoption of the place of effective management test in relation to shipping and air transport profits that are covered by Article 8 of the OECD Model Convention.[51] According to Skaar, the starting point in determining the place of effective management is to look to the place where the major decisions of an enterprise are made, which should be reflected in the balance sheet of the enterprise.[52] Vogel further suggests that the place of effective management test in the OECD Model Convention is similar to the place of management test used under German domestic law.[53] According to German case law, the place of management is where the management's policies are actually made; what is decisive is not the place where the management directives take effect but rather the place where they are given. It is therefore the 'centre of top level management of an enterprise' that

---

48 Lord Loreburn in his speech took the view that: 'In applying the conception of residence to a company, we ought, I think, to proceed as nearly as we can upon the analogy of an individual. A company cannot eat or sleep, but it can keep house and do business. We ought therefore to see where it really keeps house and does business. The decision of Kelly, CB, and Huddleston, B in Calcutta Jute Mills v Nicholson and Cesena Sulphur Co v Nicholson (1876) 1 Ex D 428, now 30 years ago, involved the principle that a company resides for purposes of income tax where its real business is carried on. Those decisions have been acted upon ever since. I regard that as the true rule, and the real business is carried on where the central management and control actually abides.'

49 *North Australian Pastoral Co Ltd v. FCT* (1946) 71 CLR 623.

50 *Malayan Shipping Co Ltd v. FCT* (1946) 71 CLR 156. This case decided that the company was an Australian resident as the managing director exercised complete management and control over the business operations of the company from Australia, despite the fact that the trading operations of the company took place overseas.

51 Vogel, *Double Taxation Conventions*, (1997), p. 483 as cited in Pinto (2005) 'A New Three-Tire Proposal for Determining Corporate Residence Based Principally on Individual Residence', Asia-Pacific Tax Bulletin, IBFD January/February.

52 Skaar, Permanent Establishment: Erosion of a Tax Treaty Principle, p. 233 (1991).

53 Vogel (1997) *Double Taxation Conventions*.

determines where its place of effective management lies.[54] The place of effective management test has operated hitherto with reasonable success, especially since the determination of important management and commercial decisions would normally be at a board meeting which would be held in a single location, such as the head office.[55] This would also be the place where the top-level management activities occur and accordingly, the OECD has stated that it has therefore been 'rare in practice for a company, to be subject to tax as a resident in more than one State'.[56]

In conventional (closed economy) tax parlance, the residence principle may be viewed more as approximating the ability to pay approach to taxation while the source principle may be viewed as akin to the benefits approach to taxation. The principles of both capital export neutrality (CEN) and capital import neutrality (CIN) could also be theoretically attained if all countries choose a single tax principle (either one) and apply a uniform proportional tax rate. In the absence of such harmonization/ coordination, this outcome will not occur. The residence principle is seen as being preferable as a second-best alternative to tax harmonization, as it will not induce tax competition between countries to attract mobile factors, and will lead to maximization of global production. Economists tend to favour residence jurisdiction, both because they consider the source of income to be hard to pin down (income often has more than one source) and because they think residence jurisdiction promotes economic efficiency since the decision where to invest should be unaffected by the tax rate. However, pure residence taxation is unrealistic for three reasons. First, countries are unlikely to give up the right to collect tax from foreigners doing business within their economy and territory. Second, pure residence-based taxation would reduce revenues in poor developing countries which rely heavily on source-based taxation, in favour of the rich developed countries where investors reside. Third, and most important, residence taxation is much easier to evade or avoid by channelling international investments through tax havens. Strong protection of bank confidentiality and other secrecy provisions in havens make it hard for the residence country to get information about its residents' foreign source income. Residents can channel their income from the source country through a country with an appropriate tax treaty and then park them in a convenient haven. It is very hard for the residence country to try to tax this income, since it is very hard to find out about it. Even countries with highly sophisticated tax administrations find it difficult to combat this and for poorer countries it is virtually impossible.[57] A residence-based tax system also has very high informational requirements. In particular, it requires that either the authorities in the factor-importing country provide the necessary information to tax authorities in

---

54 Vogel (1997) *Double Taxation Conventions*, p. 488 as cited in Pinto (2005) 'A New Three-Tire Proposal for Determining Corporate Residence Based Principally on Individual Residence', Asia-Pacific Tax Bulletin, IBFD January/February.

55 Pinto (2005) 'A New Three-Tire Proposal for Determining Corporate Residence Based Principally on Individual Residence', Asia-Pacific Tax Bulletin, IBFD January/February.

56 Para. 21 of the Commentary to Art. 4 of the OECD MC.

57 Tax Justice Briefing (2005) *Source and Residence Taxation*, Tax Justice Network.

the factor-exporting country, or that the mobile factors truthfully report their foreign incomes.

Direct taxation becomes highly convoluted in an interdependent world, since both source and residence are fluid concepts which can be manipulated. As stated earlier, nearly all countries assert jurisdiction to tax based on the principles of both source and residence. The policies of the various countries whose constituents engage in international trade regarding source- and residence-based taxation may create the potential for the double taxation of certain cross-border flows of income. Zee (1998) argued that the problem could be avoided simply by adopting either one of the two tax principles by all countries. The adherence to a single principle has, however, proved to be either politically unfeasible or (arguably) economically undesirable in the traditional framework of analyses. For example, a system of pure residence-based taxation could require net capital importing (usually developing) countries to surrender their rights to tax a significant proportion of income generated from activities carried out within their national borders. In contrast, a system of pure source-based taxation, in addition to having the effect of moving the tax base in the opposite direction to that of the pure residence-based system, would violate horizontal equity as the foreign-source income of a domestic resident could be taxed differently from its income generated domestically. If the effective tax burden abroad is lower than that at home, a pure source-based system would (all other things being equal) distort investments in favour of foreign locations. For this reason, it is commonly believed that such a system would encourage excessive tax competition.[58]

2.4   Double Taxation: Implications of Tax Treaty Rules

2.4.1 Double Taxation

As stated in the previous section, most countries exercise both their jurisdiction to tax residents on worldwide income and their jurisdiction to tax non-residents in respect of local source income. As a result, a resident of one state who receives income from a source in another country will often be subject in respect of that income to double taxation because of concurrent application of residence-based and source-based taxation.[59] For example, a company resident in country A conducting business through an affiliate in country B, could be taxed in country A on its worldwide income (including that derived through the branch) if country A has a residence-based taxation system. At the same time, the affiliate could be taxed by country B on the income derived through the affiliate if country B has a source-based taxation system. The concurrent exercise of their taxing rights by the country of residence (A) and the source country (B) leads to double taxation. Thus, double taxation can be defined, in a non-exhaustive way, as the imposition of

---

58 Zee (1998) 'Taxation of Financial Capital in a Globalized Environment: The Role of Withholding Taxes,' National Tax Journal, Volume 51 no. 3 (September 1998) pp. 587–599.

59 Doernberg and Hinnekens (1999)Electronic Commerce and International Taxation, Kluwer Law International, p. 17.

comparable taxes by two or more sovereign countries on the same item of income of the same taxable person for the same taxable period.[60] However, it does not just mean that the same transaction is effectively taxed more than once; it means that the sum of these separate taxes is higher than it ought to be.[61] Other causes of double taxation include divergent characterization of facts for tax purposes and divergent personal attribution of income. This can be the case for individuals maintaining habitual abode or conducting professional activities in two or more countries. It can also be the case for companies operating in countries with different corporate laws. For example, a company may be incorporated under the laws of country A which determines residence by reference to the place of incorporation (that is, it considers as a resident any company incorporated under its laws). At the same time, the company may be effectively managed and controlled from country B which determines residence by reference to the place of effective management. Such a company would meet the residence test in both countries and can therefore be taxed as a resident by both countries A and B. Likewise, two or more states which each deem, by their own definition, an item of income to arise from sources within their territory can concurrently tax the same item of income. Finally, double taxation can also result from mismatches in accounting standards or in the timing of income recognition. Double taxation comes in three basic forms:

- residence-residence double taxation;
- residence-source double taxation; and
- source-source double taxation.

Residence-residence double taxation occurs when a taxpayer is deemed a resident of more than one nation and each asserts the right to tax on a residence basis. Residence-source double taxation arises when one nation seeks to tax income on a residence basis and another country asserts the right to tax the same flow of income on a source basis. Finally, source-source double taxation exists when each of two nations that tax on a source basis considers a particular flow of income to have a domestic source.[62] To avoid double taxation, in principle, there would be two solutions to this problem. States could delegate the power to tax international income to an international authority (con-joint taxation) or they agree on some rule to share the jurisdiction to tax between them. Leaving aside the European Union, the first option has never seriously been contemplated and is generally believed to be utopian.[63] Consequently, the problem of double taxation has been dealt with along the lines of the second option. Framed in this way, the basic question that has to be answered is:

---

60 Arnold and McIntyre (1995) *International Tax Primer* (The Hague: Kluwer Law International).

61 Bracewell-Milnes (1980) T*he Economics of International Tax Avoidance*, Kluwer pp. 27–30.

62 Mitchell (1997) 'United States-Brazil Bilateral Income Tax Treaty Negotiations', 21 Hastings International & Computer Law Review. 209, pp. 213, 214–15.

63 Tanzi (1999) 'Is There a Need for a World Tax Organization?' In Razin, and Sadka (eds.), *Economics of Globalization: Policy Perspectives from Public Economics*. pp. 173–186. Cambridge: Cambridge University Press.

which country has the right to tax the income and which country has to restrict its tax claims?[64]

2.2.2   Tax Treaty Rules

The principal methods of relieving international double taxation are the tax-credit method and exemption. Bilateral tax treaties, or tax conventions as they are often called, attempt to resolve issues of double taxation of multinational income, discriminatory tax treatment of foreign enterprises and the promotion of information exchanges between tax authorities. More than 2000 bilateral treaties have been concluded worldwide, based on the recommendations of the OECD model double taxation convention.[65] There are several reasons why tax treaties are useful and important. From the perspective of a capital-exporting country, a tax treaty is important in that it affords its own enterprises, to the extent possible, a level playing field in a given foreign market, in comparison with enterprises of other capital-exporting countries.[66] At the same time, bilateral tax treaties also create possibilities for the exchange of information between capital-exporting and capital-importing countries and can support the prevention of fraud and abuse. Common bilateral tax treaties solve the double taxation problem by restricting the taxing rights of the source country, which correspondingly increases the taxing jurisdiction of the residence country. Where a source country retains its rights to tax a particular flow of income, the country of residence may avoid double taxation on that income in one of two ways:

- by granting a credit to its resident taxpayers for taxes paid to the foreign jurisdiction; or
- by exempting the foreign source income from the taxable income base of its taxpayers.[67]

Under the current international tax system,[68] it is generally left to the residence country to alleviate double taxation. The first is the 'worldwide' or 'credit' method in which the residence country taxes foreign source income but provides a credit for taxes paid to foreign jurisdictions. A variation of the credit method is the 'tax sparing' or 'matching credit' method, under which the country of residence in effect grants a credit for a tax that is higher than the tax actually levied in the source country. The credit method attempts to achieve full 'horizontal equity' more effectively than

---

64 Genschel and Rixen (2005) *International Tax Cooperation and National Tax Sovereignty*, Paper prepared for the Conference on 'Market Making and Market Shaping in the Global Political Economy' Open University Hagen, December, 2005.

65 Haufler (2001) *Taxation in a Global Economy*, Cambridge University Press, p. 51.

66 UNCTAD (2000) *Taxation:* On issues in international investment agreements, UN, New York and Geneva.

67 Treasury Paper at p. 7.1.2.

68 Avi-Yonah (2000) 'Commentary to International Tax Arbitrage and the 'International Tax System', 53 Tax Law Review p. 167.

the deduction or exemption method.[69] However, the credit method is complex from both compliance and an enforcement perspective, as the foreign income needs to be recomputed according to domestic rules.

> It may also discourage investments abroad or encourage the deferral (i.e. non-repatriation) of types of foreign income, such as dividends, which are normally not assessed for tax in the country of residence until actually received. Since the taxpayer's ultimate tax liability is the higher of the country of residence and source country tax, the source country can manipulate the credit method to its advantage by increasing its own tax up to the amount of the country of residence tax without, on balance, aggravating the ultimate tax position of the investor.[70]

The second is the 'exemption' method under which the residence country cedes all taxing jurisdiction to the source country.[71] The foreign tax is, therefore, the only tax burden borne by that income. This method is most favourable to the taxpayer if the source country tax is lower than the country of residence tax. It is also easily enforceable, fosters CIN and, in principle, does not encourage deferral of income. However, it is more prone to abuse and can cause discrimination between residents, depending on whether they realize domestic or foreign income. Normally, the exemption method is applied by the country of residence. For certain types of income, however, tax arrangements may require the source country to exempt the income. This is generally the case for passive income, including royalties and capital gains.[72]

Most tax treaties restrict the taxation of multi-jurisdictional business income in the source country, unless a sufficient nexus can be established. Under the current system of international taxation, the determination of the source of active business income is critical because it ultimately determines the allocation of tax revenues between jurisdictions. Domestic source rules that allow unfettered taxation of enterprises carrying on business within the country invariably cede priority to treaty provisions that limit host country taxation in certain circumstances. However, jurisdictional rules for the taxation of multinational income vary significantly from one nation to another and from one income type to another.[73] If an enterprise is

---

69 Equity is discussed in detail in Chapter 4.

70 UNCTAD (2000) *Taxation:* On issues in international investment agreements, UN, New York and Geneva.

71 Some countries, such as France, do not tax their residents on a worldwide basis but simply exempt certain foreign income from domestic tax. Under the exemption or territorial method, the taxpayer is unilaterally relieved from double taxation by the country of residence exempting foreign source income from the resident taxpayer's taxable income base. Under the United States and Canadian tax systems, this exemption or territorial system for double taxation relief is utilized only for a few designated types of income, such as in respect of exempt dividends of certain foreign affiliates.

72 UNCTAD (2000) *Taxation:* On issues in international investment agreements, UN, New York and Geneva.

73 Many developed countries have established some form of foreign income accrual rules to protect against the avoidance or excessive deferral of tax on passive income. These rules are necessary because even though countries purport to tax worldwide income on the basis

a resident of a country that has a bilateral tax treaty with the country where the buyer of the enterprise's product resides, then most tax treaties provide that the non-resident business must have a PE in the host country before that country can tax the income derived from such sales.

The concept of PE as evidence of the physical presence nexus for taxation is introduced through the provisions of international tax treaties. These tax treaty provisions effectively override the domestic source rules of both countries when dealing with a foreign enterprise resident in a treaty partner country. By stipulating that there must be a PE within the host or source country before the income of the foreign business can be taxed by the host or source country, the treaty serves to allocate taxing jurisdiction (and revenues) away from the treasury of the source country in favour of the country where the enterprise is resident. So by entering into a bilateral tax treaty, a nation agrees to forego its taxing authority over non-resident enterprises that do not maintain a PE within the country. Tax treaties also establish a set of rules for the attribution of business income and expenses to the activities of foreign enterprises. Most model tax conventions provide that only business income attributed or connected to a PE within the source country will be subject to taxation in accordance with the source country's domestic income tax laws.[74]

Foreign tax credits, however, do not always alleviate the burden of double taxation. The United States, for example, will not allow a tax credit in a source-source double taxation situation, where both the United States and another country deem a certain item of income to have a domestic source. In such a situation, the taxpayer, for U.S. tax purposes, does not derive any foreign source income. Since the existence of foreign source income is essential to generate a foreign tax credit for U.S. tax purposes double taxation will persist in such a case. Because the source-source situation creates the potential for double taxation without any corresponding relief from foreign tax credit provisions, it remains particularly problematic. Conversely the source-source situation also carries with it the risk of tax avoidance. A tax avoidance opportunity could arise when each of two countries considers an income flow to have a foreign source, and neither country asserts jurisdiction to tax on a residence basis. Since most countries employ residence-and source-basis taxation, this tax avoidance scenario should not arise too often.[75]

The relief from double taxation in global trade and investment is often cited as the primary motivating force towards bilateral and multilateral cooperation in the

---

of residency, they generally do not tax foreign income until it is repatriated to the residence country. Since resident companies would be inclined to defer repatriation of income in order to avoid taxation, tax authorities around the world have designed rules that permit the residence country to tax certain forms of investment income, such as interest, dividends and royalties, on an accrual basis regardless of whether or not the profits are actually distributed back to the home country.

74 See OECD Model Treaty, Article 7(2).

75 Sweet (1998) 'Formulating International Tax Laws In The Age Of Electronic Commerce: The Possible Ascendancy Of Residence-Based Taxation In An Era Of Eroding Traditional Income Tax Principles', 146 U. Pa. L. Rev. p. 1949, *University of Pennsylvania Law Review*, 1998 August.

field of international taxation.[76] The reality of international taxation, however, is that the foreign tax credit rules or exemption systems found in the domestic laws of most developed countries effectively alleviate the incidence of double taxation of multinational business income. Given that countries have unilaterally taken steps to protect their residents from double taxation of foreign source income, what is the primary force that drives the conclusion of tax treaties?

In order to understand the development of the current tax treaty system, one must appreciate that international tax rules have been motivated not by concerns of the plight of the taxpayer as much as by the fiscal demands of taxing nations. Tax treaties do not levy any new taxes but provide rules by which nations can accommodate competing tax claims, but in essence they achieve nothing more (and nothing less) than disentangling the transnational tax base and assigning it to different jurisdictions so that these can apply their own domestic rules to their share of the tax base.[77] The bilateral treaties merely help to 'coordinate divergent national tax laws';[78] they regulate the interface of autonomous national tax systems. A nation's tax treatment of the multinational income of its residents is modified by the rules and principles established by bilateral tax treaties. Where income is derived by a resident of one country from sources in a foreign country, and if both countries assert a legitimate claim to tax that income, then either country may view an agreement to grant the other the primary right to tax that income as a loss of tax revenue.[79] The assignment of primary tax jurisdiction to one country will result in the loss of tax revenue to the other treaty country. In effect, the allocation of tax jurisdiction in a bilateral treaty constitutes a fiscal transfer mechanism between nations. Neither the foreign tax credit nor the exemption method would eliminate instances of double taxation that result from overlapping source of income rules.[80]

The lack of worldwide uniformity in establishing jurisdictional rules can be attributed to numerous factors, but the primary factors appear to be differences in historical antecedents and the conscious attempt by governments to expand or protect territorial claims.[81] Similarly, uniformity of tax systems around the world

---

76 Warren. 'A Income Tax Discrimination Against International Commerce' (2001) 54 *Tax L. R.* p. 131. Many bilateral tax treaties are invariably referred to as a 'Convention to Prevent Double Taxation'.

77 Genschel and Rixen (2005) International Tax Cooperation and National Tax Sovereignty, Paper prepared for the Conference on 'Market Making and Market Shaping in the Global Political Economy' Open University Hagen, December, 2005.

78 Li (2003). International Taxation in the Age of Electronic Commerce: A Comparative Study. Toronto: Canadian Tax Foundation p. 33.

79 International treaty negotiation is, to some extent, a zero-sum game: see Avi-Yonah, The Structure of International Taxation: A Proposal for Simplification (1996) Texas Law Review, p. 1301.

80 Kaufman (1998) Fairness and the Taxation of International Income, 29 *Law and Policy in Intentional Business* 145, pp. 149-150. Taxpayers caught in overlapping source of income rules must usually rely on the provisions contained in an income tax treaty to prevent double taxation.

81 Palmer (1989) Toward Unilateral Coherence in Determining Jurisdiction to Tax Income 30 *Harvard International Law Journal*, p. 6

is not feasible because countries will not cede national tax sovereignty, and consequently the diversity of nations' tax rules must be handled by special rules at the interface of tax systems. A corollary that has been found to apply in practice is that the different features of each interface of two tax systems mean that reconciliation is done on a case-by-case basis, that is, bilateral rather than multilateral treaties have become the rule.[82] 'In this sense, the term "international tax" is a misnomer, since there is no overriding international law of taxation'.[83]

2.5   Development of the 'Permanent Establishment' Concept

The concept of a PE is probably the single most important concept found in tax treaties since it serves to establish taxing jurisdiction by the source country over a foreigner's unincorporated business activities (including activities of a branch).[84] The non-resident enterprise's profits from business activities are taxable by the source country only if the enterprise has a PE located in the source country.[85] As will be seen further, 'the purpose of the PE rules is to specify under what conditions a resident of one country will be subject to taxation in a second country. If a resident of the first country has a PE in the second country, he may be subject to tax in that second country, otherwise he is not taxable on business profits.'[86] Source-country income taxes are generally only applied to active business income when a PE (that must be an unincorporated company and thus not a legal entity) exists within its borders. If no PE exists within the source country, the business profits would thus either escape taxation or, as is typically the case, would be taxed by the residence country. Hence, PE is a defined term in each bilateral tax treaty and generally consists of 'a fixed place of business through which the business of an enterprise is wholly or partly carried on'.[87] Tax treaties offer examples of PE including stores, offices, branches or factories. In addition, tax treaties typically exclude from the definition of a PE activities related to a physical presence within a source country that are merely preparatory or auxiliary in nature such as the maintenance of a warehouse to store goods.[88]

---

82 Vann (1991) A Model Tax Treaty for the Asian-Pacific Region? (Part I). Bulletin for International Fiscal Documentation 45(3): 99-111.

83 Li (2003). International Taxation in the Age of Electronic Commerce: A Comparative Study. Toronto: Canadian Tax Foundation p. 31.

84 Levine and Weintraub (2000) 'When Does E-Commerce Result in a Permanent Establishment? The OECD's initial response' 04 Tax Management International Journal, p 219, April 14, 2000.

85 Organisation for Economic Co-Operation and Development, Model Tax Convention on Income and on Capital (2003) as they read on 28th January 2003 (hereinafter OECD Model Treaty).

86 Peschcke-Koedt (1998) 'A Practical Approach to Permanent Establishment Issues in A Multinational Enterprise', 98 Tax Notes International 95-15, May 1998 Para. I (B) (1) p. 1601.

87 See OECD Model Tax Treaty, at Art. 5(1).

88 Ibid. at Art. 5(4).

So where does the rule come from? A detailed explanation of the historical background of PE is beyond the scope of this chapter. The earliest version of the PE principle has been traced to the late 1800s when European nations negotiated bilateral tax treaties to govern the tax treatment of cross-border economic activity.[89] The modern version of the rule arose after the First World War when nations became concerned that international double taxation was inhibiting international trade and investment.[90] In his study of the application of the principle by national tax authorities, Skaar notes that the principle has undergone a significant dilution during the past half century to take into account emerging commercial practices. Enhanced global trade, the rise of the service sector, increased mobility of capital and other factors of production all contributed to a perceived need to modify the physical presence requirement of the traditional PE. The definition of a PE within the current OECD model treaty is the commonly accepted standard for double tax treaties throughout the world. It uses the PE concept to define the contact required to support source taxation of foreign goods and 'business profits' in general. It 'requires a definitive, organized contact or presence so that casual business connections or even a steady stream of exports without a "business presence" of the foreign exporter will not trigger source taxation'. PE is defined in Article 5(1) of the OECD Model Tax Convention and is interpreted in the commentary as containing three conditions:

- the existence of a 'place of business', that is, a facility such as premises or, in certain instances, machinery or equipment ('place-of-business test');
- this place of business must be 'fixed', that is, it must be established at a distinct place with a certain degree of permanence ('permanence test'); and
- the carrying on of the business of the enterprise through this fixed place of business. This usually means that persons who, in one way or another, are dependent on the enterprise (personnel) conduct the business of the enterprise in the state in which the fixed place is situated ('business-activities test').

Each of these three conditions must be met before activity of a business enterprise can be deemed to result in a PE and together they are often termed the 'fixed place of business test'. The place of business is usually the location where the business activity of the foreign company occurs, but the necessity of satisfying all three requirements sometimes leads to different results. The term 'fixed' is typically broken into two components: 'spatial and temporal'. One refers to a geographical status within the taxing state; the other refers to a time component. In other words, the business activity must be able to be linked to a specified geographical area[91] and the activity must not

---

89 The requirement for a fixed place of business within source countries is typically traced back to the tax treaty between Austria-Hungary and Prussia in 1899. For background, see Skaar, Permanent Establishment: Erosion of a Tax Treaty Principle pp. 65–101 (1991).

90 Cockfield (2004) 'Reforming the Permanent Establishment Principle Through a Quantitative. Economic Presence Test', vol. 33, no. 7 *Tax Notes International*.

91 Geographical status was easily identifiable as a plant, office or factory.

be of a purely temporary nature.[92] However, many businesses are able to function without the use of a traditional fixed status, thereby complicating the determination of the geographical status requirement. The PE definition was broadened to include dependent agents that habitually conclude contracts in source countries.[93] Further, construction projects lasting more than 12 months constitute a PE (often reduced to six months in tax treaties).[94] There are, however, a number of 'fictions' set out in provisions of the model tax treaties that attempt to circumvent the requirement of geographical and temporal 'permanence'. These fictions ensure that certain temporary and mobile activities are caught by the definition of PE. For example, there are provisions to ensure that the income generated by entertainers could be taxed in the source state despite the absence of any real fixed place of business.[95] In addition to this, commentary accompanying the OECD Model Tax Convention[96] and other convention models specifically identifies certain types of activities that may be considered a PE which include especially: place of management; a branch; an office; a factory; a workshop; a mine, an oil or gas well, a quarry or any other place of extraction of natural resources. This list is illustrative and non-exclusive.

> A general principle to be observed in determining whether a permanent establishment exists is that the place of business must be fixed in the sense that a particular building or physical location is used by the enterprise for the conduct of its business, and that is must be foreseeable that the enterprise's use of this building or other physical location will be more than temporary.[97]

Certain treaty provisions negotiated between countries further dilute the PE principle beyond the developments within model tax treaties.[98] For example, the tax treaty between Norway and the United Kingdom includes provisions to ensure pure source state taxation of offshore petroleum related activities, which 'implies that several of the traditional conditions for PEs under the basic rule are completely abandoned'.[99] Finally, the United Nations model tax treaty has broadened the definition of PE to strengthen source state taxation, which is typically in the interest of developing nations. For example, a PE within this model tax treaty is defined

---

92 OECD Model Treaty, commentary to Art. 5, at p. 5 'the place of business has to be a "fixed" one. Thus in the normal way there has to be a link between the place of business and a specific geographical point.' ('Permanent establishment can be deemed to exist only if the place of business has a certain degree of permanency, i.e. if it is not of a purely temporary nature.') (as they read on 28th January 2003).

93 OECD Model Tax Treaty, at Art. 5(5).

94 Ibid. at Art. 5(3).

95 OECD Model Treaty, Art. 17.

96 OECD Model Treaty, commentary to Art. 5, at p. 2–30.

97 United States Model Income Tax Convention, Technical Explanation, paragraph 69.

98 For a detailed discussion see Cockfield (2004) 'Reforming the Permanent Establishment Principle through a Quantitative. Economic Presence Test', vol. 33, no. 7 *Tax Notes International*.

99 For a detailed discussion see Cockfield (2004) 'Reforming the Permanent Establishment Principle through a Quantitative. Economic Presence Test', vol. 33, no. 7 *Tax Notes International*.

to include independent agents in certain circumstances as well as the performance of services that last longer than six months.[100] A 'restricted force of attraction' rule additionally expands source state taxation by permitting states where non-residents maintain traditional PE to tax other income that is attracted to the PE even though this income is not directly related to the PE.[101] Other multilateral tax treaties such as the Andean Pact moved to exclusive sourced-based taxation, downplaying physical presence tests. Increased economic integration along with information technology developments like the internet represent a renewed threat to the usefulness of the PE concept.[102]

Hence the question here is can the rule be justified? Contemporary international tax policy analysis often employs guiding principles to evaluate a particular legal rule such as the PE principle. Cockfield argues that,

> on the equity side, various entitlement theories such as the benefit principle, economic allegiance or inter-nation equity are used to justify a particular tax policy choice. On the efficiency side, commentators typically trot out goals such as promoting capital export neutrality, capital import neutrality, the need for low compliance and tax administration costs and so on.[103]

However, the truth is that there is very little agreement on the appropriate set of guiding principles for international tax policy and an honest view might suggest that current justifications suffer from a certain degree of arbitrariness.[104] The arbitrariness can be partly explained by the absence of any world tax authority to unify the disparate theories. In contrast, tax systems at the national level can at least theoretically be brought into concordance with accepted guiding principles through political measures as electorates can toss out legislators that impose politically unacceptable taxes. Due to the absence of any world tax organization, developments in international tax policy result less from the application of accepted guiding principles, but rather take form from a combination of the exercise of economic power and the pragmatic need to promote cross-border economic activity to enhance domestic welfare through international trade and investment. In other words, countries strive to collect as much tax revenue as possible from international trade and investment without upsetting the apple cart by provoking retaliations from major trade partners.[105] For example, there is no sacred reason why a physical presence requirement should be used to determine nexus for international income tax purposes. Commentators have noted that the exertion of tax jurisdiction over significant sales into a source country can be

---

100   United Nations Model Tax Treaty, at Art. 5.

101   Ibid. at Art. 7.

102   Cockfield (2004b) 'Reforming the Permanent Establishment Principle through a Quantitative. Economic Presence Test', vol. 33, no. 7 *Tax Notes International.*

103   Cockfield (2004b) 'Reforming the Permanent Establishment Principle through a Quantitative. Economic Presence Test', vol. 33, no. 7 *Tax Notes International.*

104   Cockfield (2004b) 'Reforming the Permanent Establishment Principle through a Quantitative. Economic Presence Test', vol. 33, no. 7 *Tax Notes International.*

105   Cockfield (1998)Tax Integration under NAFTA: Resolving the Conflict between Economic and Sovereignty Interests, 34 Stanford Journal of International Law p. 39.

justified simply on the basis that the source country market presented opportunities for the profits to be generated in the first place. For example, Vogel suggests: 'It cannot convincingly be denied that providing a market contributes to the sales income at least to some extent as providing the goods do. There is no valid objection, therefore, against a claim of the state to tax part of the sales income.'[106]

Other potential justifications for taxation despite an absence of a physical presence include the fact that the source country government provided the means to access the market by building roads and other infrastructure.[107] Finally, permitting capital importing countries (especially developing countries) to enjoy revenues from taxing cross-border transactions offers these countries an incentive to subsidize telecommunications facilities and networks, which in turn expands market opportunities for capital exporting nations.[108]

Having noted the arbitrariness of existing rationales, it is still possible to argue that the PE principle has served well the international community or at least the developed nations that implemented and supported the principle. The principle can be justified from an efficiency perspective as it offered a relatively straightforward compliance guide to businesses and tax authorities. A multinational firm understands that it will not have to hire a foreign accountant, register as a taxpayer, maintain records pursuant to foreign tax laws, file a tax return, and so on in a foreign jurisdiction unless it sets up shop in the source country. Similarly, the physical presence requirement permitted the foreign tax authority to audit and, if necessary, seize property to satisfy an outstanding tax liability.

The PE principle can also be supported from an equity perspective. Historically, most multinational companies would typically not set up a store or branch office unless these companies intended to conduct significant business activity within the source country. In an age when international trade most often contemplated cross-border sales of manufactured goods, a physical presence within foreign markets was often necessary to engage in significant operations. Source countries hence were only permitted to tax significant and recurring cross-border activity taking place within their borders. As long as this assumption held, the PE rule enabled a relatively balanced sharing of tax revenues from cross-border activities: capital exporting countries enjoyed the revenues associated with taxing production while capital importing nations derived revenues from taxing sales functions.[109]

In any event, the proof, as they say, is in the pudding, and the PE principle appears to have promoted or, at a minimum, did not inhibit cross-border trade and investment, enhancing national and international welfare. The success of the principle, however,

---

106   Vogel (1998) Worldwide vs. Source Taxation of Income – A Review and Re-evaluation of Arguments, INTERTAX pp. 393, 400.

107   McLure (2000) Alternatives to the Concept of Permanent Establishment, Report of the Proceedings of the World Tax Conference: Taxes Without Borders 61–15 (CTF 2000).

108   Cockfield (2002d) The Real Digital Divide: Electronic Commerce, Developing Countries and Declining Tax Revenues, *UNESCO Encyclopedia of Life Support Systems*, 6.31.3.6.

109   Cockfield (2004b) 'Reforming the Permanent Establishment Principle through a Quantitative. Economic Presence Test', vol. 33, no. 7 *Tax Notes International.*

is almost certainly related to the flexibility of the concept, which has adapted to changing commercial practices. A more cynical view might suggest that the PE concept arose from the economic dominance of industrialized nations who favoured residence-based taxation since they were generally capital exporters when the rules were initiated. In fact, it cannot be overlooked that many developing nations have opposed the PE principle almost since its inception.[110]

2.6   Characterization of Income

Income characterization, or the classification and assignment of income method, was adopted as the backbone of tax treaties by the League of Nations in the 1920s and has been the basis for bilateral divisions of taxing powers since then. Income derived from commerce activities can be divided into two main categories: (1) business profits; (2) remuneration from the use of technology, know-how or royalties. This distinction is important because the tax treatment of the different types of income often varies under the tax legislation of most countries. Certainly in cross-border situations, this may lead to problems, for instance, on the applicability of withholding taxes on royalties. Tax rules under domestic laws, as well as treaties, impose different tax treatment on different types of cross-border income. For example, business profits are sourced (in the absence of a PE within foreign markets) to the country where the income-producing business is based and taxed on a net basis. Royalty income, on the other hand, is generally sourced to the country where the intellectual property was used (for example, the country where the consumer of the intellectual property is resident) and may be subject to gross withholding taxes.[111]

In addition to the geographic rules that source income to taxing jurisdictions, there exists a series of rules that allocate taxing jurisdiction and taxing method depending on the character of the income produced by a cross-border transaction. In fact, a determination of the character of income is the first step towards analyzing the appropriate tax treatment for a cross-border transaction.[112] For international income tax purposes, characterization rules are important in the context of tax treaties as well as domestic laws for situations where tax treaties do not exist. The proper characterization of income and accompanying source rules are often important to determine the availability of foreign tax credits. For example, the United States provides relief from double taxation by offering a foreign tax credit for foreign taxes paid on foreign source income alone. The analysis herein focuses on characterization issues in the tax treaty context. Tax treaties impose different tax treatment on different

---

110   Zapata (1998)The Latin American Approach to the Concept of Permanent Establishment in Tax Treaties with Developed Countries, 52 Bulletin for International Fiscal Documentation p. 252.

111   Cockfield (2006) 'The Rise of the OECD as Informal 'world tax organization' Through the Shaping of National Responses to E-commerce Tax Challenges,' *Yale Journal of Law and Technology.*

112   Cockfield (2002b) The Law and Economics of Digital Taxation: Challenges to Traditional Tax Laws and Principles, Berkeley-Keio Seminar on International Tax Law Concerning Digital Financial Innovation at Keio University in Tokyo on June 6–7, 2002.

types of income. For example, normal business profits are sourced (in the absence of a PE within foreign markets) to the country where the income-producing business is based.[113] While these classification principles often bear little relationship to economic reality, the classification rules have formed part of traditional international tax norms and have been relatively straightforward to administer from a tax authority perspective. Traditional economic activity was slotted into the appropriate classification and profits or gross receipts (and corresponding tax revenues) were allocated to the appropriate tax sovereign.[114]

2.7   Transfer Pricing

The difficulty of characterizing income payments and identifying their source has been at the heart of most international tax disputes. A particular problem these issues give rise to is that of transfer pricing. With growing specialization in production of components in different locations across the globe, intra-firm transactions account for a growing share of world trade. With the global dominance of the multinational companies in trade and related transactions, one of the major issues of tax policy is the allocation of the tax base for these firms between countries. Transfer pricing refers to:

> a means of allocating costs between units of a large organization or multinational company for goods or services supplied. The pricing may be based on allocating true profits to the individual units, although in the case of multinational companies, the price may be chosen to avoid paying excessive taxes or duties in one particular country.[115]

For the sake of simplicity, it should be highlighted that transfer pricing occurs between a company and its subsidiaries in other countries or country. 'Allocating costs' refers to when multinationals sell/buy products between themselves and the prices would be either extremely high or extremely low depending on which jurisdiction they wanted money to remain in. These transactions could help avoid in some cases millions of dollars. Governments realized the problem and implemented legislation accordingly. Among some of the different methods that governments implemented, the 'arm's length principle'[116] was instituted, which basically established that the sale prices would have to be according to market prices, in other words, 'what the price would have been if the entities really had been independent of one another'.[117] But in many cases – and perhaps most – there is no 'arm's length price' – the price that would prevail in transactions between unrelated parties – against which to judge whether transfer prices are reasonable. Thus, it is difficult to know whether 'separate accounting' (accounting intended to measure the income of the various members of

---

113   US Model Tax Treaty, at Art. 7; OECD Model Tax Treaty, at Art. 7.

114   Cockfield (2002b).

115   *A Dictionary of Finance and Banking*. Oxford University Press, 2nd Ed. p. 357.

116   Ogley (1993) The principles of international tax. (Intersfisc Publishing) p. 155.

117   Dorgan (2000) 'Global Shell Games', Washington Monthly. Obtained from: http://www.alternet.org/story/9464.

a corporate group) accurately determines the income of various entities. Transfer prices can be manipulated to minimize taxes (or for other reasons).

Manipulation of transfer prices is not the only reason separate accounting often cannot be used to divide the income of affiliated firms. Pervasive economic interdependence is inherent in the nature of the modern corporation; that is, the activities of one part of a firm may influence the income of other parts in ways that defy quantification. Where this occurs, it is often appropriate to use a formula to apportion the total income of the firm among jurisdictions. The need for formula apportionment does not arise only within a given legal entity; it may also be difficult to know where a group of affiliated firms earns its income.[118] Economic interdependence and transfer pricing problems may be every bit as great between affiliated corporations as within a single legal entity. In response to these and other problems, some of the states of the United States employ combined reporting, under which the income and apportionment factors of related corporations are 'combined' to determine the income subject to tax by a given state.[119] The transfer pricing regimes of most countries possess two fundamental characteristics – to require a transactional approach (that is, to consider each transaction separately) and to establish comparability (taking into account functions performed, assets used and risks assumed) between the controlled and the uncontrolled transactions. Comparability is broadly the link between the arm's length principle and the operation of arm's length pricing methodologies.

---

118   See, for example, McLure (1984) and (1986).

119   There is substantial disagreement about the proper scope of combination. Some states (and some taxpayers) prefer worldwide combination, while others prefer to limit combination to the 'water's edge'. Bowing to pressures from multinational corporations, the U.S. government, and the governments of other developed countries, the states no longer require worldwide combination.

Chapter 3

International Taxation: Indirect Taxation

Introduction

Taxation has either direct or indirect effects on almost every aspect of production and distribution in modern economies.[1] Taxes such as tax on goods and services which include general sales tax, VAT, excise duty, import and export duties form the indirect taxes. These taxes are an important source of revenue for most of the governments around the world. They either follow the European model of VAT or the US model of sales tax. VAT is an indirect, multi-stage consumption tax. As an *indirect tax*, the VAT is levied upon the articles of trade before they reach the customer, who eventually pays the tax-inclusive market price. The label 'indirect' follows from the fact that the payer of the VAT does not suffer a corresponding reduction in their income from such purchases. VAT is insensitive to the individual circumstances of the taxpayer following from its 'indirectness' and it is not an effective means of redistribution. Sales tax is a tax on the retail sale of specified tangible property or services, which have historically been sold over the counter to the buyer and collected at the location where the good is transferred from the seller to the buyer. This will include personal property and in some cases intangible property is also subject to sales tax as tangible personal property, for example computer software is sometimes considered tangible and therefore taxable. Real property is usually not subject to sales tax, but may be subject to transfer tax. Three factors determine whether sales tax liability in a particular state exists for a transaction: (i) the type of good being sold; (ii) *situs*, or the location where the transaction takes place; and (iii) nexus. This chapter contains a comprehensive overview of the principles of the European VAT system and the sales and use tax system of the United States.

3.1   Indirect Taxation

I have discussed in the previous chapter that direct tax is based on the equity or income of corporate or individual entities. In the case of indirect taxation, however, taxes are levied on the taxpayer's consumption activities and the value of those taxes is added to the price of the product that is being sold or of the service being provided. In indirect taxation, the actual taxpayer, that is, the person who bears the financial burden of the tax, does not pay the tax directly to the public treasury.[2] Since this type

---

1   James (2001) *Taxation Research as Economic Research* Paper number 01/07 ISSN No: 1473 2939, University of Exeter Research Discussion Paper.

2   The distinction between direct and indirect taxes relates to 'whether the person who actually pays the money over to the tax collecting authority suffers a corresponding reduction in his income. If he does, then – in the traditional language – impact and incidence are on

of tax is levied on the operations that are carried out by business owners or service providers, they are the ones who are liable for payment to the state. Considering the types of charges, there are three kinds of indirect taxes: cumulative indirect taxes, indirect taxes on value-added, and indirect taxes on sales (retail and excise taxes).

In the first case, the tax is levied on each operation and includes the tax levied on its respective input. In other words, the tax calculation basis of a sales operation includes the tax that has been levied on the previous operation. Cascading taxes of this type represent a heavier tax burden for products whose production or commercialization processes involve a number of different stages. Since no offsetting mechanisms are included in their calculation, it is easier to levy and to pay such taxes. Though the procedure for calculating and levying cumulative indirect taxes is simpler, such taxes do not favour the competitiveness of national products vis-à-vis their foreign counterparts. The successive levying of this tax on the different stages of production makes it difficult to quantify the amounts that have been collected and that must be included in the calculations of an item's production cost. The fact that it is impossible to eliminate all the taxes that are levied on export products offers comparative advantages to imported products which, as a rule, are not submitted to a similar treatment in their countries of origin.

Value added tax (VAT) makes use of the billing/credit type of method and a tax is imposed only on the portion of additional revenue that is generated at each stage of the production and commercialization process. This type of tax provides the governments with a regular inflow of revenue because it is levied according to the development of the chain of production. It is a more sophisticated type of levy that involves a more complex technique for calculating the tax to be collected since the tax that has already been levied on the previous stages is not included in the calculation basis of an operation. The sales tax category includes two types of indirect taxes: the retail sales tax and the excise tax. They are imposed at a single specific moment of the chain of production or commercialization. A general sales tax is applied to the sale of all commodities and services. As such, it is distinguished from an excise tax imposed upon the sale of particular commodities or services.[3] 'A general sales tax by its comprehensive nature tends to be more neutral than excise taxation.'[4]

3.2   Comparison of Income and Consumption Taxation

From an economic viewpoint, sales tax and VAT taxation are consumption-based. 'They are an indirect tax on the consumption of economic wealth.'[5] The intellectual

---

the same person and the tax is direct; if not and the burden is shifted and the real income of someone else is affected (i.e., impact and incidence are on different people) then the tax is indirect.' See Alan Schenk and Oliver Oldman(2006) Value Added Tax: A Comparative Approach, (Cambridge University Press).

   3   Doernberg, Richard L. and Hinnekens, Luc (1999) Electronic Commerce and International Taxation Kluwer Law International, p 21.

   4   Doernberg, Richard L. and Hinnekens, Luc (1999) Electronic Commerce and International Taxation Kluwer Law International, p 21.

   5   Doernberg, Richard L. and Hinnekens, Luc (1999) Electronic Commerce and International Taxation Kluwer Law International, p 21.

arguments for consumption taxation can be traced back to Thomas Hobbes. Writing some 350 years ago,[6] his argument was based on the logic that the state provides protection for the enjoyment of life and that taxes are the price of that protection. Because consumption is the material manifestation of the enjoyment of life, so should consumption be the base of taxation.[7]

> Consumption taxation of a certain transaction can take place in one country and taxation of the profit related to that transaction in another country. The difference in principle between the existing systems of income taxation compared to consumption taxation is that income taxes are subjected oriented and turnover taxes are transaction oriented.[8]

However, this distinction is essential when formulating tax policies.[9]

'Some commentators are optimistic about the prospects of consumption based taxation, especially when it is compared with the fiscal degradation of income taxation.'[10] Doernberg and Hinnekens found that VAT and sales taxes are a steadier and more dependable source of tax revenue than income taxes as a consumption tax base is less vulnerable to international tax fight. Consumption-based taxation is an increasingly important source of national revenues. It represents, on average, 30 per cent of the total OECD member states' tax revenue. A recent study for the European Commission pointed to consumption taxes as the single most important source of EC average tax revenue. A similar statistical study also reveals the fact that developing economies primarily depend on consumption-based tax to meet the various needs of the state.

There are three major reasons that many economists have advocated a shift from income to consumption taxation: simplicity, efficiency and fairness.[11] Kaldor argued that the difficulties associated with taxing income are so great that a shift to an expenditure tax would in fact raise more revenue from the very wealthy than income tax does – a view at sharp variance with conventional wisdom.[12] Professors Bankman and Weisbach have recently argued for the superiority of an ideal consumption tax

---

6   Hobbes, T. *Leviathan*. New York: Penguin Books, 1651 (Penguin edition published in 1968) as cited in Metcalf, Gilbert E. (1999) 'Consumption taxation', *The Encyclopaedia of Taxation and Tax Policy*, edited by Joseph J. Cordes, Robert D. Ebel, and Jane G. Gravelle (Urban Institute Press), p 75.

7   Metcalf, Gilbert E. (1999) 'Consumption taxation', *The Encyclopaedia of Taxation and Tax Policy*, edited by Joseph J. Cordes, Robert D. Ebel, and Jane G. Gravelle (Urban Institute Press), p 75.

8   Westberg, Bjorn (2002) Cross-border Taxation of E-Commerce, IBFD p 146.

9   Income and consumption can be viewed as different aspects of 'consumption' in a broad sense. In this respect, income represents the potential power to consume and consumption represents the exercise of the power by consuming goods and services. See Alan Schenk and Oliver Oldman (2006) Value Added Tax: A Comparative Approach, (Cambridge University Press).

10   Doernberg, Richard L. and Hinnekens, Luc (1999)Electronic Commerce and International Taxation Kluwer Law International, p 22.

11   Metcalf, Gilbert E. (1999) 'Consumption taxation', *The Encyclopaedia of Taxation and Tax Policy*, edited by Joseph J. Cordes, Robert D. Ebel, and Jane G. Gravelle (Urban Institute Press), p 75.

12   Kaldor, Nicolas (1955) An *Expenditure Tax*. London: George Allen and Unwin as citied by Metcalf, Gilbert E. (1999) 'Consumption taxation', *The Encyclopaedia of Taxation*

over an ideal income tax on three grounds. First, consumption tax is more efficient because it does not discriminate between current and future consumption, while both income and consumption taxes have identical effect on work effort. Second, consumption tax is at least as good at redistribution as income tax and thus can equally satisfy vertical equity. Third, consumption tax is easier to administer than income tax because it does not attempt to tax income from capital and thus can omit many of the vexing complications that arise from such an attempt, like accounting for basis.[13] However, the common perception is that a consumption tax would be highly regressive compared with an income tax. This follows from the fact that the savings rate relative to income rises with income. Whether a consumption tax need be more regressive than an income tax depends on: (1) the degree of progressivity of the income tax being replaced; (2) the structure of the consumption tax being contemplated; and (3) the way in which progressivity is measured.[14]

One of the ways by which the effects of this regression could be reduced would be to establish differentiated rates for products and services based on their essentiality. Non-essential products that are preferably consumed by high-income taxpayers would be subject to higher rates. The products that ensure the subsistence of lower-income groups would be subject to lower rates or even to exemption. Differentiated taxation on non-essential products has met with general acceptance in the practical context of modern tax structures. This differentiation has been implemented both by the establishment of higher tax rates for such products and by excise taxes, which are specific indirect taxes levied on certain types of products. In practice, however, it has been observed that with the adoption of differentiated tax rates, tax administration tends to become more complex and, as a result, the costs are higher than the benefits thus obtained.

Indirect taxation is associated with efficiency because it is easier for the public authorities to administer and collect this type of tax. First, it requires less complex calculation and payment procedures. Second, the universe of taxpayers to be controlled by tax administration is smaller, and third, the fact that business enterprises and service providers are subject to the registration rules set forth in the commercial legislation is an ancillary element for verifying compliance with tax liabilities. Though most authors support it, the regressivity of indirect taxation is still the subject of much discussion. Thomas Hobbes, whose views were taken up again and expanded by Nicholas Kaldor in his book *An Expenditure Tax*,[15] proposes a tax based on expenditures. This line of argument qualifies the act of saving as a positive attitude for society while consumption is considered an individualistic and antisocial

and Tax Policy, edited by Joseph J. Cordes, Robert D. Ebel, and Jane G. Gravelle (Urban Institute Press), p 75.

13 Bankman, Joseph and Weisbach, David A (2005) The Superiority of an Ideal Consumption Tax Over an Ideal Income Tax (working paper) as citied in Avi-Yonah, Reuven S (2005) 'The Three Goals of Taxation' Available at SSRN: ssrn.com/abstract=796776.

14 Metcalf, Gilbert E. (1999) 'Consumption taxation', *The Encyclopaedia of Taxation and Tax Policy*, edited by Joseph J. Cordes, Robert D. Ebel, and Jane G. Gravelle (Urban Institute Press), p 75.

15 Kaldor, N. (1955) *An Expenditure Tax*. 4.ed, Unwin University Books, London, 1955.

attitude. According to this principle, the levying of taxes on consumption would be the fairest way by which to obtain resources from society.[16] Avi-Yonah argues that consumption tax is needed to raise revenue whenever public sector requires more revenue than can be raised by income tax. Further redistribution can largely be achieved more effectively by taxing consumption broadly and using the spending side of the budget to achieve progressivity. In addition, consumption itself is more easily regulated by consumption taxes than by an income tax.[17]

Whether income or consumption is a fairer base for taxation is widely debated. The main guidelines for an analysis of the distributional features of a tax system can be found in the optimal taxation theory. The structure of optimal taxation contemplates three aspects: the representation of individual preferences, of technology and of market structure; the government's need to raise a fixed amount of revenue with a limited set of tax instruments; and the criterion function, which ranks outcomes and chooses the best tax system within the limited set available. This theory is based on the notion that taxation efficiency is highly cost intensive and that attempts to minimize such costs are worthwhile. Thus, the models that evolve from this theory may represent mere attempts to minimize efficiency costs or even to evaluate the distribution of income by balancing efficiency costs against distributional implications.

The fairness of a particular tax structure would, therefore, be evaluated in terms of the proportion of direct and indirect taxes to the total revenues collected by the government. However, this type of evaluation is incapable of objectively determining the concepts of equity and ability to pay. Musgrave and Musgrave approach the problem by arguing that the essence of modern welfare economics precludes distributional considerations.[18] The basic issue is not equity per se, a concept that is considered desirable by the vast majority of authors, but rather how this abstract concept can materialize within the practical elaboration of a tax system.

Two lines of thought have attempted to shed light on the definition of the concept of tax equity: one is based on the benefit principle, the other, on the ability-to-pay principle.[19] The former sees equity as the extent to which the amount of taxes paid by taxpayers is proportional to the quantity and quality of the public services provided or available to them. The benefit principle does not confine the concept of equity to a structural analysis of a tax system but considers it in the context of government expenditure policies as well. The latter line of thought, which was originally developed by Rousseau, Say and Stuart Mill, approaches the concept of equity from the ability-to-pay perspective. It restricts the concept of equity to the area of government revenues and does not consider government expenditure policies

---

16 Kaldor, N. (1955) *An Expenditure Tax.* 4.ed, Unwin University Books, London, 1955.

17 Avi-Yonah, Reuven S (2005) 'The Three Goals of Taxation' Available at SSRN: ssrn. com/abstract=796776.

18 Musgrave, R.A. and Musgrave P.B. (1973) *Public Finance in Theory and Practice,* McGraw-Hill Book Company, 1973.

19 As mentioned in Chapter 2, a more detailed discussion follows in Chapter 4.

relevant to the analysis of the concept at hand. Equity would therefore have two components: a horizontal one, related to the requirement of equal taxes for people in equal positions, and a vertical one, corresponding to the pattern of unequal taxes among unequal incomes.[20] In a comparative analysis of these lines of thought, Musgrave and Musgrave point out that the merely comparative character of these approaches is already a clear indication of their respective limitations.[21] According to these authors, 'neither approach is easy to interpret or implement. For the benefit principle to be operational, expenditure benefits for particular taxpayers must be known. For ability-to-pay approach to be applicable, we must know just how this ability is to be measured. These are formidable difficulties and neither approach wins on practicality grounds'.[22] Similarly:

> however inadequate the system of income taxation may be in relation to the objectives, which it seeks to attain, it is inconceivable that, within any foreseeable period, it should be wholly abandoned in favour of an alternative system based on personal expenditure. The most that can be hoped for therefore is to introduce a spending tax that can be operated side by side with the income tax, and that would take some of the weight off the income tax without imposing an excessive administrative burden.[23] [24]

3.3   Consumption Taxation: Destination or Origin Principle

The application of the benefit principle to consumption taxation leads to taxation in the country where the consumption takes place.[25]

> With respect to the taxation of trade in goods among sovereign nations, a distinction can be drawn between the destination principle and the origin principle of taxation. Under the destination principle, exports are exempt from consumption tax – for example, a value-added tax (VAT) or a sales tax – and are subsequently taxed at the rate levied by the importing country, resulting in taxation at the place of consumption.[26]

---

20 I have discussed in more detail in Chapter 4.

21 Musgrave, R. A., Musgrave P. B. (1973) *Public Finance in Theory and Practice*, McGraw-Hill Book Company, 1973.

22 Musgrave, R. A., Musgrave, P. B. (1973) *Public Finance in Theory and Practice*, McGraw-Hill Book Company.

23 Kaldor, Nicolas (1955) An *Expenditure Tax*. London: George Allen and Unwin as citied by Metcalf, Gilbert E. (1999) 'Consumption taxation', *The Encyclopedia of Taxation and Tax Policy*, edited by Joseph J. Cordes, Robert D. Ebel, and Jane G. Gravelle (Urban Institute Press).

24 Policymakers should focus on developing a broadly based, efficient, and easily administered tax system with moderate marginal rates. Although the primary goal of the tax system should be to promote efficiency, policymakers also need to consider how to distribute the burden of taxation so the system is seen as fair and just. See 'Fiscal Affairs Department of the International Monetary Fund' *Financial Development* 35(3), p 4.

25 Westberg, Bjorn (2002) Cross-border Taxation of E-Commerce, IBFD p 143.

26 Ligthart, J.E. (2004) Consumption Taxation in a Digital World: A Primer, Canadian Tax Journal, Volume 52, No. 4 p 1078.

The destination and origin principles for indirect taxation are analogous to the source and resident principles for direct taxation. The difference between the destination and origin principles is that the destination principle imposes tax where consumption takes place, whereas the origin principle imposes tax where production takes place. As with source taxation, one might argue that the origin principle distorts the location of production. As with resident taxation, one might argue that the destination principle causes distortions in relative savings decisions across countries. 'Tax revenue accrues to the country in which the final sale occurs. In a world of perfect competition, the destination principle implies that all firms receive the same tax-exclusive price from selling in any location irrespective of their country of residence.'[27] The destination principle is considered to generate a fair distribution of the tax burden: the private consumption base is viewed as a much better proxy for the benefits of public goods than other tax bases, such as production.[28]

Under the origin principle, consumption tax is collected at source – that is, at the place where the goods are produced or exported. Imported commodities are exempted to avoid double taxation. The origin principle implies that consumer prices (or tax-inclusive prices), adjusted for transportation costs, are equated across countries. Origin-based taxation induces firms to locate in low-tax countries, which, it is feared, will give rise to a 'race to the bottom' in taxes, undermining countries' ability to raise revenue. The OECD speaks of 'harmful tax competition'.[29] Some authors have challenged this notion;[30] tax competition may also have the beneficial effect of reducing a country's incentives to expand an already inefficiently large government. Moreover, tax competition may induce government officials to offer public-good packages that are more in line with the preferences of voters.[31]

Under any destination-based regime, governments typically find it impossible to collect consumption taxes from purchasers. Hence, they must use the sellers of goods and services as a chokepoint and collection agent. This causes two imperative

---

27 Ligthart, J.E. (2004) Consumption Taxation in a Digital World: A Primer, Canadian Tax Journal, Volume 52, No. 4 p 1079.

28 Origin and destination taxes have equal effects on neutrality within a closed economy. General imposition of both forms of taxation is neutral if factors are fixed in supply. Neutrality is not likely to be realized with either regime in an open economy setting with decentralized taxing authority across sub-national jurisdictions, given the different rates that will be imposed. However, the source of non-neutrality differs across the two regimes. Cross-state producer prices (as seen by the consumer) are altered by origin-based taxes, and consumer prices (as seen by the producer) are affected by destination taxes. See Fox, William F, Murray, Matthew N and Luna, LeAnn (2005) How Should a Subnational Corporate Income Tax on Multistate Businesses Be Structured? *National Tax Journal*, Vol. LVIII, No. 1.

29 OECD (1998) *Harmful Tax Competition: An Emerging Global Issue* (OECD: Paris) as citied in Ligthart, J.E. (2004) Consumption Taxation in a Digital World: A Primer, *Canadian Tax Journal*, Volume 52, No. 4 p 1079.

30 Wilson, J.D. (1999) Theories of Tax Competition, *National Tax Journal*, Vol. 52, pp 269-304 as cited in Ligthart, J.E. (2004) Consumption Taxation in a Digital World: A Primer, *Canadian Tax Journal*, Volume 52, No. 4 p 1079.

31 Ligthart, J.E. (2004) Consumption Taxation in a Digital World: A Primer, *Canadian Tax Journal*, Volume 52, No. 4 p 1079.

consequences. First, it generates extravagant compliance costs, especially for smaller and medium-sized firms as destination-based taxation compels sellers to calculate, report and remit consumption taxes for each jurisdiction in which sales occur.[32] Second,

> even with the best intentions (and the best tax software), companies find it inordinately difficult to determine their tax remittance obligations in thousands of jurisdictions with different and constantly changing tax rates, definitions, and reporting requirements. Tax authorities, for their part, confront a regime of daunting administrative complexity. An origin-based system in principle can reduce these costs.[33]

Destination-based taxation requires a high degree of intergovernmental cooperation, since the imposition and enforcement of tax collection obligations on sellers who conduct their business abroad often requires their home government's cooperation.

> The only equilibria under a destination-based regime, moreover, are perfect collusion among *all* governments or competition that drives each government to the same set of policies. A government that withholds its consent effectively places its domestic firms beyond the reach of foreign tax collectors and, in that manner, hands them a competitive advantage vis-à-vis others that have joined a cooperative.[34]

However, destination-based taxation is the international norm and is supported by the OECD, the European Union and the World Trade Organization (WTO). The origin principle is rarely applied in practice to trade, except for trade among the former members of the Soviet Union.[35] As Lockwood[36] argues, the case for preferring destination-based taxation over origin-based taxation on efficiency grounds is strong but not absolute. Only fewer than two very restrictive assumptions – which typically are not encountered in practice – are the principles equal. First, within each country the consumption tax rate should be the same for all commodities, although that uniform rate may differ across countries. Uniformity implies that relative producer prices are equated to relative consumer prices in each country; thus, equating one set of relative prices across countries – for example, relative producer prices under the destination principle – would also equate the other. Second, bilateral goods trade between countries should be balanced, so that a change from taxing imports to taxing

---

32 Cline, Robert J. and Neubig, Thomas S. (1999) Masters of Complexity and Bearers of Great Burden: The Sales Tax System and Compliance Costs for Multistate Retailers (Ernst & Young, September).

33 Greve, Michael S.(2003) Sell Globally, Tax Locally: Sales Tax Reform For The New Economy, in Kevin A. Hassett (ed) Aei Studies On Tax Reform, (The Aei Press, Washington DC).

34 Greve, Michael S.(2003) Sell Globally, Tax Locally: Sales Tax Reform For The New Economy, in Kevin A. Hassett (ed) Aei Studies On Tax Reform, (The Aei Press, Washington DC).

35 Ligthart, J.E. (2004) Consumption Taxation in a Digital World: A Primer, Canadian Tax Journal, Volume 52, No. 4 p 1079.

36 Lockwood, B (2001) Tax Competition and Tax Coordination under Destination and Origin Principles: A Synthesis, *Journal of Public Economics*, Vol.81 pp 279-319.

exports would not have a significant effect on revenue.[37] It is important that in order to avoid double taxation or non-taxation it is essential to achieve agreement among countries on the place of taxation.[38] In the case of VAT in the absence of international convention, double taxation seems to be unavoidable.[39] Given a transaction could be taxed in more than one jurisdiction; it is possible that the tax burden could rest on one or more person. There is a need for international conventions which would clarify whether the right to tax belongs to the country of deemed consumption or for specific reasons to another country. The risk of conflicts is obvious.[40]

3.4   Value Added Tax

At the time of its foundation in 1957, the primary concern of the European Economic Community (EEC) was with commodity rather than factor trade. This reflected in an explicit legal base for indirect tax harmonization (Article 99 of the EEC Treaty). VAT is an indirect, multi-stage consumption tax. As an *indirect tax*, the VAT is levied upon the articles of trade before they reach the customer, who eventually pays the tax-inclusive market price.[41] The label 'indirect' follows from the fact that the payer of the VAT does not suffer a corresponding reduction in such purchases. VAT is insensitive to individual circumstances of the taxpayer following from its 'indirectness' and it is not an effective means of redistribution. Therefore, its chief role is to raise government revenue without influencing consumption patterns. Indeed, it is the unprecedented revenue-productivity of this tax that makes it appealing to many states.[42] In order to preserve neutrality, the VAT system should provide a comprehensive tax base, be of a uniform rate, and have limited exemptions. Application of multiple rates and a broad range of exemption increases administrative and compliance burdens and distorts consumer choices.

As a *multi-stage tax*, the modern VAT collects revenue at all stages of production and distribution.[43] In close connection with the multi-stage nature of this tax, VAT provides for the right to recoup the tax paid by the business participants of the supply-chain. The right to regain the VAT is put into practice by the application of the credit-invoice administrative method.[44] The credit-invoice method requires

---

37 Ligthart, J.E. (2004) Consumption Taxation in a Digital World: A Primer, Canadian Tax Journal, Volume 52, No. 4 p 1078.

38 Westberg, Bjorn (2002) Cross-border Taxation of E-Commerce, IBFD p 145

39 Terra, Ben (1998) *The Place of Supply in European VAT*, (Kluwer Law International) pp 2-3.

40 Westberg, Bjorn (2002) Cross-border Taxation of E-Commerce, IBFD p 145

41 Schenk, Alain and Oldman, Oliver (2000) *Value Added Tax*, 26 (Transnational Publishers ed., 2000 p 12.

42 Tait, Alain A. (1998) *Value Added Tax*, 3 (International Monetary Fund ed., Washington, DC. pp 21-24.

43 Schenk, Alain and Oldman, Oliver (2000) *Value Added Tax*, 26 (Transnational Publishers ed., 2000 p 29.

44 Schenk, Alain and Oldman, Oliver (2000) *Value Added Tax*, 26 (Transnational Publishers ed., 2000).

taxable persons to calculate VAT at the appropriate rate on all taxable supplies made (outputs) throughout the chain of supply. Through this invoice/credit mechanism, a business is responsible only for that part of the VAT attributable to the value that it adds in its stage of production.[45] The right to recoup the tax makes it possible to avoid the negative consequences of tax 'cascading'.[46] Being exactly proportional to the price makes VAT neutral both with respect to the length of the production and distribution chain (internally) and with respect to the relative tax burdens on domestic and imported goods in the market place (externally). Because it is proportional to the price and it is measured by the contribution of value added, it is also neutral as to the method of commerce.

As a *consumption tax*, VAT is applied to a base consisting of personal expenditure.[47] The last link in the chain bears the tax: normally the consumer. If taxes are fees for public services, burdening the VAT on final consumption is justified by the fact that consumers are the main beneficiaries of public services.[48] Being a consumption tax, VAT not only aims at taxing final consumption but also at taxing it at the place of consumption.[49] This ambition gains the most importance in the context of the inter-jurisdictional application of VAT. In the case of cross-border transactions, more tax jurisdictions are concerned with the taxation of the sale. To designate the country of taxation there is a need for special, so-called 'place of supply' rules.[50] These rules, by resolving potential conflicts between the jurisdictions, pursue the goal of avoiding double taxation or accidental non-taxation.[51]

The administration of the border tax adjustments under the destination principle requires close cooperation from the tax administrations of the countries involved in the transaction. To avoid double or non-taxation it is necessary to keep track of the cross-border movement of physical goods.[52] This is only possible through the checking of the documentation of the merchandise at the border. As a result, there is a need for border controls. As opposed to the destination principle, the origin principle assigns

---

45 Taylor, A, Scott (2000), An Ideal E-Commerce Consumption Tax in A Global Economy', *BILETA 2000:World Wide Law* website:www.bileta.ac.uk.

46 Unless the tax paid by the business can be reclaimed the value previously taxed and the previously paid tax itself are again subjected to tax in the next stage of sale. This practice leads to serious price distortions or to vertical integration of businesses to avoid accumulation of tax through several stages of sale.

47 Schenk, Alain and Oldman, Oliver (2000) *Value Added Tax*, 26 (Transnational Publishers ed., 2000) pp 7-12.

48 Terra, Ben (1998) *The Place of Supply in European VAT* (Kluwer Law International).

49 Schenk, Alain and Oldman, Oliver (2000) *Value Added Tax*, 26 (Transnational Publishers ed., 2000) p 260.

50 Schenk, Alain and Oldman, Oliver (2000) *Value Added Tax*, 26 (Transnational Publishers) pp 269-272.

51 This object of the place of supply rules has also been acknowledged by the ECJ, see Case 168/84 *Berkholz v Finanzamt Hamburg-Mitte-Altstadt* (1985) ECR 2251, and Case C-327/94 *Dudda v Finanzamt Bergisch Gladbach* (1996) ECR I-4595.

52 Schenk, Alain and Oldman, Oliver (2000) *Value Added Tax*, 26 (Transnational Publishers) p 262.

taxing jurisdiction to the exporting country.[53] The destination country charges no tax. Under this solution, importers in each country compare the tax-inclusive prices of domestic and foreign goods. There are no border tax adjustments under this scheme. Consequently, there is no need for border controls. Application of this principle is not common, since it directs all revenues from the VAT imposed on international trade to the country of origin. As seen above, this practice conflicts with the ambition of the VAT to tax consumption at the place of consumption. The most common way of determining the place of supply rules is based on the destination principle. According to this principle, the exporter receives a tax rebate in the amount of the VAT levied on the goods and services that are being exported.[54] This practice is referred to as zero-rating. Zero-rating is a special type of exemption under which the exporter charges a rate of 0 per cent on the tax base and retains the right to claim back his input-credits.[55] As the outcome of the destination principle, the international trade in goods and services is based on net-of-tax prices,[56] therefore the effects of the differences between national tax rates are neutralized. Eventually, the destination country taxes the imported product usually only upon resale by applying its own rate.

The VAT system also relies on the reverse charge or self-assessment method for applying and accounting for VAT in the case of cross-border transactions. Where a person outside the country supplies relevant services to a person in the country in connection with the recipient's business, the recipient is treated as though the recipient supplied and received the service and thus accounts for output VAT based on the value of the service received and at the same time recovers this VAT as input VAT if it relates to a taxable supplier. This obligation of the local person to account for reverse charge VAT addresses the problem of tax avoidance or evasion on the part of the foreign supplier and of the competitive advantage of lower VAT rates applicable to suppliers established in certain member states.

In the European Community, the application of the VAT scheme is governed by a series of Directives and Regulations. The First VAT Directive is fundamental to the EC VAT system, setting out in its recitals and first two articles the principles on which the system is designed. The recitals record the necessity of a common form of consumption tax to avoid both distortions of competition and hindrances to the free movement of goods and services.[57] They also record that the aim of establishing the highest degree of simplicity and neutrality is best achieved when the tax is as general as possible, but that this aim may not be achieved immediately.[58] The principle of VAT is stated in Article 2 of the First VAT Directive (1967)[59] as follows:

---

53 Terra, Ben (1998) *The Place of Supply in European VAT* (Kluwer Law International).

54 Schenk, Alain and Oldman, Oliver (2000) *Value Added Tax*, 26 (Transnational Publishers) p 260.

55 Schenk, Alain and Oldman, Oliver (2000) *Value Added Tax*, 26 (Transnational Publishers) p 227.

56 Terra, Ben (1998) *The Place of Supply in European VAT* (Kluwer Law International) p 5.

57 Directive 67/277/EEC, Recital 2.

58 Directive 67/277/EEC, Recitals 5, 6.

59 Directive 67/227/EEC (OJ 1967 1301).

The principle of the common law system of value added tax involves the application to goods and services of a general tax on consumption exactly proportional to the price of the goods and services, whatever the number of transaction which takes place in the production and distribution process before the stage at which tax is charged. On each transaction, value added tax, calculated on the price of the goods or services at the rate applicable to such goods or services, shall be chargeable after deduction of the amount of value added tax borne directly by the cost components.

The detail of the common VAT was left to the Second Directive. However, the Second Directive answered only the issues necessary to establish a truly common form of VAT in the community. It also allowed member states to retain significant derogations from the common form of VAT in a number of sensitive areas. The most important area of inconsistency left by the Second Directive was that it was for member states to decide which goods and services were to be taxed and which were to be exempted. Other deficiencies included national differences in identifying which should be subject to VAT and how VAT was to be applied to both imported goods and cross-border supplies of services. In other words, the VAT adopted in each member state might have common principles, but it was short of being a common tax. The concern for harmonization arose because a portion of member states' VAT revenue was to become a main Community resource. Work therefore started to replace the Second Directive with a more detailed provision consistent with the principle of the First VAT Directive.

3.4.1   VAT Harmonization

There is no dispute as to the importance of tax harmonization for the consolidation of economic unions. Since its first moments, the EU put out a well conceived project for harmonizing the tax systems of its members and worked together to have it implemented. The EU has established an 'internal market' regime that provides for the free exchange of goods and services. The internal market requires, among other things, a uniform consumption tax. While member states retain their tax jurisdiction under the EU Treaty, the EU is authorized to promulgate VAT Directives and Regulations that are binding on member states. In particular, member states are required to 'transform' the Sixth VAT Directive into domestic law by passing legislation which is consistent with the Directive and its amendments. Further, it also requires broadening the basis of taxation and applying uniform rules. Under the system of 'VAT harmonization', however, EU member states reserved the right to set VAT tax rates and to exempt certain supplies of goods and services. As a result, national regular tax rates range from 15 per cent to 25 per cent, and while the supply of certain goods may be taxed at a reduced rate in one member state, it may be tax exempt in another.

The lack of uniformity in the implementation of EC Directives on VAT across EU countries and procedural complications that the cross-country differences in the VAT regime entail in a single market create further distortions in trade flows. The 'transitional' VAT regime for cross-border trade, implemented since the abolition of custom controls between EU countries in 1993, embodies a wide variety of rules for determining the place where the transaction is taxed and, consequently, the place where the tax is deducted or refunded. Hence, it may not come as a surprise that these national peculiarities tend to have a distorting effect on competition among suppliers from different EU member states. In fact, the 'level playing field' for domestic and foreign businesses championed in the political discussion with the US has not yet been fully realized within the EU itself.

3.4.2   Sixth VAT Directive

The Sixth VAT Directive was adopted to replace the Second Directive in 1977 and this Directive is the most comprehensive one in the series of VAT Directives and provides the grounds for further harmonization. It provided a common set of rules for several questions: taxable persons subject to the tax; territory covered by the tax; common definition of taxable transactions; common rules for identifying where and when a taxable transaction occurs; common valuation rules; a common list of exemptions. The following summary confines itself to the rules of the consolidated Sixth Directive relevant for the purposes of this thesis. By 1990, the common form of VAT was becoming a reality. Besides the Framework Directives, several other Directives had provided regulation for mutual assistance of tax authorities,[60] measures allowing traders from other states and from outside the EC to claim VAT refunds in appropriate cases,[61] and some moves towards various national derogations.[62] The European Court began to provide interpretation of the directives although the first substantive VAT case did not come before the European Court until 1976.[63] The first case alleging specific infraction under a VAT Directive against a member state was not heard until 1984.[64] By 1990, however, the case law was becoming an important aspect of the development of tax.

Despite comprehensive legislation and judicial activity, VAT was still a tax requiring border controls. Each exporting state removes any VAT from exported products and refunds it to the exporter. The importing state then intercepts the imported goods in the same way as for custom duty and imposes a VAT charge on the value of goods at the import. In effect, therefore, much of VAT on goods is collected in exactly the same way as if VAT on imports was a customs duty. This approach could not be maintained in a single market without internal frontiers. The reason why border controls are needed is because VAT was imposed as a destination-based tax. In the view of the Commission, and various committees, VAT could avoid the problems of border controls only if it became an origin-based tax, or at least an origin-collected tax.[65] However, the Commission failed to persuade all the member

---

60 Article 28 of the Sixth Directive preserves the right to continue existing derogation from the Second Directive.

61 The Eighth VAT Directive (79/1072/EEC) of 6 December 1979 (1979OJ L 331/ 11), dealing with traders in other EC states and the Thirteenth VAT Directive (86/560/EEC) of 17 November 1986 (1986 OJ L 326/40), dealing with traders in third states.

62 The Eighteenth VAT Directive (89/465/EEC) of 18 July 1989 (1989 OJ L 226/21) abolishing some of the derogation permitted by art. 28(3) of the Sixth Directive.

63 *Mazzalai Case 111/75*, (1976) ECR 657.

64 *EC Commission v Belgium Case 325/82*, (1984) ECR 777.

65 An origin-based VAT is one where liability is imposed in, and revenue is retained by the export state. An origin-collected tax is one where liability is imposed in the state of

states, although a compromise was adopted.[66] Under the agreed approach, the origin basis of VAT was adopted (without any clearance procedure) for mail order goods, excise goods and new means of transport. In all other cases, the existing system was to remain. In order to make a VAT charge on imports work without customs controls, a series of inward processing controls were used instead, requiring accounts from persons to whom goods bought by cross-border acquisition were delivered. Article 2 of the Sixth VAT Directive defines the scope of VAT to include: the supply of goods and services within the territory of the country by a taxable person, the intra-Community acquisition of goods within the territory of the country by a taxable person or a non-taxable legal person and the importation of goods.

At the beginning of 1993, a 'transitional system' was introduced which retained the destination principle for transactions between VAT-registered traders but applied the origin system to sales to final consumers. Since 1 January 1993, the system of taxation of 'imports of goods' from other member states has been replaced by 'intra-Community acquisitions of goods'. That of 'intra-Community supplies' has replaced the system of 'exports of goods' to another member state. The new system is still based on the principle of taxation according to destination but the formalities take place at the destination point rather than the border. The following conditions must be exchanged between taxable persons, dispatched or transported to the acquirer by, or on behalf of, one of the taxable persons, from one member state to a member state other than that from which the goods are dispatched or transported. Intra-Community supplies are exempt in the member state of the enterprise which sells them and are taxable in the member state where the goods arrive. The taxable person thus reports the output VAT on his VAT return and deducts the input VAT on the same return, if he has the right. Member states thus fully preserve their fiscal sovereignty: the member state of arrival ensures that the goods acquired are subject to taxation; the member state of the seller, or of origin, does not have to ensure that the goods are effectively intra-Community supply, goods purchased (origin-based VAT included) by a private individual, in a member state. However, purchases from mail-order companies, including all sales in which the vendor is responsible for shipments are taxable in the country to which they are sent, if the dispatch is on behalf of a supplier whose total sales in that country exceed a threshold value. This is the 'distance selling exception' to the system of origin-taxation applicable to private consumers affecting their purchases in another EC-jurisdiction.

The transitional system was due to last until 1996. However, moves towards a definitive system have stalled although the principles for the definitive system have been set out by the Commission. The fundamental principle of the definitive system is that the 'place of taxation' would no longer be where goods are located, or services provided, but where the suppliers' business was established. In other words, the origin principle would form the basis of the system with the difficulties of revenue

---

export on behalf of the state of import. The export state must therefore account in some way to the import state for the VAT on any export between the states. In effect, VAT is collected as a sort of withholding tax in this case. An origin-collected tax therefore requires some kind of clearing system at Community or national level between member states.

66 Art 28 and following articles of Sixth VAT Directive.

allocation to be dealt with by a new system of allocation based on consumption levels in each member state and a narrowing of the range of rates charged across the EU. There was, however, an exception for distance sellers such as mail-order companies who were required to apply the rate prevailing at the place of delivery and, if required, to appoint fiscal agents to account for the tax on their behalf.

The preference for the origin principle may well be a matter of high principle for some in the Commission, but it is interesting to note that many of the perceived problems with the destination system concerned the practicalities of enforcement. The reason for the need to move to a transitional system was that the destination system required physical border controls to make it work. The elements of the destination system that remain are policed by the mutual exchange of information which is possible where both supplier and recipient are VAT registered, even if they are resident in different member states. Given these identified difficulties, it seems surprising that the EU believes that a system involving a non-EU supplier where the services by their very nature cannot be subject to border controls will be enforceable. In the context of inter-EU trade, such a system is acknowledged to work only where the return in one member state can be checked against that in another.[67]

3.4.3   Taxable Person

Within the current VAT regime, the taxable person is a central player. The VAT system is built up around the concept of the taxable person. Under Article 4(1) of the Sixth VAT Directive, a taxable person shall mean any person who independently carries out, in any place, any economic activity defined to include all activities of producers and traders. An economic activity is defined as 'all activities of producers, traders and person concerning services ... A person who carries on an economic activity under an act of employment, does not carry on the activity independently'.[68] The operation of this provision is again a mixture of EC provisions and national law. Hence, a taxable person is defined under the Value Added Tax Act 1994 as a person who is, or is required to be, registered under the Act.[69] The status of such persons can take the form of a private individual, a partnership, a private or public incorporated body, government bodies and non-profit making organizations. A person is a 'taxable person' if registered or required to be registered under the VAT law of a member state. It is for the member state to determine precisely how and when the registration duty arises and is fulfilled. The Sixth Directive provides only a framework within which this duty arises.[70] The Directive also gives member states discretion to exempt taxable persons from duty to collect the tax below a nationally determined threshold.[71] Taxable persons are obliged to report the commencement of, and any change in, their taxable activity. They should keep sufficient accounts

---

67 Ivinson, Jonathan (2004) Overstepping The Boundary - How The EU Got it Wrong on E-Commerce, *Computer and Telecommunications Law Review*, 10(1), 1-4.

68 Sixth VAT Directive, Directive 77/338 Art.4 (2) and Art 4 (4).

69 VATA 1994, S. 3(1).

70 Art 4.

71 Art 24.

of their finances and issue an invoice when supplying to another taxable person. Taxable persons are required to submit their return at the end of each taxing period and pay the VAT due.

Once a person is registered or required to be registered under national law, every taxable person is allocated a unique identification number by the tax administration, which is usually distinguishable solely for VAT purposes. Verification of the taxable status bears outstanding importance in cases of cross-border supplies to businesses, where the Sixth Directive assigns tax liability to the business recipient of certain services under the so-called 'reverse charge'[72] method. To be able to disregard further VAT obligations, the supplier should be certain about the taxable status of its customer. Identification of registered business with regard to intra-Community transactions is facilitated by the VAT Information Exchange System[73] (VIES). According to Article 6 of the Council Regulation on Administrative Cooperation in the Field of Indirect Taxation (EEC) No. 218/92 governing the VIES, the competent authority of each member state shall ensure upon request that persons involved in the intra-Community supply of goods or services obtain confirmation of the validity of the VAT registration number of any specified person.

3.4.4   Taxable Transaction

Taxable transactions include the supply of goods and the supply of services. The *Supply of goods* is defined as the transfer of a right to dispose of tangible property as owner.[74] The *supply of services* means any other transaction not constituting a supply of goods.[75] By means of this catch-all definition, the Directive intends to ensure that intangible supplies do not escape taxation.[76]

---

72 As discussed earlier in this chapter, the rationale behind the reverse charge or self-assessment system is the wish to ensure taxation at destination. However, application of reverse charge is only viable in the case of business recipients, who have the sufficient means to fulfil such obligation and are motivated for compliance by the right to deduct the input credits. Final consumers lack both; moreover the lack of audit-trail would render enforcement impossible. Consumption Tax Aspects of Electronic Commerce, A Report from Working Party No. 9 on Consumption Taxes to the Committee on Fiscal Affairs, OECD, 15 (2001).

73 The VIES was established by Council Regulation on administrative cooperation in the field of indirect taxation (EEC) No 218/92 (hereinafter; 'the VIES Regulation') OJ L024 01/02/1992 p 1. It is a common system for the exchange of information on intra-Community transactions for tax purposes. It was set up for the supplementation of the Sixth Directive after the introduction of Council Directive amending the Sixth Directive with a view to the abolition of fiscal frontiers (91/680/EEC) OJ L376 31/12/1991 p 1. Elimination of border controls necessitated closer cooperation between national tax administrations. *See* Recital 3 of the VIES Regulation.

74 Article 5 of the Sixth Directive, Sixth Council Directive on the harmonization of the laws of the Member States relating to turnover taxes (77/388/EEC) OJ L145 13/06/1977.

75 Article 6 of the Sixth Directive.

76 Schenk and Oldman (2000) Value Added Tax, at p 139; Tait (1998) Value Added Tax, at p 387.

3.4.5   *VAT Jurisdiction: Place of Supply*

The place of taxation with respect to *goods* is determined upon the physical location of the goods concerned regardless of where the parties reside.[77] The meaning of a supply of goods has received judicial consideration. In the ECJ decision, known as the *Theotrue* case, the following explanation of what is a supply of goods is given: 'supply for such purposes in relation to goods requires the transfer of goods from one taxable person to another, either immediately or at a future date, and implies the existence of the goods at such time of transfer'.[78] It is important to make a distinction between the physical product and the property that exists within that product. A VAT charge only arises where the property in the goods is transferred by sale; the possession of goods is transferred under an agreement for sale of the goods; or the possession of goods is transferred under agreements, which expressly contemplate that the property will also pass at some time in the future. Goods imported from outside the EU are liable to VAT at importation; goods delivered from one member state to another are taxed in the country where the transport of the goods begins, unless supplied to VAT-registered customers, in which case they are taxed as an acquisition in the member state of receipt. Supplies of goods to non-taxable persons may be taxed in the supplier's member state, subject to the total value of supplies in any single member state remaining below a threshold.[79] The place of supply rules for services is much more complicated and can be either the place where the supplier is situated or the place where the customer is situated depending on the category of the services in question.[80] For purposes of administrative feasibility, place of supply rules for services may further differ in accordance with the type of service.

As discussed before, the Community faces a serious dilemma when trying to choose among the principles underlying the place of supply rules. How to choose between these principles? Both the destination and the origin principles have their positive and negative points when considered within the special context of the internal market. The precise and expeditious border tax adjustments of the destination principle satisfy the requirement that intra-Community competition should not be distorted and the free flow of goods and services should not be hindered through the application of indirect taxes.[81] It also satisfies the general requirement of VAT of allocating the tax into the country of consumption. The serious drawback of this principle is its essential co-existence with border controls. These border controls, by necessitating the presence of the same infrastructure at the borders as would be in place were the Community not a customs union, are incompatible with the idea of a

---

77 Article 8 of the Sixth Directive. General rules in Art 8 apply to determine where goods are supplied: 'for goods dispatched or transported: the place where the taxable transaction is effected is where the goods are at the time dispatch or transport begins. For goods not dispatched or transported: the place where the goods are when supply takes place'.

78 In the ECJ decision, known as the *Theotrue* case (1983) VATTR 88 at p 92.

79 As discussed earlier in the section Taxable Person.

80 Article 9 of the Sixth Directive.

81 Articles 2 and 14 of the Treaty of Rome Treaty Establishing the European Community, March 25, 1957, consolidated version in Official Journal C340 10/11/1997 at pp 173-308, Tait (1998).

true European common market described in the Treaty of Rome.[82] The most appealing feature of the origin principle is the lack of need for border tax adjustments. The inability of the origin principle to concentrate the VAT revenue to the country where consumption takes place conflicts with the general requirements of a consumption-based taxation scheme. With respect to the interests of the Community, dislocation of VAT revenues among member states would distort competition within the common market.[83]

Abolishing the tax frontiers has been the ultimate goal of the Community from the outset of the harmonization process.[84] Accomplishment of this goal only seems possible through the application of the origin principle; despite this fact, place of supply rules have been guided predominantly by the destination principle since the adoption of the First Directive. The fragmentation of the internal market following from the operation of border controls, has indeed been acknowledged by the Commission in its White Paper[85] issued in 1985. This document proposed a so-called 'definitive system' of VAT built on the origin principle and the parallel operation of a clearing house. Fearing to lose fiscal sovereignty, the members have not yet been unwilling to take the measures necessary for the introduction of a clearing house. According to Terra and Kajus,[86] introduction of the clearing house is impossible if there are significant tax and consequent price differences between the member states. Agreement on the way of determining the shares of the member states from the VAT revenue would also be essential. However, the Commission made persistent efforts in its subsequent series of proposals during the last decades to reconcile the conflicting interests of the internal market and the member states.

At present, place of supply rules are based on an 'interim system' that was introduced by a Council Decision, which, as the first step toward the implementation of the origin principle, terminated border controls from 1993.[87] According to this regime, sales to consumers have become subject to the origin principle, while the destination principle remained effective for sales to business customers. The 1993 system is known as the 'transitional system'; it will probably be replaced by a

---

82   Tait (1998) at p 158.

83   Application of the origin principle results in a VAT burden on imported products. The country of import therefore should grant an input credit to the importer to avoid tax cascading. This, however, would mean that the importing country did not only miss the revenue from tax but suffered a positive loss by granting the input. In case of not granting input credit to the importer, imported products will become more expensive following from the tax cascading. Tait (1998) Value Added Tax, at pp 437-444.

84   Report of the Fiscal and Financial Committee in The EEC Reports on Tax Harmonization (International Bureau of Fiscal Documentation, 1963) 'Neumark Report', cited in Schenk, Alain and Oldman, Oliver (2000) *Value Added Tax*, 26 (Transnational Publishers) 2000 p 437.

85   Completing the Internal Market: White Paper from the Commission to the European Council, June 28-29, 1985 (COM (85) 310).

86   Terra, Ben and Kajus, Julie (1992) *Value Added Tax in the EC after 1992* (Kluwer Law and Taxation Publishers).

87   Council Directive amending the Sixth Directive with a view to the abolition of fiscal frontiers (91/680/EEC) OJ L376 31/12/1991 p 1.

'definitive system for taxation of trade between member states based in principle on taxation of origin of the goods or services supplied'.[88] The definitive system should be effective, modern and neutral, treating intra-Community transactions in much the same manner as domestic transactions, in accordance with the concept of an internal market. However, as the Council had not reached a replacement decision by 31 December 1996, the transnational arrangements of 1993 continue to apply until the Council decides on the definitive system.

3.5   Sales Tax

Sales tax is a tax on the retail sale of specified tangible property or services, which have historically been sold over the counter to the buyer and collected at the location where the good is transferred from the seller to the buyer, unless the property is specifically exempted from tax. The sales tax issue involves not only questions about states in which sellers must collect tax – it involves determinations of what is taxable. This will include personal property, and in some cases intangible property is also subject to sales tax as tangible personal property, for example, computer software is sometimes considered tangible and therefore taxable. Real property is usually not subject to sales tax but may be subject to transfer tax.[89] Three factors determine whether sales tax liability in a particular state exists for a transaction: (i) the type of good being sold; (ii) *situs*, or the location where the transaction takes place; and (iii) nexus. 'The general sales or turnover tax thus applies in principle to the supply of goods and services, irrespective of their distribution through traditional or electronic channels and irrespective of the physical or digital form of the goods.'[90]

In a single-stage tax model, a sales tax is applied only once in the production and distribution channels, whereas in a multi-stage tax model, sales tax is imposed at all stages in production and distribution.[91] Thus, sales tax may be applied to the sale by manufacturer to the wholesaler or to the retail sale. In the traditional 'consumer levy' tax jurisdiction, the buyer pays the tax at the time of the sale and the seller collects and remits the tax as an agent for the taxing jurisdiction; they are not collected directly by the government. Purchases by businesses either for resale or as inputs to production are (in theory if not always in practice) exempted from sales taxes in order to avoid double taxation. In the absence of a remedial provision, the mere imposition of a sales tax by the purchaser's state could easily be circumvented by arranging for the sale to take place in the seller's state or a third state even though the purchase item is used in the purchaser' state. Consequently, the states that impose sales tax also impose a use tax for goods purchased outside the state that are used

---

88 Art 35a of Sixth Directive.

89 Hellerstein, Jerome, R and Hellerstein, Walter, (1992) 'State Taxation: Sales and Use, Personal Income, and Death and Gift Taxes', *State Tax Notes* pp 13.01, 13.05.

90 Doernberg, Richard L. and Hinnekens, Luc (1999)Electronic Commerce and International Taxation (Kluwer Law International) p 21.

91 Doernberg, Richard L. and Hinnekens, Luc (1999)Electronic Commerce and International Taxation (Kluwer Law International) p 21.

within the state.[92] Hence, a sales tax regime is actually made up of two separate taxes: sales tax and use tax.

3.5.1   Use Tax

What is use tax? 'Use' is defined typically as an exercise of a right or power to use, consume, possess or store that is acquired by a sale for use of tangible personal property or a taxable service. The use tax is an 'Ingenious legal device that was developed to safeguard state sales tax[93] by imposing tax on the privilege of using, consuming, distributing or storing tangible personal property after it is brought into the State from without the State'.[94] It generally applies to the same kinds of taxable receipts as the sales tax. Use tax is meant to apply only if a sale has not been subjected to sales tax. This usually occurs only when the sales tax does not apply because the seller is outside the buyer's state. Use tax usually applies if the product or service is purchased remotely and used or consumed in the buyer's state. The seller must collect the use tax if it has nexus in the state. Use taxes are most commonly due when an item is purchased from a business in another state and the business does not have sufficient presence (nexus) in the consumer's state for the sale to be subjected to sales tax. In the event that a consumer purchases an item and the sales tax is not collected, the consumer is required to remit use tax according to the location of consumption of the item.[95]

The use rates are generally the same as the sales tax rates and the payment of a sales tax to an out of state vendor will usually qualify as a credit towards the use tax.[96] This credit mechanism attempts to prevent double taxation of the same item. Most states require the consumer to self-assess the use tax, since the only collection agent (the seller) in the transaction does not have a taxable, physical presence in the reporting state. However, if the seller has the requisite taxable nexus in the consumer's home state, the state can impose a sales tax collection obligation on the seller, thus guaranteeing the collection of the tax.[97] The obligation is imposed in return for the seller having purposefully availed it of, and benefited from, the taxing state's laws and market.[98]

---

92 State's authority to levy these taxes is derived from the 10th Amendment of the US Constitution, which states 'The powers not delegated to the United States by the Constitution, nor prohibited by it to the States, are reserved to the states respectively, or to the people.' U.S. Const. amend. X.

93 *National Bellas Hess, Inc. v. Department of Revenue of Ill.*, 386 U.S. 753 (1967).

94 Hellerstein, Jerome, R and Hellerstein, Walter (1998) *State Taxation*, 3rd edition p 16.01.

95 Simon, Steven John (2002) Electronic Commerce: A Taxing Dilemma, *Informing Science*, Volume 5 No 1, pp 29-41.

96 Hellerstein, Jerome, R and Hellerstein, Walter (1998) Walter, *State Taxation*, 3rd edition at pp 16.01, 16.11(3).

97 Cline, Robert J. and Thomas S. Neubig (1999), 'Masters of Complexity and Bearers of Great Burden: The Sales Tax System and Compliance Costs for Multistate Retailers', *Ernst & Young Study* Sept. 8. p 3.

98 Hellerstein, Jerome, R and Hellerstein, Walter (1998) Walter, *State Taxation*, 3rd edition, pp 16.01, 16.11(3).

The use tax is theoretically effective when applied to sales of tangible personal property but cannot ordinarily be enforced as a complementary tax against services purchased out of state but performed in state. As a practical matter, however, use taxes are often totally avoided unless a collection burden is imposed on the seller.[99] This is especially true for individual consumers, as opposed to business consumers, since unlike individuals, many business consumers undergo regular use tax audits.[100] The United States is an ideal example of myriad and multiple sales tax systems, hence it can be used to illustrate the international sales tax principles of cross-broader e-commerce sales tax issues. The first barrier to state taxation is the United States Constitution. Under the Constitution,[101] states may not tax out of state sellers unless the imposition of the tax meets the Due Process Clause requirement of minimum contacts and the Commerce Clause requirement of physical presence.

3.5.2   Due Process Clause

The Due Process Clause of the Fourteenth Amendment to the United States Constitution requires that governmental action must be fundamentally fair. The Due Process Clause[102] ensures fairness in the operations of the state governments towards its citizens. No one should be deprived of 'life, liberty, or property' including tax dollars, without due process of law. This 'fundamental fairness' test, when applied to a state's power to impose on a remote vendor the duty to collect and remit use taxes, has resulted in the United States Supreme Court consistently holding that due process requires some minimum connection between a state and the person, property or transaction taxed.[103] The Due Process analysis centres on whether a taxpayer's connections with the jurisdiction are sufficient to give notice that it may be haled into court or subject to a tax, in that jurisdiction.[104] For present purposes, the Due

---

99 Cline, Robert J. and Thomas S. Neubig (1999) 'Masters of Complexity and Bearers of Great Burden: The Sales Tax System and Compliance Costs for Multistate Retailers', *Ernst & Young Study* Sept. 8. p 5.

100   National Governor's Association data located at <http://www.nga.org/internet/ Proposal.asp>, last visited on 2 November 2000, indicating up to 500 audits per annum for multistate sellers.

101   *National Bellas Hess, Inc. v. Dep't of Revenue of Ill.*, 386 U.S. 753 (1967), holding that an Illinois use tax statute violated the Fourteenth Amendment's Due Process Clause and created an unconstitutional burden on interstate commerce. The Court imposed the minimum contacts requirement in context of Due Process.

102   The Due Process Clauses of the United States Constitution (Fifth and Fourteenth Amendments) state: 'No person shall ... be deprived of life, liberty, or property, without due process of law.' U.S. Const. amend. V. 'Nor shall any State deprive any person of life, liberty, or property, without due process of law ....' U.S. Const. amend. XIV, 1.

103   *International Shoe Co. v. Washington*, 326 U.S. 310, 316 (1945). The Court found that due process requires that a defendant have minimum contacts with the jurisdiction.

104   *Burger King Corp. v. Rudzewicz*, 471 U.S. 462, 476 (1985). The Court held that if one purposefully engages in significant economic activities in the state, he 'manifestly [avails] himself of the privilege of conducting business there', and because his activities are subject to the 'benefits and protections' of the forum's laws it is presumptively not unreasonable to require him to submit to the burdens of litigation in that forum as well.'

Process Clause requires that a seller meet minimum thresholds of activity (which need not equate to physical presence) with a state before that state can impose a tax on the seller or an obligation to collect that tax from in-state buyers.[105] However, even if a taxpayer exceeds the Due Process limitation, it must also exceed the physical presence requirement of the Commerce Clause before taxation can occur.

3.5.3   Commerce Clause

The US Constitution was, in part, a compromise between national and state sovereignty and the distribution of power between larger and smaller states. As part of this compromise, the 'Commerce Clause' contained in Article 1, Section 8 of the Constitution granted the federal government broad powers with respect to interstate commerce. Through judicial interpretation, this federal power was broadened further and states were restricted in the burdens that they could impose on interstate commerce.[106] The Commerce Clause of the US Constitution is the source of federal power to regulate federal and state taxation:[107] 'Congress shall have the power to regulate commerce ... among the several States.' The Due Process and Commerce Clauses are closely related and many courts consider the Clauses concurrently when resolving the constitutionality of state taxation. Despite this close relationship, the Clauses impose separate and distinct limits on the powers of the states. The Due Process Clause focuses on the individual and the fundamental fairness of governmental activity upon the individual. In contrast, the Commerce Clause focuses on the effects of state regulation on the national economy.

However, the Commerce Clause is more restrictive than the Due Process Clause, in that it requires more than a minimal connection with the taxing state before taxation can occur.[108] The Commerce Clause requires that a taxpayer establish a 'substantial nexus', defined as physical presence within a state, before the state can impose a tax. However, the Commerce Clause has a negative implication, the so-called 'dormant Commerce Clause', which prohibits a state from taxing if the tax has the effect of restraining interstate business. The dormant Commerce Clause allows Congress to prevent the states from imposing taxes that are restrictive of interstate commerce. It also allows Congress to require minimum standards, such as physical presence in the state, before taxation can occur.[109] Congress could eliminate (or expand upon) the judicially created physical presence test; the minimum connection required by the Due Process Clause, by contrast, can only be changed by an amendment to the Constitution.

---

105   *National Bellas Hess, Inc. v. Department of Revenue* of Ill., 386 U.S. 753 (1967). However, it was not until the Court's ruling in *State of North Dakota v. Quill Corp*, 504 US 298 (1992), that the distinction between Due Process (minimum connection) and Commerce Clause (physical presence) nexus was established.

106   Ward, Burke T. and Sipior, Janice C. (2004) To Tax or Not To Tax E-Commerce: A United States Perspective, *Journal of Electronic Commerce Research*, Vol. 5, No.3, pp 172-180.

107   US Constitution; Art. I, 8 cl.3.

108   *State of North Dakota v. Quill Corp*, 504 US 298, 313 (1992).

109   Edson, Christina R (1996) 'Quill's Constitutional Jurisprudence and Tax Nexus Standards in an Age of Electronic Commerce', *49 Tax Law*, pp. 893, 937.

3.5.4 Judicial Interpretations

In 1967, the Supreme Court first applied the dual analysis of the Due Process Clause and the Commerce Clause to a tax imposed on an out-of-state mail-order seller. In *National Bellas Hess, Inc. v Department of Revenue*,[110] the Supreme Court addressed a challenge involving the application of the Illinois use tax to a Missouri mail-order house that owned no property and had no sales outlets or employees in Illinois. National Bellas Hess simply used the postal system to deliver catalogues to its customers twice a year; to deliver its products it used either the postal system or a common carrier. The business disputed Illinois's levy of its use tax upon the goods delivered to Illinois customers because its only connection with the state was by common carrier and mail. The State of Illinois argued that Bellas Hess had established a minimal connection with Illinois and should therefore be subject to the law that required the collection of Illinois tax. Under the relevant Illinois statute, any 'retailer maintaining a place of business[111] in the state was required to collect the tax. That Clause was further defined to include a retailer that was 'engaging in soliciting orders within this State from users by means of catalogues ... whether such orders are received or accepted within or without this state'. Illinois asserted that it had provided a market for Bellas Hess to exploit and Bellas Hess therefore owed Illinois this collection duty. The Supreme Court held that the levy violated the Dormant Commerce Clause because the 'Constitution requires some definite link, some minimum connection, between a state and the person, property or transaction it seeks to tax'. Thus, it held that the Due Process Clause and the Commerce Clause required that the seller maintain some sort of presence in the taxing state and the Court made note of the distinction between the taxpayer's physical presence in the state and a presence established solely by common carrier or through US mail.

The Supreme Court held in *Complete Auto Transit v Brady*[112] that a tax imposed by a state must meet the following four-prong test to withstand Commerce Clause scrutiny. The tax must: (i) apply to a taxpayer with a 'substantial' nexus with the taxing state; (ii) be fairly apportioned; (iii) not discriminate against interstate commerce; and (iv) be fairly related to the services provided to the taxpayer by the state. To date, the majority of litigation arising out of the Complete Auto Transit test has focused on the definition of the substantial nexus requirement leading to the creation of the physical presence requirement as discussed in *State of North Dakota v Quill Corp.*[113] In this case, the Supreme Court declined to eliminate the physical presence test and adhered to the rule that taxpayers had been relying on for 25 years: that physical presence with a state was required before taxation could occur. Quill was a mail-order seller of office supplies and equipment, with no physical presence in North Dakota. The State imposed a use tax collection obligation on Quill, claiming that Quill was a 'retailer maintaining a place of business' in North Dakota. The state

---

110 *National Bellas Hess, Inc. v Department of Revenue of Ill.*, 386 U.S. 753 (1967).
111 120 Ill. Comp. Stat. 439/2 (West 1965).
112 *Complete Auto Transit, Inc. v. Brady*, 430 U.S. 274, 279 (1977).
113 *State of North Dakota v. Quill Corp*, 504 US 298, 313 (1992).

acknowledged that Quill did not meet the physical presence requirement of *Bellas Hess*,[114] but argued that it did have a significant economic presence in North Dakota, sufficient to require Quill to collect tax on items sold into North Dakota.

The North Dakota Supreme Court agreed that *Bellas Hess* was obsolete, based on the changes in society and the mail-order industry since 1967. The *Quill* Court indicated that the Due Process analysis strayed from the physical presence requirement, speaking more to a minimal connection that seemed to embrace North Dakota's economic presence argument. While the Due Process and Commerce Clauses are closely related in their impact on state taxing jurisdiction, *Quill* notes that, because they promote disparate goals, different nexus standards apply under each Clause.[115] Due Process Clause physical presence is based on whether a taxpayer's connections with a state are substantial enough to legitimate that state's exercise of power over him.[116] By analysis, this requirement is satisfied if: (i) there is sufficient and purposeful direction of the taxpayer's activities aimed at a state's residents; and (ii) there is rational relationship between the tax imposed and the benefits the taxpayer received through access to the taxing state's market.[117] Therefore, since Quill had directed its activities towards North Dakota with an intention to profit therefrom, under a pure Due Process analysis the tax was fairly imposed.

However, while physical presence is not required under the Due Process Clause, it is still required under the Commerce Clause. In a vain attempt to prevent future confusion, the Court explicitly stated that 'a [out-of-state seller] whose only contact with the taxing State is by mail or common carrier lacks the 'substantial nexus' required by the Commerce Clause'. The Court specifically upheld an important part of its ruling in *Bellas Hess* by emphasizing the 'continuing vitality of *Bellas Hess*' sharp distinction between mail-order (sellers) with a physical presence in a taxing state' and those without such a physical presence. Thus, since Quill did not have the requisite physical presence, North Dakota's tax was unconstitutional as a restriction on interstate commerce and a violation of the dormant Commerce Clause.

The physical presence standard remains in force and is the standard applied currently to all remote sellers, internet sellers included. But defining exactly what qualifies as physical presence has proven to be a formidable task. The Supreme Court in *Quill* noted that a 'few floppy diskettes' did not rise to the level of physical presence but did not offer much beyond that. However, the Supreme Court did suggest that Congress has the power to impose uniform state tax rules on the states and acknowledged that 'Congress is free to decide whether, when and to what extent the States may burden interstate mail-order concerns with a duty to collect use taxes'.[118] In reality, as the task of identifying physical presence becomes far more nebulous, the only clear rule to emerge from the discussion is that *any physical*

---

114 *National Bellas Hess, Inc.* v. *Department of Revenue of Ill.*, 386 US 753 (1967).

115 The Commerce Clause serves to promote a stable national economy, while the Due Process Clause serves to insure notice and fair warning to the taxpayer.

116 *State of North Dakota v. Quill Corp*, 504 US 298, 313 (1992).

117 *State of North Dakota v. Quill Corp*, 504 US 298, 313 (1992).

118 504 US 298 at p 318 (1992).

connection, no matter how slight, could equate to physical presence.[119] However, without a clear definition of what qualifies as physical presence, it will be difficult to apply the physical presence standard to e-commerce sellers with sales activity across the nation.

---

119 *Tyler Pipe Industries, Inc. v. Washington Dep't of Revenue*, 483 U.S. 232, (finding nexus based on the permanent presence of a representative in state) as cited by Silhan, Sidney s. (1999) 'If It Ain't Broke Don't Fix It: An Argument For The Codification Of The Quill Standard For Taxing Internet Commerce', at p 13.

Chapter 4

The Relevance of E-Commerce for Taxation

Introduction

It is indisputable that the development of e-commerce and new business models has allowed all kinds of businesses to change their trading practices in ways that were unimaginable when tax rules were developed. Hence, before I look in detail at the impact of e-commerce on tax systems, it is worthwhile spending a little time on tax policy. This chapter will have a detailed discussion about the policies and principles behind taxation. The question is why do we tax the way we do? What are the political, economic, social and administrative pressures that have contributed to the shape of our tax system?

Taxation is clearly part of a political economy. Tax principles naturally involve ethical and political questions. The primary purpose of taxation is to raise revenue for the government. Another purpose behind taxation is the redistribution of wealth and income. Changes in taxation can and do affect the economy but control is exercised by adjusting the money supply and credit. Choosing taxes and reasons for taxes is in itself a fascinating topic, which requires detailed analysis; the effect of e-commerce has made it more complicated. This chapter will also look into the nature of e-commerce and will discuss the attributes of e-commerce that have significant implications for taxation and taxing jurisdictions. Most fundamentally, should e-commerce be taxed at all? What makes taxation of e-commerce so unique? What about arguments that e-commerce should not be taxed during its infancy? Can e-commerce actually be taxed as it should be?

4.1 Principles and Objectives of Tax Policy

Taxation has been a much discussed subject in the literature on economics. Many authors have put forward views of what qualifies as 'good' taxation and what constitutes undesirable tax policy. Consensus on these issues has changed over time, depending upon historical circumstances and the prevailing mode of economic thinking.[1]

The question is do we have generally accepted taxation principles? According to Ronald Dworkin, a principle is a 'standard that is to be observed because it is a

---

1   Hettich, Walter and Winer, Stanley L (2002) Rules, Politics and the Normative Analysis of Taxation, in Richard Wagner and Jurgen Backhouse (eds), *Handbook of Public Finance*, Kluwer Academic Publishers.

requirement of justice or fairness or some other dimension of morality'.[2] Westberg argues that 'principles may provide the supporting argument, but do not require a certain solution to a legal problem. They may even conflict with one another'.[3]

It is widely agreed upon in public finance that a tax system should be designed according to the principles of neutrality, efficiency, certainty, simplicity, effectiveness, fairness and flexibility. Each of these terms requires a definition and a description of the context in which it is to be used. Some of these principles may also be contradictory. Even if not all of them have the rank of general principles, they are valuable expressions of a code of conduct for tax authorities.[4] In practice, it is difficult to pursue all principles simultaneously as a variety of trade-offs exist among them. Equity versus efficiency is the most discussed trade-off in the literature of public finance. Here, the relevant trade-off exists among efficiency and low compliance cost. This trade-off can best be explained if the process of taxation is understood as a state action which takes place in an asymmetric information environment. In general, the state has little information concerning the characteristics and behaviour of the taxpayer, making it difficult to define and control a tax base. The state tries to overcome the information asymmetry by increasing the requirements for reporting the tax base which, in turn, leads to higher compliance costs.[5] However, this is not a book about the economics of taxation. That subject is a study in itself. Still, we should understand something about the economic logic of choice that undergirds the selection of taxes.

4.1.1   Why Do We Tax the Way We Do?

A government that cannot tax cannot survive. Taxation has always been a mechanism for the stabilization and regulation of the economy. In a modern economy, governments must achieve two primary goals, which are controversial but which also have been widely employed by the states. They must provide public goods and services demanded by the population and they must find ways to implement changes in the distribution of income that is generated by market forces if such changes are desired by the collective.[6] This, in turn, must be financed through taxation. However, because taxation inevitably impinges on most aspects of economic activity, careful consideration must be given to its design. This requires design of a tax system in the most efficient and equitable way possible. Setting up an efficient and fair tax system is, however, far from simple. Tax scholars use criteria of 'efficiency' and 'equity' in order to evaluate the appropriateness of a particular

---

2   Dworkin, Ronald (1977) Taking Rights Seriously, p 22 as citied in Westberg, Bjorn (2002) Cross-border Taxation of E-Commerce, IBFD p 53.

3   Westberg, Bjorn (2002) Cross-border Taxation of E-Commerce, IBFD p 53.

4   Westberg, Bjorn (2002) Cross-border Taxation of E-Commerce, IBFD p 56.

5   Köthenbürger, Marko and Rahmann Bernd (1999) *Taxing E-commerce*, in: T. Gries and L. Suhl: Economic Aspects of Digital Information Technologies (Wiesbaden).

6   Hettich, Walter and Winer, Stanley L (2002) Rules, Politics and the Normative Analysis of Taxation, in Richard Wagner and Jurgen Backhouse (eds), *Handbook of Public Finance*, Kluwer Academic Publishers.

tax policy choice.[7] Efficiency concerns include the desired neutral tax treatment of comprehensive forms of economic activity in order to avoid welfare-reducing market distortions, ease of tax administration in order to promote tax collection and low compliance costs for businesses in order to ensure that economic activity is not unduly discouraged. Equity concerns involve considerations such as fairness among similarly situated individuals (horizontal equity) and fairness among individuals with different economic circumstances (vertical equity). Taxation also has a regulatory component; it can be used to steer private sector activity in the directions desired by governments. This function is also controversial, as shown by the debate surrounding tax expenditures.[8]

Three features of taxation are especially important. First, tax law should be simple to enable taxpayers to better understand the tax consequences of their economic decisions, and it should not influence their economic decisions. That is, taxpayers should not be unduly encouraged or discouraged from engaging in certain activities or taking certain courses of action primarily due to the effect of the tax law on the activity or action. Second, the distribution of taxation's impact across the population raises issues of equity, or fairness, which must be given substantial weight even if it entails costs in terms of economic efficiency. Third, the practical enforceability of tax rules and the costs arising from compliance are important considerations; more so since these are both affected by, and have implications for, the efficiency and public perceptions of the fairness of tax systems.[9] From an overall policy perspective, perhaps the best tax system is one that matches the benefits received with the costs of the system, providing the greatest utility to citizen taxpayers who, through political measures, can determine the desired amount of public services they wish to see funded.

The tax rules should specify when the tax is to be paid, how it is to be paid, and how the amount to be paid is to be determined. A person's tax liability should be certain rather than ambiguous. A tax system's rules must enable taxpayers to determine what is subject to tax (the tax base) and at what tax rate(s). Taxpayers should be able to determine their tax liabilities with reasonable certainty based on the nature of their transactions. If the transactions subject to tax are easy to identify and value, the principle of certainty is more likely to be attained. On the other hand, if the tax base is dependent on subjective valuations or transactions that are difficult to categorize, the principle of certainty might not be attained. In addition, how the taxes are paid and when the taxes are due should be spelled out in the applicable laws, as well as in the tax forms and instructions. Certainty is important to a tax system because it helps to improve compliance with the rules and to increase respect for the system. Certainty generally comes from clear statutes as well as timely and

---

7   Basu, Subhajit (2003) 'Relevance of E-Commerce for Taxation: an Overview', *Global Jurist Topics*: Vol. 3: No. 3, Article 2, http://www.bepress.com/gj/topics/vol3/iss3/art2.

8   Reuven, Avi-Yonah, S (2005) 'The Three Goals of Taxation' (September 2005). Available at SSRN: http://ssrn.com/abstract=796776.

9   Noord, Paul van den and Heady, Chistopher (2001) 'Surveillance Of Tax Policies: A Synthesis Of Findings In Economic Surveys', *Economics Department Working Papers, No. 303, OECD*, website at http: www.oecd.org/eco/eco, p 16.

understandable administrative guidance that is readily available to taxpayers. The principle of certainty is closely related to the principle of simplicity. The more complex the tax rules and system, the greater is the likelihood that the certainty principle will be compromised.

4.1.2   Efficiency Considerations

Taxation is not only a pure transfer of resources from the private sector to the state, but it also affects the behaviour of the taxpayer. The efficiency principle encompasses notions of both fiscal and economic efficiency. Fiscal efficiency characterizes any system which can be both administered and complied with at a low cost free from unduly complicated processes and improper burdens. One of the most important factors in achieving fiscal efficiency is the establishment of administrable demarcations such that taxable items can be easily identified and taxation cannot be easily avoided by simply restructuring the transaction. Economic efficiency is about maximizing economic output given the resources available to the community. If the only concern were to minimize efficiency losses associated with taxation, taxes generally should be designed to leave economic behaviour unaffected. While such a tax system would avoid distortions in economic behaviour, it would be highly unlikely to yield sufficient revenues to fund socially useful expenditure without producing substantial inequity. A more useful guideline is that the tax system should be as 'neutral' as possible, that is, minimize discrimination in favour of or against any particular economic choices. According to Noord and Heady:

> as a rule of thumb, in the absence of compelling considerations to the contrary, improvements in efficiency can be achieved by: (i) broadening tax bases by eliminating exemptions and special regimes; (ii) flattening rate structures; and (iii) integrating or aligning different tax rate structures to avoid arbitrage opportunities.[10]

Although an efficient tax system is desirable, it is not the only criteria by which tax systems are judged. Indeed, equity in the tax system is very important. People want tax systems to be fair at least as much as they want them to be efficient. When equity goals are similar to efficiency goals, no conflict arises in the formation of tax policy, but when the goals of equity and efficiency conflict, as they often do, normative judgments must be made.[11]

4.1.3   Equity Considerations

When dividing the principles of taxation into equity and efficiency issues, the efficiency issues tend to be more straightforward because they deal with the facts

---

10 Noord, Paul van den and Heady, Chistopher (2001) 'Surveillance Of Tax Policies: A Synthesis Of Findings In Economic Surveys', *Economics Department Working Papers, No. 303, OECD*, website at http: www.oecd.org/eco/eco.

11 Holcombe, Randall G. (1999) *Public Finance Government Revenues And Expenditures In The United States Economy*, (West Publishers), DeVoe Moore Center at Florida State University, DeVoe Moore, Centre p 203.

about the effects of taxation. As discussed before, an efficient tax is one that minimizes the excess burden of taxation, has low compliance costs and is easy to monitor and administer. Equity issues, on the other hand, are inherently normative in nature. This implies that there are indisputable principles of tax equity in the same way that there are with regard to efficiency. Nevertheless, there are a number of generally accepted principles of tax equity. Because in the real world citizens collectively choose their tax policies, and because people want their tax systems to be fair, equity issues are at least as important as efficiency issues in the determination of tax systems.

There are two fundamental principles which undergird most taxes and have different economic and political ramifications.[12] These are the 'ability-to-pay' principle and the 'benefit' principle. According to the benefit principle, people should pay taxes in proportion to the benefits they receive from government output. This principle has obvious appeal from an equity standpoint. It seems only fair that people should pay for the benefits they receive and, conversely, that people should not be forced to pay for benefits that go to others. The benefit principle, in effect, views a tax as the price that is paid for a government-supplied good. Just as it is fair for people to pay for the goods they receive in the private sector, so it is also fair that they pay for the benefits they receive from the public sector. According to the ability-to-pay principle, people should pay taxes in proportion to their ability to pay.[13] However, as Holcombe[14] suggested, there is a close correspondence between the benefit and ability-to-pay principles under the presumption that the demand for government goods and services is correlated with the income and wealth of citizens. If this is true, then those with the greatest ability to pay also are those who derive the greatest benefits from government expenditures. The argument is worth further consideration, for not only is there a certain logic to it but it also is an old idea in economics dating back to Adam Smith. In Smith's classic treatise, *The Wealth of Nations*, originally published in 1776, he said:

> The subjects of every state ought to contribute towards the support of the government, as nearly as possible, in proportion to their respective abilities; that is, in proportion to the revenue which they respectively enjoy under the protection of the state. The expense of government to the individuals of a great nation is like the expense of management to the joint tenants of a great estate, who are all obligated to contribute in proportion to their respective interests in the estate.[15]

---

12 Peters, B. Guy (1991) *The Politics of Taxation: A Comparative Perspective*, (Blackwell: Cambridge) p 50.

13 Holcombe, Randall G. (1999) *Public Finance Government Revenues And Expenditures In The United States Economy*, (West Publishers), DeVoe Moore Center at Florida State University, DeVoe Moore Centre.

14 Holcombe, Randall G. (1999) *Public Finance Government Revenues And Expenditures In The United States Economy*, (West Publishers), DeVoe Moore Center at Florida State University, DeVoe Moore Centre.

15 Smith, Adam The Wealth of Nations (New York: Modem Library, 1937, originally 1776), at p 777.

In other words, Smith viewed the benefit principle and the ability-to-pay principle as implying similar things about the tax structure. Smith stated that one's benefits from government are in proportion to the income that one receives under the protection of the state but that one's income is also a good measure of a person's ability to pay. However, as a general principle, 'ability-to-pay' has much more appeal. Two main issues arise in assessing the fairness of taxes under the ability-to-pay principle. These are the concepts of 'horizontal equity' and 'vertical equity'. The principle of horizontal equity is satisfied when people with an equal ability to pay end up paying the same amount of tax. The principle of vertical equity is satisfied when people with a greater ability to pay end up paying the appropriate amount more than people with a lesser ability to pay. The notion of vertical equity is important to the design of a fair tax code. In business taxation equity is normally more easily achieved than in the taxation of individuals. The principle of equity is often viewed as a fairness principle. There is widespread agreement that high-income individuals should pay their fair share of taxes and that low-income individuals should not be burdened with excessive taxation. However, there is less agreement on exactly what a high-income individual's fair share of taxes is and to what degree low-income individuals should be able to avoid taxation on equity grounds.[16] 'In the context of optimal tax theory, a fair tax is one that guarantees a socially desirable distribution of the tax burden.'[17]

Until recently, most theoretical formulations associated direct taxation with the attainment of equity and indirect taxation with the efficiency requirements that a tax structure was expected to meet. Progressive taxes levied on income or equity are directly proportional to the taxpayer's ability to pay, therefore wealthier individuals contribute with larger portions to the costs of general social welfare. In turn, indirect taxes are characterized by their regressivity and by the fact that they are equally applied among taxpayers in unequal positions from a contribution point of view. Because they are levied only on the portion of income that is to be spent on consumption, taxes of this type penalize taxpayers that spend the larger portion of their income on consumption. Considering that the smaller a taxpayer's income,

---

16 That is, many people view a tax as fair if taxpayers with the greatest ability to pay have the highest tax burdens. Nevertheless, the term *fair* tends to have different meanings to different people. For example, with respect to an income tax, an income tax system might be considered fair if:

- All taxpayers are taxed at the same tax rate (a flat tax) because those with higher incomes will pay more than taxpayers with lower incomes;
- Taxpayers with higher incomes pay tax at higher rates than lower income taxpayers (a progressive tax);
- Many different types of income are taxed the same (meaning, for instance, that few or no types of income are excluded from taxation).

Therefore, use of the word fair in describing a tax might be better used in the context of whether a tax system is *perceived* as fair. This approach acknowledges some of the subjectiveness of the term *fair*. Generally, in evaluating the principle of *equity*, consideration should be given to the entire range of taxes a taxpayer is subject to, rather than to just one type of tax.

17 Rosen, Harvey S (1995) *Public Finance*, (Irwin 4th edition US).

the larger the proportion that consumption represents in relation to that income, it becomes evident that the tax burden of low-income taxpayers is heavier than that of high-income taxpayers.

4.1.4   Principles of Neutrality

A tax that is generally seen as unfair or arbitrary in its incidence can generate reluctance among taxpayers to comply. One of the most important economic criteria concerning taxes is fiscal neutrality. The principle of tax neutrality requires that any equitable tax system treat economically similar income equally.[18] This criterion argues that the tax system should not impose any special barriers, or provide any special advantages, to citizens or businesses choosing to use their funds or energy one way versus another or to invest in one industry versus another. Instead, the tax system should be neutral among all uses of resources, allowing the market to determine the most productive utilization of those resources available.[19] All sources of income and all expenditures should be, according to this criterion, treated equally. A more discriminatory tax system will distort the operations of the market and, at least in theory, produce lower real economic growth and income. If different tax rates or other distinctions related to income taxation require legal definitions of different sources, and different allowances, and if these definitions do not correspond to basic economic thinking then there are clear incentives to avoidance.[20] Neutrality in respect of consumption taxation requires a consistent tax policy with, as a matter of principle, no exemptions. Neutrality is important not only for its favourable efficiency and for horizontal equity effects but also because it usually helps tax rules to be clear and simple to understand, reducing both the administrative and compliance costs of taxation.

4.1.5   Enforceability and Compliance

Evidently, the relationship between equity and neutrality on the one hand and enforceability on the other goes in both directions. It is only by firm and equitable enforcement that a theoretically desirable tax system can be both equitable and neutral in effective terms. Hence, providing a better service to taxpayers, particularly the vast majority who wish to pay the correct amount of tax, should encourage the development of a simplified and effective compliance system. The main thrust of this discussion of tax policy to this point has been to emphasize the importance of an efficient and equitable tax system. An inefficient tax code with a large excess burden hinders the productivity of the economy, which means that there is less output for everyone and everyone is potentially worse off. While most individuals would accept

---

18 Cigler, James D and Stinnett, Susan E. (1997) 'Treasury Seeks Cybertax Answers with Electronic Commerce' Discussion Paper, 8 *Journal of International Taxation* 56, 58.

19 Peters, B. Guy (1991) *The Politics of Taxation: A Comparative Perspective*, (Blackwell: Cambridge) p 51.

20 Stiglitz, Joseph E (1988) Economics of the Public Sector, pp 388 and 390-391 as cited in Westberg, Bjorn (2002) Cross-border Taxation of E-Commerce, IBFD p 60.

that both efficiency and equity are desirable in a tax system, it may not be possible to achieve both. An efficient tax system may not necessarily be considered fair and one that is considered equitable may not be efficient. The challenge in this case is to establish the tax structure that gives the best trade-off between the two. Therefore, a complete understanding of tax policy requires knowledge of the principles of equity and efficiency in taxation, as well as an awareness of the political environment in which tax policy is formulated. If generally agreed upon principles of tax equity can be identified, and if those principles can be applied to the tax system consistently, then it is possible to produce a tax system that people will agree is fair.

4.2   Taxes as a Source of Revenue

The revenue goal of taxation explains why all OECD members, and most other countries, have both an income tax and a consumption tax as their principal sources of revenue. Data from government finance statistics shows that taxes are the principal source of government revenue, accounting on average for about 80 per cent of total revenue (all countries). Domestic taxation of goods and services makes up the largest share in tax revenues (36.5 per cent).[21] Revenues from import duties account on average for 13.2 per cent of total revenue and 17.5 per cent of tax revenue. Major differences exist between developing and developed countries: for the developing countries import duties as a share of total government revenue are 15.8 per cent (compared with 2.6 per cent for developed countries) and as a share of tax revenue 21.2 per cent (compared with 3 per cent for developed countries).[22] The combined tax revenues from goods, services and those from imports account for 54 per cent of tax revenues (all countries) or 58.3 per cent of developing countries' and 37 per cent of developed countries' tax revenue.[23] These forms of taxation make up a major source of government revenue.[24] Income taxes generate about a third of total tax revenue in developing countries. Therefore, they play a much less important role in developing countries than in developed countries where they generate a large proportion of total revenue. Data on the ratios of tax revenue to gross domestic product (GDP) for a number of developing countries for two years, 1978 and 1988, show that most developing countries collect tax revenue that ranges between a higher ratio of 30 per cent and a lower ratio of 10 per cent with an average

---

21 Mainly sales and value added taxes.

22 In the case of the EU, individual member countries do not report revenues from import duties (some report very low values). This is because EU import duties are directly passed on to the EU common budget as a traditional own resources payment, and only 10% is retained by the importing country (this share increased to 25% as of 2001). Therefore, the calculations of EU member States' import revenues are based on their individual contributions to the EU budget (Commission of the European Community, 1998c).

23 Teltscher, Susanne (2000), 'Tariffs, Taxes and Electronic Commerce: Revenue Implications for Developing Countries', UNCTAD Study Series on 'Policy Issues in International Trade and Commodities' No.5 UNCTAD/ITCD/TAB/5, Geneva, p 1.

24 Other important sources not considered here are income taxes and social security contributions.

of around 18 per cent of GDP.[25] VAT has been successful in raising revenue even in developing countries with weak tax administrations, which are largely unable to collect personal income tax from the majority of the population. In Latin America, for example, consumption taxes accounted for 52 per cent of total revenue in 1996–2002, compared with only 27 per cent for (mostly corporate) income taxes; in Africa the figures for the same period were 35 per cent for consumption taxes, 32 per cent for taxes on international trade (which are equivalent to consumption taxes) and 30 per cent for income taxes.[26] For all developing countries in 1999–2001, income taxes accounted for only 24.3 per cent of total tax revenue, compared with 38.6 per cent for all developed countries; the remaining revenue was mostly based on consumption taxes.[27]

Consumption taxes have a very good track record in terms of raising revenue. VAT, specifically, is second only to the individual income tax in its ability to raise revenue in most OECD member countries and in some it raises more revenue than income tax. The distribution of tax revenue among major taxes for OECD and the European Union shows that the vast bulk of tax revenue, that is, over 80 per cent, comes from three main sources: income taxes, taxes on goods and services and social security contributions (other payroll taxes are zero or very small in most countries). The European Union relies more on consumption taxes and social security contributions and less on personal income tax than the OECD average. VAT is a critical source of tax revenues throughout the European Union. The EU countries generally derive about 30 per cent of their overall tax revenue from taxes on domestic goods and services (mainly VAT); in 1996–2002, the individual income tax accounted for 32 per cent of total tax revenue.[28] In addition, VAT extra charges contribute 45 per cent to the EU Community budget (supplemented by customs duties and other contributions). Effective tax rates on consumption in the EU area are, on average, higher than in most other OECD countries. This not only reflects a higher tax to GDP ratio but also a tax mix relying heavily on consumption taxes. If one adds excises and the corporate income tax, total income taxes account for 44 per cent of all government revenues in the same period, while consumption taxes account for 49 per cent.[29] In North America, on the other hand, income taxes accounted for 82 per cent of all revenue for the same period, and only 15 per cent came from consumption taxes (including state level sales taxes).[30]

---

25 Tanzi, Vito and Zee, Howell (2001) *Tax Policy for Developing Countries*, March 2001 International Monetary Fund, Economic Issue No 27 http://www.imf.org/external/index.htm.

26 Richard M. Bird and Eric M. Zolt, Redistribution via Taxation: The Limited Role of Personal Income Tax in Developing Countries, -- UCLA L. Rev. – (2005).

27 Richard M. Bird and Eric M. Zolt, Redistribution via Taxation: The Limited Role of Personal Income Tax in Developing Countries, -- UCLA L. Rev. – (2005).

28 Bird, Richard M. and Eric M. Zolt, Redistribution via Taxation: The Limited Role of Personal Income Tax in Developing Countries, -- UCLA L. Review.

29 Bird, Richard M. and Eric M. Zolt (2005) Redistribution via Taxation: The Limited Role of Personal Income Tax in Developing Countries, -- UCLA L. Review.

30 Bird, Richard M. and Eric M. Zolt (2005) Redistribution via Taxation: The Limited Role of Personal Income Tax in Developing Countries, -- UCLA L. Review.

State and local governments in the United States rely on sales taxes for financing the services they provide. The taxes have typically yielded about one-third of state tax collections (far more than the contribution for any tax other than the personal income tax), around 10 per cent of local government tax revenue (a distant second to property taxes but more than twice the revenue from any other tax), and about one-quarter of combined state and local tax revenue (US Bureau of Census, 2000). From fiscal 1947 to fiscal 1998, general sales taxes produced more revenue than any other state tax. However, the US$159 billion they produced in fiscal 1998 was roughly two billion dollars less than was produced from individual income taxes. State sales tax bases have been declining relative to state personal income for many years.

4.3 Nature of E-Commerce and Taxation

E-commerce can be intangible, multi-jurisdictional, and easily located in tax havens. It poses great challenges to tax authorities. Effective administration relies on the tax authorities' power and means to obtain information in order to assess a taxpayer's tax liability by identifying taxpayers, identifying and verifying transactions, and establishing a link between taxpayer and the transactions. E-commerce has the potential to make it difficult or impossible for tax authorities to obtain information or to enforce tax collection. Taxpayers may disappear in cyberspace, reliable records and books may be difficult to obtain, and taxing points and audit trails may become obscure.[31]

When transactions generating income, or resulting in sales, have cross-border connections, international tax mechanisms have been developed to rationalize concurrent claims to taxing jurisdiction over the income or the sale.[32] As discussed earlier in the book, an extensive network of bilateral income tax treaties link most of the developed and many of the developing nations. Within the EU, extensive steps have been taken by each member state to coordinate each nation's separate taxes on goods, services and corporation profits. The technologies that made e-commerce possible have challenged those existing mechanisms with transactions that cannot readily be identified under existing definitions in the treaty networks, nor in the domestic statutory provisions for sales and income taxation.[33]

The issues surrounding taxation of e-commerce transactions comprise a complex intersection of developments in information technology and multinational taxation issues. Discussion in the earlier two chapters showed that existing taxation systems have developed in an economic environment characterized by the exchange of tangible goods and personal services. However, because of the growth of global e-commerce, a major shift is happening in favour of intangible goods and electronically provided services where suppliers need not be present at the point of sale. Exactly the same book, computer, software or automobile (or other tangible

---

31 Doernberg, Richard L., et al. (2001) Electronic *Commerce and Multijurisdictional Taxation* (London: Kluwer Law International) p 388.

32 Salter, Sarah W (2002) E-Commerce and International Taxation, New Eng. Journal of Int'l & Comp Law, Vol.8:1 pp 6-17.

33 Salter, Sarah W (2002) E-Commerce and International Taxation, New Eng. Journal of Int'l & Comp Law, Vol.8:1 pp 6-17.

product) could be bought from a website or from a local bookstore, computer outlet or car dealer (or other retail outlet). Similarly, software, music and movies delivered online are quite nearly perfect substitutes for the same products delivered in tangible forms. Perhaps the most important feature of e-commerce is the ease with which shoppers can gain information and the competitive pressure on price. Whereas prior revolutions either drove prior technology to extinction or niche markets (the telephone and telegraph; printed books and illuminated manuscripts) or created sufficiently different products that competition between the old and the new technology was relatively limited (television and drive-time radio; TV news coverage and printed news media), the digital revolution is creating competition between technologies that deliver essentially the same products in different ways. E-commerce exacerbates the problems globalization poses for tax collection. It will become more difficult to locate income streams and transactions in physical space and for governments to know that a transaction has taken place. In some instances, the geographic 'location' of a firm or a buyer or seller may actually be ambiguous.[34] What, then, are the attributes of e-commerce that have significant implications for taxation? Professor Hellerstein described the problem as:

> The new technology and the concomitant reconfiguration of telecommunications and related industries play havoc with traditional standards for determining jurisdiction to tax; the sourcing of income; the nature, value, situs, and timing of sales; the classification of property and taxpayers; and the collection of taxes.[35]

Jeffrey Owens, Head of Fiscal Affairs for the OECD, has identified six characteristics of the internet that influence the operation of tax systems.[36]

1. The ability to establish public and private global communications systems, which are secure and inexpensive to operate. The opportunities that this opens up for new forms of commercial activities will not be limited to large companies. Small- and medium-size enterprises will find it easier to engage in international commerce. Start-up capital requirements on the internet are typically very low. This, in turn, will lead to a rapid expansion in cross-border activities.

2. The process of 'disintermediation' whereby the internet eliminates or substantially reduces the need for intermediaries in the sale and delivery of goods and services and in the provision of information. Commerce, which uses the internet, requires a small number of distribution, sales representative, broker and other professional intermediaries. Already it is possible for a producer of software to sell and deliver its products directly to the final

---

34 Kobrin J. Stephen (2001) 'Territoriality and Governance of Cyberspace', Journal of International Business Studeis, Vol. 32, No 4, pp 687-704.

35 Hellerstein, Walter (1997) 'Telecommunications and Electronic Commerce: Overview and Appraisal', *State Tax Notes*, Volume: 12, p 525.

36 Owens, Jeffrey (1997) 'The Tax Man Cometh to Cyberspace', paper presented at the *Harvard Law School International Tax Program Symposium on Multi-jurisdictional Taxation of Electronic Commerce.*

consumer. Similarly, an airline company can deliver tickets directly to passengers. Financial and other information may become available without the intermediation of banks and other financial institutions.

3. The development of encrypted information that protects the confidentiality of the information transmitted on the internet. Whilst it is possible to detect a message sent by one person to another over the internet, encryption generally precludes understanding the content of the message.

4. An increased scope for the integration of business functions, for example, design and production. Private intranet networks are now widespread in Multinational Corporations (MNEs). The OECD estimates that at least two-thirds of internet transactions take this form. This development produces a closer integration of transactions within an MNE and makes it increasingly difficult to separate the functions carried out by related enterprises. This integration may also produce a dramatic synergistic effect, the sum of the parts being much less than the integrated whole.

5. The internet provides greater flexibility in the choice of the organization form by which an enterprise carries out its international activities.

6. The internet has led to a fragmentation of economic activity. The physical location of an activity, whether in terms of the supplier, service provider or buyer of goods or user of the service, becomes less important and it becomes more difficult to determine where an activity is carried out.

Operating almost exclusively on the global online environment of the internet, e-commerce has a number of features that distinguish it from traditional commercial activities. These include the blurring of national boundaries; the elimination of distance; no or minimal physical presence; the reduction of intermediaries (or disintermediation); the lack of physical regulatory control; and the potential for increased intra-firm integration and the capacity of firms to outsource non-core functions (Figure 4.1). These features do not eliminate traditional physical trade as such, but are complements to it. To the extent that these features create potential new opportunities for the participants in both the conventional and new economy, they create equally significant challenges to the existing international tax system.

4.3.1　Borderless Commerce

Most national tax systems, as well as the international tax regime on which many of these systems are based, assume that commercial activities can be linked to a particular territory. Westberg argues that there are at least three types of problems.

> Firstly, there can be difficulties pinning down a certain business entity in a certain location. The jurisdiction may be unknown to the purchaser and to the tax authorities. Secondly, there, may be problems in assigning a certain business activity to a certain place. Thirdly, there may be problems in relating a transaction to certain business entity.[37]

37　Westberg, Bjorn (2002) Cross-border Taxation of E-Commerce, IBFD p 23.

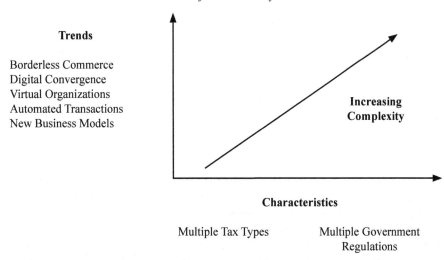

Trends

Borderless Commerce
Digital Convergence
Virtual Organizations
Automated Transactions
New Business Models

**Increasing
Complexity**

Characteristics

Multiple Tax Types   Multiple Government
                            Regulations

Figure 4.1   The Increasing Complexity of Global E-Commerce Taxation

E-commerce challenges this assumption because it is inherently non-territorial. This disjuncture between the geographical foundations of modern taxing systems on the one hand and the territorial character of e-commerce on the other is at the heart of the challenge that e-commerce poses to taxation. Cross-border transactions have historically been one of the most problematic areas of taxation. The process of disintermediation, in which remote vendors sell directly to customers in other jurisdictions without the buffer of a wholesale distributor or retail outlet, will result in hundreds of thousands of entities dealing with taxes in additional states or countries for the first time. This will expand disputes of both business tax compliance efforts in multiple new foreign jurisdictions, and nexus and jurisdictional disputes over which states or nations can impose income or transactional taxes on e-commerce vendors. Any resolution of how to tax e-commerce transactions will have to take into account the inherent difficulties of verifying the location, identity and residence of a seller or purchaser over the internet.

4.3.2   Digital Commerce

Over time, technological innovations have been incorporated into commercial activities, changing the products and services themselves, their delivery and how processes underlying the completion of a transaction are performed. Digital communications have produced an integrated digital platform. There is a wide array of products and services offered in digital format that are both purchased and delivered through this digital connectivity. Digital transactions involve downloading software, a film or a symphony, for example, and paying with electronic cash.[38] The problem posed by digitally downloaded goods is radically different. When bits are

---

38 Kobrin, Stephen J. 1997. Electronic Cash and the End of National Markets. *Foreign Policy*, Vol. 107 Summer, pp 65-77.

exchanged for bits, the seller has no need to know where the buyer is located or even his identity and in the absence of a 'product' delivery, the relevant authorities may not ever know that a transaction has taken place.[39] The taxation of such services and intangibles raises complex tax issues. Current tax rules are simply inapplicable to these digital products and services. The absence of tax rules adaptable to the digital economy will cut across both direct (income) and indirect (transactional) tax systems.

4.3.3   The 'Virtual' Corporation

The internet is also accelerating the trend toward 'virtual' corporations with narrowly defined core competencies. In the information age, there is less need for vertical integration. Companies are more likely to narrowly define their core competencies and leave manufacturing, distribution, fulfilment, customer service and other functions to third parties. In part, this is because of the ease with which companies can enter into joint ventures, partnerships, outsourcing agreements and other affiliations to bring products to market. For instance, Cisco Systems is primarily a virtual corporation. Cisco Systems sells many of the routers, circuits and other equipment used to construct the infrastructure of the internet. Over three-quarters of all Cisco Systems's product orders are made online. Over two-thirds of all Cisco Systems's manufacturing is outsourced to other companies. As a result, for a large percentage of its product sales, no Cisco employee ever meets either the customer or the actual product involved in a transaction. An even more dramatic example of the virtual corporation is *eMachines*. This personal computer reseller sold 1.7 million computers globally in 1999, producing over US$1 billion in revenue. Incredibly, the company used only 20 employees to conduct its business, relying on other entities for virtually all of its operational functions. With the narrowing of core competencies, e-commerce businesses will frequently have more flexibility to relocate (or initially locate) their property and payroll in jurisdictions with more favourable income tax rules and rates. It is far easier to shift the location of computer servers, headquarter employees or information technology personnel than it is to move around large factories. Thus, the emergence of the virtual corporation is going to put pressure on tax laws particularly in the income tax arena to develop new rules for apportioning the income of more mobile and dynamic businesses. In a complementary development, e-commerce also places a premium on intangible values (such as brand names and customer information), leading to more tax compliance, planning and litigation over the value and location of such intangibles.

4.3.4   Real-time Commerce

The internet also facilitates a significant increase in real-time, paperless transactions. This trend is likely to enhance the momentum toward tax compliance reengineering and automated tax solutions for transactional taxes. It also will increase the pressure

---

39 Kobrin J. Stephen (2001) 'Territoriality and Governance of Cyberspace', *Journal of International Business Studies*, Vol. 32, No 4, pp 687–704.

on taxing authorities to simplify the substantive and procedural tax rules to make an automated system more workable and less costly. During the 1990s, the growing interest in the automation of sales and use tax or VAT compliance was part of a larger movement toward the use of enterprise resource planning (ERP) software to automate corporate finance, distribution and other operational functions. The explosion of e-commerce and the growth of internet-based transaction processing for both B2B sales and B2C sales will accelerate the creation of a less paper-oriented environment in which electronic databases largely supplant filing cabinets filled with sales invoices and purchase orders. E-commerce has contributed to the ease with which companies can enter into joint ventures, partnerships, outsourcing agreements and other arrangements transforming them into virtual organizations. For example, at Cisco Systems, a leader in networking solutions for the internet, over two-thirds of manufacturing is outsourced to other companies and over three-quarters of sales occur online. Such an agile virtual enterprise would find relocation of property and payroll functions to jurisdictions with more favourable income tax rates and rules to be relatively easy. The emergence of virtual organizations will put pressure on taxing authorities to develop new rules for apportioning the income of these more mobile and dynamic businesses.

4.3.5 Changing Business Models

The internet is also causing a revolution in business models that is creating new and challenging issues for state, federal and international tax systems. The internet is characterized not just by remote selling but also by a range of evolving business models such as online auctions, reverses auctions, virtual communities, infomediaries, aggregators and brokers. Traditional businesses have also undergone changes. Traditional industries such as automobiles, clothing, book publishing and pharmacies are being turned upside down by the potential of online retailing to replace conventional store purchases. Many manufacturers are being transformed into retailers; many conventional intermediaries such as wholesalers and distributors are disappearing or being replaced by new web-based intermediaries, such as telecommunication companies, internet access providers, certification authorities related to digital signatures, business entities or authorities in charge of handling the domain name system. The role of intermediaries will also change. Many traditional forms of intermediation carried out by banks and travel agencies will disappear. This development could negatively influence tax compliance as previous reporting sources will no longer be available. In international taxation the lack of intermediaries for the withholding of tax on royalties and certain other payments to foreign persons could be problematic.[40] These business models are significantly altering the landscape of interactions between suppliers, sellers and buyers, creating many new tax issues. Before the internet, gift certificates were primarily purchased at retail outlets. In the last few years, however, a number of internet start-ups such as GiftCertificates.com and Giftpoint.com have begun to build an online marketplace for gift certificates. These entities buy the gift certificates from retail outlets at a discount and resell

---

40 Westberg, Bjorn (2002) *Cross-border Taxation of E-Commerce*, IBFD p 20.

them over the internet. This new business model raises new taxation issues such as the identity of the actual retailer, the sourcing of consumption, the classification of the good or service sold and the relevant sales price upon which the transactional tax would be based. New tax rules incorporating these new business models must also allow adaptability to future business models which emerge. As the discussion in this section makes clear, the problem is not merely one of changing rules that no longer make sense; taxation of e-commerce also faces technological constraints. According to Professors Abrams and Doernberg 'what may be a sound rule from a tax policy perspective may be totally unworkable in light of available technology. Perhaps the most significant implication of the growth of electronic commerce for tax policy may be that technology rather than policy will determine the tax rules of the 21st century'.[41]

4.4   To Tax or Not to Tax E-Commerce

There is no consensus as to what extent e-commerce should be made subject to taxation. This issue lies at the intersection of trade policy, economic policy and tax policy and it is not always possible to reconcile the three. Therefore, it seems worthwhile to go through the arguments for and against the taxation of e-commerce in a systematic way. The first issue to be dealt with is to what extent e-commerce can be taxed. It will not be useful to discuss the desirability of taxing e-commerce if it is simply not possible (or administratively prohibitively expensive) to do so. The administrative procedures necessary for taxing e-commerce are also considered. The next issue to be considered is to what extent it is socially desirable to tax e-commerce at the same rate as goods being sold through traditional retail trade or whether some degree of preferential tax treatment of e-commerce is called for. Since the taxation of e-commerce is a relatively new research area, there are many potentially important questions to be answered before a definite conclusion can be reached on this topic. The lack of clarity on the taxation of e-commerce is an impediment to its development.[42] In the broader sense, international coordination is required because of globalization and the involvement of multinational corporations. Accordingly, norms to remove distortions in international direct taxation should be introduced. International consensus is needed to avoid double taxation and unintentional non-taxation.[43]

4.4.1   Is E-Commerce Taxable?

In order to find out whether it is possible to tax e-commerce, we should consider the problems that arise because of e-commerce for taxation. I have discussed the nature of e-commerce, which makes it difficult for taxation. In this section, I deal with the problems; I will consider the issue of classification and jurisdiction. However, as I have explained before, there could be many challenges for the enforcement of

---

41 Abrams, Howard E. and Doernberg, Richard L. (1997) 'How Electronic Commerce Works', *State Tax Notes*, Volume: 13, at 136.

42 Westberg, Bjorn (2002) Cross-border Taxation of E-Commerce, IBFD p 31.

43 Westberg, Bjorn (2002) Cross-border Taxation of E-Commerce, IBFD p 32.

transactions related to e-commerce. These are anonymity of identity and location of parties, anonymity of transactions and accounts, disintermediation, transfer pricing issues, online delivery and digital cash, easy access to tax havens and low tax jurisdictions, identification of taxing jurisdiction, new evasion opportunities, recovery of tax and exchange of information. The general opinion seems to be that existing tax rules are applicable and should be applied in a digital environment. The problems caused by new forms of communication are not seen as new problems, only as bigger ones.

4.4.1.1 Issue of Classification The problem of classifying digital products has been a subject of attention for several decades and has become more important with the arrival of e-commerce. In taxation, it is often necessary to classify a transaction or the object of a transaction. Transactions are classified, for example, as income from employment or from royalties, and the objects of the transactions are classified, for example, as products or services. I will focus here on the classification of products and services. Traditionally, distribution of information has depended on the distribution of the media. When the information has been fixed, for example on a CD, the information has been distributed in fixed form. These transactions have traditionally been taxed as transactions in goods, without regard to the fact that the actual object of the transaction is the information contained in the physical product. In these cases, the information product is an object that exists and can be observed in the physical world.

The classification problems connected to e-commerce are primarily related to the principle of neutrality. An information product, for example a music album, can be delivered either physically, in the form of a record, or digitally. According to current tax law, the same information product will be taxed differently depending on how it is delivered. It is hard to find a way to classify information deliveries within the framework of current tax law, which at the same time satisfies fundamental taxation principles and considers the characteristics of information. Classification problems occurred in the traditional physical environment. As long as information was distributed mainly in physical form, these problems were of little importance. As production and distribution move out into the networks, the problems grow more pressing.

In the end, the neutrality problem may seriously endanger the legitimacy of the tax system. The dominant view among the tax subjects is or will be that the two forms of delivery are just that: different forms of delivery of the same product. The law, which treats them as different products, will then seem out of touch with the real world. These problems may to some extent be problems of terminology. However, underlying them there are more fundamental assumptions related to tax law. These assumptions are deeply rooted in the history of tax law and its connection to trade in goods. The discussion regarding classification can contribute to the discussion of information taxation mainly by highlighting the fact that products in networks are neither goods nor services in a traditional sense. Information simply does not fit into tax law because tax law is rooted in the production and distribution of physical products, and not services, still less information. This is even more evident from the discussion of localization problems.

4.4.1.2 Issue of Jurisdiction   The key issue that the internet poses for tax policy is not so much its potential to create a world without borders but rather to create a world of only borders – a world in which everyone is as responsive to local taxation as people who live on geographic borders.[44] In legal terminology, 'jurisdiction' describes the legal authority of the state. The scope of that authority is manifest either in terms of a 'prescriptive jurisdiction, the power to legislate or otherwise prescribe legal rules; or enforcement jurisdiction, the power to apply such rules through judicial or executive action'.[45] The state exerts its legal sovereignty over physical and conceptual spaces. The application of state law requires that a territorial connection can be made between the legal question and this physical or conceptual state place. That connection is an imperative of international law and is necessary to distinguish the applicability of one state's laws from another's. Even when expressed in terms of 'prescription' and 'enforcement', the concept of jurisdiction evokes certain geography, one that articulates the scope of state sovereignty in territorial terms.[46] There are two aspects that disconnect between geographic jurisdiction and the internet.[47] First, *enforcement* of law or regulation based on territorial jurisdiction may become problematic in the e-commerce environment. As Dryden[48] notes, the internet is not a lawless frontier; the issue is not the absence of law and regulation, but rather problems of enforcement through territorial jurisdiction. Second, and perhaps more important, there are serious questions about whether territorial jurisdiction provides a legitimate *conceptual* basis for the governance of the internet.[49]

Difficult jurisdictional issues arise when the world's principal tax systems begin to collide with the emerging world of global e-commerce. Several taxation concepts relate to the physical or geographical location of a person, a company or a transaction. This is because taxes are national. Tax jurisdictions are very much dependent on the territorial nexus principle and the status of a taxpayer.[50] It is therefore always

44 Goolsbee, A. (2000) 'In a World without Borders: The Impact of Taxes on Internet Commerce', *National Bureau of Economic Research (NBER) Working Paper No. 6863*, Cambridge, MA.

45 Ott, D.H (1987) *Public International Law and the Modern World* (London: Pitman Publishing, 1987) at 137 as citied in Gordon, Suzanne E. (2001) Changing Concepts of Sovereignty and Jurisdiction in the Global Economy: Is there a Territorial Connection? Working Paper Series # 1, The Canadian Centre for German and European Studies.

46 Gordon, Suzanne E. (2001) Changing Concepts of Sovereignty and Jurisdiction in the Global Economy: Is there a Territorial Connection? Working Paper Series # 1, The Canadian Centre for German and European Studies.

47 Kobrin J. Stephen (2001) 'Territoriality and Governance of Cyberspace', *Journal of International Business Studies*, Vol. 32, No 4, pp 687-704.

48 Dryden, John. 2000. *The Work of the OECD on Electronic Commerce*. Paris: OECD.

49 Kobrin J. Stephen (2001) 'Territoriality and Governance of Cyberspace', *Journal of International Business Studies*, Vol. 32, No 4, pp 687-704.

50 Hellerstein has divided the issue of jurisdiction to tax into two components – substantive jurisdiction to tax and enforcement jurisdiction to tax – though he recognizes that these may not be mutually exclusive concepts. Substantive jurisdiction refers to states' power to tax the activity and enforcement jurisdiction refers to states' ability to compel collection of the tax. He argues that substantive jurisdiction arises from either a source or a residence connection. Enforcement jurisdiction normally arises because a state has personal jurisdiction

necessary to attribute a transaction to a certain geographic location. The aim is always that the creation of value should be taxed where the value is actually created. The connection can be formal, for example connected to where an organization is registered. It can also be based on where a transaction is regarded as taking place. Whether or not the physical location of an internet user can be determined with any degree of accuracy is still controversial. An IP address is a network organizational construct only loosely related to a geographical location. The question is whether and how geography can be inferred from the available data.[51] Kobrin argues that the idea of territorial jurisdiction is compromised if it is not possible to describe a transaction in cyberspace vectorially, in terms of two-dimensional geographic coordinates. Given the lack of clarity about the meaning of a virtual presence, there may well be circumstances when it is difficult, if not impossible, to locate a transaction geographically.[52] If the parties to a transaction cannot be located geographically with any degree of certainty, and if regulatory authorities are unaware of the transaction, enforcement becomes difficult.

Conceptually, there are two distinct issues. The first is the issue of when it is appropriate for a state to subject persons outside its borders to the economic burden (as opposed to the administrative burden) of a particular tax because of contacts with that state, which are in whole or part electronic in nature. The second significant issue is to determine when a state can legitimately ask that a foreign person be asked to assist in the collection of a tax on others, where those others are within the state's legitimate taxing jurisdiction. The distinction made here, between jurisdiction to impose the burden of a tax and jurisdiction to impose a duty to help collect a tax, is not one that is reflected in the actual law of jurisdiction that has developed, but in a more global and technologically sophisticated economy it may become increasingly important to make this distinction. However, governmental entities should be cautious about imposing jurisdictional oversight and protections that will have extra-jurisdictional implications.

When an online purchase is made, either directly or through the intervention of an electronic agent, programmed with the background, assets and preferences of its human principal/buyer, has the buyer stepped into a new place or simply used a different means of communication, much like a phone, fax or satellite link, to affect that purchase? More specifically, if I order a book online from my home in Belfast from a seller physically located in California, is it as if the bookseller boarded a plane and delivered the book to me in Belfast, or is it as if I flew to California to purchase the book off his shelf? Does the 'push' and 'pull' of technology make a difference in how the law should be applied?

---

over the earning entity or jurisdiction over a withholding entity. See Hellerstein, Walter (2003) *Jurisdiction to Tax income and Consumption in the NewEconomy: A Theoretical and Comparative Perspective*, 38 Georgia Law Review pp 1-70.

51 Kobrin J. Stephen (2001) 'Territoriality and Governance of Cyberspace', *Journal of International Business Studies*, Vol. 32, No 4, pp 687-704.

52 Kobrin J. Stephen (2001) 'Territoriality and Governance of Cyberspace', *Journal of International Business Studies*, Vol. 32, No 4, pp 687-704.

The internet penetrates deeply into domestic economic, political and cultural structures; tax issues go to the heart of a wide range of social issues from beliefs about social spending and the role of government to the distribution of income and wealth. Tax codes are used to discourage activities deemed undesirable by society. They are the basis of attempts to redistribute wealth and income though a graduated income tax or inheritance taxes. What is seen as an appropriate rate of taxation reflects social views about the role of government and collective versus individual solutions to social problems.[53] Although the principle of formal sovereignty, in theory, remains the underpinning of international taxation, developments such as economic integration and global e-commerce challenge the state's ability to adhere to or invoke this principle. It is beyond any argument that e-commerce, particularly digital e-commerce, has impaired the state's ability to tax the income generated by confusing traditional source rules thus making it more difficult to characterize income. If a state cannot characterize income according to traditional source rules, it cannot effectively determine whether it has a right to tax that income. This could result either in double taxation or non-taxation, thus inhibiting the growth of e-commerce or allowing these transactions to go completely untaxed.[54]

The autonomy and the anonymity with which people are able to move through the electronic world prevent any legitimate chance of effective self-governance. The virtual identity of a person most of the time has no relation to their actual identity. I have argued in other places that it is possible to govern cyberspace with a set of norms, which could banish a user from a community electronically. However the technology is not developed yet to prevent them from wreaking havoc under a new identity. Even if it were possible to virtually govern online activity, such governance ignores the impact that virtual activity has on the physical world. Jurisdiction is the area of law that deals most directly with the contact between the two worlds. 'It is more important that the applicable rule of law be settled than that it be settled right.'[55] The question is then how to settle this point of law within the bounds of the traditional legal framework. It is my submission that incremental and conservative change in jurisdiction law is right because it is the best choice. This means that the defined parameters of the law should be applied to the new factual situations. Governments should take steps to align 'enforcement jurisdiction' with 'substantive jurisdiction' to ensure that technological developments do not undermine sound tax policy.[56]

4.4.2   Should E-Commerce be Taxed?

So far I have analyzed to what extent e-commerce can be taxed and, apart from trade in digitalized goods, the conclusion has been that it is possible to tax e-commerce.

---

53 Kobrin J. Stephen (2001) 'Territoriality and Governance of Cyberspace', *Journal of International Business Studeis,* Vol. 32, No 4, pp 687-704.

54 Basu, Subhajit (2003) 'Relevance of E-Commerce for Taxation: an Overview', *Global Jurist Topics*: Vol. 3: No. 3, Article 2, http://www.bepress.com/gj/topics/vol3/iss3/art2.

55 *Burnet v Coronado Oil and Gas Co.*, 285 US 393, 447 (1932).

56 Hellerstein, Walter (2003) 'Jurisdiction to Tax income and Consumption in the New Economy: A Theoretical and Comparative Perspective', 38 *Georgia Law Review* pp 1-70.

However, just because it is possible to tax (part of) e-commerce it is not obvious that it is socially desirable to do so.[57] However, two related concerns have focused the international response:[58] (1) that a transaction with a cross-border aspect may be taxed more lightly than a similar purely domestic transaction, stimulating tax evasion and tax competition between governments; and (2) that reallocation of resources in response to tax conditions rather than market conditions will create economic distortions that diminish productivity.[59] International tax regimes are 'sets of implicit or explicit principles, norms, rules and decision-making procedures around which actors' expectations converge in a given area of international relations'.[60] A general theme in tax research is how the necessary tax revenue to support the public services can be raised in the most efficient and equitable way. The debate about e-commerce taxation divides into two primary groups.

The first group, the pro-taxation group, believes that e-commerce should be taxed just like regular commerce. Arguments for taxing e-commerce are based on equity, economic neutrality, revenue (or lower tax rates) and simplicity of compliance and administration. First, failure to impose the tax on online purchases would cause significant revenue losses for state and local governments. Second, if e-commerce is given a no-tax status, then businesses can locate themselves in states where there is no sales tax or VAT (and still serve almost all of their audience online) for electronic purchases, thus making the loss of tax revenues a bigger problem. Differential taxation can also keep businesses from adopting the best business practices. In the case of companies with both traditional and online operations, the need to avoid nexus may prevent some otherwise desirable business practices. For example, in order to prevent nexus, Barnes and Noble stores may not be able to accept returns of merchandise purchased from its online sister company. Companies may be required to maintain separate call centres and warranty and repair operations for their traditional and online customers. Companies operating only through e-commerce may need to avoid locating warehouses in the best sites, building demonstration centres for their products, in order to prevent establishing nexus. Third, allowing tax exemption for electronic goods and services that are identical to goods and services purchased in traditional stores is not fair, for example, not taxing an electronic book that is downloaded directly online while taxing the hardcopy of the same book sold in a store. Fourth, it is also unfair to consumers when their tax liability depends on how they buy a good rather than how much they buy. Especially since mostly the richer consumers have access to e-commerce services, banning taxes on electronic transactions allows the richer community to pay less consumption taxes while the poorer part of the

---

57 Some commentators have argued that it is desirable to tax e-commerce and conventional retail trade differently.

58 Bolkestein, Frits (2001) *Harmful tax competition, VAT on digital deliveries, taxation of savings*, Address to European American Business Council, Washington D.C. (May 9).

59 Salter, Sarah W (2002) E-Commerce and International Taxation, *New Eng. Journal of Int'l & Comp Law,* Vol.8:1 pp 6-17.

60 Paris, Roland (2001) 'Global Taxation and the Transformation of the State', Department of Political Science, University of Colorado at Boulder, Paper presented at the 2001 Annual Convention of the American Political science association, San Francisco, August 30–September 2, 2001 p 3.

community still has to pay VAT or sales tax. Many studies have found the sales tax or VAT to be regressive against current income, meaning the percentage of income paid in sales taxes or VAT falls with income.[61] The evidence indicates that ownership of computers and e-commerce access by low-income households is much below that for high-income households.[62] This digital divide can result in uneven taxation that disadvantages low-income households. In effect this means even more regressive sales tax or VAT.

I have also discussed before that a basic principle of taxation is economic neutrality[63] and it is difficult to argue that web-based vendors deserve the advantage of a tax holiday versus their bricks and mortar competitors. If e-commerce is not taxed consistently with other forms of commerce, market distortion and a consequent inefficient allocation of resources would arise.[64] Issues of equity and fairness also arise. The digital revolution may lead to a shift in the tax burden to assets and individuals who are 'nailed down', the more immobile elements of society. While some shifts in tax assessment and collection are unavoidable, revisions to the tax code should be made because of a deliberate societal process that considers revenue needs, equity, efficiency and effectiveness, rather than by default. Finally, some seem to believe that e-commerce should receive preferential treatment in order to encourage its development. There are several problems with this view, which is reminiscent of 'infant industry' arguments for tax incentives often heard in developing countries. A differential tax treatment must not be adopted as it offers an easy tax avoidance mechanism and creates administrative complexity. What is crucial is that e-commerce represents a fast growing base, which no country can afford to exclude from the tax net.

There is no evidence that e-commerce needs preferential treatment and as Goolsbee says, it appears that 'most arguments regarding externalities are based on politics, not economics'.[65] E-commerce is growing rapidly and is likely to continue to do so, with or without preferential tax treatment.[66] The situation commonly found in developing countries contemplating tax incentives is vastly different from the present situation in one important respect. In developing countries, there is generally no competing local economic activity to be harmed by the tax-motivated development of new tax-preferred industries. By comparison, much of e-commerce

---

61 Fox, William F. (1998) 'Current Conditions and Policy Options,' Editor: Philip Dearborn, *Taxing Simply, Taxing Fairly, (Greater Washington Research Centre)*.

62 This estimation is based on study conducted by National Telecommunications and Information Administration and US Census Bureau, U.S. Department of Commerce using population surveys for the year 2000 as cited by Fox and Luna in 'Taxing E-Commerce: Neutral Taxation is Best for the Industry and the Economy'.

63 Committee on Fiscal Affairs (1998) Electronic Commerce: Taxation Frame- work Conditions. Paris: OECD, Directorate for Financial, Fiscal and Enterprise Affairs, October 8.

64 Salter, Sarah W (2002) E-Commerce and International Taxation, New Eng. *Journal of Int'l & Comp Law,* Vol.8:1 pp 6-17.

65 Goolsbee, Austan (2001) The Implications of Electronic Commerce for Fiscal Policy, *Journal of Economic Perspectives,* 15 p 19.

66 For a detailed discussion on growth of e-commerce see Chapter 2.

does compete with local vendors who would be disadvantaged by preferential tax treatment of e-commerce.

The broader issue of the taxation of access to the internet is often confused with the issue of the taxation of e-commerce. 'Whether the idea is to impose a tax on the flow through the pipeline, on the size of the pipeline, or on the size of the connection, however, it has little merit.'[67] The proponents of a tax-free internet argue that internet access taxes and fees result in rate hikes making access more expensive for the consumer and thus restricting the growth of internet use and e-commerce. Further, these proponents argue against imposing the requirement to collect and remit transactional taxes on remote e-commerce vendors because of the cost of compliance with multiple taxing jurisdictions. Such cost is viewed as a barrier to market entry for small, start up e-businesses.

On the other hand, believers of anti-taxation argue that the internet has created many jobs by moving retailing to the net. Among these jobs, they count trucking and package-delivery sectors. They also argue that by lowering the cost of products for the consumer, e-commerce allows the consumer to buy more things, thus benefiting a wider number of manufacturers. In addition, taxing e-commerce the same way as conventional businesses brings about other concerns and complications because first, due to the internet, many small businesses are now able to serve consumers outside of their area. Imposing taxes on e-commerce will keep these businesses from going on the net resulting in huge losses for these businesses as well as the economies they support. Second, the opponents of e-commerce taxation commonly argue that because the internet has had such a profound effect on productivity, there is no need for states to collect the revenues on these transactions. The internet has been the driving force of the economy in many countries and imposing taxes on e-commerce would result in slowing down its growth, costing the governments huge revenues in the end. Given the future higher revenues expected from e-commerce, a tax ban on e-commerce could be viewed as a reasonable government subsidy for a developing industry. Favouring e-commerce over other commerce thus may lead to short-term market distortion and inefficiency, but that has been perceived as a rational price to achieve longer-term objectives.[68] Third, the existing tax laws are inappropriate for the internet due to its electronic and border-spanning nature. Serious modifications and different enforcement mechanisms are necessary in order for these laws to work for the electronic marketplace. Finally, some advocates of exempting taxation e-commerce have adopted a theory advanced by the mail-order industry that remote vendors should not be required to collect tax because they do not benefit from services provided by the states where their customers are located. This argument and counter-arguments that accept the validity of its basic premise confuse the issue by focusing on services provided to remote vendors, which should be essentially irrelevant. The point is that purchasers pay the sales tax or VAT and it is to them that states provide services; the remote vendor would merely collect the

---

67 Bird, Richard M (2005) 'Taxing Electronic Commerce: The end of the Beginning', ITO Paper 0502, International Tax program, Institute of international business.

68 Salter, Sarah W (2002) E-Commerce and International Taxation, New Eng. Journal of Int'l & Comp Law, Vol.8:1 pp 6-17.

tax. There is no reason to believe that a consumer of a given product consumes fewer state services simply because the product is bought from a remote vendor.

Taxation raises a number of fundamental issues, which illustrate the more general regulatory problems involving international e-commerce. As I have discussed before, a basic principle of taxation is economic neutrality,[69] and it is difficult to argue that web-based vendors deserve the advantage of a tax holiday versus their bricks and mortar competitors. Issues of equity and fairness also arise. The digital revolution may lead to a shift in the tax burden to assets and individuals who are 'nailed down', the more immobile elements of society. While some shift in tax assessment and collection are unavoidable, revisions to the tax code should be made because of a deliberate societal process that considers revenue needs, equity, efficiency and effectiveness, rather than by default. Although arguments both for and against taxation exist, the important thing is for authorities to understand the internet and its unique nature as well as its potentials and weak points before a decision is made. Especially, understanding the border-spanning and global nature of the internet is very important before a global tax agreement is reached. The future lies in developing a system suitable for the digital world of e-commerce, which is simplified in terms of compliance and administration.

4.5   Tax Avoidance and Tax Evasion

The two critical problems in taxation are first to identify the tax base and then to enforce the tax. 'The anonymity and mobility associated with e-commerce make both of these tasks more difficult.'[70] Even if they can identify and measure the tax base, how can they enforce taxation in view of the disappearance of the third party intervention that has for long served as the practical basis of tax withholding, not to mention the possibility of basing activities in such no-man's-lands as satellites and off-shore ships?[71] Tax avoidance and tax evasion are important issues when it comes to concerns about tax compliance in relation to e-commerce.[72] In an e-commerce environment the possibilities of hiding transactions are vast and the possibilities of identifying parties to a transaction are in many cases virtually non-existent. The opportunities for tax evasion seem endless. Tax evasion is always unlawful. Tax avoidance and tax evasion have always been problems with which tax authorities have had to contend. There have always been certain businesses that choose to locate their corporate headquarters or to conduct their business activities from states that offer low or no tax regulation. The cost of conducting offshore activities, however, can often outweigh the benefits of tax relief. For this reason, tax avoidance and evasion opportunities of this nature have generally been exploited by only a small number

---

    69 Committee on Fiscal Affairs (1998) Electronic Commerce: Taxation Frame- work Conditions. Paris: OECD, Directorate for Financial, Fiscal and Enterprise Affairs, October 8.

    70 Bird, Richard (2003) Taxing Electronic Commerce: A Revolution in the Making, *C.D. Howe Institute Commentary*, No.187.

    71 Cockfield, A.J. (2001) 'Transforming the Internet into a Taxable Forum: A Case Study in E-Commerce Taxation.' *Minnesota Law Review* 85 (5): pp 1171–1266.

    72 Westberg, Bjorn (2002) *Cross-border Taxation of E-Commerce*, IBFD p 79.

of businesses, as the majority are unable to support such schemes. Traditionally, businesses have also been deterred from locating in tax haven countries by other problems inherent in these countries. Although they can offer appealing tax rates, businesses must also consider other characteristics that may not be conducive to maintaining a globally competitive business. Such characteristics include a climate or geography that is not suitable to the particular business, high labour costs, low education levels, poor infrastructure, political instability or a small consumer base.

A business operated through a commercial website, however, is not subject to the same physical constraints as a 'bricks and mortar' business. For example, a small- or medium-sized business in the UK can easily post its website with a host who operates from a tax haven country. Here it will still be able to access profitable consumer bases while having its financial information hidden by the privacy protection that tax haven countries often provide. The fact that an e-commerce business requires no physical presence other than a server also makes the problems identified above irrelevant. It is now not only affordable for virtually any e-commerce business to locate in a tax haven but all of the incentives for doing so remain while the disincentives are gradually disappearing. Therefore, when business is conducted on the internet. the problem of tax competition reaches a new level of complexity. For some businesses, many of the physical constraints on tax evasion or avoidance remain. However, now a category of digital goods and services can be transacted entirely over the internet. With respect to these transactions, states cannot rely on physical controls to prevent or deter tax avoidance and evasion.

Chapter 5

Direct Taxation and E-Commerce

Introduction

The shift from a physically-oriented commercial environment to a knowledge-based electronic environment poses significant issues in relation to taxation and taxation regimes. One of the most important effects of e-commerce has been to de-emphasize the significance of the place where economic activity is carried out, which makes it difficult to determine which jurisdiction has the right to tax. It has also blurred the traditional distinction between the form of delivery and the substance of what is delivered. Thus, the specific tax implications of e-commerce and the threat it imposes on the established tax systems can be examined by reference to how much e-commerce tends to disrupt the concepts and principles of direct taxation and international tax treaty rules. This chapter will explore the effect of e-commerce on the principles of direct taxation, including source- and residence-based taxation, the tax treaty concept of PE, treaty characterization, issues of payments on various transactions, classification of payments resulting from digital transactions, classification of payment of services and know-how and transfer pricing. The principal emphasis throughout this chapter will be on the issue of whether and to what extent a particular taxpayer or potential taxpayer can be brought into a particular tax system. One can always question the continued validity of these rules in a digital world.

5.1   Principles of Direct Taxation and E-Commerce

The discipline of international taxation is governed by national tax laws that react to international dimensions of how and by whom income is earned. Even before the advent of e-commerce it was not always easy to determine where income arose. Countries might differ over whether the presence of a facility, the location of customers, the passage of title or a number of other factors determine where the income arises.[1] E-commerce facilitates cross-border transactions and as a mechanism has particular relevance to international taxation. Consequently, accordingly to Li, while e-commerce may not introduce any new problems, it is apparent that any problems already associated with an inability to synchronize or inter-relate a variety of disparate taxing systems became exacerbated by a model that facilitates the very types of transactions that result in such problems in the first instance.[2] A

---

1   Doernberg, Richard L. and Hinnekens, Luc (1999) *Electronic Commerce and International Taxation,* Kluwer Law International.

2   Li, Jinyan (2003) *International Taxation in the Age of Electronic Commerce: A Comparative Study* (Toronto: Canadian Tax Foundation).

fundamental change in existing tax rules does not appear to be requisite. However, internet and e-commerce has increased the need for efficient and equitable tax treatment of firms operating in multiple tax jurisdictions. Current procedures used by most countries to allocate the tax base between jurisdictions and to avoid double taxation through a network of more than 1,500 bilateral double taxation treaties, most of which are modelled after the OECD conventions,[3] is not only cumbersome, but will also come under increasing pressure as the scope and volume of cross-border activities expands sharply. This is because the double taxation treaties are based on the assumption of national sovereignty in tax policy, which will become less relevant as globalization progresses. Most discussion with respect to income taxes to date has focused on three problems: how can we attribute income arising in the 'internet' to a particular jurisdiction? How can we characterize such income? And most important, how can it be taxed? 'Every country wishes to benefit from its fair share of taxation on the profits.'[4] 'Yes, but what is a fair share and, even more basically, what are the profits that are subject to tax?'[5]

A hypothetical electronic transaction as illustrated by Paris[6] shows the complexities that arise. Suppose an e-commerce firm has its headquarters in country 'A' and the company accepts customer orders through a website that is maintained in country 'B'. The website then transmits orders to the company's sales department in country 'C'. A customer residing in country 'D' places an online order. The order is channelled electronically through a chain of servers in a number of locations, ultimately arriving at the company's website in country 'B', which in turn would transmit the order to the sales office in country 'C'. Let's further assume that the company has 'storage facility' in yet another jurisdiction country, 'F'. After approving the order, the sales office arranged for shipment of the product from the storage facility in country 'F' to the customer. If the product is digitized then it might be delivered electronically directly to the customer who could be located anywhere in the world. The company, in other words, has no idea of where in the physical world its digitized product would be delivered. Furthermore, if the product was digitized, the company's storage facility could amount to nothing more than a computer hard drive or server or an array of 'mirror' servers located in several different jurisdictions. In this case, the storage facility from which the company's product was delivered might be just as mobile as the customer receiving the product. However, not all the e-commerce transactions today are as complicated as this hypothetical example, but the hypothetical transaction illustrates the difficulties

3   Owens, J (1998) 'Taxation within a Context of Economic Globalization', *Bulletin for International Fiscal Documentation,* 52, pp 290-6.

4   Bernstein, Jack (2000) 'Canadian Taxation Issues for Electronic Commerce.' *Tax Notes International* 21 (July 17): pp 263-71.

5   Bird, Richard (2003) Taxing Electronic Commerce: A Revolution in the Making, *C.D. Howe Institute Commentary*, No.187.

6   Paris, Roland (2001) ' Global Taxation and the Transformation of the State', Department of Political Science, University of Colorado at Boulder, Paper presented at the 2001 Annual Convention of the American Political science association, San Francisco, August 30 September.

involved in determining the geographical source of income, and the residency status of those engaged in income-producing activities within the world of e-commerce.

The question is where is the source of income in the above example? Is it country 'A' where the company has its headquarters? Country 'B' where the company has its website? Country 'C' where the sales office processed the order? Or is it the country from which the product was delivered? Much of this would depend on the definition and application of the concept 'PE', to the extent that income-generating activities took place in a country where the company had a 'PE' or a 'fixed place of business', which country would be entitled to tax the profits attributable to the establishment? How does a website fit into the structure of a PE? Is a website a 'fixed place of business'? If so, where is it located? Is it in the jurisdiction where the retailer is physically present or on the electronic server that serves the website? Even if it is a fixed place of business in a taxable jurisdiction, is the website merely used solely for the display, delivery or advertising of goods or services?

Income tax treaties do not provide easy answers to these questions because they were developed in a non-digital era when transactions and commercial law dealt primarily with tangible property. As noted earlier, there are two prevailing approaches to direct taxation: one based on the 'source' principle and another based on the 'residence' principle. Taxation based on the source principle, however, presupposes that taxing authorities can determine the geographical source of income, while taxation on the residence principle requires information about the identity and residency status of those engaged in income-producing activities. E-commerce, however, breaks down the necessary and clear connection between territory and commerce, and makes this type of information more difficult to obtain, thus complicating the task of taxing income based on source or residence. To complicate matters further, there is a real difference of opinion between the developed and developing countries as to the appropriate approach in allocating taxable jurisdiction.

Developed countries generally prefer to allocate taxable jurisdiction based on the enterprise's residence. Hence, if residence is used as the principal criterion to decide taxable nexus for e-commerce, the bulk of the revenues generated from such commerce will accrue to the developed countries. If, however, taxable nexus is based upon the site of the server, it is entirely possible that the developing countries might accrue some revenues on the basis that the source of the income is within their jurisdiction. Residence-based taxation creates problems because of the difficulties in placing the central mind and management of an enterprise, particularly with e-commerce, which by its very nature is mobile. It is undeniable that the traditional concepts of residence, characterization and source of income do apply to e-commerce transactions, however, as Li argues, forcing their application onto transactions undertaken through a radically different medium necessarily results in uncertainty in the application of the traditional source- and residence-based taxation models to e-commerce.

5.2   E-Commerce and the Concept of Residence and Source

Countries generally exercise jurisdiction to tax income based on residence or source. Both of these concepts are likely to become more elusive in the context of e-commerce;

the issue might be posed as follows: 'if all value is created in state R, but all the customers that determine value are in state C, where is the income generated?'[7]

5.2.1   Residence Based Taxation

Determining the residence of a taxpayer is generally uncomplicated because a country of residence essentially is the geographic location where a taxpayer has the closest personal links.[8] However, with the growth of e-commerce, place of registration of a company has become even more irrelevant than before. Does e-commerce have implications for taxation based on residence? The basic principles have not changed. The highest level of key commercial decisions is still a crucial factor.[9] However, the artificial nature of the place of incorporation test may become an even more artificial test because of e-commerce.[10] The advances in communication technology make it possible for directors sitting in different countries to easily, and simultaneously, communicate with each other through video-conferencing. It is no longer necessary for the boards to meet at a fixed place, as was the practice in the past. This makes the determination of the '*place of effective management*' extremely complicated. Where does the board meeting take place or where is an essential decision taken? More than one country could consider that a certain meeting has taken place within its jurisdiction and that it is entitled to tax the revenue. Given that the process of incorporation is purely a formal one, it therefore becomes relatively easy in an e-commerce environment for a company to change its incorporation to another country. For example, the residence of a company may be changed by creating a new entity in another country and transferring the business to it or by simply re-registering the company in another country. At the same time, it must be recognized that some limits on this type of activity may be placed by countries that have capital gains tax regimes as these provisions may be triggered when such reorganization occurs.[11] There is already evidence that many e-commerce companies are establishing themselves in tax havens.[12] This type of business structure would be quite conceivable and especially applicable to businesses that deal in intangible content, such as software, pornography

7   Doernberg, Richard L (1998) Electronic Commerce and International Tax Sharing (Mar. 30) Tax Analysts, available at http://www.tax.org/ritp.nsf?OpenDatabase&Start=1&Count=300&Expand=1.

8   Department of The Treasury (1996), Selected Tax Policy Implications of Global Electronic Commerce (Washington D.C.: Office of Tax Policy) paragraph 7.1.5.

9   Inland Revenue, Electronic Commerce: The UK's Taxation Agenda (1999), paragraph 8.4.

10   Pinto, Dale (2005) 'A New Three-Tire Proposal for Determining Corporate Residence Based Principally on Individual Residence', *Asia-Pacific Tax Bulletin*, IBFD January/February, p 15.

11   Pinto, Dale (2005) 'A New Three-Tire Proposal for Determining Corporate Residence Based Principally on Individual Residence', *Asia-Pacific Tax Bulletin*, IBFD January/February, p 15.

12   Cockfield, A.J. (1999) 'Balancing National Interests in the Taxation of Electronic Commerce Business Profits', 74 *Tulane Law Review pp* 133, 172.

or gambling activities.[13] In these types of businesses, it would therefore be possible for the parent company of a multinational organization to be set up and incorporated[14] in a tax haven from which its e-commerce operations could be conducted.[15]

It can be argued that there is nothing necessarily wrong with this course of action if the company is actually established in the tax haven.[16] However, because the 'place of incorporation' test is purely a formal one, a company only needs to incorporate itself in a tax haven, while its business operations can be produced, controlled and supplied from another country, without the need for any employees or other business presence to exist in the tax haven country. For example, in the case of computer software, a foreign company could be incorporated in a tax haven such that it would be the manufacturer and developer of the software, also retaining ownership of the software product during the complete production cycle.[17] Specialized development services, for example computer programming or debugging services, could be provided by so-called 'virtual migrants', who could be specialist computer programmers drawn from countries such as India and the Philippines.[18] In this way, the taxing nexus that may otherwise be found to exist by using domestic employees of the foreign company would be avoided and also anti-deferral rules would likely be inapplicable in this type of situation.

Another possible test for determining corporate residence is to look to the place of central management and control of the company. A number of countries already apply this approach.[19] However, in an e-commerce context, determining the place of central management and control may still be problematic for a number of reasons.[20]

First, as electronic commerce allows residents to more easily influence the operations of offshore subsidiaries (which could include tax haven entities), it will become more difficult to determine where such a business is really being carried on. Second, the use of

---

13 Pinto, Dale (2005) 'A New Three-Tire Proposal for Determining Corporate Residence Based Principally on Individual Residence', *Asia-Pacific Tax Bulletin*, IBFD January/February, p 15.

14 Pinto, Dale (2005) 'A New Three-Tire Proposal for Determining Corporate Residence Based Principally on Individual Residence', *Asia-Pacific Tax Bulletin*, IBFD January/February, p 17.

15 Reuven S. Avi-Yonah, (1997) 'International Taxation of Electronic Commerce', 52 *Tax Law Review* 507, No. 83.

16 Pinto, Dale (2005) 'A New Three-Tire Proposal for Determining Corporate Residence Based Principally on Individual Residence', *Asia-Pacific Tax Bulletin*, IBFD January/February, p 17.

17 Pinto, Dale (2005) 'A New Three-Tire Proposal for Determining Corporate Residence Based Principally on Individual Residence', *Asia-Pacific Tax Bulletin*, IBFD January/February, p 17.

18 Allen R. Myerson (1998) 'Ideas & Trends: Virtual Migrants: Need Programmers? Surf Abroad', *The New York Times* (New York), 18 January 1998, available at <www.nytimes.com.

19 Pinto, Dale (2005) 'A New Three-Tire Proposal for Determining Corporate Residence Based Principally on Individual Residence', *Asia-Pacific Tax Bulletin*, IBFD January/February, p 16.

20 Pinto, Dale (2005) 'A New Three-Tire Proposal for Determining Corporate Residence Based Principally on Individual Residence', *Asia-Pacific Tax Bulletin*, IBFD January/February, p 17.

new technologies such as intranets and videoconferencing facilities, which allow directors to maintain residences in different jurisdictions, presents challenges to the effective application of this test.[21]

Apart from dispensing with the need for boards of directors to meet in a physical place such as a head office, such technologies allow for management of corporate groups to be dispersed in different countries, with communications being possible through either e-mail or videoconferencing facilities. In other words, e-commerce not only poses a challenge to existing tax rules by allowing a business to earn income from another country without maintaining a physical presence in that country, but it also allows the management and control of a business to be conducted from a country (or countries) different to the one the company earns its business income from. The fact that e-commerce makes it possible for a company to run without a physical presence in any single country is central to the problems of applying traditional tests of corporate residence in an e-commerce environment.[22] As mentioned earlier, Article 4(3) of the OECD Model Convention uses the place of effective management as a tie-breaker rule in cases of corporate dual residency. However, e-commerce can fundamentally change the way people conduct business and because of these changes, the place of effective management test will also be subject to the same problems as exist with the central management and control test.[23] Adding to the difficulties of applying the place of effective management test in an e-commerce setting is the likelihood of mobile places of effective management.[24]

It is clear from the above analysis that there are difficulties with applying all of the existing tests for determining corporate residence in an e-commerce context and these difficulties will need to be overcome to ensure that residence-based taxation can continue to operate effectively in an electronic commerce environment.[25] The OECD has issued a discussion paper in which it has considered various alternatives to resolving these difficulties,[26] which gives a unique solution in all the cases and not just for most of the cases. These are:

---

21 Pinto, Dale (2005) 'A New Three-Tire Proposal for Determining Corporate Residence Based Principally on Individual Residence', *Asia-Pacific Tax Bulletin*, IBFD January/ February, p 17.

22 Pinto, Dale (2005) 'A New Three-Tire Proposal for Determining Corporate Residence Based Principally on Individual Residence', *Asia-Pacific Tax Bulletin*, IBFD January/ February, p 17.

23 Pinto, Dale (2005) 'A New Three-Tire Proposal for Determining Corporate Residence Based Principally on Individual Residence', **Asia-Pacific Tax Bulletin**, IBFD January/ February, p 17.

24 Boards of directors may arrange to meet in different places, perhaps on a global rotational basis, and managing directors today are much more mobile than in the past. In such cases, decisions may be made while on the move (e.g. while flying between countries) or in many different locations.

25 Pinto, Dale (2005) 'A New Three-Tire Proposal for Determining Corporate Residence Based Principally on Individual Residence', Asia-Pacific Tax Bulletin, IBFD January/February.

26 OECD (2001) 'The Impact of the Communications Revolution on the Application of 'Place of Effective Management' as a Tie Breaker Rule' (February 2001), available at www. oecd.org/daf/fa/e_com/ec_4_POEM_Eng.pdf.

- replace the 'place of effective management' concept;[27]
- refine the 'place of effective management' test;[28]
- establish a hierarchy of tests so that if one test does not provide a solution the next applies; or
- combine the second and third alternatives.

Pinto has argued that

> while this last approach is designed to achieve some flexibility, it is surprising, for two reasons, that the place of incorporation test is listed as the second alternative in the OECD's hierarchy of tests. First, as discussed, the place of incorporation is arbitrary, artificial and formalistic and often will have little to do with the location from which a business is conducted. Second, given that the application of the place of incorporation test will almost always yield an answer, having any tests below it in a hierarchy of tests would therefore seem to be largely redundant and superfluous.[29]

There is no real alternative to the concept of 'place of effective management'. It is not possible to set down a single rule. The 'place of effective management' has to be determined based on the facts and circumstance of each case. The existing concept gives a unique solution in most cases. Where in the case of a globally integrated enterprise, no unique solution is available through the concept of 'place of effective management'; the solution could be 'source-based' taxation only. However, in contrast to the relative simplicity in finding a country of residence, many uncertainties and difficulties arise when determining whether a source country may impose tax upon the company for a cyberspace transaction. OECD work in this area is commendable, however it has failed put forward any model in its discussion paper to overcome the identified problems.[30]

5.2.2   Source-Based Taxation

Origin (source) is the specific place where income is produced. The source country should have the priority to tax profits resulting from activities conducted within its jurisdiction if the taxable entity participates accordingly in the economic life.[31]

---

27 The OECD Residence Report puts forward three possible replacements for the place of effective management test: the place of incorporation test, the place where directors or shareholders reside and finally the place where a company has its strongest 'economic nexus', a term not defined in the report.

28 By determining residence in accordance with a list of predominant factors, the factors listed in Para. 24 of the Commentary to Art 4 of the OECD MC.

29 Pinto, Dale (2005) 'A New Three-Tire Proposal for Determining Corporate Residence Based Principally on Individual Residence', *Asia-Pacific Tax Bulletin*, IBFD January/February, p 18.

30 Pinto, Dale (2005) 'A New Three-Tire Proposal for Determining Corporate Residence Based Principally on Individual Residence', *Asia-Pacific Tax Bulletin*, IBFD January/February, p 18.

31 Schäfer, Anne and Spengel, Christoph (2002) *ICT and International Corporate Taxation: Tax Attributes And Scope of Taxation* Centre For European Economic Research (ZEW) and University of Mannheim.

Consequently, in a *first step*, it is questionable from which threshold business activities in the source country are deemed to be sufficient in order to be taxed and, thus, how the tax attributes shall be defined adequately.[32] In a *second step*, it is necessary to analyze if there are feasibility problems in the case of taxation based on the given tax attributes in the source country. In order to determine the scope of taxation in the source country, an appropriate threshold and thus a tax attribute has to be defined.[33] Under current tax rules, business income is taxable only if an enterprise maintains a PE in the country. Income from 'services' is taxed in the country where the service is provided and not where it is delivered or utilized. Taxation of income in the source country, therefore, depends on the existence of PE and characterization of income. Would the existence of a computer server located in a foreign jurisdiction elicit such a presence? As the cross-border e-commerce expands, it may turn out that source of income becomes more difficult to reasonably determine. The conditions of economic life have changed due to the internet and e-commerce. It is argued that, today, enterprises could participate more easily to a substantial extent in the economic life of another country without having a 'fixed place of business'. Since income could be derived and value could be added by a corporation without having a physical presence in the source country, the level of the company's physical presence within a jurisdiction would not necessarily equate with the level of participation in the economic life of that jurisdiction. Thus, the use of a specific location by the company might no longer constitute a significant factor for deriving income.[34] Due to this weakening connection between physical and economic presence, the current definition of a PE, which largely relies on physical manifestations of an economic presence, might give rise to anomalous results.[35]

Taxation based on the source principle means that all income generated in a country is finally taxed in the source country. The *principle of feasibility* implies that the effective enforcement of a tax system has to be guaranteed in order to achieve equity and efficiency. For the purpose of taxation according to the source principle, the tax attributes in the source country need to be clearly determinable and possibilities of manipulation have to be prevented.[36] However, due to the changed economic structures because of e-commerce, there are serious problems in determining the amount and location of income as well as avoiding manipulation in the case of tax attributes in the source country.[37]

---

32 Schäfer, Anne and Spengel, Christoph (2002) *ICT and International Corporate Taxation: Tax Attributes And Scope of Taxation* Centre For European Economic Research (ZEW) and University of Mannheim.

33 Schäfer, Anne and Spengel, Christoph (2002) *ICT and International Corporate Taxation: Tax Attributes And Scope of Taxation* Centre For European Economic Research (ZEW) and University of Mannheim.

34 Australian Taxation Office (1999), Tax and the Internet: Second Report December 1999, Canberra.

35 Discussed in more detail later in this chapter.

36 Schäfer, Anne and Spengel, Christoph (2002) *ICT and International Corporate Taxation: Tax Attributes And Scope of Taxation* Centre For European Economic Research (ZEW) and University of Mannheim.

37 Schäfer, Anne and Spengel, Christoph (2002) *ICT and International Corporate Taxation: Tax Attributes And Scope of Taxation* Centre For European Economic Research (ZEW) and University of Mannheim.

The most obvious benefit of residence taxation is ease of administration. It is not necessary to identify the source of economic activity when income is subject to taxation only in the country of residence. This in turn helps those companies engaged in e-commerce in the calculation of tax liabilities whose income may not be attributable to any specific geographic location. The US Treasury paper suggested that 'source based commerce could lose its rationale and be rendered obsolete by e-commerce'.[38] It also suggested that e-commerce will 'accelerate' a trend towards preferring residence-based taxation to source-based taxation due to the difficulty of implementing a source-based regime in the world of cyberspace:

> The growth of new communications technologies and e-commerce will likely require that principles of residence-based taxation assume even greater importance. In the world of cyberspace, it is often difficult, if not impossible, to apply traditional source concepts to link an item of income with a specific geographical location. Therefore, source based taxation could lose its rationale and be rendered obsolete by e-commerce. By contrast, almost all taxpayers are resident somewhere. United States tax policy has already recognized that as traditional principles lose their significance, residence-based taxation can step in and take their place. This trend will be accelerated by developments in electronic commerce where principles of residence-based taxation will also play a major role.[39]

Hellerstein[40] argued that this view of the US Treasury is hardly uncontroversial for a variety of reasons. First, as Professor Reuven Avi-Yonah has observed, 'the recommendation to tax income from electronic commerce primarily or exclusively on a residence basis is inconsistent with generally accepted international consensus, as embodied in tax treaties and in the U.S. international tax regime'.[41] That consensus is based on the principle that the residence jurisdiction has the primary right to tax passive (investment) income while the source jurisdiction has the primary right to tax active (business) income. Abandoning the source-based principle in favour of the residence-based principle in the context of e-commerce would therefore violate accepted international norms of tax policy. Second, it is by no means clear that residence-based taxation provides a panacea for the difficulties of assigning income from electronic commerce on a source basis. While the task of administering a residence-based regime may be somewhat less daunting than the task of administering a source-based regime with respect to income from e-commerce, Cigler was of the opinion that 'many international tax professionals have experienced cases which are much more complex leading to the conclusion that the ultimate solution for electronic commerce will not rely on the "resident somewhere" principle'. Moreover,

---

38 Department of The Treasury (1996) Selected Tax Policy Implications of Global Electronic Commerce (Washington D.C.: Office of Tax Policy) paragraph 7.1.5.

39 Treasury White Paper at p 20.

40 Hellerstein, Walter (2001) 'Electronic Commerce and The Challenge For Tax Administration' Paper presented to the United Nations Ad Hoc Group of Experts on International Cooperation in Tax Matters in Geneva, Switzerland, on September 12, 2001 pp 16-18.

41 Avi-Yonah, Reuven S. (1997) 'International Taxation of Electronic Commerce', 52 *Tax Law Review*, p 527.

the 'relative meaningless of corporate residency',[42] and the ease with which an internet-based enterprise may establish a corporate residence divorced from any of its 'tangible' activities, suggest that the general adoption of a residence-based regime for electronic commerce could raise as many problems as it resolves. Third, and having particular importance to developing countries and countries with economies in transition, a residence-based rule raises troublesome questions of international tax equity. As Charles McLure has observed, 'a shift to residence-based taxation would be a boon to the United States, the world's leader in the production of electronic content'.[43] 'But', he continues, 'it is troubling to those who worry about the ability of source countries and countries where consumption occurs – especially developing countries – to tax income and consumption'.[44] David Tillinghast expressed similar concerns:

> The changes wrought by the internet, which drastically reduce the need for a seller or a service provider to have a physical presence in the country where its customer is located, threaten fundamentally to alter this division of revenue by shifting the balance of taxing jurisdiction, and revenue, decisively in favour of the country of residence. Since income flows between countries are not necessarily balanced and in the case of flows between developed and developing countries are often severely imbalanced, such a shift could have profound revenue consequences.[45]

According to Hellerstein, 'wholly apart from the dictates of sound tax policy or practical considerations about enforcement we cannot lose sight of the fact that the choice of tax principles may well create winners and losers'.[46] Accordingly, when distributional implications are added to the calculus, a residence-based approach to taxing income from e-commerce may not be particularly attractive. It favours developed countries at the expense of developing countries. Tax havens may undermine fiscal sovereignty if taxation is based on residence. Tax havens have benefited due to sovereign control over fiscal policy in an age of interdependence. Corporations and individuals can easily shift resources to realize gains from low tax locations, aided by information and communications technology (ICT).

---

42 Cigler, James D. (1997) 'International Taxation of Electronic Commerce: An Evolution Requiring Planning and Action' (unpublished paper presented to the International Tax Reform Forum, Tax Policy Group, Silicon Valley Joint Venture, Dec. 4, 1997), quoted in Charles E. McLure, Jr., Taxation of Electronic Commerce: Economic Objectives, Technological Constraints, and Tax Laws 269, at 419-20.

43 McLure, Charles E Jr (1997) 'Taxation of Electronic Commerce: Economic Objectives, Technological Constraints, and Tax Laws', Tax Law Review, Symposium on Taxation and Electronic Commerce.

44 McLure, Charles E Jr (1997) 'Taxation of Electronic Commerce: Economic Objectives, Technological Constraints, and Tax Laws', Tax Law Review, Symposium on Taxation and Electronic Commerce.

45 Tillinghast, David R. (1996) 'The Impact of the Internet on the Taxation of Informational Transactions', 50 Bulletin International Fiscal Document, pp 524, 525.

46 Hellerstein, Walter (2001) 'Electronic Commerce and The Challenge For Tax Administration' Paper presented to the United Nations Ad Hoc Group of Experts on International Cooperation in Tax Matters in Geneva, Switzerland, on September 12, 2001 pp 16-18.

Residence-based taxation empowers corporate entities to incorporate themselves in tax havens and outsource work anytime anywhere.[47] Revenue collection will shift to low tax locations. This would lead to revenue losses for public authorities whose utilities were used for the human endeavour that generated profit and will contradict the benefit principle.[48] If residence-based taxation leads to the empowerment of tax havens in an era of digitization, this will affect revenue collection in the US. Residence-based taxation will erode the tax base of countries like India, Australia, Ireland, China, Philippines, Russia, Ukraine and Canada, which are involved with value creation, when the major firms doing business along the digitized route and markets reside in the US. Of the total worldwide software sales in 2000/01 of US$440 billion, US$219 billion occurred in the US. The US consumed 61.1 per cent of India's exports and 39.2 per cent of Australia's ICT-related exports in 2000/01.[49] The US as the dominant country of source will gain from source-based taxation. According to one estimate, US e-tailers served 20 per cent of the West European market and 14 per cent of the Asian market.[50] Given the US dominance in financial, software, publishing and entertainment services, sourced-based taxation has the potential of creating substantial revenue for the US.

Australia has argued for the continuing vitality of source-based taxation. To quote from the Australian White Paper: 'unless income is derived from property used in Australia or from acts done in Australia there would seem little likelihood that an Australian court would find that the source of the income was in Australia.'[51] The Australian White Paper noted, if the result of the performance of a service becomes more important than the location where the service was really performed, by giving undue emphasis to the place of contract, the place of payment, or even where the services were utilized, this could encourage tax planning. The suggestion is that residence can be more easily relocated to tax havens than the relocation of the actual performance of a highly skilled service (source).[52]

The Indian Finance Ministry's Report[53] expressed concern about the distributional consequences involved with the shift from source- to residence-based taxation. Especially worrying for India's tax authority was the fact that equilibrium in revenue sharing between countries of source and countries of residence was not one of the stated objectives of the OECD or the US. It stated the problems of determining residence. It opined that there was no substitute to the 'place of effective management

---

47 McLure, Charles E. (2001), 'Globalization, Tax Rules and National Sovereignty,' Bulletin for International Fiscal Documentation 55, 8, pp 328-41.

48 Li, Jinyan (1999), 'Rethinking Canada's Source Rules in the Age of Electronic Commerce: Part 2,' Canadian Tax Journal 47, 6, pp 1411-78.

49 Desai, Ashok V. (2002), 'India's market shares,' Business Standard (New Delhi).

50 Cairncross, Frances (2001), The Death of Distance (Harvard Business School Press, Boston) p 123.

51 Australian Taxation Office (1999) Tax and the Internet: Second Report December 1999(Government Printing Service, Canberra) p 79.

52 Australian Taxation Office (1999), Tax and the Internet: Second Report December 1999(Government Printing Service, Canberra) p 91.

53 Central Board of Direct Taxes (2001) Report of The High Powered Committee on Electronic Commerce and Taxation (New Delhi: Ministry of Finance).

test'. When the 'place of effective management' was tough to determine after giving due consideration to a variety of factors, source-based taxation should prevail.[54]

5.3   Permanent Establishment in E-Commerce

The ability of a state to claim its share of income from an enterprise engaged in e-commerce depends upon its ability to establish that the entity has a sufficient presence in the state to justify the exercise of taxing authority. The rise of e-commerce seriously challenges the concept of PE for determination of the source of income. Permanent establishment is focused on physical presence to find out whether or not an income is subject to tax. E-commerce dissolves most physical nexus. The internet provides an environment where automated functions, by their very nature, are able to undertake a significant amount of business activity in a source jurisdiction with little or no physical activity or participation in the economic life or use of infrastructure in any jurisdiction anywhere. Geographic location becomes hard to determine and easy to influence, giving businesses geographical independence and facilitating tax planning. This highlights the inappropriateness of allocating taxing rights on a concept based on geographical fixedness in an e-commerce environment.

Article 5(1) of the OECD Model Tax Convention defined PE as: 'a fixed place of business through which the business of the enterprise is wholly or partly carried out.'[55] There is a clear attempt to distinguish substantive economic activity, which creates a taxable presence, from mere 'preparatory or ancillary' activity; the latter, although conducted through a 'fixed place of business', does not create a taxable PE. Although not free from doubt, the PE concept, with its requirement of a 'fixed place of business', tends to lend some certainty to the circumstances in which a non-resident person would be subject to tax in a host country. However, the OECD has been struggling with the application of the PE definition in the context of e-commerce. In late 1999, the OECD's Working Party No. 1 on Tax Conventions and Related Questions released a discussion draft of commentary (OECD Draft) that clarifies the definition of PE in Article 5 of the OECD Model Treaty.[56] The OECD Draft concluded that while fixed automated equipment operated by an enterprise and located in a country may constitute a PE, a distinction needed to be drawn between computer equipment and the software used by such equipment. Thus a website, which is a combination of software and electronic data, does not have a location that can constitute a 'place of business' as there is no '*facility such as premises or, in certain instances, machinery or equipment*'[57] as far as the software and data constituting that

---

54 Central Board of Direct Taxes (2001), Report of The High Powered Committee on Electronic Commerce and Taxation (New Delhi: Ministry of Finance) pp 60-65.

55 OECD (1998) Model Tax Convention on Income and Capital, June 1998. Art 5 (1).

56 OECD (2000) Application of the PE, Definition in the Context of Electronic Commerce: Proposed Clarification of the Commentary on Article 5 of the OECD Model Tax Convention, Revised Draft for Comments, March 3.

57 Para 2 Commentary on Article 5 OECD Model Tax Convention.

website is concerned. Hence, it does not have any tangible property. Its exact location is also unknown. Accordingly, the website by itself cannot be treated as PE.[58]

Article 5 of the OECD Model Tax Convention also distinguishes when, and in what circumstances, the activity within the host country of an agent of the non-resident principal would establish the requisite nexus to permit direct taxation of the principal's business activities by the host country where there is no 'fixed place of business'. A non-resident person would not have a taxable presence solely because of using an agent, regardless of the type of activity carried out on behalf of the principal. Rather, the agent must be 'dependent', that is, dependent both legally and economically, on the principal. Beyond that, the agent must be able to enter into contracts in the name of the principal, which, at least, means that the agent must be able to bind the principal to a contract as a matter of local law. If, however, the agent is independent, a PE does not exist because of the agency.[59] Regarding this, the OECD Draft[60] concluded that since a website is not a person, as defined in Article 3,[61] a website could never be the dependent agent of an enterprise. Even if 'artificial intelligence' software is loaded on a server, it will not create a PE for an enterprise under paragraph 5 of the Model Tax Convention. An internet service provider does not constitute an agent of the enterprise for the purposes of PE because it does not have the authority to conclude contracts.[62]

Although the OECD Model Tax convention specifically referred to a dependent agent as a 'person', that term was not exhaustively defined (Article 3) and was intended to be interpreted widely. The website performs the tasks that the enterprise programmed it to do, similar to the tasks that an agent performs based on instructions from his principal. Sophisticated websites can actually solicit customers by sending e-mails to potential customers and are capable of carrying on the business of the company per its instructions. Using 'artificial intelligence', it can refine the list of customers and actually target likely customers based on past responses. This means that a website has the capability to provide instantaneous information concerning products and services. Further, by means of intelligent software, a website acting on behalf of an enterprise may have the authority to conclude contracts in the name of the enterprise. It can also be programmed with all the required instructions from the enterprise with the power to accept sales and allow the conclusion of a sale. This activity is similar to a person having the authority to conclude contracts in the name of the enterprise. The same thing is happening when a purchase is made online. The user inputs the information required by the website and, being in accordance with the instructions and requirements programmed, the purchase is authorized automatically without the need of human approval. It is important to note that the website alone cannot perform these functions. It must work with the server to accomplish these

58 OECD (2001) *Taxation and Electronic Commerce* (Paris: OECD).

59 OECD Model Convention, Articles 5(5) and 5(6).

60 OECD (2000) 'The Application of the Permanent Establishment Definition in the Context of Electronic Commerce: Revised Draft', 20 Tax Notes International 1199, March 13.

61 Article 3 of the OECD Model defines the term 'person' including an individual, a company, and any other body of persons.

62 OECD (2001) *Taxation and Electronic Commerce* (Paris: OECD) pp 80, 84-85.

tasks. Thus, the website itself does not constitute a dependent agent for the enterprise, but working along with a server it satisfies the conditions of Article 5(5) and thus may constitute a PE in the state where the server and the website are located.

A server is a special type of computer, which works as the hub of a computer network. The server can function as the primary site where information is stored, if part of a network, or as a gateway for incoming and outgoing information. A server may perform as stand-alone equipment and not as part of a network. In this case, the server earns its name because it is 'serving' web pages to users over the internet. When a server is part of a network of computers, it acts as the brain of the network allowing other computers to send and receive information as a network.[63]

After several years of deliberation, the OECD member countries agreed that a computer server (that is, a computer that has been networked to the internet) will fulfil the physical presence requirement.[64] Servers around the world will now constitute PEs if the software within the servers performs the integral functions of a cross-border transaction, enabling countries to tax any profits attributable to the servers' operations. As discussed earlier, the server on which the website is hosted would be a PE provided it constitutes a *'fixed place'*. Therefore, to constitute a 'fixed place of business' a server needs to be located at a certain place for a sufficient period to become fixed within the meaning of paragraph 1 of Article 5. In addition, the activities carried on through the website hosted on it relate to the *'core functions'* of the business of the enterprise and are not merely preparatory or auxiliary in nature. Accordingly, a server in which a website is stored and used is a piece of equipment having a physical location and may thus be a 'fixed place of business' of the enterprise that operates it.[65]

The OECD Draft further emphasizes that the distinction between a website and the server on which the website is stored and used is important since the enterprise that operates the server may be different from the enterprise that carries on business through the website. For example, it is common for the website through which an enterprise carries on its business to be hosted on the server of an ISP. Although fees paid to the ISP under such arrangements may be based on the amount of disc space used to store the software and data required by the website, these contracts typically do not give to the enterprise to which the website belongs any right to a particular space or control over the operation of the server (as opposed to the operation of the website software itself). In such a case, the server and its location are not at the disposal of the enterprise, even if the enterprise has determined that its website should be hosted on a particular server at a particular location; but the enterprise does not even have a physical presence at that location since the website does not involve tangible assets. In these cases, the enterprise cannot be considered to have

---

63 Sher, Judd A (1999) 'A Band-Aid or Surgery: It is time to Evaluate the Health of the Permanent Establishment Concept', *07 Tax Management Journal* 415, Washington, July 9. pp 414, 416.

64 OECD, Committee on Fiscal Affairs, *Model Tax Convention on Income and on Capital*, Condensed Version (5th ed., 2003) at 102-105.

65 OECD (2000) The Application of the Permanent Establishment Definition in the Context of Electronic Commerce: Revised Draft, *20 Tax Notes International*, p 1199.

acquired a place of business by virtue of that hosting arrangement. However, if the enterprise carrying on business through a website also owns (or leases) and operates the server on which the website is stored and used, the server could constitute a PE of the enterprise if the other requirements of Article 5 of the OECD Model Tax Convention are met.[66]

It can be argued that the situation of renting space on the server of an internet provider is similar to renting an office or a building through which the enterprise carries on its business. In both cases, the enterprise is renting a physical location. The only difference is that in the case of the building or office rental, the enterprise has the option to choose the state in which it will operate while under the server arrangement the enterprise may not have this option. It is the ISP which controls and operates the server. If, however, the server is owned or leased by the enterprise owning the website then it is '*at the disposal*' of the enterprise and would constitute a PE. Hence, some argue that the mere maintenance of a website on a server located in a taxing jurisdiction satisfies the requirements for a PE.[67]

However, e-commerce is largely indifferent to the location of hardware, thus the fact that, for instance, a clothing retailer's electronic catalogue resides on a server in a given country does not give the clothing retailer a fixed, vested economic interest in that country in the same manner that a factory or office would. For example, if the clothing retailer's only physical presence in a country was through a server, the clothing company would not particularly care about the composition of the country's workforce, whether the country's transportation system was functional or whether the country was politically stable. All of these considerations would be more important if the clothing retailer had a factory or office in that country. All these aspects are taken into consideration only when an enterprise intends to carry on business in a certain state. Those facts and circumstances are a part of a business decision as to where an enterprise would open an office or build a factory and demonstrate the character of permanence intrinsic to the concept of PE.[68]

What happens when the business may be said to be wholly or partly carried on through equipment such as a server that it controls and operates? Some countries believe that the issue is already dealt with in paragraph 10 of the OECD commentary, which expressly recognizes that the business of an enterprise may be carried on through automatic equipment. Other countries, however, draw a distinction between the example, given in that paragraph, of a gaming or vending machine and servers used in e-commerce operations. These countries consider that in the case of a gaming or vending machine, the machines are in a fixed place of business and enter

---

66 OECD (2000) The Application of the Permanent Establishment Definition in the Context of Electronic Commerce: Revised Draft, *20 Tax Notes International*, p 1199.

67 For example, the Income Tax Department of the India working group to examine the tax implications of e-commerce transactions recommended that a computer terminal which is used to receive and send information across national boundaries and a website used in e-commerce should be regarded as a PE. In addition, the Australian Tax Office in its discussion paper stated that even a website located on a server that is fixed in time and location, and through which business is carried on might constitute a PE.

68 Forst, David L (1997) 'The Continuing Vitality of Source-Based Taxation in the Electronic Age', *15 Tax Notes International* pp 1455-1458.

into completed transactions with customers to provide goods or services. They note that a vendor who changes locations each week would quickly lose its customers. The location of a server is, however, irrelevant to the customer of an e-commerce operation, since the customer has access to the business goods or services wherever the customer has an internet connection. Thus, an *e-tailer's* business is carried on, not through the server, but through the enterprise's offices, warehouses, research facilities and other locations in which its income-generating activities take place. According to these countries, the server in these circumstances does not, therefore, meet the requirement that e-tailers have a 'fixed place of business'.[69]

The commentary also provides that a PE can exist where the business of the enterprise is carried on mainly through automated equipment with the activities of the enterprise's personnel being restricted to setting up, operating, controlling, and maintaining such equipment. As an example, the commentary addresses gaming and vending equipment and provides that whether such machines constitute a PE depends on whether the enterprise carries on business activity besides the initial setting up of the machines.[70] If the enterprise merely sets the machines up and then leases them to operators in the other state, then no PE results. However, if the enterprise also operates and maintains them for its own account, then a PE will occur and this result follows if the machines are operated and maintained by the enterprise's dependent agent.

A further issue is to what extent human intervention is necessary for automatic equipment to be considered to constitute a PE of an enterprise. In one view, automated equipment that does not require human intervention for its operation may constitute a PE. The relevant question, in such a case, would be the nature of the business and whether the activities performed through the equipment are the core income-generating activities of the business. This view is taken because it would be illogical to conclude that personnel are necessary to have a PE when no personnel are in fact necessary to generate income.[71]

There is another view that some human intervention would be necessary for a PE to exist. However, there are different views as to the exact parameters of that requirement. Those differences relate to the following questions:

- whether the intervention must necessarily take place in the country or can be done from abroad;
- whether the intervention needs to be that of employees of the enterprise or of any person, whether or not employed by the enterprise;
- what level of human intervention is required?

---

69 OECD (2000) 'The Application of the Permanent Establishment Definition in the Context of Electronic Commerce: Revised Draft' (OECD: Paris).

70 Contrast gaming and vending machines, ATMs, and juke boxes, where a user's entire transaction is conducted by interaction with the machine, with the activities conducted or functions performed at the site of a computer server on the internet, which are normally more limited.

71 An example of equipment that operates automatically is the automatic pumping equipment used in the exploitation of natural resources.

On the first question, some consider that the intervention must be that of persons who are present for that purpose in the country where the equipment is located. According to this view, it is only under these circumstances that an enterprise could be regarded as participating in the economic life of that country like domestic enterprises.[72]

On the other hand, in the 'pipeline' case, The Second Chamber of the German Supreme Court held that an underground oil pipeline, located in Germany, but regulated by computer from the Netherlands, constituted a PE in Germany for the purposes of German business property tax. German law defines PE in the same manner for both its income tax and net worth tax. Clearly, the pipeline was integral to the taxpayer's business and there was a significant degree of permanence to the pipeline. The court held that the pipeline constituted a fixed place of business in Germany. With respect to the requirement that the pipeline must serve the taxpayer's business, the court stated that a fixed place of business serves a business activity when a taxable person exploits it for a certain period for business purposes. Did the Dutch company exploit the German stretch of the pipeline by operating it by remote control from the Netherlands? According to the court, a taxpayer need not be physically present at the fixed place of business to exploit it. The deployment of persons (an entrepreneur, an employee, independent contractors or other) to the fixed place of business is not always required; rather in the case of fully automated equipment the exploitation of the fixed place of business for the purpose of the taxpayer's business is sufficient. The court did not elaborate on this statement but its ramifications for e-commerce are obvious. The statement could be interpreted to mean that even though a taxpayer is not physically present in a particular country, it could have a PE in that country through its virtual presence.[73] The German tax authorities issued a pronouncement which provides that 'for the time being' (that is, pending the discussions at the OECD level), German authorities would take the position that a server does not create a PE pursuant to Article 5, paragraph 4 of the OECD Model Tax Convention because the activities have to be classified as being of a preparatory nature, despite the view taken by the German Supreme Court in its so-called 'Pipeline Decision'.[74]

A related question could be about the passive use of an asset for operational reasons. The European Court of Justice had the occasion to consider whether such use would amount to a PE in a judgment of 4 July 1985.[75] The European Court held that the definition of a fixed place of business presupposes both physical resources as well as personnel who assist the entrepreneur in the use and implementation of the physical resources. The court stated that a fixed place of business could be a piece of equipment (such as a vending machine), but subject to the proviso that it is permanently installed at a specific location and that it requires the employment

---

72 OECD (2000) 'The Application of the Permanent Establishment Definition in the Context of Electronic Commerce: Revised Draft' (OECD: Paris).

73 Forst, David L (1997) 'The Continuing Vitality of Source-Based Taxation in the Electronic Age', *15 Tax Notes International*, p 1459.

74 Hey, Friedrich, E.F. (1999) 'German Authorities Rule That Server Does Not Constitute PE', *19 Tax Notes International* 635.

75 Judgments of the European Tax Court.

of human energy for its operation. There are different views regarding the level of human intervention required. Some commentators argue that what matters is whether or not the equipment is operated, and not merely set up and maintained, by persons, while others think that it may be difficult to distinguish the operation from the maintenance of computer equipment, especially when databases are updated or software upgraded.

As seen above, it is possible that a server would satisfy the general rule of Article 5(1) of the OECD Model Convention and thus constitute a PE. However, paragraph 4 contains an exception to the rule of paragraph 1, listing a number of activities that might be carried on through a fixed place of business, without creating a PE. A facility is not a PE if it is used solely for purchasing, storing, displaying or delivering goods, collecting information or carrying on any other type of activity of a 'preparatory or auxiliary character'.[76] Is it possible to think of a server as a storage facility, as falling within one of the exceptions of paragraph 4? The US Treasury, in its White Paper, took the position that the use or lease of a computer server generally does not create a PE, because of paragraph 4, seeing the server as analagous to facilities used for storage and display.[77] Where a business sells information instead of goods, the White Paper provides that 'a computer server might be considered the equivalent of a warehouse, which is accepted from the definition of PE'.[78] Nevertheless, where the server is integral to the business (for example an ISP), the White Paper recognizes that the exception may no longer apply.[79] However, even though a server hosts a website, what could be seen as storing or displaying data and software, a server does more than that. In fact, it also operates the website and allows the connection between the website and its user. As a result, the exception provided in paragraph 4(a) of Article 5 is not applicable to a server and thus a fully automated server may give rise to a PE.

As in the case of a website, the server could possibly be treated as a dependent agent under paragraph 5 of Article 5 of the OECD Model Tax Convention to constitute a PE.[80] I discussed earlier in this section that the OECD Model

---

76 Bittker, Boris I and Lokken, Lawrence (1997) *Fundamentals of International Taxation U.S. Taxation of Foreign Income and Foreign Taxpayer*, 2nd Edition, (Warren, Gorham & Lamont, Boston, 1997) pp 66-97.

77 *Selected Tax Policy Implications of Global Electronic Commerce*, Department of the Treasury, Office of Tax Policy), (Treasury White Paper).

78 Id. Art. 5, paragraph 4(a) excludes from the definition of permanent establishment the use of facilities solely for the purpose of storage, display or delivery of goods or merchandise belonging to the enterprise.

79 Levine, Howard J. and Weintraub, David A (2000) 'When does e-commerce result in a permanent establishment? The OECD's initial response' *04 Tax Management International Journal*, p 229.

80 The server performs the tasks of the corporation that programmed it. As with a website, the server acting as the brain of the agent performs its functions in furtherance of its master (the party responsible for programming it). Thus, in this manner a server may be seen either as a dependent agent itself or as extending the foreign enterprise in such a way as to establish its business presence within the other country Sher, Judd A (1999) 'A Band-Aid or Surgery: It is time to Evaluate the Health of the Permanent Establishment Concept', *07 Tax Management Journal* p 425.

Convention reference to a dependent agent as being a 'person' must be examined taking into consideration that the Model was drafted at a time when the existence and the development of the internet and e-commerce were unforeseeable and hence dependent agents were expected to always be persons. The Treasury White Paper rejects this view because the activities or services performed by the server do not include contractual authority that is normally associated with a dependent agent. As seen above, by means of intelligent software, the website is able to conclude contracts for the enterprise. Hence, Italy has taken the position that where the server is loaded with 'intelligent software' that can conclude simple contracts, the server's actions become similar to that of an agent and thus may be sufficient to give a business a PE.[81] It seems, however, that the server needs to host a website in order to perform such tasks for an enterprise. The server by itself will not act on behalf of the enterprise. A server is more likely to constitute an independent agent for the enterprise acting in the ordinary course of their business, as evidenced by the fact that they host the websites of many different enterprises.

In the end, an expansive view of PE may have theoretical appeal, especially where, for example, the human presence has been replaced by a form of 'virtual' presence, such as the remote control of equipment from a foreign country. In such a case, neutrality would require that the enterprise conducting the activities from a remote location receive the same treatment as the enterprise that physically sends its employees to the site of the equipment for its operation and maintenance. According to the neutrality principle, if the latter activity gives rise to a PE, so should the former. Furthermore, a broad interpretation would apparently ensure the vitality of the PE concept in the age of e-commerce. However, at least in the case of computer servers, such an interpretation is problematic. The views of the OECD are consistent with the existing rules and principles. However, it is important to point out that treating the server which hosts the website, which is at the disposal of the enterprise and performs 'core business functions' of the enterprise, as a PE will not address the crucial issues arising from the growth of e-commerce. Nevertheless, one may question whether that premise makes sense in the context of e-commerce. At a fundamental level, one can argue that it makes little sense to attempt to fine-tune a definition of PE, rooted in concepts of physical presence, for a universe of transactions in which physical presence is often irrelevant.[82] Treating the server as PE will not create certainty of tax burden or ensure maintenance of the existing equilibrium in revenue sharing between countries of residence and source. More than one server may be used by the

---

81 Fairpo, Anne (1999) 'Electronic Commerce-U.K. Policy Document', *1 Tax Planning International's E-commerce*, No 5, p 4.

82 In fact, the OECD itself has recognized these concerns by mandating its Technical Assistance Group on Monitoring the Application of Existing Norms for Taxation of Business to consider and comment on the following questions:

1. Whether the concept of permanent establishment provides an appropriate threshold for allocating tax revenues between source and residence countries with respect to the use of tax havens in the context of electronic commerce;
2. Whether there is a need for special rules relating to electronic commerce and whether such rules would be a viable alternative to existing international norms.

enterprise, making the location of the server actually performing specific functions in the source country difficult to determine. The location of the server is easy to manipulate. There is nothing to prevent it being located in a low tax jurisdiction or a tax haven and not in the source country. Even if the server is located in the source country, in e-commerce a huge volume of transactions can be conducted without any requirement of office and staff in the source country. The attribution of income to the PE and taxation in the source country, in terms of Article 7 of the Convention, would be negligible.

At a fundamental level, one can always argue that it makes little sense to attempt to fine-tune a definition of PE, rooted in concepts of physical presence, for a universe of transactions in which physical presence is often irrelevant. In fact, the OECD itself has recognized these concerns by mandating its Technical Assistance Group on Monitoring the Application of Existing Norms for Taxation of Business to consider and comment on the following questions:

- whether the concept of PE provides an appropriate threshold for allocating tax revenues between source and residence countries with respect to the use of tax havens in the context of electronic commerce;
- whether there is a need for special rules relating to electronic commerce and whether such rules would be a viable alternative to existing international norms.[83]

Having examined e-commerce under the existing rules of PE, the following conclusions could be reached. First, websites, web hosting arrangements, and ISP should generally not be treated as a PE. Second, since the server is a piece of equipment having a physical location, it may constitute a PE. Nevertheless, the server itself does not conduct business for the enterprise without the website. Thus, if an enterprise carrying on business through a website also operates (by owning or leasing) a server on which the website is stored and used, the server, along with the website, may constitute a PE.[84] The discussion whether the concept of PE will have to be replaced by another concept is far from over. Since the current definition of the PE-rule is based on economic activities, it is reasonable and might be necessary for this threshold to be adjusted in case of changes in the nature of business and in the way the business is carried on. The assumptions underlying the existing PE-concept as a measure of economic activity might no longer be correct. Therefore, it is questionable whether the definition of a PE and thus the *de minimis* threshold for the right to tax of the source country is still appropriate with regard to the changed

---

83 OECD, 'The Application of the Permanent Establishment Definition in the Context of Electronic Commerce: Proposed Clarification of the Commentary on Article 5 of the OECD Model Tax Convention, Revised Draft for Comments', March 3, 2000.

84 See Lodin, Sven-Olof (2001), 'International Tax Issues in a Rapidly Changing World,' *Bulletin for International Fiscal Documentation* 55, p 5; and Kobrin, Stephen J. (2001), 'Territoriality and the Governance of Cyberspace,' *Journal of International Business* 32, 4, p 694.

organizational structures of the economy.[85] However, as Bourgeois notes, it seems unlikely that the divergent views on this, presumably held in accordance with national interests, can easily be reconciled at the international level.[86] The UK has opposed the possibility that servers may constitute PE.[87] The Indian Finance Ministry's Report criticized the definition of servers as PE. It noted the problem of enriching tax havens and the consequent uncertainty with regard to the collection of tax revenues. It suggested the search for an alternative to the concept of PE within the OECD or the UN. It was concerned that the server as PE could threaten the existing revenue distribution equilibrium between countries of residence and countries of source. To avoid this problem, the Finance Ministry proposed that when the 'place of effective management' is tough to establish, source-based rules should apply.[88] The views of most of the developing countries are clearly in favour of a change; while most developed countries are in favour of adopting the existing views. According to Lee, 'maintaining existing rules and concepts benefits the countries that export goods, services and capital'.[89] In addition, the rule that business profits are not taxable without PE in the source country presupposes that any massive sales are not possible without a PE. It is also implicitly presumed that without sales activity in a country, no sales are possible, which is no longer the case with the advance in technology.[90]

It goes without saying that the definition of PE primarily refers to the traditional manufacture of, and trade in, physical products. This does not mean that the provisions cannot be applied to new phenomena, but it seems far-fetched to apply it to non-physical objects. The discussion of this provision has been mainly concerned with how transactions in computer networks can be connected to physical objects and thereby to states where those objects are located. This calls for a method of unambiguously connecting the transactions in the networks with physical locations. In the debate, many more or less elaborate attempts have been made to find a connection between physical and logical infrastructure. In these attempts it often seems as if the networks are perceived merely as the means of delivery. Information is treated as if it were transported through the networks. One is looking for information factories and information shops in the networks. The server is seen as an information tap, where information flowing through the network can be drawn off.

In some sense this is correct, since the information is in fact transmitted from one physical point to another through the physical network in the form of electromagnetic

85 Schäfer, Anne and Spengel, Christoph (2002) *ICT and International Corporate Taxation: Tax Attributes And Scope of Taxation* Centre For European Economic Research (ZEW) and University of Mannheim.

86 Bourgeois, Pierre J. (2000). 'Income_Taxes.Ca.Com: An Update.' *Canadian Tax Journal* 48 (4): 1274–98.

87 OECD (2001) Taxation and Electronic Commerce (Paris: OECD) at p 82.

88 Central Board of Direct Taxes (2001), *Report of the High Powered Committee on Electronic Commerce and Taxation* (New Delhi: Ministry of Finance) pp 64–75.

89 Lee, Chang Hee, (1999) 'Impact Of E-Commerce On Allocation Of Tax Revenue Between Developed And Developing Countries' *18 Tax Notes International* 2569.

90 Lee, Chang Hee, (1999) 'Impact Of E-Commerce On Allocation Of Tax Revenue Between Developed And Developing Countries' *18 Tax Notes International* 2569.

impulses. The problem is that this view sees distribution of information as distribution of physical goods. In the case of physical distribution, an object is transported by physical persons and delivered to other physical persons. The transactions comprise distinct physical components: the object, the persons involved and the place where the transaction takes place. The relations between the object, the persons and the place are self-evident and uncomplicated. The reason for this is that the transaction involves distinct, physical phenomena, such as human beings.

In e-commerce, the relations between the parties involved are less clear. The physical infrastructure, computers and cables, is as tangible as the physical infrastructure for the distribution of goods. The information 'is' in some sense in the networks, but it forms its own infrastructure, which does not follow the physical infrastructure. Information is not matter that can be pumped through the networks like oil being pumped through a pipeline. The server is not a warehouse where information is stored on a shelf. It would be more correct to say that if information is a good, then information is the warehouse as well as the transport workers.

Information is the logical infrastructure's equivalent of trains and railways, ships and the sea, balloons and the air. One possible strategy from the enforcement point of view is to trace the transaction back to the persons and companies involved, thereby bypassing the several middlemen and ambiguous constellations. The problem with that strategy is that it overlooks the specific character of e-commerce, that it blurs traditional structures and makes legal categories irrelevant. The risk is that the taxation will be alienated from the economic reality. It may be possible to solve one problem by finding a tax subject, but at the same time create a new one. The purpose of the international tax rules is to mirror the transaction and tax it where it takes place. By connecting taxation to traditional tax subjects, the opposite is accomplished. The parts of the transaction where value is created are bypassed.

5.4   Characterization of Income

The next substantive issue in deciding who is entitled to tax revenues generated by electronic transactions is the characterization of income, a context in which e-commerce pushes the principles and rules of international taxation to their logical limits and beyond. Under existing international tax treaty rules, each category of income has its own source. It is, therefore, crucial to define the character of income from electronic transactions. Should we treat it as business profits from sales, services income or royalties income (which falls under the category of investment income) from the use of intellectual property? The literature on income characterization in respect of royalties has focused on 'how', rather than 'why' – that is, on the application of existing rules to electronic commerce transactions. The theories, policies and principles concerning the taxation of royalties have received little attention, even though a vast amount of literature has been published following the advent of e-commerce.[91] Under present conditions, distinguishing a 'royalty' from a 'service

---

91 Tadmore, Niv (2004) Further Discussion on Income Characterization, *Canadian Tax Journal*, Vol 52, No 1, p 125.

fee', from 'interest' from 'dividends', from a 'management fee' is often an exercise in futility.[92] Tadmore argues that although this distinction has always been difficult to make,[93] in the context of e-commerce it has become impossible, for example, some forms of income have been characterized as profits (website hosting and online auctions) and some other as royalties (downloading with right of reproduction). A wide application of the royalties definition would protect the revenue base but could catch a large number of small-value transactions. It may also be argued that minor differences in the nature or mode of delivery of a product could lead to significantly different tax results, although it could be claimed that such differences involve considerable differences in substance.[94]

Let me consider an example here: I access 'Software Unlimited', a website which provides software in order to download an 'interactive tax guide'. They offer me two options. Either I obtain a CD-ROM version or I download the program directly from their website. The question is if I choose the first option and the company ships me a CD, what kind of income is this? If, on the other hand, I choose to download the software would this then change the nature of the income? Again, while there are rules to determine source of income which work well in conventional commerce, the sourcing of income in e-commerce is much more difficult.

Characterization of income is important because both national and international income tax rules assign different categories of income to different jurisdictions. For example, under the OECD Model Tax Convention,[95] and many bilateral conventions, income from personal services is generally sourced in the country where the services are performed; income from rentals and royalties is sourced according to the location of the property or, in the case of certain types of intangible property, where the intangible property is used; and income from the sale of purchased inventory is generally sourced in the country where title passes. The principle of tax neutrality requires consistent tax treatment for electronic and conventional modes of business. However, the critical question for e-commerce would be how to analogize digital transactions to transactions in conventional commerce that are addressed in the relevant provisions of national law and international treaties. For example, the purchaser of a digitized image arguably is purchasing the services of the enterprise that purveyed the image over the internet. Under such a characterization, the income ordinarily would be sourced to the country in which services were performed.[96] Alternatively, the transaction might be viewed as the licence to use an intangible, namely, the digitized image that

---

92 Bird, Richard M (2005) Taxing Electronic Commerce: The End of the Beginning? ITP paper 0502, International Tax Program, Canada, http://www.rotman.utoronto.ca/iib/ITP0502. pdf.

93 Tadmore, Niv (2004) Further Discussion on Income Characterization, *Canadian Tax Journal*, Vol 52, No 1, p 125.

94 Tadmore, Niv (2004) Further Discussion on Income Characterization, *Canadian Tax Journal*, Vol. 52, No 1, p 125.

95 OECD (1998) Model Tax Convention on Income and Capital, (OECD Model Tax Convention).

96 Under the OECD Model Tax Convention, this would depend in part, on whether the services are effectively connected with a permanent establishment or are attributable to a fixed base in the country where the services are performed. OECD Model Tax Convention, Arts 14, 15.

is transmitted over the internet. Under such a characterization, the income ordinarily would be sourced to the country in which the intangible right was used.[97] Finally, one might view the true nature of the transaction as the purchase of a photograph, economically identical to the purchase of an item of inventory.

The problem results from the fact that international tax rules apply very different tax treatments to each of these different categories of income, despite the seeming economic similarities of the example. Under such a characterization, the income would ordinarily be sourced to the country in which title to the photograph passed.[98] Obviously, the proper characterization of a transaction will depend on its particular facts. The point is simply that the characterization of transactions in e-commerce, which has significant implications for the sourcing of income, is a task fraught with difficulties. A physical book sold from one country to the next creates active business profits that would be taxed in the source country as long as a PE exists. But, as the US Treasury Department notes, a digitized form of this same book may give rise to either sales proceeds or royalties (since copies of the book can easily be made and sold and thus the initial payment represents compensation for the use of a copyright), which are only subject to (usually low or nil) withholding tax rates in the source country,[99] or perhaps the book is updated from time to time via the internet and therefore payment for services has arguably taken place.

While analyzing the transactions involving digitized information, the US Treasury Report suggests that the form of transaction may have to be disregarded. For example, where computer software is sold on the internet with a right to make a copy, mere right to copy may be disregarded in view of the ease with which the number of copies can be made. However, if such a right to make copies is accompanied by a right to sell to the public, royalty will arise. On the one hand, it may be arguable that some of these transactions, such as the electronic purchase of a digital book, are merely substitutes for conventional transactions involving physical objects and that it would be inappropriate to treat them as creating royalty income. On the other hand, it is arguable that the transactions could involve considerable differences in substance; for example, a consumer purchasing a physical copy of a book is usually unable to manipulate the data in the book, while a consumer downloading a digital copy of the book will be able to alter its format, manipulate the date. Whether, and to what extent, the definition of royalties needs to be adapted needs further consideration. Digitized information also poses problems for the definition of services income, as distinguished from sales of goods income or royalties. Previously, a reference work, such as an encyclopaedia, would have been sold as a set of bound volumes and the sale of the bound volumes would have resulted in the sale of goods income, notwithstanding the fact that the cost of printing and binding represented only a

---

97 Under the OECD Model Tax Convention, this would depend in part, on whether the royalties are effectively connected with a permanent establishment or arise from a fixed base in the country in which the royalties arise. OECD Model Tax Convention, Art 12.

98 Under the OECD Model Tax Convention, this would depend in part on whether the 'business profits' from the sale are 'attributable to' a permanent establishment in the country where title passes. OECD Model Tax Convention, Art 7.

99 Treasury White Paper at p 23.

small fraction of the encyclopaedia's value. Now, instead of purchasing a bound volume, a potential purchaser might be able to choose between a set of CD-ROMs and a computer online service through which the encyclopaedia's content can be accessed. If the customer has a sufficiently fast modem connection, there may be little practical difference between accessing the online service and the CD-ROMs on the customer's personal computer. Yet the sale of the CD-ROMs still results in sale of goods income while the character of the income arising from the online service is not clear.

The OECD income characterization report indicates that one of the most important characterization issues arising from e-commerce is the distinction between business profits and payments for the use of, or the right to use, a copyright.[100] In deciding whether or not payments arising in transactions concerning digital products constitute royalties, the main question to be addressed is the identification of that for which the payment is essentially made. Although the rationale of a substantive test is attractive, the task of identifying the essence of the consideration can be fraught with difficulties. The essence of the consideration test involves questions that are to be determined in the context of the transaction itself, thus connoting subjective elements, and hence inherent ambiguity and uncertainty.[101]

A majority of the TAG believed that such transaction should be characterized as giving rise to 'business profits' under Article 7 of the OECD Model Convention on the theory that the transaction was equivalent to the electronic ordering of tangible products and that the form of delivery should not change the Treaty classification of the transaction. The minority, however, believed that this type of transaction constituted payment for 'royalties', and should therefore be treated under Article 12 of the OECD Model Convention, on the theory that the substance of the transaction was for the right to copy the program onto the customer's hard drive. According to the OECD:

> e-commerce transactions give rise to business income, unless the transaction involves the transfer of a copyright right (mostly referring to the right to reproduce the copyrighted material for commercial exploitation purposes). Three out of 28 'typical' types of transactions are characterized as resulting in royalties. The main advantage of this approach is that it simplifies the characterization problem and provides more certainty to taxpayers. The main disadvantage is the potential erosion of source taxation.[102]

Li contends it is reasonable to predict that the OECD guidelines will provide a useful reference to national tax authorities in applying Treaty and domestic rules to argue that income characterization and, in particular, the OECD guidelines, require further consideration.[103]

---

100   Tadmore, Niv (2004) Further Discussion on Income Characterization, *Canadian Tax Journal*, Vol 52, No 1.

101   Tadmore, Niv (2004) Further Discussion on Income Characterization, *Canadian Tax Journal*, Vol. 52, No 1.

102   OECD (2003) Model Tax Convention on Income and on Capital: Condensed Version (Paris: OECD, January 2003) p 444.

103   Li, Jinyan (2003) International Taxation in the Age of Electronic Commerce: A Comparative Study (Toronto: Canadian Tax Foundation), xxi.

The OECD guidelines have significant drawbacks. Moreover, no bright-line criteria may be available to distinguish between royalties and business profits from e-commerce. 'Rough and ready' guidelines may address some issues, but they will not resolve the practical and conceptual difficulties triggered by a distinction that lacks a sound basis.[104] Tadmore[105] demonstrates that they in fact do not provide reliable bright-line tests for distinguishing between business profits and royalties in all sorts of increasingly common transactions. He then reviews the historical reasons for distinguishing between business profits and royalties and concludes that although the distinction never had a strong rationale, in the context of electronic commerce the same reasons that justify the source-based taxation of business profits also justify the source-based taxation of royalties. In both cases, 'the source state provides the communications infrastructure that facilitates the trade online; it offers the market where demand exists; and most important, it provides the protections that shield the value of the digital supplies by the non-resident'.[106] He concludes by summarizing other adverse implications and the enforcement problems entailed in retaining a distinction between royalties and business profits in taxing income from e-commerce.[107]

E-commerce has blurred the traditional distinction between the form of delivery and the substance of what is delivered. The potential conflicts over characterization of e-commerce payments is no doubt exacerbated by the 'all or nothing' consequences of characterization under the current rule – if payments are treated as royalties or technical fees, both the source country and the provider country share taxing rights, but if the payments are considered business profits and the provider has no PE in the source country, the source country loses all its taxing rights. Commentators have suggested various approaches to avoid these precipitous outcomes.[108] One that has received some publicity is a proposed '10 per cent' withholding tax rule. This proposal contemplates the identification of foreign vendors who would have relied on domestic distributors prior to the advent of e-commerce. On the assumption that payments to such vendors erode the customer nation's tax base, that jurisdiction would be permitted to levy a creditable 10 per vent withholding tax on payments to the foreign e-commerce vendors.[109] The tax would be collected only by business customers of e-commerce vendors (and not final consumers) and it would be enforced by deduction for income tax purposes for the cost of acquisitions on which withholding tax should

---

104   Tadmore, Niv (2004) Further Discussion on Income Characterization, *Canadian Tax Journal*, Vol. 52, No 1.

105   Tadmore, Niv (2004) Further Discussion on Income Characterization, *Canadian Tax Journal*, Vol. 52, No 1.

106   Tadmore, Niv (2004) Further Discussion on Income Characterization, *Canadian Tax Journal*, Vol. 52, No 1, p 126.

107   Tadmore, Niv (2004) Further Discussion on Income Characterization, *Canadian Tax Journal*, Vol. 52, No 1, p 126.

108   Krever, Richard (2001) Electronic Commerce and Taxation: An Overview of Key Issues, *Asian-Pacific Tax Bulletin*.

109   Doernberg, R.(1998) 'Electronic Commerce and International Tax Sharing' (1998) vol. 16, *Tax* Notes International, p 1013.

have been, but was not, collected.[110] Proposals for the increased use of withholding taxes by either characterizing payments as royalties or adopting the proposed 10 per cent rule, are only feasible if they are adopted by all relevant trading nations. Otherwise, there is a risk of double taxation if the jurisdiction to which payment is made does not adopt a similar characterization of the transaction.[111] A second problem is the difficulty (or impossibility) of imposing the royalty withholding obligation or a 10 per cent withholding obligation on individual consumers. Since these customers will not seek to deduct the cost of their purchases, the denial of a deduction where they have failed to withhold tax will have no effect on these payers.[112] In the cases of individual consumers, a jurisdiction might simply have to concede the *de facto* exclusive taxing rights of the vendor's home jurisdiction under the withholding tax options.[113]

Li, on the other hand, proposes the introduction of a uniform withholding tax and the application of the global profit split method. The uniform withholding tax would be a final tax if the taxpayer was not subject to residence-based taxation on the same income and a creditable tax if the income was taxed by the residence state.[114] Li divides income into two broad categories. 'Business profits' would include payments of portfolio income between related corporations and 'portfolio income' would include dividends, interest, rent, capital gains and, significantly, royalties.[115] However, Li does not explain how royalties may be distinguished from 'active' business profits or suggest specific rules by reference to which this distinction could be made. In the e-commerce context, such rules are obviously vital to the effective implementation, operation and administration of any reform that preserves the distinction between royalties and business profits.[116]

OECD guidelines simplify this characterization problem and provide a degree of certainty. Although some degree of agreement has been reached in principle on some of these matters at the OECD, experience demonstrates that it can be a very long way from principle to practice in international tax matters. To sum up, the views of the TAG do not necessarily imply unanimity of view amongst all nations of the world. The view is that the different positions taken by countries are in the background of concern for protecting the integrity of their respective tax bases. This concern makes

110   Doernberg, R.(1998) 'Electronic Commerce and International Tax Sharing' (1998) vol. 16, *Tax* Notes International, p 1013.

111   Sweet, J (1998) 'Formulating International Tax Laws in the Age of Electronic Commerce: The Possible Ascendancy of Residence-Based Taxation in an Era of Eroding Traditional Income Tax Principles' vol. 146, *U. Pa. L. Rev.*, 1949 at pp 1957ff.

112   Krever, Richard (2001) Electronic Commerce and Taxation: An Overview of Key Issues, *Asian-Pacific Tax Bulletin.*

113   Doernberg, R (1998) 'Electronic Commerce and International Tax Sharing' (1998) vol. 16, *Tax* Notes International, p 1013.

114   Li, Jinyan (2003) International Taxation in the Age of Electronic Commerce: A Comparative Study (Toronto: Canadian Tax Foundation).

115   Li, Jinyan (2003) International Taxation in the Age of Electronic Commerce: A Comparative Study (Toronto: Canadian Tax Foundation).

116   Tadmore, Niv (2004) Further Discussion on Income Characterization, *Canadian Tax Journal*, Vol. 52, No 1, p 126.

it unlikely that an international consensus would be reached on the issues relating to characterization of incomes. The possibility of some incomes being taxed twice or remaining unintentionally untaxed, in both the country of residence and the country of source, cannot, therefore, be ruled out. However, until there is some international consensus as to the characterization of the above concepts, there would be no definite way to determine the source of income, which would result in two possible outcomes. The first would be that both countries, recognizing the ambiguities in the transaction creating the income, fail to characterize the income at all. In this case, the income would go untaxed and neither country would benefit from the tax revenue. In isolated cases, this result would be of little consequence, but if states remain incapable of characterizing income, as e-commerce activity increases, the loss of tax revenue would be significant. The second possibility would arise when both countries would try to manipulate the source concepts to justify exercising their taxing prerogative. Because each state has the sovereign right to tax within its territory, each country can legitimately make a claim to the tax value of that income. However, because of this the taxpayer would be taxed twice for the same activity. This uncertainty would also reduce the incentives for taxpayers to carry on e-commerce activities internationally, which would have the overall effect of stifling this form of economic activity. Because states and businesses have recognized the economic potential of e-commerce, this also would be an undesirable result.

At the heart of the current difficulties is the erosion of the traditional relationship between the service provider's and the service consumer's location. The link has weakened with each improvement in communications technology, such as fax transmissions and e-mail. In an earlier era, the location of the service provider was generally fixed and physically determinable. With electronic information, however, the service provider is mobile and can easily move to a tax haven or a low-taxed treaty jurisdiction. These opportunities for tax planning can ultimately erode the taxable base. At the policy level, I agree with the view that the characterization of payments should not change with the mode of delivery from physical to digitized form. This will ensure uniformity of approach among all the assessing officers. For the taxpayer, it would ensure certainty of the tax burden. The only long-term solution of the problems created by characterization lies in making direct taxation identical for all streams of income in a manner aimed at ensuring equitable sharing of revenues between residence and source countries.

5.5   Transfer Pricing

Experience from dealing with multinational companies shows that accounting manipulations allow for a transfer of tax bases (paper profits) even if physical capital (real activity) remains intact as multinational companies attempt to exploit differences in marginal statutory tax rates across countries, either actual or *de facto* (if there exist differing laxities with which tax administration is carried out). In most situations, this involves maintaining a judicious setting of the imputed values on the internal transfer of goods and services between operations in different countries. Such tax-shifting manipulations in which intra-firm sales are invoiced (that is, 'transfer pricing') is often arbitrary, since no formal sales occur, and firms can play strategic games in an effort to lower their tax liabilities. Each subsidiary of the parent company located in different tax jurisdictions is currently taxed as a separate entity. This provides incentives for firms engaged in activities in multiple tax jurisdictions to lower their worldwide tax liabilities through transfer pricing, that is, manipulation of costs of inputs imported from subsidiaries in different tax jurisdictions and through the allocation of joint costs of the headquarters, and research and development. They also inflate the income of the enterprise in a low tax jurisdiction and reduce the enterprise's income in a relative high tax jurisdiction.

Tax authorities are naturally concerned that global enterprises may establish prices for transfers of products and services among related entities in a manner that shifts taxable revenues beyond the jurisdiction of the authorities. The customary notion of 'arm's length transaction' is not always easy to apply in practice. Evidence suggests that multinational companies reduce their tax burden by between 3 and 22 per cent by shifting reported incomes from high- to low-tax countries.[117] The fact that transfer pricing is pervasive in the US, despite the fact that US tax authorities are among the most technically well equipped in the world and thus most effective in imposing penalties on flagrant tax violations, suggests that its existence on a global scale is indeed widespread.

The incidence of preferential transfer pricing appears to have gained momentum with the increase in global trade and the growth of e-commerce. E-commerce is more collaborative and dispersed than traditional forms of commerce, and its supply chain is intrinsically connected. It facilitates connectivity both intra-group and inter-group.[118]

The growth of e-commerce, particularly in the B2B sector, presents a tremendous challenge to existing transfer pricing mechanisms because digital products and services tend to be highly integrated and intangible in nature. Technology and e-commerce businesses rely upon valuable intangible properties, patents, trademarks and licences to earn income in multiple jurisdictions. The establishment of preferential royalty or licence fee arrangements is relatively easy when dealing with transfers of intellectual property rights and other intangible assets between related or affiliated entities. E-commerce uses its own payments system, referred to as 'cyber-payments', and the weakening or elimination of convenient points of taxation in the production–distribution process due to disintermediation.[119] B2B e-commerce transactions could facilitate the use of transfer pricing by multinational enterprises and makes them increasingly difficult for governments to detect. As noted by Owens 'the communications revolution presents no new problems, no fundamentally or categorically different dimensions, for transfer pricing. It just presents all the old

---

117   Harris, D., R. Morck, J. Slemrod and B. Yeung (1993) 'Income Shifting in US Multinational Corporations', in A. Giovannini, R. Hubbard and J. Slemrod (eds.), Studies in International Taxation, Chicago: University of Chicago Press.

118   Lau, Collin and Halkyard, Andrew (2003) From E-Commerce to E-Business Taxation, Asia-Pacific Tax Bulletin.

119   Owens, Jeffrey (1997) The Tax Man Cometh to Cyberspace, *Tax Notes International* 14.

problems more quickly'.[120] This makes it even more difficult than at present for tax authorities to determine what a given transaction actually is and to find a transaction between independent enterprises about which enough is known to conclude that it may be considered a comparable transaction to that undertaken between related enterprises.[121]

Application of the arm's length principle is generally based on a comparison in transaction with the conditions in transactions between independent enterprises.[122] The comparison must be performed at the transactional level; an analysis based on consolidated results from a number of distinct trading activities is unlikely to meet the required standard of reliability.[123] 'E-commerce transactions may not be directly compared with similar trade in physical goods. The cost structure and risks involved in the supply of digital music or software are not comparable to the deliveries of CDs.'[124] The development of private intranets within multinational enterprises puts pressure on the traditional application of the arm's length principle,[125] by stimulating the fuller integration of multinational operations, particularly in the provision of services. The main argument is that the arm's length method fails to capture the transfer of know-how and other intangibles within multinational enterprises.

Current practice in all jurisdictions is to combat transfer pricing by substituting an 'arm's length' price for the price nominated by the parties in cross-border transactions between related persons. The substitution of a so-called arm's length price that represents the price that unrelated persons would pay for the same supply is problematic at the best of times. Unless the parties are selling raw goods subject to uncontrolled world prices, ascertaining a genuine market price is at best difficult and often next to impossible. The difficulties are compounded many times when the supply is intellectual property or services in a digital form as it will be impossible to find an exactly comparable supply available elsewhere to use as a benchmark when determining the uncontrolled market price.[126]

The solution proposed by many observers is the adoption of a worldwide unitary tax system that allocates the worldwide income of corporate groups to all countries in which the groups operate on the basis of a pre-agreed formula.[127] The potential technical stumbling block to all unitary tax proposals is the identification

---

120   Owens, Jeffrey (1997) The Tax Man Cometh to Cyberspace, *Tax Notes International* 14, p 1849.

121   Electronic Commerce Answering The Emerging Taxation Challenges Jeffrey Owens.

122   Transfer Pricing Guidelines (OECD 1997) Chapter I(C)(i)(a) para. 1.15.

123   Westberg, Bjorn (2002) Cross-border Taxation of E-Commerce, IBFD p 129.

124   Westberg, Bjorn (2002) Cross-border Taxation of E-Commerce, IBFD p 129.

125   The principle that transactions between the related enterprises of an MNE should be treated as though they were undertaken between independent enterprises.

126   Technical Advisory Group on Monitoring the Application of Existing Treaty Norms for the Taxation of Business Profits, (draft discussion paper) 'Attribution of Profit to a Permanent Establishment Involved in Electronic Commerce Transactions' (Paris, February, 2001).

127   R. Bird (1986) 'The Inter-jurisdictional Allocation of Income', 3, *Australian Tax Forum*, p 333.

and weighting of income allocation criteria. The criteria currently used to reallocate profits in unitary tax systems (such as the Canadian provinces or US states) are relevant to traditional commerce but may not be appropriate for e-commerce. The value of real estate, size of the payroll, number of executive employees, and so forth, may not reflect the actual contributions of different parts of an e-commerce organization. Quite often, e-commerce businesses rely heavily on independent and seconded contractors rather than traditional employee relationships. Because they have no need of raw materials, access to transportation and so forth, comparatively valuable product development and servicing centres can be located far from expensive urban centres and employ relatively few people. Applying an allocation formula designed to apply to traditional industries may produce a highly distorted distribution of profits for tax purposes. Devising an alternative formula better suited to e-commerce would be a formidable and thus far untried task.

The significant potential technical barriers to a unitary tax solution to income allocation are probably outweighed by the political hurdles in the path of this approach. To date, no governments or international organizations have supported a move from the current water's edge rules to unitary taxation. In the current political environment under which nation states are not willing to cede tax sovereignty to a multilateral approach, the prospects for a shift to unitary taxation are terribly dim at best. For the foreseeable future, therefore, allocation of profits between jurisdictions and solutions to transfer pricing will continue to be based on attempts by tax authorities to find arm's length prices in situations where genuine market alternatives may not exist.

As e-commerce fosters the proliferation of cross-border activities, international tax planning will become increasingly important and increasingly complex. Examining the totality of facts, it will be difficult in terms of determining appropriate transfer pricing to decide which business functions should carry greater weight, particularly given that e-commerce has changed the way of intermediation and distribution of business flows to a significant extent. It is no small wonder, therefore, that taxpayers and tax collectors alike are struggling to determine which business functions are significant and agree a suitable allocation of profits thereto.[128] There is a need to establish transfer pricing guidelines which are internationally acceptable for e-commerce, and other high priority sectors to provide comfort and security to investors, so as to preserve the revenue base.

5.6   Conclusion

The US suggestion to shift from source-based taxation to residence-based taxation seems to be motivated by its worry regarding revenue collection via the source-based route in the internet age. This is unlikely, as the US's market share in the retail sector, the dominance of Wall Street, Hollywood, Silicon Valley and Seattle would enable the US to collect substantial revenue via the source-based route.

---

128   Li Jinyan, (2001) 'Slicing the Digital Pie With a Traditional Knife – Effectiveness of the Arm's Length Principle in the Age of E-Commerce', *Tax Notes International*, p 775.

Australian and Indian proposals pleading for the continuing vitality of source-based taxation deserves serious consideration. First, the suggestion that source is tougher to determine than residence due to digitization seems improbable because of the absence of a widely accepted standard governing the definition of residence. Moreover, source is less elusive than residence, because it is impossible to take Silicon Valley to Monte Carlo. Second, it is cheaper to continue with an established standard (source) than negotiating numerous treaties based on a new one (residence). Third, residence-based taxation is likely to empower tax havens. This will erode the fiscal sovereignty of all source countries which produce goods and services that benefit due to digitization. Revenue authorities should monitor tax collection. The perceived uncertainty regarding the global distribution of revenue can be guarded through an 'escape clause', in the case of drastic shortfall in revenues because of unforeseen happenstance. Escape clauses need to be moderately priced so that the cost of escape avoids defection; to be an enduring standard, 'escape' must guard against the easy use of the residence principle.[129] PE is the threshold of commercial activity beyond which a firm can be taxed in a foreign country. The OECD has defined automated servers, using a fixed location for a certain period, and performing certain core functions of the firm, to be a candidate worthy of PE. The traditional understanding is that human intervention is required in addition to the above requirements. While the new definition may benefit the server-abundant US in the short-run, it would lose in the long-run if automated servers migrate to tax havens. PE based on substantial human and financial investment in a foreign country will leave fewer incentives for firms to indulge in tax planning, compared with a situation where automated servers can constitute PE. Server-scarce countries are likely to oppose automated servers being defined as PE. India and the UK have opposed this move. Source-based taxation along with the traditional definition of PE continues to be relevant in the digital economy.

Until there is some international consensus as to the characterization of the above concepts, there will be no definite way to determine the source of income, resulting in two possible outcomes. The first is that both countries, recognizing the ambiguities in the transaction creating the income, fail to characterize the income at all. In this case, the income will go untaxed and neither country will benefit from the tax revenue. If states remain incapable of characterizing income, as e-commerce activity increases, the loss of tax revenue will be significant. The second possibility is that both countries will try to manipulate the source concepts so as to justify exercising their taxing prerogative. Because each state has the sovereign right to tax within its territory, each country can legitimately make a claim to the tax value of that income. The result for the taxpayer, however, is that he is taxed twice for the same activity.

Many of the participants in the ongoing debates over international taxation of e-commerce have strongly urged the importance of having a higher degree

---

129   Rosendorff, B. Peter and Helen V. Milner (2001), 'The Optimal Design of International Trade Institutions,' *International Organization* 55, 4, pp 829-57.

of international cooperation in this area. During the second half of the twentieth century there had been a variety of attempts to create international organizations with sufficient authority to propose, though seldom to impose, solutions to problems with substantial international dimensions. The United Nations would be the most obvious example, but the International Monetary Fund (IMF) and the World Trade Organization (WTO) would be more appropriate in this context. However, there is no such organization dealing with issues of taxation. The Committee on Fiscal Affairs (CFA) of the OECD would perhaps be the closest approximation, but many countries are not members of the OECD. Tanzi had suggested the formation of a World Tax Organization, which would not have actual authority to impose or collect any taxes but which would be a forum for the collection and reportage of tax data and trends on a worldwide basis, the formulation of basic norms for tax policy and tax administration and which would provide technical assistance and arbitration services to countries that request it.[130] Some of the substantive suggestions for coping with the global income-taxation of e-commerce would appear to require some form of international organization to make them work. For example, some commentators had suggested that ultimately some type of apportionment approach, similar to that used by the states of the US, would be the only effective way of taxing global enterprise income. One would expect that some international analogue of the Multi-State Tax Commission (US) would be a necessary part of any such system. In order for taxation rules to match economic reality, taxation authorities cannot afford to stagnate.[131]

It will be misleading to suggest that the internet and e-commerce has only produced problems for international taxation as they also offer some benefits to tax administration. Technological changes create new problems but also make available a new range of tools to be used to ensure tax compliance and collection and to improve taxpayer service. These include, possibilities of more accurate and efficient record-keeping, faster and easier compliance with tax requirements, including through electronic filing of returns and automated deductions of certain taxes such as payroll and social security taxes and provision of information to taxpayers. There is a possibility that it could also assist in the improved exchange of information among the tax administrators of different countries. However, the advantages of the internet revolution for tax administrators, particularly those in developing countries, will definitely not be automatic. The governments would need transparent, consistent and realistic policies for taxing e-commerce.

---

130 Tanzi, Vito (1998) paper given at the 32nd General Assembly of the Inter-American Centre of Tax Administration, Bahia Brazil, in May 1998. Similar view had also been expressed by Central Board of Direct Taxes (2001), *Report of the High Powered Committee on Electronic Commerce and Taxation* (New Delhi: Ministry of Finance).

131 Lau, Collin and Halkyard, Andrew (2003) From E-Commerce to E-Business Taxation, *Asia-Pacific Tax Bulletin*.

Chapter 6

The Effect of E-Commerce
on Consumption Taxes

Introduction

The problems concerning the application of consumption taxes on e-commerce are generally recognized as having more immediacy than the issues concerning direct taxation. This chapter will examine generically two different tax systems and the effect on them of e-commerce: the European VAT and the US sales and use tax. The chapter begins by describing the effect of direct e-commerce on VAT. Most of the current VAT rules were developed at a time when the ability to digitize and deliver goods and services cross-border was limited. This section of the chapter will include a descriptive account of the serious dysfunction of the present VAT rules by closely scrutinizing the application thereof to electronic supplies. In order to have an effective international system of VAT in the context of cross-border trade, the rules must be capable of answering three questions with respect to a particular cross-border supply transaction: (i) Is the transaction subject to tax? (ii) Who is required to pay the tax? (iii) To whom should the tax be paid? However, answers to these questions will differ frequently depending on whether the supply at issue is classified as a good or a service and, if as a service, into which category of service it falls.

The second part of the chapter covers the US sales tax, particularly the issues of 'nexus' and '*situs* of sale'. Any application of state sales and use tax to e-commerce must be considered in the light of the decision of the US Supreme Court in *Quill Corp. v North Dakota*, which effectively exempts many remote sales of tangible products. Conceptually pure versions of these two taxes have similar effects, but inherent administrative differences in the two taxes and deviations from the conceptual model enacted by the states or forced on them by judicial interpretations of the US Constitution create important differences in their effects. Particularly important for present purposes are: (i) the treatment of sales of services and intangible products under the two taxes (such products are generally taxable under the VAT, but not state sales taxes); (ii) the treatment of purchases by business (VAT on such purchases are almost universally creditable against VAT on sales, but many such purchases are subject to state sales tax); and (iii) the treatment of sales between jurisdictions (they are commonly subject to VAT in the country of destination but exempt from sales and use tax in states where the vendor lacks a physical presence).

6.1   Indirect Taxation and E-Commerce

Commerce in the physical world has been mostly governed by relatively independent discrete geographic domains and tax obligations have been enforced based on physical presence. However, problems arise for governments that seek to impose laws determined by geography, such as VAT and sales tax, on e-commerce transactions. This is the heart of the debate. The fact that consumption tax revenues relative to e-commerce transactions are being lost is generally accepted. Most would even agree that a tax model treating the sale of goods and services equally, regardless of where the retailer is located or the nature of its business model, would correct this. It is the translation of this general desire into the specific where disagreement arises. Any resolution of how to tax e-commerce transactions will have to take into account the inherent difficulties of verifying the location, identity and residence of a seller or purchaser over the internet.

In order to examine the impact of e-commerce on consumption taxes, it is essential to distinguish between national and sub-national consumption taxes, more particularly, between VAT adopted by members of the EU and the sales/use tax in force in the US states. Although both levies in principle are consumption taxes, and both levies encounter certain common problems raised by e-commerce, there are also dramatic differences between VAT and sales tax. From a US perspective, tax collectors already have a huge difficulty in collecting sales and use taxes from sellers, irrespective of whether such sales were effected online or offline from out-of-state sellers who have no presence there to create 'nexus'.[1] The US Supreme Court interpreted 'substantial nexus' as the requirement of a taxpayer to have a 'physical presence' in a state.[2] However, the EU position is characterized by the effort that seeks to enforce VAT collections on supplies of digitized products from online sellers situated outside Community territory to consumers in an EU member state. Tax rules have historically emphasized the taxation of transactions that involve tangible goods or the taxation of income derived from the economic activity associated with these tangible goods. Further, intangible goods are often exempted from sales taxation. Additional problems are created when taxable and non-taxable services or intangible goods are bundled together and sold for one price. In contrast, value-added taxes generally subject the consumption of most tangible and intangible goods and services to taxation. I will first discuss the e-commerce issues raised by VAT and then turn to the special problems of the US sales/use tax system.

---

1   This problem arose from the principle enshrined in the 14th Amendment to the US Constitution, which gave a State the right to impose its tax jurisdiction on a person who 'purposefully directs its business activity into a State and the what is commonly referred to as the Commerce Clause of the Constitution which prohibits a State from extending its tax jurisdiction to persons that do not have a "substantial nexus" with that State'

2   The 1992 case *Quill Corp. v. North Dakota* 504 U.S. 298 (1992) established that businesses are not responsible for collecting a use tax unless they have a physical presence or nexus in a customer's home state and the advent of internet and e-commerce only further complicates the problem.

6.2   Value added Tax (VAT)

The implications of e-commerce for VAT are dependent upon the four categories of transactions involving e-commerce. Briefly, first, transactions involving B2B sales of tangible property consummated through electronic means (for example, the purchase over the internet of a computer by a business taxpayer from a remote computer vendor). Second, transactions involving B2B sales of digital products (for example, the purchase over the internet of an electronic database by a business taxpayer from a database vendor). Third, transactions involving B2C sales of tangible property consummated through electronic means (for example, the purchase over the internet of clothing by an individual from a remote vendor). Fourth, transactions involving B2C sales of digital products (for example, purchase of anti-virus software over the internet by an individual). I have discussed in Chapter 3 that VAT levied in the EU is a destination-based tax. The discussion in the following sections focuses on how the destination principle is actually implemented under the EU's transitional[3] VAT system.

6.2.1   VAT and Indirect E-Commerce

The debate on the taxation of e-commerce was initially focused on the sale of tangible products to businesses and consumers; these transactions still account for the largest percentage of internet sales. The sale of a tangible product does not raise any fundamental taxation issues because the proper destination-based consumption tax can be levied once the consignment passes through customs. Thus, if a US customer purchases a book over the internet from a seller in the United Kingdom, the proper destination-based consumption tax and applicable customs tariff can be levied when the consignment crosses customs control at the US border. Such a sale does not raise any fundamental taxation issues. As these types of transactions become more common, customs authorities will have to handle significantly greater flows of small consignments.

However, if both the product and the payment method are digitized – for example, downloaded software paid for with electronic cash – complicated enforcement issues

---

3   I have discussed about the EU 'transitional' VAT system in Chapter 3. Briefly, in 1967, the European Common Market decided that the origin principle should eventually be adopted for trade within the Common Market, (rebate of VAT on exports and collection of VAT on imports) so that the border adjustments required for implementation of the destination principle would not interfere with creation of a single market. In 1987, the Commission proposed a shift to the origin-based system internally by 1993. In 1989, it was realized that the 1987 proposals would not be implemented by 1993; the 'transitional' system was adopted as a means to implement the destination principle for internal trade in goods (Services are taxed on an origin basis as discussed later in the chapter). The key components of this system are reverse charging of VAT on sales to registered traders and collection of tax on distance sales to households and unregistered traders by vendors making substantial amounts of such sales to customers located in a given Member State. Genser, Bernd (2001) 'Coordinating VATs between Member States', presented at a conference on 'Tax Policy in the European Union', held at the Research Centre for Economic Policy, Erasmus University, Rotterdam, 17-19 October 2001 as cited by McLure, Charles E. Jr. (2001) 'Taxation of Electronic Commerce in the European Union' Hoover Institution, Stanford University.

arise because the origin and the destination of the transaction are obscured. The cardinal point in the workings of VAT in the EU is the importance ascribed to the distinction between the delivery of goods and the rendering of services. The review of online commercial activities indicates that it is digital e-commerce[4] which causes major problems to taxing authorities. While utilizing the opportunities offered by the internet, the indirect form of e-commerce retains physical forms of distribution and therefore puts much limited pressure on conventional tax concepts built on the physical reality of trade.[5] Distance selling has existed for many years, and there is no difference in principle between a cross-border transaction in tangible goods effectuated by fax or a telephone call than one effectuated by the 'click of a mouse'. However, e-commerce increases the opportunity for cross-border trade and the increase in the volume of such transactions counsels that attention be paid to existing procedures to assure that they ensure the efficient collection of taxes as well as the speedy expedition of goods to their destination.[6]

As discussed in Chapter 3 the tangible products moving between member states of the EU are treated differently, depending on whether they are bought by registered traders or by others. In the former case, exports are zero-rated and, under the system of 'reverse charging', purchasers are expected to self-assess the tax of the destination state. Sales from a vendor in one member state to consumers and unregistered traders located in another (for example, mail order and telephone sales) are treated differently, depending on the volume of sales the vendor makes to customers located in the other member state. If sales fall below the threshold, they are subject to the VAT of the state where the vendor is located. If they exceed that threshold, the vendor must register in the state where customers are located and collect the VAT of that state.[7]

However, this becomes more complicated when aside from the object itself the transaction is also characterized by other rights besides those of physical ownership. Hence, special attention must be given to the VAT treatment of software purchased through indirect e-commerce. The sale of computer software is an ensemble of

---

4　Also termed as Direct E-Commerce.

5　OECD (1997) Electronic Commerce: The Challenges to Tax Authorities and Taxpayers, 4, Nov. 18, 1997, at pp 9-20 Website: http://www.oecd.org/daf/fa/e_com/turku_e.pdf; Schenk, Alain and Oldman, Oliver (2000) *Value Added Tax*, 26 (Transnational Publishers) at pp 489-490.

6　The OECD has pointed out that many Member countries have a *de minimis* standard for low value packages sold by distant sellers that allows them to escape taxation altogether. In the context of a global market in which local consumers can more easily acquire such packages from distant suppliers, the OECD has suggested that Member countries may wish to re-evaluate the *de minimis* threshold to assure that local suppliers are not being harmed by tax-free competition from distant sellers. OECD Committee on Fiscal Affairs, Electronic Commerce: A Discussion Paper on Taxation Issues (1998) at p 22.

7　EU concluded with respect to the likely increase in purchases of physical goods by private consumers over electronic networks. Commission of the European Communities, Proposal for a Council Directive amending, and Directive 388/77/EEC as Regards the Value Added Tax Arrangements Applicable to Certain Services Supplied by Electronic Means (2000) Explanatory Memorandum at p 4.

a number of transactions put into one. A customer is given the right to use the software and in limited cases to make and keep a specified number of copies of the software. The customer would therefore be purchasing the data carrier in a tangible way but would be receiving only rights over the usage of the software and not over the software itself. It is important to understand that, due to the peculiar nature of software, what is transferred during the sale of a computer program, whether it is bought off-the-shelf or custom-made to suit individual needs, is a good or a service for purposes of VAT.

The principal element in a transaction for the transfer of bespoke software[8] is not the physical delivery of the medium which contains the program (later to be used for the installation of the program on the customer's resident disks) but the development of the software itself. Such a transaction can consist of a multiplicity of aspects: the development of the software and the delivery of the diskettes. In order to determine the nature of the supply to determine whether the object of the transaction for the purposes of the Sixth Directive is a good or a service depends upon what is considered as being the principal element of the transaction for both the seller and the buyer. As the principal element in the transfer of bespoke software is the development of the program, which cannot be considered a tangible thing as defined in Article 5 of the Sixth Directive, therefore, the sale of a custom-made computer program is deemed a supply of service.[9]

In the case of shrink-wrapped software, after a number of decisions and statements by the EU, there is strong support the view that the sale of off-the-shelf software[10] should be considered as supply of good. As early as 1996, a number of countries, including Germany and the Netherlands, approved regulations, which place the sale of shirk-wrapped software as the supply of goods for the purposes of VAT.[11] This view was opposed by dissenting interpretations put forward, mostly constructed on the argument that the principal transaction in the sale of shrink-wrapped software is not the physical transfer of the tangible medium but rather the transfer of some other right, generally the right to use and in some cases to make a specified number of copies of the software.

Under accepted tenants of copyright law, it is not the diskette or CD-ROM which are important in themselves but what they contain and the right to use the software. Moreover, the right to use the software is not contained in the diskette, thus reducing the possibility that the data medium is the principal element in the transaction. Since a consumer buys a computer program to use on his computer and this use makes the principal element of the transaction, software cannot be considered a supply of good but that of a service since the right transferred is not tangible or found on the

---

8 Bespoke or 'customized software' is the software, which is tailor-made based on the specific needs of the customer.

9 This was decided in the German case Faabourg-Gelting Linien A/S - Case C-251/94. As cited in Kabisch, Volker (2000)*'Tax Aspects of International Electronic Commerce'*, Electronic Commerce Legal Issues Platform, ECLIP - Esprit project 27028 at p 137.

10 'Shrink-wrap software' is the readily available software, which is sold 'off-the-shelf.

11 Germany - VAT Directions, German Ministry of Finance at Sec.25 (2)98/620, following the deliberations of the 30th and 38th sessions of the EU VAT Committee.

diskette as would be required under Section 5 of the Sixth Directive. Unlike books and music CDs, a computer diskette cannot be used on its own but has to be installed on a hard disk, and it is only after such installation that the software can be used. Therefore, the diskette is only a 'data carrier' and only 'ancillary to the possibility to use the software', making the purchase of software the supply of a service in terms of Section 6 of the Sixth Directive. As opposed to books and other objects, which can be purchased from a website, both shrink-wrapped and bespoke software should be deemed supplies of services and not of goods.

However, a different view was taken by HM Customs and Excise, which defines goods for the purposes of computer software as the physical device upon which information is recorded. By contrast, services are defined as comprising data, programs or instruction.[12] Customs and Excise Notice No. 702 provides that where the goods (that is, the physical form such as a CD-ROM) and services (that is, the information) are not separately identified, the import is to be treated as an importation of goods.[13] If the value of the supply of goods and services are separately identified, VAT is paid on the importation of goods.[14] VAT is charged on the cost or value of the carrier medium. In relation to separately identified services, VAT must be accounted for in respect of those services, which were specified in the Value Added Tax Act 1994, Schedule 5, on the basis of the reverse charge.[15] Which would normally be the case where the recipient receives the supply for business purposes? The service element of the supply is the information on the carrier, and the charge is for use of the information, which is subject to copyright protection. Both these cases are subject to reverse charge.[16] If a supply is made to a non-business consumer, import VAT is payable solely upon the physical carrier. Since normalized software is typically regarded as a supply of goods, this would mean that supplies to countries outside of the member states of the EU would typically be zero-rated.[17] The supplier under these circumstances would be entitled to recover all its VAT incurred on the components in making the supply. It is perhaps still too early, however, to speak in definite terms as regards the categorization of shrink-wrapped software because of contradictory views and more importantly the absence of a corpus of court decisions in the EU.

6.2.2 VAT and Digital Content

The digital environment of direct e-commerce causes problems for the VAT system in three ways. The first problem is related to the exponential growth in the number of cross-border B2C transactions.[18] VAT systems were designed with the assumption

---

12   HM Customs and Excise Notice No. 702/4/94, para. 2.1.
.13 HM Customs and Excise Notice No. 702/4/94, para. 3.2.
14   HM Customs and Excise Notice No. 702/4/94, para. 3.2.
15   VATA 1994, s 8, sch 5.
16   VATA 1994 Sch5 para. 1 and 3.
17   VATA 1994, s 30.
18   OECD, Report On The Turku Conference at p 17 'Explanatory Memorandum' to the Proposal for a Council Directive amending the Sixth Directive as regards the value added tax arrangements applicable to certain services supplied by electronic mean (COM (2000) 349 final) June 7, 2000, pp 6-7.

that B2C transactions would predominantly take place within national boundaries. The emergence of mail-order systems did increase the cross-border transaction[19] but it still did not result in such a boost of international B2C transactions, as did e-commerce. As a second problem, Hinnekens (1998) argued that direct e-commerce questions the classification of supplies as goods or services. Within the sphere of e-commerce, where electronic transactions compete with physical forms of supply, the goods originally supplied through conventional channels become digitized.[20] Upon digitization, the products lose physical appearance; therefore, the regime governing the taxation of goods cannot be applied anymore.[21] The question, therefore, is how to tax these supplies or whether to tax them at all. The same doubts arise with respect to new types of digital supplies.[22] In addition, new types of transactions are difficult to fit into the existing lists of goods and services to which different rules are applicable under the present systems of VAT.[23] The concepts of fixed establishment, use and enjoyment, location of property, the place where services are performed and distance covered by transport was developed for tangible goods and services developed in a different technological era. Third, tax administrations are overwhelmed by the evasive nature of online commerce. Under all existing VAT systems, suppliers need to tell the tax status and the location of their customers if they wish to discharge their administrative and payment obligations properly.[24] Accordingly, enforcement in lack of voluntary compliance is based on the authority's knowledge of the identity and geographical data of the supplier.[25] Based on the anonymous series of digital signs representing the transactions, it is almost impossible to identify and locate the supplier and the customer.[26]

The VAT distinctions among e-commerce activities are not purely academic. There are several differences between the treatment of goods and services throughout the VAT system. Differences may involve a taxable event (for example, import from non-EC supplier applies to goods and not to services), the place of taxable supply (for example, intra-community acquisition deals with goods and not with services), exemptions (for example, distance selling rule applies to goods and not to services), formalities (for example, reverse charge procedure applies to services and not to goods) and applicable rates (for example, zero-rate may apply to books in printed form but not in digitized form). It is important that for these differences distinction be made between services according to their type. For different services there are different VAT rules particularly with respect to the place of supply. In the following

---

19 Coopers and Lybrand Belgium (1998) 'Does Cyber-Commerce Necessitate a Revision of International Tax Concepts?' *International Bureau of Fiscal Documentation* at p 2.

20 Hinnekens, Luc (1998) 'The Challenges of Applying VAT and Income Tax at p 55.

21 Hinnekens, Luc (1998) 'The Challenges of Applying VAT and Income Tax at p 55.

22 Houtzager, Mark and Tinholt, Jeroen (1998) *E-Commerce and VAT in Caught in the Web: The Tax and Legal Implications of Electronic Commerce* at pp 99-102.

23 Hinnekens, Luc (1998) 'The Challenges of Applying VAT and Income Tax at p 57.

24 OECD (1997) Report on the Turku Conference, at pp 9-12.

25 OECD (1997) Report on the Turku Conference pp 9-12; Explanatory Memorandum, at pp 9-11.

26 Report by the Technology TAG of the OECD, (2000) on the technological questions of tax collection.

sections, discussion will focus on these functional problems along with theoretical and practical weaknesses of the Sixth Directive in handling inter-jurisdictional digital transactions.

6.2.2.1　Supply of Goods or of Services　The first issue to be decided by the Community was whether the Sixth Directive should tax digital services at all. The goal of the Sixth Directive was to levy VAT as broadly as possible,[27] so the answer should be positive because apart from the use of a new medium, digital supplies have all the characteristics of a taxable transaction.[28] They are affected for consideration, supplied by businesses registered for VAT purposes to businesses with the same status and to final consumers. In addition, these supplies represent a benefit that forms an increasing portion of the GDP.[29] The next question is whether these supplies are capable at all of fulfilling the criteria of the definition of either goods or services. In a modern world, the solicitation of a customer, the conclusion of a contract or the payment of the consideration often involve means of electronic communication. Therefore, it is obvious that use of the internet as a communications link or as a payment tool does not require a new category of VAT transaction if physical goods are delivered to the customer or if services are physically performed. These transactions can be dealt with under the existing source rules of Article 8 (supply of goods) and Article 9 (supply of services), under which the place of supply for an 'offline' delivery of goods is generally the place where the shipping of the goods begins. The business model of the online book seller Amazon.com falls into the category 'offline' delivery because Amazon. com ultimately ships physical products to its customers.

Some authors, like Houtzager and Tinholt,[30] argued that all internet transactions should be treated as supply of goods. Central to this categorization is the tangibility of the product and its transfer to the consumer as owner, as is required under Article 5 of the Sixth Directive. These commentators justify their interpretation on the inclusion of '*electricity and like*' in the definition of 'goods' in the Sixth Directive. However, the reason why trade in electrical current is regulated under the rules on goods is not its 'tangibility' but because of the fact that the authorities usually closely control such activity, as provision of public utility, therefore its trade route is transparent enough to apply the place of supply rules for goods. This cannot be said about electronic deliveries. Their very nature would render taxation impossible under the regime designed for taxing the supply of goods.

27　This has been the goal of the European VAT system since the issuance of the First Council Directive: The Preamble of First Directive. First Council Directive on the harmonization of legislation of member states concerning turnover taxes (67/227/EEC) OJ 071 14/04/1967. This intention has also been reinforced by Article 2 of the Sixth Directive.

28　OECD (1997) Report on the Turku Conference, at p 4. OECD (1998) 'Electronic Commerce: Taxation Framework Conditions', A Report by the Committee on Fiscal Affairs of the OECD at p 3.

29　E-commerce is predicted to rise to between 4 per cent and 7 per cent of the GDP in the UK, Germany, Italy, and France by 2003. As mentioned in UK Online (2000) 'Where Does the UK Stand Now?' website: http://www.e-envoy.gov.uk/2000/progress/anrep1/030.htm.

30　Houtzager, Mark and Tinholt, Jeroen (1998) E-Commerce and VAT in *Caught in the Web: The Tax and Legal Implications of Electronic Commerce* p 99 (Deventer ed.).

The European Court of Justice seems to hold the view that characterization of a good or service should not depend on the mode of distribution. In the *Datacenter* case, it found that the mode of distribution was irrelevant for purposes of defining tax-exempt services.[31] The European Commission back in 1998 proposed the following uniform guideline:[32]

> A supply that results in a product being placed at the disposal of the recipient in the digital form via an electronic network is to be treated for VAT purposes as supply of services... Products that, in their tangible form, are treated for VAT purposes as goods are treated as services when they are delivered by electronic means.

In the light of the European Council's adoption of Directive 2002/38/EC and Regulation No. 792/2002,[33] the EU treats all products that are distributed electronically as services. Consequently, the online transactions are sourced under Article 9 of the VAT Directive without exception and regardless of the fact that the supply of an electronic book or sound file, for instance, may be taxed differently from the supply of a comparable physical product. Furthermore, Article 9 applies to B2B transactions as well as to B2C transactions. International consensus behind this interpretation had already come to existence within the OECD framework[34] which was in favour of classifying these supplies as supplies of services.

6.2.2.2 VAT and Place of Supply Rules The VAT rule for supply of goods is the destination principle; the rules for services are more complicated: place of supply can be either where the supplier or customer is located depending on the specific type of service being delivered.[35] Article 9 of the Sixth VAT Directive provides for two categories of place of supply rules: the first is based on the identification of the place of business of the supplier or the customer, depending on the service. The second is based on the place of effective use and enjoyment, irrespective of the place of business. This Article pursues the double aim of concentrating VAT revenue to the country of consumption, while preserving administrative feasibility.[36] This twofold objective has resulted in a rather extensive and complicated framework of place of supply rules.

The place of supply of a service is under the general rule of Article 9(1), deemed the place of the supplier's business or fixed establishment from which the service is

---

31 E.C.J. Case C- 2/95, *Sparekassernes Datacenter (SDC) v Skatteministeriet.*

32 'Electronic Commerce: Commission sets out guidelines for indirect taxation,' *EU Business,* June 17, 1998, available at http://www.eubusiness.com/finance/980617co.htm.

33 Detailed discussion about the EU Directive and its consequences appears in Chapter 8.

34 OECD (1998) Taxation Framework Conditions. By this document, the OECD countries voted for classifying digital deliveries as services for the purposes of taxation.

35 The Sixth VAT Directive was based on the destination principle. Exports between member states were zero-rated and taxed according to the prevailing rate at the place of consumption or, in the language of the Commission, goods were de-taxed on leaving the state of origin and re-taxed on entering a second state.

36 Terra, Ben (1998) *The Place of Supply in European VAT* (Kluwer Law International at p 57).

supplied.[37] The expressions '*place of business*', 'fixed establishment'[38] and 'permanent address or usual residence'[39] are not defined in the Sixth Directive. The relevance of place establishment under the Sixth Directive is divided between a numbers of sections, namely Article 9, Article 17 and Article 21. The general rule, based on the origin principle was designed to catch B2C transactions or national supplies to business customers and was based on the already mentioned belief that due to technical limitations supply of services to consumers normally takes place within one country, therefore the supplier, the customer and the consumption are all located within the same jurisdiction. Under this section, the responsibility to account for and pay the tax lies with the business supplier.[40] This rule was in line with the administrative realities of B2C transactions, since business suppliers are the ones in possession of necessary data and equipment for the discharge of this obligation.[41] Section (2) of Article 9 laid down special rules with respect to certain services. Most relevant to the conduct of e-commerce is the fact that '*cultural, entertainment, or artistic*' services are taxed where they are performed and intangible or intellectual services such as copyrights, licences, financial transactions and professional consultations are taxed where the customer who receives the service is established. This nature of the services makes the central business establishment of the supplier relatively mobile.[42] Therefore, apart from the intention to realize taxation in the country of consumption as best as possible, this subsection also aims at preventing the suppliers from establishing their businesses in the countries with the lowest tax-rates, which they would probably do, and was the general rule applicable.[43] Both B2B and B2C supplies of the listed services are meant to come under this subsection regardless of whether the two parties reside within the borders of the same country. According to this subsection, the business supplier should discharge its VAT responsibilities in

---

37   As a result, exports of services are subject to EU VAT, imports are not. Within the EU, this rule could have achieved competitive neutrality if tax rates were uniform (which they are not).

38   The concept of fixed establishment is interpreted by Customs and Excise 'as establishment (including business establishment) from which business activities are carried out and which has both the human and technical resources necessary for making or receiving the supplies of services in question'.

39   Case law that has contributed to elucidate the meaning of PE for the VAT liability of non-e-Commerce services should assist in defining the parameters also for e-commerce operations. Lambert stresses that the application of principles from non-e-commerce operations to e-commerce business should not be automatic, but only follows an analysis into whether a particular interpretation, building on what was decided on previous occasions by the ECJ, would result in a fair application of Art. 9. This object of the place of supply rules has also been acknowledged by the ECJ in *Gunter Berkholz v Finanzamt Hamburg* (1985) 3 CMLR 667. Gaming machines were installed on ferries operating between Denmark and West Germany, the tax authority sought to apply VAT on the gaming machines.

40   Subsection (a) section (1) of 28g of the Sixth Directive.

41   Terra, Ben (1998) *The Place of Supply in European VAT* (Kluwer Law International p 56).

42   Terra, Ben (1998) *The Place of Supply in European VAT* (Kluwer Law International).

43   Terra, Ben (1998) *The Place of Supply in European VAT* (Kluwer Law International).

compliance with the tax rate and other requirements of the national VAT regime in the country where it carries out its supplies.[44]

Subsection (e) of section (2) contains regulations with regard to intangible services, such as consultancy, advertising or data processing. Following from their nature, these services are primarily supplied to taxable entities. Therefore, they are presumed by the Sixth Directive to be more susceptible to cross-border delivery.[45] Consequently, in case the central businesses of the supplier and the recipient are not established within one member state, the section stipulates as the place of supply the location of the recipient's business in line with the destination principle. This rule is coexistent with the application of the 'reverse charge' method under which the liability to account for and pay the tax is imposed on the business recipient. The supplier in turn does not have to charge VAT, that is, the supply is zero-rated in the country of origin.[46]

This rule together with subsection (b) of section (1) of Article 21 makes it clear that the reverse charge also applies to cases where a taxable person established outside the Community renders services to a European taxable person.[47] The subsection also applies to instances where the customer, regardless of its tax status, is established outside the European Community. Within its scope, Article 9(2)(e) of the VAT Directive achieves competitive neutrality for EU suppliers as well as non-EU suppliers. This solution naturally follows from the underlying theory of taxing in the country of consumption. When the recipient of the services listed in subsection (e) section (2) is a final consumer residing in the Community, the supply is taxable according to Article 1. The general rule also applies to cases where the supplier and business recipient both have their central businesses within the borders of one member state.[48] In order to avoid the possibility of double or non-taxation of these services following from the possible manipulation of the place of business or residence,[49] the Sixth Directive contains a provision complementing the preceding place of supply rules. According to section (3) of Article 9, national VAT systems may deem the place of 'effective use or enjoyment' of these services as the place of supply, when this place is different from the location of the supplier or the consumer, and when these different rules lead to different results as to the applicability of the Sixth Directive. By limiting the application of the 'country of destination principle' to a few types of services, Article 9(2)(e) subjects some online business models to

---

44 Terra, Ben (1998) *The Place of Supply in European VAT* (Kluwer Law International at p 75).

45 Terra, Ben (1998) *The Place of Supply in European VAT* (Kluwer Law International pp 155-156).

46 The current position is that supplies of e-commerce supplied from outside the EU are taxed according to the destination principle, with the origin principle applying in respect of EU suppliers. However this is about to change as it is proposed that VAT on services is to be made payable in the country of consumption instead of the supplier's country.

47 Terra, Ben (1998) *The Place of Supply in European VAT* (Kluwer Law International p 157).

48 Terra, Ben (1998) *The Place of Supply in European VAT* (Kluwer Law International at p 155).

49 Terra, Ben (1998) *The Place of Supply in European VAT* (Kluwer Law International at pp 220-222).

taxation while exempting others. This is not consistent with the EU's objective to provide uniform rules for the sourcing of all types of online transactions. What is more, the current catalogue of services covered by Article 9(2)(e) is too vague to produce clear-cut answers as to the categorization of B2B transactions.

As discussed earlier, the internet makes it possible for more intangible goods and services to be delivered to customers by suppliers who have no physical presence in the country where consumption takes place. As a result, both businesses and consumers may be able to structure their buying patterns to avoid paying the VAT. Most of the problems seem to follow from the application of section (1) to B2C transactions more often than would be justified by the requirement of taxing at the place of consumption.[50] Section (1) was designed to deal with national supplies, based on the already mentioned assumption on the model of transactions to consumers. Despite the fact that this underlying assumption has been set aside by the explosion in the number of private internet users, section (1) remains applicable in many cases in lack of a better rule. A better rule would be one of the special place of supply rules. However, the special rule is applicable only in case of services specifically listed therein and under special conditions stipulated thereby. This interpretation has been acknowledged by the ECJ in the *Dudda-case*: 'in every situation, the question, which arises, is whether it is covered by one of the instances in Article 9 (2); if not, it falls within the scope of Article 9 (1)'.[51] It follows that those new types of services[52] or traditional services supplied in a novel constellation fall under the general rule.[53]

The over-application of the general rule leads to two undesirable consequences. The first of these consequences appears within the Community. Namely, taxing at origin leads to the misallocation of VAT revenues among the member states under a given pattern of consumption.[54] Moreover, it has the potential of distorting consumption patterns and intra-Community competition by offering the opportunity

---

50 Commission of the European Community (1998) DG XXI, 'Interim Report on the Implications of Electronic Commerce for VAT and Customs', XXI/98/0359-EN, April 3, 1998 at p 11; Commission of the European Community (1999) 'Harmonization of Turnover Taxes', Working Paper of see Directorate General XXI, June 8, 1999 at p 13.

51 Case C-327/94 *Dudda v Finanzamt Bergisch Gladbach* (1996) ECR I-4595 Recital 21.Cited in Terra, Ben and Kajus, Julie (1992) *Value Added Tax in the EC after 1992* (Kluwer Law and Taxation Publishers.

52 New types of services include, for example, web hosting, web design, online arbitration services, collocation services. Commission of the European Community (1999) 'Harmonization of Turnover Taxes', Working Paper of see Directorate General XXI, June 8, 1999 at p 14; Eriksen, Nils and Hulsebos, Kevin (2000) Electronic Commerce and VAT – An Odyssey towards 2001 in VAT Monitor July/August, at p 138.

53 Commission of the European Community (1999) 'Harmonization of Turnover Taxes', Working Paper of see Directorate General XXI, June 8, 1999 at p 14; OECD, Report on the Turku Conference, at p 17.

54 The Commission, in the 'Explanatory Memorandum' to the Proposal, has denounced application of the origin principle with regard to cross-border supplies as distorting competition within the Community for the Sixth Directive, cited in Terra, Ben and Kajus, Julie (1992) *Value Added Tax in the EC after 1992* (Kluwer Law and Taxation Publishers, Place of Supply in the EC, at p 55).

to consumers to make their purchases from member states with the lowest VAT rates.[55] It is obvious that, for example as Coppers and Belgium pointed out for a Swedish consumer who has the choice to order supplies from Luxembourg with a VAT of 15 per cent, the decision to do so will be of no small consequence keeping the fact in mind that the Swedish rate is 25 per cent.[56] The other undesirable consequence of the overwhelming application of the general place of supply rule occurs on the global playing field. In cases of inbound international supply of services not listed by the special rules, the place of supply is deemed to be outside of the Community. Therefore, supplies of these services to European businesses or consumers are not taxable under the Sixth Directive.[57] If the country of the supplier does not have a VAT regime, the service remains untaxed. On the other hand, outbound international supply of the same services is taxable in both cases.[58]

Consequently, under the general rule, situations may occur where European businesses charge VAT on their supplies to European and third-country customers, while third-country suppliers provide services without tax both within the Community and internationally. This situation is disadvantageous to European businesses on both the European and the international playing field.[59] Moreover, it potentially distorts the pattern of transactions for two reasons. First, this situation induces European businesses to supply their services through websites set up in third countries to retain their competitiveness.[60] Second, due to the difference in prices, final consumption will shift to VAT-free international supplies.[61]

The application of the *lex specialis* might cause some problems with regard to digital deliveries. Namely, the place of supply of services listed under subsection (c) of section (2) might be different from the place of receipt or consumption when supplied digitally.[62] This possibility follows from the special features of digital

---

55 Terra, Ben and Kajus, Julie (1992) *Value Added Tax in the EC after 1992* (Kluwer Law and Taxation Publishers).

56 Coopers and Belgium, Lybrand (1998) 'Does Cyber-Commerce Necessitate a Revision of International Tax Concepts?' *International Bureau of Fiscal Documentation* at p 5.

57 Commission of the European Community (1998) DG XXI, 'Interim Report on the Implications of Electronic Commerce for VAT and Customs', XXI/98/0359-EN, April 3, 1998 at p 7; Explanatory Memorandum, at 6; Schenk, Alain and Oldman, Oliver (2000) *Value Added Tax*, 26 (Transnational Publishers ed., 2000) p 489; David Hardesty (2000) 'EU Proposes New Taxes on Non-EU Sellers in E-Commerce Tax News'.

58 Commission of the European Community (1998) DG XXI, 'Interim Report on the Implications of Electronic Commerce for VAT and Customs', XXI/98/0359-EN, April 3, 1998 p 7; Explanatory Memorandum, at p 6.

59 Commission of the European Community (1998) DG XXI, 'Interim Report on the Implications of Electronic Commerce for VAT and Customs', XXI/98/0359-EN, April 3, 1998.

60 OECD, Report on the Turku Conference, at p 18; Hinnekens, Luc (1998) 'The Challenges of Applying VAT and Income Tax Territoriality Concepts and Rules to International Electronic Commerce' 26 Intertax at p 57.

61 OECD, Report on the Turku Conference, at p 18; Hinnekens, Luc (1998) 'The Challenges of Applying VAT and Income Tax Territoriality Concepts and Rules to International Electronic Commerce' 26 Intertax at p 57.

62 Harmonization of Turnover Taxes, Working Paper of Directorate General XXI, June 8, 1999. at p 14.

delivery. For example, in cases of receiving music or motion pictures online in one of the member states, performance thereof might have occurred previously outside of the EC or in another member state.[63] When the place of performance does not coincide with the place of receipt or consumption there is chance of non-taxation or misallocation of VAT revenues. It is important to note here that some of these problems were addressed by the European Community with the adoption by the European Council of Directive 2002/38/EC applying VAT on digital products.[64]

6.2.2.3 Consumer and Tax Status, Place of Effective Use and Enjoyment Determination of the tax status of the recipient when necessary is facilitated by the VIES.[65] In the process of verifying the registration number, the supplier and the tax authorities make use of traditional media for the exchange of information. However, in the sphere of e-commerce, the transaction between the supplier and the customer is taking place online. Clearly, the inability of the VIES system to provide online, real-time verification prevents the suppliers from fully exploiting the comfort and speed offered

63 Harmonization of Turnover Taxes, Working Paper of Directorate General XXI, June 8, 1999. at p 14.

64 The preference for the origin principle may well be a matter of high principle for some in the Commission but it is interesting to note that many of the perceived problems with the destination system concerned the practicalities of enforcement. The reason for the need to move to a transitional system was that the destination system required physical border controls to make it work. The elements of the destination system that remain are policed by the mutual exchange of information which is possible where both supplier and recipient are VAT registered, even if they are resident in different member states. Given these identified difficulties it seems surprising that the EU believes that a system involving a non-EU supplier where the services by their very nature cannot be subject to border controls will be enforceable. For more detailed discussion refer to Chapter 8.

65 The VIES was established by Council Regulation on administrative cooperation in the field of indirect taxation (EEC) No 218/92 OJ L024 01/02/1992 p 1. It is a common system for the exchange of information on intra-Community transactions for tax purposes. It was set up for the supplementation of the Sixth Directive after the introduction of Council Directive amending the Sixth Directive with a view to the abolition of fiscal frontiers (91/680/EEC) OJ L376 31/12/1991, The EC has set a VAT registration threshold of euro 100,000 a year for distance sales of tangible products to consumers and unregistered traders within the EU; If sales exceed the threshold, remote EU vendors must register in the EU member state where the customer is located and collect the VAT of that state, in keeping with a true destination based system. This registration system does not apply to tangible services, which are taxed on an origin basis. Sales between registered traders in the EU are based on a reverse charging system, in which exports are zero-rated16 and purchasers are expected to self-assess the tax of the destination member state. Thus, remote vendors must be able to differentiate between sales to registered traders and sales to others. The VAT Information Exchange System (VIES) was set up to enable companies to easily confirm the validity of VAT registration numbers and to allow tax administrators to monitor and control the flow of intra-EU trade. On June 14, 2002, the Commission introduced the online validation service. The online service, which any member of the public can now access free of charge, allows checking of the databases of VAT registration numbers which each Member State maintains as part of the VIES. DN IP/02/864 'VAT: New Commission On-Line Validation Service Saves Time And Costs For Businesses', Brussels, 14th June 2002. I shall discuss VIES further in Chapter 8 (online registration).

by electronic trade and therefore potentially hampers the pursuance of such activity.[66] The location of the customer is required to be verified in order to determine the tax status of the customer. For business purchasers, if the verification process through the VIES system was successful, the location of the business can be inferred from the registration number.[67] In the case of final consumers, there is no such supplementary system.[68] When dealing with the consumer during a physical sale, VAT was either paid on the spot or it was a requirement to let the supplier know the address of the customer for the purposes of delivery and payment. When ordering online, consumers use electronic mail for communicating with the seller but e-mail addresses do not provide enough information about the real, physical residence of its user.[69]

The most evident means of finding out their location is to ask the customers to self-declare this information.[70] However, unless underlining this practice with reliable verification, buyers might feel tempted by the anonymity of online trade to disclose false information.[71] Despite the diverse efforts to solve this problem, there is still no reliable and feasible means of identifying and locating consumers in lack of voluntary compliance.[72] For the time being suppliers might verify disclosed data by using the credit card information requested from the purchaser previous to the conclusion of the contract.[73]

In the case of services listed under section (2) subsection (e) of Article 9, establishing the fact that the location of the customer is inside or outside of the Community is not always satisfactory. The VAT systems of member states that implemented the derogation provided by section (3) of Article 9 require the determination of the place of effective use or enjoyment of these services. If such place is different from the location of the customer, it should be considered as the place of supply to realize taxation at consumption. In the light of the difficulties with establishing the location of the customer, the conclusion that determining the place of effective use or enjoyment is almost impossible within the digital environment may

---

66 Explanatory Memorandum, at p 7; Jenkins, Peter (1999) 'VAT and Electronic Commerce: The Challenges and Opportunities', *10/1 VAT Monitor* On June 14, 2002, the Commission introduced the online validation service. The online service, which any member of the public can now access free of charge, allows checking of the databases of VAT registration numbers which each Member State maintains as part of the VIES. DN IP/02/864 'VAT: New Commission On-Line Validation Service Saves Time And Costs For Businesses', Brussels, 14th June 2002. I shall discuss VIES further in Chapter 8 (online registration).

67 Subsection (d) section (1) of Article 22 of the Sixth Directive.

68 I shall discuss more on this in Chapter-8 while discussing the Technological constraint in implementation of collection mechanism for VAT on digital sales.

69 Working Paper - 1998, at pp 7, 14; Eriksen and Hulsebos (2000) at p 139; Jenkins (2001) at p 4.

70 OECD (2001) Consumption TAG Report, at p 13.

71 It is possible, by disclosing false information as to their location that consumers can save significant VAT costs thanks to the differences in the VAT rates of the Member States and third countries. Coopers (1998) at p 128.

72 OECD (2000) Technology TAG Report The conclusion of the Report is that work should be continued in the field of defining reliable technology for jurisdictional identification.

73 Explanatory Memorandum, at p 8.

be drawn without a long analysis.[74] The evasive nature of e-commerce necessitates new tools for detecting the flow of digital services through the internet.[75] In the lack of reliable technological means, the supplier remains dependent upon the information revealed by the customer voluntarily.

The invoice is the heart of the EU VAT system.[76] It records information necessary for the proper taxation of a transaction and it is a prerequisite for claiming VAT deduction.[77] In order for businesses to be able to realize the advantages, following from paperless transactions, the facilitation of electronic invoicing is crucial.[78] Such an idea, however, is absent from the Sixth Directive. Although Article 22[79] allows member states to accept this type of invoice, this is clearly an inadequate basis for uniformly implementing electronic invoicing in the Community. Member state legislation already in place in this matter is often solely focused on domestic electronic invoicing.[80] In addition, such rules are generally accompanied by cumbersome administrative requirements.[81]

The above factors have a negative impact on the fulfilment of obligations under the Sixth Directive. On the other side of the coin, these practical deficiencies also undermine the effective enforcement of VAT rules in lack of voluntary compliance.[82] The pieces of information needed by the supplier for compliance are also essential for the tax authorities for enforcement.[83] To recognize and fight infringement of VAT rules, they need to identify the transaction and gather data on the supplier and the customer. It is obvious that without re-tailoring the rules of the Sixth Directive according to the needs of e-commerce, and finding the necessary technological means for their implementation, value added taxation of electronic trade remains

---

74 Jenkins, Peter (1999) 'VAT and Electronic Commerce: The Challenges and Opportunities', *10/1 VAT Monitor* at p 4.

75 OECD (2000) Technology Technical Advisory Group (TAG), '*Report on Tax and e-Commerce*', December.

76 Tait, Alain A (1988). *Value Added Tax*, 3 (International Monetary Fund Ed., Washington, D.C., 1988) at p 279 Final Report on Invoicing, PriceWaterhouse Coopers on behalf of the European Commission, August 23, 1999 at p 4.

77 28h of the Sixth Directive.

78 Explanatory Memorandum, at p 4; Taxation Framework Conditions, p 5; OECD, Report on the Turku Conference, p 12; David Hardesty, 'EU Proposes Electronic VAT Invoices in E-Commerce', Tax News 1, 4, Nov. 19. 2000 website: http://www.ecommercetax.com; Eriksen, Nils and Hulsebos, Kevin (2000) Electronic Commerce and VAT – An Odyssey towards 2001 in VAT Monitor July/August p 138.

79 Subsection (c) section (3) of Article 22 of the Sixth Directive.

80 Eriksen, Nils and Hulsebos, Kevin (2000) Electronic Commerce and VAT – An Odyssey towards 2001 in VAT Monitor July/August, p 138.

81 Eriksen, Nils and Hulsebos, Kevin (2000) Electronic Commerce and VAT – An.

82 Tait (1998) pp 315-317; Working Paper - 1998, p 13; OECD, Report on the Turku Conference, pp 9-11; OECD, Taxation Framework Conditions, p 6.

83 Tait, Alain A (1988). *Value Added Tax*, 3 (International Monetary Fund Ed., Washington, D.C., 1988).

vague and incidental.[84] The steps taken by the Community to find viable solutions are detailed in Chapter 8.

6.2.2.4 VAT Liability of ISP An ISP gives a private user an IP address to call to gain access to the web. The access services provided by ISPs can be regarded as the other side of the coin of e-commerce, since companies would be unable to sell their products if nobody was able to connect through to their servers. However, internet access is not the only service provided by ISPs. ISPs spend a considerable amount purchasing the technology and hardware to enable them to offer access to the internet. ISPs also provides ancillary services, which include e-mail, website hosting, the assignment of domain names and the creation and maintenance of chat groups and news groups. If these services were provided in exchange for payment then the ISP would be liable to collect VAT from customers according to the rates applicable in each member state. In the supply of products by ISPs there is nothing which can be tangible; hence, for the purposes of the Sixth Directive, such transactions shall be deemed to fall under the definition of services and not of goods.

ISP provides 'access to global information networks' and therefore, by virtue of Section 9(2e) of the Sixth Directive, belongs to the definition of telecommunication services following an amendment in June 1999. The amendment to Article 9 by means of 199/59/EC was partly inspired by the fact that non-EU companies offering telecommunication services to Community residents had an advantage over their EU competitors. Before the coming into force of 1999/59/EC, ISP services were taxed under the general rule found in Section 9(1) under which the place of establishment of the ISP, or rather the country where it would be registered for VAT, would be considered as the place of supply for taxation purposes. To address the competitive disadvantage suffered by European ISPs, particularly about services rendered to non-taxable individuals and enterprises, in March 1997 the Council allowed member states to derogate from the rule under section 9(1).[85] In order to protect the commercial interests of ISPs operating within their national territories, in a matter of a few months all member states had implemented 97/203/EC,[86] but it was evident that a more clear and definitive answer to this question should be sought, thus laying the grounds for the introduction of the definition of telecommunication services under the exceptional rules to the place of supply of services in section 9(2). With the enactment of 1999/59/EC, the scope of these derogations, an interim arrangement, was fulfilled. Finally, 1999/59/EC opted for the reverse charge system through section 21(1b) for telecommunication services introduced by section 9(2e). By means of the new section 9(4) EU members could change the determination of the place of supply by virtue of Section 9(3b) in the case of services to non-taxable persons in the EU by non-EU ISPs when such services are 'effectively used or enjoyed' in Community territory. Section 9(3b), however, can only be applied in the

---

84 Tait, Alain A (1988). *Value Added Tax*, 3 (International Monetary Fund Ed., Washington, D.C., 1988).

85 European Council Decision of the 17th March 1997, 97/203/EC.

86 Taylor, Dominic and Ogely, Adrian (1997) 'VAT and Telecommunications in the European Union: An Update', *Tax Notes International*, 3rd November 1997.

case when the services were supplied to 'non-taxable persons established'[87] and not necessarily to EU residents only. This presents a much wider net for VAT taxation including non-Europeans using or enjoying ISP services of non-EU providers while passing through Community territory. It was argued that also this could potentially have double-taxation implications.[88]

As regards ISPs, a final point raised by Kabisch could be discussed.[89] If an ISP provides ancillary services besides access to a 'global information network', such as separate special support services which are charged separately, the tax rate that should be levied is determined with reference to the rate that would be applicable for the principal element in the transaction, in this case access to the internet. Some types of paid-for support services would clearly not fall under the definition of 'telecommunication services'. An analogy could be drawn with an ECJ judgment[90] in which the court decided that the place of supply of a composite service was to be determined according to the place of supply of the dominating supply in the transaction. Following this line of thought therefore ancillary services supplied by ISPs in connection with the access to the internet offered to customers should be viewed as falling within the parameters of the definition of telecommunication services, albeit indirectly.

6.3 Sales Tax

The earlier discussion about the nature of the retail sales tax provides an overview of the constitutional restraints that are imposed on its implementation in relation to out-of-state sales. US jurisprudence regarding federal taxation of out of state transactions began to emerge in 1941. In that year, a Mexican radio station broadcasting from near the US border persuaded US federal courts that it should not have to pay US income tax on its advertising revenues obtained from US customers.[91] In accordance with that precedent, the US taxing authority (Internal Revenue Service (IRS)) refrained from taxing mail-order sales originating outside the US and directed to US customers.[92] Presently, for instance, a US state may not levy a sales or use tax on a mail-order transaction originating from outside the state and directed to a customer within that state, unless the tax is imposed on the in-state customer rather than on

---

87 Sec. 9 (4) Sixth Directive.

88 Lejeune Ine, Vanham Bart, Verlinden Isabelle, Verbeken Alain (1988) 'Does Cyber-Commerce Necessitate a Revision of International Tax Concepts?' Part I, *European Taxation*, 1998, volume 38, p 4.

89 Kabisch, Volker (2000) '*Tax Aspects of International Electronic Commerce*', Electronic Commerce Legal Issues Platform, ECLIP - Esprit project 27028.

90 Faaborg-Getling Linien A/S, European Court of Justice Case C-251/94, which dealt with the provision of catering services on board a passenger ferry.

91 *Piedras Negras Broadcasting Co. v. Commissioner*, 43 B.T.A. 297 (1941) *nonacq.* 1941-1 C.B. 18, *aff'd*, 127 F.2d 260 (5th Cir. 1942).

92 Treas. Reg. § 1.864-4(b) Example (3) as cited by David Thomas (2001) 'Current Issues in US State and Federal Taxation of Electronic Commerce', Paper presented at 16th Annual Conference BILETA (2001).

the out-of-state seller.[93] The practical problems with identifying those customers and collecting the tax are so great as to discourage almost all effort to impose the tax.

This virtual US tax exemption for out-of-state mail-order transactions can easily by extended by analogy to e-commerce; similarly, state and local taxing authorities found that out-of-jurisdiction e-commerce sales are not as readily taxable as counterpart mail-order sales. Indeed, one could view e-commerce sales as simply a form of mail-order sales initiated through electronic media and completed by the same couriers as used in mail-order sales. If one questions why taxing authorities should show so much interest in e-commerce sales when they have been basically content to leave mail-order sales untaxed, 'the answer is that, potentially, the dollar volumes involved in e-commerce transactions far surpass anything we have seen in the area of mail order sales'.[94] In addition to potentially enormous volumes of traditional transactions in tangible goods, electronic sales of digitized products and services will soon explode and, in addition, could easily be so positioned as to originate outside the United States. Hence, the use of the internet changes only the magnitude of sales transactions; it does not change fundamental complexities arising out of constitutional restraint on enforcement and collection of sales/use taxes.[95]

The discussion in this chapter is not about the issues of fixing the sales and use tax structure, namely, how the states' sales tax regimes can be modified to accommodate massive amounts of economic activity conducted through e-commerce by remote service providers engaged in non-traceable transactions from unidentifiable locations. Instead, the focus of the discussion is on how these restraints limit the states' ability to apply their laws to e-commerce – although consideration of various forms of federal legislation to restrain, expand or otherwise prescribe the way in which states may or may not tax e-commerce are important questions. However, it is more of political will that can obtain national sales tax simplification, rationalization and restructuring with constraint on local sales tax authority that would reduce the compliance burden by giving remote vendors a near uniform sales tax landscape. This is particularly relevant if there has to be a speedy outcome from the state legislative processes. Attaining consensus across states on what the rationalized model will be and then getting individual state legislatures to adopt that 'reform' structure would promise a long struggle and would radically change how state and local tax policy is designed in the US. In principle, an in-state consumer stands nothing to gain by making an out-of-state or interstate purchase free of sales tax because they will ultimately have to pay an identical use tax when they use, store or consume the property or services in their home state. If, for example, a Washington resident was to go to Oregon to purchase a car, he would pay no sales tax in Oregon, which does not have sales tax, but he would pay use tax in Washington, equal to the sales tax that he would have paid had he bought the car in Washington.

In theory, this basic sales/use tax regime also applies to transactions in e-commerce in the same manner that it applied to transactions in the above example

---

93 *Quill Corp. v. North Dakota*, 504 U.S. 298 (1992).

94 Fleming, J. Clifton (2000) 'Electronic commerce and the State and Federal Tax Bases, Brigham *Young University Law Review* at pp 1, 4.

95 Thomas, David (2001) 'Current Issues in US State and Federal Taxation of Electronic Commerce', Paper presented at 16th Annual Conference BILETA (2001). www.bileta.ac.uk.

involving the car. Thus, when a book is bought from Amazon.com by a buyer in Georgia, there is no question that the buyer owes a Georgia use tax equal to the sales tax that he would have paid had he bought the book in a bookstore in Georgia. There is, however, one significant difference between the purchasing from Amazon.com and the purchase of the automobile as described above. With respect to the purchase of the car, the state has a practical means of requiring the purchaser to pay the use tax namely, collecting it upon registration of the vehicle. However, states do not require consumers to register books they purchase. Consequently, unless the consumer voluntarily remits the use tax on the purchase from the out-of-state vendor, the state has no practical means for collecting the use tax unless it can require the out-of-state vendor to collect the use tax in the same way that it relies on the in-state vendor to collect the sales tax. E-commerce facilitates transactions between remote vendors, thus increasing the likelihood of non-payment of state sales and use taxes.

The three factors used in determining whether sales tax liability exists for retail transactions creates problems in an e-commerce environment. First, regarding the content or substance of the transaction, e-commerce retail transactions mainly involve intangible goods and services. Some intangible goods, like music, which are normally transferred through a tangible medium, such as a compact disk, can also be delivered through an electronic medium and avoid classification as a tangible good. As long as sales taxes are only imposed on tangible goods, this shift in the type of goods being purchased results in an erosion of the sales tax base and a subsequent reduction in sales tax revenues. The second factor, is *situs*, the location of the transaction. This is readily determinable in a transaction where a consumer goes to a retail store and purchases a tangible good; the taxing jurisdiction is the state where the vendor's store is located. However, if a resident of one state purchases a tangible good from an online catalogue on the internet from a vendor in another state, to be delivered to someone else in still another state, then it becomes unclear in which state the transaction occurred. A physical concept such as *situs* does not adapt easily to a non-physical environment like the internet. Third, the concept of nexus deals with whether the taxing jurisdiction has sufficient connection to the transaction to have the power to impose a sales or use tax on the transaction or collection duty on an out-of-state vendor.[96] Since the buyer and seller need not have direct contact to engage in a transaction over the internet, a nexus problem may develop if the buyer and seller reside in different jurisdictions. The 'US problem' with consumption taxation of e-commerce has a similarity with remote selling. However, for the US and other countries having sales tax, the magnitude of the problem is more for e-commerce because of the taxation requirements of digital products. Hence, in the following sections I will be discussing these three issues.

6.3.1   Sales Tax Nexus

'Nexus rules' determine whether a state can tax income or require remote vendors to collect sales tax or pay business activity taxes and act as a connection between the vendors and state such that subjecting the vendor to the state's sales tax rules

---

96 Adams, Sally (1997) *Danger: Internet Taxes Ahead*, Taxes Sept. pp 495, 501.

is neither unfair to the vendor nor harmful to interstate commerce. These two requirements of fairness to the vendor and no impediment to interstate commerce stem from the US Constitution respectively, from the Due Process Clause and the Commerce Clause. In *Bellas Hess*,[97] the Supreme Court ruled that, under the Due Process and Commerce Clauses, states could not impose a requirement to collect use taxes on the sale of tangible products on a 'seller whose only connection with customers in the State is by common carrier or the US mail'.[98] The Court did not distinguish between the Due Process and Commerce Clauses as foundations for this decision. However, in 1992, in *Quill*, partially overturning the decision in *Bellas Hess*, the Court clarified that the Due Process and Commerce Clauses provide two distinct tests.[99] The first of these requires only some definite link, some minimum connection, between a state and the person, property or transaction it seeks to tax. Thus, the Court said,

> If a foreign corporation purposefully avails itself of the benefits of an economic market in the forum State, it may subject itself to the State's in personam jurisdiction even if it has no physical presence in the State...Comparable reasoning justifies the imposition of the collection duty on a mail-order house that is engaged in continuous and widespread solicitation of business within a State.[100]

It is thus unlikely that the Due Process Clause will provide protection from taxation for a business that purposefully seeks to exploit the market of a state, if its contacts with the state are more than minimal. By comparison, the Commerce Clause requires 'substantial nexus'; mere 'minimum connection' or economic presence in the state is not enough to establish taxable nexus. The distinction between the two nexus requirements is potentially crucial. The Constitution gives Congress the power to regulate interstate commerce; it does not give it the power to override the constitutional guarantee of due process. Mail-order houses had argued that the physical presence test of *National Bellas Hess* applied to the Due Process Clause as well as the Commerce Clause. If the Supreme Court had accepted this view, it would have made it impossible for Congress to enact legislation requiring out-of-state vendors to collect use taxes. The Court pointedly said that, 'Congress is now free to decide whether, when, and to what extent the States may burden interstate mail-order concerns with a duty to collect use taxes'.[101]

E-commerce, especially in content, raises interesting questions of Due Process nexus. Presumably, a vendor must intend to exploit the market for nexus to exist. However, what demonstrates intent? Does the mere fact of advertising over the internet establish intent to exploit a market, and thus nexus, since it is common knowledge that the internet has no geographic boundaries? At least one decision, not involving taxation, *Bensusan Restaurant Corp. v King*,[102] suggests that it may not. In

---

97　386 U.S. 753 (1967).

98　386 U.S. 753 (1967) p 758.

99　*Quill* 504 US at p 306.

100　*Quill* 504 US at p 306.

101　386 U.S. 753 (1967).

102　937 F. Supp. 295 (S.D.N.Y. 1996), aff'd, 126 F.3d 25 (2d Cir. 1997).

this case, the court said that placing an advertisement on a website did not establish jurisdiction in the courts of the state where the advertisement is seen. Is intent to market in a given state established unless the vendor explicitly says that it will not make sales to the state and in fact does not (in which case there would be no issue of liability for collecting use tax, in any event)? Such a rule would be workable and perhaps appropriate in the case of tangible products, where shipping addresses can be used to determine destination of sales. However, how does the vendor implement the intention not to market electronic content in a given state, since there is generally no way of knowing where sales of content are received?[103] McLure Jr[104] is of the view:

> On balance, I am inclined to agree with Bruce Reid of Microsoft who has said (presumably referring to both income and sales taxation): The Quill ruling reduced the Due Process threshold for nexus to such a de minimis level that the protection afforded by that Clause is a virtual myth. Consequently Internet and online service providers, as well as those selling content via the Internet or private online networks, cannot depend upon the Due Process Clause for any protection against state taxing authorities.[105]

In the light of the preceding discussion, it should come as no surprise that the application of federal constitutional nexus principles to e-commerce is fraught with difficulties. The proposition of finding out if a company has physical presence in a particular state is far more difficult than it seems. For instance, in the case, *America Online v Johnson*, a Tennessee court decided that America Online did not have sufficient physical presence to create nexus, despite the fact that it owned and leased to others a substantial amount of telecommunications equipment in the state. This case has demonstrated the uncertainty involved in determining nexus.

However, under the non-electronic physical presence standard for nexus, an online vendor that has employees, equipment or property in a state will have physical presence that establishes nexus in that state.[106] An in-state office or warehouse is not necessary. Even if a business lacks physical presence in a state, that state may be able to claim taxing jurisdiction through the activities of a third party that are attributable to the business. This principle has been established in *Scripto v Carson*,[107] where the Supreme Court held that an out-of-state seller could be required to collect and remit use tax in Florida based on orders that its independent sales representatives solicited for it in that state. The presence of sales representatives, and of technicians performing occasional repair or installation services, and providing on-site technical advice or support will create nexus for both corporate income and sales and use tax purposes. Similarly, a computer software company that sends its representatives into

---

103   McLure, Charles E. Jr (1997) 'Taxation of Electronic Commerce: Economic Objectives, Technological Constraints, and Tax Laws', *Tax Law Review*.

104   McLure, Charles E. Jr (1997) 'Taxation of Electronic Commerce: Economic Objectives, Technological Constraints, and Tax Laws', *Tax Law Review* at pp 322-31.

105   McLure, Charles E. Jr (1997) 'Taxation of Electronic Commerce: Economic Objectives, Technological Constraints, and Tax Laws', *Tax Law Review* at pp 322-31.

106   *Quill* and *National Bellas Hess*.

107   362 US 207 (1960).

a taxing jurisdiction to conduct business activities, such as the design and creation of a home page, may also be creating nexus in the taxing jurisdiction. If an employee is permanently located in a state, and works out of a business location of the taxpayer, the employee likely causes nexus. It should not matter what the employee does, so long as the employee works out of the employer's business location. However, as Hardesty[108] has pointed out, there is some disagreement on this question. Most of the decided cases relating to employees in a state involved salespeople. Some have concluded that only a salesperson in a state can cause nexus. However, there seems to be little support for this notion.

Some level of negligible or '*de minimis*' physical presence in a state will not create taxable nexus. States have taken a very narrow view of what amount of physical presence will be considered negligible to safeguard their revenue base. The New York Court of Appeals, in *Orvis Co. Inc. v Tax Appeals Tribunal*[109] and *Vermont Information Processing Inc. v Tax Appeals Tribunal*,[110] held that sporadic visits by a mail-order company's sales personnel for the purpose of soliciting orders from retailers, and occasional visits by a computer software and hardware developer's personnel to install software, train employees and correct difficult or persistent problems, were sufficient to satisfy the substantial nexus standards of *Quill*.[111] Questions regarding '*de minimis*' activities arise not only with the presence of employees in the taxing jurisdiction but also with the location of certain kinds of property in the state. For instance, a taxing authority may argue that a computer company that sends dozens or hundreds of floppy disks containing its software into a state may be deemed to have sufficient physical presence in the state.

The same questions about '*de minimis*' physical presence also arises with property in the state. In *Quill*, the out-of-state mail-order company also licensed software to some of its North Dakota clients. According to the Court, 'although title to a few floppy diskettes present in a State might constitute some minimal nexus ... [the Court] expressly rejected a "slightest presence" standard of constitutional nexus'. Accordingly, the Court concluded that Quill's licensing of the software in that case did not meet the substantial nexus requirement of the Commerce Clause. Because the Court did not define what would constitute more than a few disks, some states may argue that the presence of a substantial amount of licensed software creates substantial nexus under *Quill*. In this regard, it is unclear whether states will make a distinction between 'canned' (that is, not customized) software that is licensed

108   Hardesty, David (2001) Sales *Tax and E-Commerce*, EcommerceTax.com 2001 Edition.

109   *Orvis Co. Inc. v. Tax App. Tribunal, Docket* No. 138 (N.Y. Ct. App. 1995).

110   Vermont Info. Processing Inc. v. Tax App. Tribunal, Docket No. 139 (N.Y. Ct. App. 1995).

111   In Orvis, employees who did not live in New York visited customers at least 12 times over a 3-year period. In Vermont Information Processing, the taxpayer's personnel made 30 to 40 trips into New York over a period of 3 years. The New York Court of Appeals held that while a physical presence of the vendor is required under Quill Corp., it need not be substantial. Rather, the presence must be more than a 'slightest presence' and may be manifested by the presence in the taxing state of the vendor's property or the conduct of economic activities in the taxing state performed by the vendor's personnel or on its behalf.

(essentially 'sold') to in-state customers for personal use or consumption, differently from software sent to the customer to permit the remote vendor to commercially exploit the market state where the customer is located. It is common practice for online service providers to ship thousands of 'free copies' of software to consumers around the country so that the consumers can begin to access their commercial online services or information databases.

A Tennessee court, in *AOL v Johnson*[112] held that, there is 'no authority that supports a finding of substantial nexus based upon the physical presence in the state of equipment leased to, or leased by, the taxpayer'. The court meant, by this statement, that personal property alone does not result in nexus. Indeed, the court seemed to work from the assumption that nothing short of employees, agents or business premises in a state will cause nexus. The case has received some negative comments with some experts wondering if the court simply got it wrong and the appeal is pending. However, the surprising result of this case highlights the difficult determinations in applying the physical presence rule. For companies engaged in e-commerce, the question of personal property will most likely come up in the context of the presence of a company's equipment, web server, or inventory in a state.

One of the primary issues in relation to online sellers is the effect of a web server in a state, since every company needs a server and it is often necessary to use a server in another state. The issue is important enough that several states have issued guidance on the effect of a web server in a state. CCH,[113] a major publisher of tax related materials, in a recent survey of state tax administrators, asked whether nexus would result from the presence of a website on a third party web server in the state. Results showed that while a number of states did not answer the question, or indicated that they were not certain of the answer, no state said yes: websites arguably are electronic advertising or intangible property. However, some states may argue that those sites that are located on a third-party computer server in the state, and for which a monthly or annual fee is paid, constitute leases of tangible personal property (for example, the computer). As such, they could be said to create a physical presence in the state. This is particularly problematic because vendors with websites may not know the location of the computer server(s) they 'rent' from third parties. Hence, under the theory of attributional nexus, even if a corporation *itself* does not have sufficient presence in a taxing jurisdiction, the jurisdiction may assert nexus by attributing the presence or activity of another person or entity to the corporation.[114] In the same CCH survey, tax administrators were asked if nexus would result where a website was hosted in a state and the hosting company also provided services, such

---

112 *America Online, Inc. v. Johnson*, Docket: No. 97-3786-III, Tenn. Chancery Ct. (3/13/01).

113 Sales and Use Taxation of E-Commerce – State Tax Administrator's Current Thinking with CCH Commentary, (CCH, 2000) As cited in Hardesty (2001).

114 *Scripto Inc. v. Carson 362 U.S. 207 (1960)* The U.S. Supreme Court held that Florida could require an out-of-state seller to collect use tax on orders solicited on its behalf in Florida by independent contractors. Scripto, the seller, which was based in Georgia, had 10 independent contractors conducting continuous local solicitation in Florida and forwarding the resulting orders from Florida to Georgia for shipment of the ordered goods.

as design, advertising or order processing. A number of states answered this question 'yes'.

Where a company operating retail stores in many states opens a website to serve the same customer base, and the website is owned and operated by the same corporation, it would likely have sales tax nexus in any state in which a store is located. However, by using separate corporations, a company apparently hopes to use '*entity isolation*' to avoid nexus. Whether it will work in the case of any particular online company depends entirely on the actions of the two corporations, and especially on services performed on behalf of each other. According to the '*entity isolation*' strategy, a retailer with stores in most states avoids nexus for its online company by placing it in a separate corporation. If the corporation operating bricks and mortar stores is operated separately from the one operating the online store, the presence of the stores in the states should not be attributed to the online company and will not cause it to have nexus. For this strategy to work, the corporations must be operated separately. For instance, the physical stores cannot be agents or representatives of the online store.

Merchandise returns can result in nexus, where a store is shown to be the agent or representative of an online company. Indeed, in California's assertion of nexus against Borders Online, returns of merchandise to Borders Books stores are reportedly the primary basis for the state's claim.[115] Whether nexus exists because of merchandise returns, however, depends on the motivation of the store in accepting returns. A store may be acting on behalf of the online company in accepting returns, in which case nexus is likely to result. However, if it acts on its own behalf, it cannot be said to be the agent or representative of its affiliate and there is no nexus.

It is important to note that with substantial online sales there will be need for a convenient way to return unwanted goods. What can possibly be more convenient than a local store affiliated with the online company; especially if the online store tells the buyer exactly where to find a local store? One of the reasons why states lost their bids to assert nexus in the mail order cases was that the numbers of returns to stores were relatively minor. The courts cited the inconsequential financial impact of the returns, though they did not give an indication of the effect of a larger number of returns. Hence, a court may find that a large number of returns indicate, on its face, that a store is the agent or representative of an online company. Even if the court does not accept this view, a large number of returns accepted by a local store can act as an indication that the store is part of an integrated retailing operation that includes its online affiliate, and that the store is not acting on its own behalf. On its face, this appears a strong argument that stores act on behalf of the online affiliate in accepting returns, thus creating an agency or representative relationship, and nexus.

Unlike most products, sellers of computer products require a relatively high amount of service. Because it would not be practical for customers to ship a computer to an out-of-state seller for servicing, sellers often arrange with local companies to provide their customers with warranty services. The Multistate Tax Commission (MTC) argued that contracting with a third party to provide warranty repair services

---

115 Hardesty, David, 'California to Assert Nexus Against Online Bookseller', EcommerceTax.com (7/22/01) (http://ecommercetax.com/doc/072201.htm).

in a state creates substantial nexus. An important point in analyzing nexus from in-state warranty services is the fact that often it is the manufacturer, not the seller that provides the warranty. If warranty services are arranged for and paid for by the manufacturer, it seems doubtful that warranty service providers can be agents of the seller. This should let most online sellers off the nexus hook, since they do not sell their own branded products, and do not offer their own warranties.

Hence, it is clear under existing law that states possess the constitutional power to impose a tax on the in-state use, storage or consumption of digital or non-digital products sold over the internet. It is equally clear, however, that states lack the constitutional power to require a non-physically present, out-of-state vendor of digital or non-digital products to collect use taxes that a state may seek to impose on the in-state use of such products. As a consequence, any use taxes that a state may impose on internet-related transactions involving non-physically present vendors are likely to go uncollected, just as use taxes that are legally due on many interstate mail-order sales currently go uncollected.

6.3.2   Taxable Sales

Current state sales taxes were designed for a world in which local merchants sold manufactured products. Thus, they apply primarily to *tangible* products; in general, they do not apply to *services*, except on a selective basis, or to *intangible* products. The first and most obvious issue in the debate over taxation of e-commerce is whether sales taxes should apply to services and intangible products delivered over the internet (and presumably to similar products delivered in other ways). If not, the burgeoning of e-commerce raises a second question: how to distinguish taxable and exempt products in a world in which traditional distinctions are becoming blurred? If the tax net is widened to include services and intangibles, a third question arises: whether these products should be exempt when bought by businesses? The answer to the question would be relatively straightforward if the states had made a deliberate legislative decision in this regard. That they have failed to do so is due not to any Hamlet-like ambivalence over the question 'To tax or not to tax?' ,but rather to the simple fact that, in many instances, states have not addressed the question specifically.[116] Moreover, since much of e-commerce involves the sale of services rather than the sale of goods, transactions in e-commerce are likely to be characterized as non-taxable unless they fall within one of the selective categories of services that the states, to a varying extent, have decided to tax. Consequently, taxpayers and tax administrators are forced to struggle with the question of whether transactions in e-commerce fall within the definition of taxable 'telecommunications services', 'data processing services', 'information services'.[117]

Hence, the starting point to determine the tax consequences of transactions in the electronic marketplace is to properly characterize the transaction based on its

---

116   Hellerstein, Walter (1997) 'State Taxation of Electronic Commerce', Symposium on Taxation and Electronic Commerce, *Tax Law Review*, at pp 431-505, *Spring* 1997.

117   Hellerstein, Walter (1997) 'State Taxation of Electronic Commerce', Symposium on Taxation and Electronic Commerce, *Tax Law Review*, at pp 431-505, *Spring* 1997.

particular facts and circumstances. This determination is critical because differing characterizations could result in different applications rules that could in turn produce different tax obligations. The most significant feature of existing state sales tax laws insofar as they apply to e-commerce is that state sales taxes generally apply only to sales of tangible personal property and not to sales of services or of intangible property. While a few states tax a wide range of services (including information and data processing services) and most states tax some services (for example, public utility services and hotel and motel services), most state sales taxes are limited to sales of tangible personal property. What impact does the limitation of most states' sales taxes to transfers of tangible personal property have on the application of the current sales tax law to e-commerce? Essentially, what it means is that most states currently seek to tax a very small portion of the transactions that constitute e-commerce. As mentioned before, if e-commerce is divided into two broad categories, the transactions involving sales of tangible personal property acquired over the internet and transactions involving sales of digital products, it is only the first category of transactions that generally falls within the scope of the states' sales taxes. Thus, if someone buys a book from Amazon. com by clicking on its website or a laptop from 'Dell.com' by clicking on its website, it is clear that most states will seek to tax that transaction. On the other hand, if someone buys software over the internet or orders plane tickets over the internet, trades stocks over the internet or enrols in distance learning courses over the internet, none of these transactions would be subject to tax in the overwhelming majority of states.

Four states, New Hampshire, Oregon, Montana and Alaska, do not impose a state level sales tax. The remaining states tax most tangible goods and exempt most services from tax. However, state-by-state differences in what is taxable and what is not make it necessary for sellers to research each state's tax rules for the status of their particular products or services. Hence, the issue that arises in this context is the meaning of the terms 'tangible' and 'intangible'. Thus, 'tangible personal property' is defined as personal property, which may be seen, weighed, measured, felt or touched or is in any other manner perceptible to the senses.[118] The statutory definition incorporates a common law (and common sense) concept of 'tangible' as perceptible to the senses. Thus, tangible personal property does not include contractual rights and other property rights, even though such rights are evidenced by documentation, which is tangible. This is consistent with the traditional common law concepts of tangible property in which the rights actually possessed are not the physical documentation but the 'intangible' contractual rights and property rights represented by the documentation. The statutory distinction between 'tangible' and 'intangible' has been relatively easy to apply in the sales tax arena. Advances in technology, however, have done much to blur this line between tangible and intangible property. The most troubling aspects of taxation of products sold online is the uncertainty regarding the taxability of digitized products, such as books, software, videos or recorded music. Currently, 17 states tax content that is transferred by electronic means.[119] These jurisdictions tax a variety of

---

118   'Tangible personal property' does not mean stocks, bonds, notes, insurance, or other obligations or securities.

119   These states include Alabama, Arizona, Colorado, Connecticut, Idaho, Iowa, Louisiana, Maine, Mississippi, New Mexico, New York, Ohio (for commercial purposes

electronic services, including, e-mail, data processing, computer bulletin boards, news and weather reports, credit reports, airline reservations, cable television, fax services, the sale of software, 900 phone number services and the like.[120] However, they differ in their approach to taxing online sales. Some tax them as part of the sales tax imposed on tangible personal property; others tax them as a separate category of services.[121]

The question presented is whether products that are clearly tangible personal property when delivered physically remain tangible personal property when delivered electronically. Is text displayed on a computer screen really the same thing as a printed book? Is a movie downloaded to a computer hard drive really the same as a video rental? The answer is not obvious. For instance, mass produced (canned) software purchased online and delivered through the mail is clearly tangible personal property and is usually subject to sales tax. Is the same software tangible personal property when a customer downloads it from a website? State tax authorities have struggled with the characterization of downloaded software for a number of years. When can sale of software be regarded as tangible and when can it be regarded as intangible?

A sale of shrink-wrapped, or canned, software is usually considered a sale of tangible personal property. Almost all states subject sales of canned software to sales and use tax. On the other hand, custom software is usually considered as not tangible property. In most cases, it is considered as 'services'. In states that subject services to sales tax, custom software may be taxable. Shrink-wrapped or canned software delivered electronically may be considered the sale of tangible or intangible property depending on the state in which it is sold. States have different rules regarding the liability to collect sales and use tax on canned software, which is transferred electronically. In Texas, the sale of canned software is taxable as tangible personal property contained on 'electronic media'. Pennsylvania taxes the sale of a licence to use canned software as a sale of a computer service. Illinois taxes the electronic transmission of software. Illinois has specific language in its sales and use tax rules that say the sale of 'canned software' is subject to sales tax regardless of how the software is transferred. Some states do not tax electronically transferred software, even though they may tax the same software sold in a box. California, for example, will not tax canned software if it is transferred electronically from the seller's place of business, to or through the purchaser's computer, and the purchaser does not obtain possession of any tangible personal property, such as storage media, in the transaction.

---

only), South Dakota, Texas, Utah and Washington. A survey of the various taxes that states impose on the internet can be found at Vertex Inc.'s web page, Internet Taxation & State Summaries <http://www.vertexinc.com/taxcybrary20/cybertax_ channel/taxtable&uscore; 72> The District of Columbia also levies such a tax.

120   Frieden, Karl and Porter, Michael (1996) The Taxation of Cyberspace: State Tax Issues Related to the Internet and Electronic Commerce, Part V, (visited October 2001) <http://www.caltax.org/andersen/contents.htm> or in 14 State. Tax Notes 1363 (Nov. 14, 1996) at part-II.

121   Frieden, Karl and Porter, Michael (1996) The Taxation of Cyberspace: State Tax Issues Related to the Internet and Electronic Commerce, Part V, (visited October 2001) <http://www.caltax.org/andersen/contents.htm> or in 14 State. Tax Notes 1363 (Nov. 14, 1996) at part-II.

The status of new products, such as electronically delivered books, videos and music has yet to be addressed by the states. The New York Department of Taxation and Finance, while replying to a petition for an Advisory Opinion from Universal Music group wanting to know if it, the music provider, is subject to sales and consumer's use tax when an item from its music catalogue is downloaded via the internet, relied upon the *New York State Tax Law*, sections 1105(a) and 1110(a)(A) for the proposition that 'sale of digitised music recordings over the internet constitutes the sale of intangible property and is not subject to sales or compensating use tax'. This opinion cited *The Stock Market Photo Agency, Inc,*[122] which held that the taxpayer's 'receipts from the electronic transfer of digital photographic images over the internet represents receipts from the sale of an intangible and are not subject to sales tax'. The Department also ruled that information and entertainment services are not considered taxable services when distributed via the internet. It is generally accepted that tax rules for the sale of intangible products and services should be the same as those for other goods – that means of delivery should not govern tax treatment. Such 'technologically neutral' taxation would not treat the sale of a paperback book any differently than the sale of a digitized book, to use one oft-cited example. On the other hand, determining which products are functionally equivalent is a tricky proposition.

States exempt most services from sales and use tax. However, what happens when property and services are bundled together? Should the result be different, depending on whether an online service 'transmits' information for others or 'sells' the same information? Even states that employ an inclusive definition of transmission must distinguish between transmission and sale of information content. The fact that online service providers (and ISPs) typically (and increasingly) 'bundle' transmission services and content further complicates matters. (At times, if non-taxable services are bundled with taxable services, both are subject to tax, unless the prices are stated separately.) Even if it were practical to unbundle charges for various services, results would probably be extremely arbitrary and subject to manipulation and thus litigation. In Texas, the term 'taxable information service' refers to information that is gathered or compiled and made available to the public. Services unrelated to the information gathered (for example, training) are not part of the taxable base of the information service. If one fee is paid for the information, as long as more than five per cent of the total charge is taxable as information services, all the charge is taxed.[123] This rule can be avoided by breaking out the taxable and non-taxable portions of the service at the time of the transaction. For practical reasons, sellers may be unwilling or unable to do this. In Alabama, amounts paid to rent equipment for receiving data are taxable but electronically transmitted information is not.[124] If the rental charges for such

---

122   The Stock Market Photo Agency, Inc, Adv Op Comm T&F November 12, 1999, TSB –A-99(48)S.

123   Frieden, Karl and Porter, Michael (1996) The Taxation of Cyberspace: State Tax Issues Related to the Internet and Electronic Commerce, Part V, (visited October 2005) <http://www.caltax.org/andersen/contents.htm> or in 14 State. Tax Notes 1363 (Nov. 14, 1996) at part-II.

124   Frieden, Karl and Porter, Michael (1996) The Taxation of Cyberspace: State Tax Issues Related to the Internet and Electronic Commerce, Part V, (visited October 2005)

equipment were not billed separately, the entire amount (including the information services) would be subject to sales tax. Thus, bundled services may sometimes present a sales tax problem for businesses providing such services.

One effective means of taxing online content is to impose the sales tax on the furnishing of the information itself. This approach avoids the difficult issues of whether the transmission of content is tangible or intangible property but it creates other problems. For example, some states impose a sales tax on 'computer services' whereas others impose it on 'information services'. In the former states, it is unclear if someone who downloads information online has also bought a taxable computer service. Similarly, it is equally unclear whether someone who purchases software online has purchased a taxable information service. The simplest way to avoid such definitional problems with the confusion and litigation sure to ensue is to adopt a broad definition of 'services' that are subject to sales tax, which includes telecommunications services, information services, data processing services and other similar online services.[125] Even if the definition of taxable services were broad, however, it would not eliminate uncertainties and avoid disputes. Thus, Texas treats charges for providing educational classes and testing over the internet as non-taxable, but separate charges by the internet service provider for maintaining the web page and for processing student information are treated as taxable data processing services.[126] There appears to be no consistent principle for taxpayers.

6.3.3   Situs *of the Sale*

Sales and use taxes are dependent on the location of the customer. Without it, it would be difficult to determine which should receive the tax revenue. The question of where a taxable sale of electronic products or services occurs is difficult because the transactions frequently have meaningful contacts with more than one jurisdiction. For example, an information provider in State A employing a server in State B can sell access to its database through an ISP or OSP in State C to a customer in State D who is billed by a financial intermediary in State E. Which states can, do and should tax the sale?[127] Hence, the third issue: whether a taxable sale has taken place. In most cases, sales have as their *situs*, the location of the customer, and the customer's state is then free to impose a tax on the sale. When e-commerce is involved, the *situs* of the sale becomes more difficult to pinpoint because the transactions are often multi-

---

<http://www.caltax.org/andersen/contents.htm> or in 14 State. Tax Notes 1363 (Nov. 14, 1996) at part-II.

125   Frieden, Karl and Porter, Michael (1996) The Taxation of Cyberspace: State Tax Issues Related to the Internet and Electronic Commerce, Part V, (visited October 2005) <http://www.caltax.org/andersen/contents.htm> or in 14 State. Tax Notes 1363 (Nov. 14, 1996) at part-II.

126   Frieden, Karl and Porter, Michael (1996) The Taxation of Cyberspace: State Tax Issues Related to the Internet and Electronic Commerce, Part V, (visited October 2005) <http://www.caltax.org/andersen/contents.htm> or in 14 State Tax Notes 1363 (Nov. 14, 1996) at part-II.

127   Hellerstein, Walter (1997) 'State Taxation of Electronic Commerce', Symposium on Taxation and Electronic Commerce, *Tax Law Review*, at pp 431-505, *Spring* 1997.

state in nature. The service provider may be in one state, the customer in another and the computer used in the transaction in still another. Therefore, multiple states may assert sales tax jurisdiction over one transaction. While the rule for sourcing product sales seems simple enough, it is not. For instance, where goods are shipped from one state to another the delivery-state rules says that the sale is taxable in the state to which the goods are shipped. However, some states have determined that, based on the terms of the sale, the sale is taxable in the state from which the goods are shipped. In these cases, the state from which the goods are shipped and the state to which the goods are delivered may both attempt to tax the sale.

Let us consider that 'ABC.com' is an online seller of clothing, with operations only in Tennessee. For customers outside Tennessee, 'ABC.com' does not collect sales or use tax. 'ABC.com' deposits goods in the mail for delivery to its customers. The statement on its order form says 'ABC.com' takes no responsibility for loss or damage to goods once placed in the mail. Tennessee has ruled, in a case with facts similar to this, that these terms of sale cause title to the goods to pass in Tennessee, when the taxpayer deposits the goods in the mail. This makes the sale taxable in Tennessee, though delivery, use and consumption take place in another state. While Tennessee insists on taxing the sale, the delivery state may determine that the sale is subject to its own use tax, thus resulting in double tax unless a sales tax credit is available.[128]

Like Tennessee, other states have their own rules for determining whether a product is taxable in the state. California, for instance, would not consider a sale taxable in the state even if it is delivered to the state, so long as the product is present in the state for only a short period of time and substantial use of the product takes place elsewhere. Problems can also arise when a single product is used in multiple states. For instance, a multi-state organization may purchase software and install it on a server in one state with the intention of enabling business locations in other states to simultaneously access the software. The question is, in which state should sales or use tax be collected and in which states should use tax be self-assessed?

Further, sales of services, especially online services used in multiple locations, present real problems for both sellers and buyers and there are not enough rules to tell what state should tax a multi-state sale of online services. A major problem is the potential for confusion between the location where an online service is billed and where it is used. For instance, buyers may use services in different locations, accessing services from different computers. Alternatively, one buyer may purchase a service but allow someone at a different location to use the service. Hardesty[129] argues that this mismatch of the use and billing locations for non-business consumers is not likely to be a problem since most use by an individual consumer is likely to take place at the consumer's billing address. More serious is online access to a service or digital product by multi-state businesses. For instance, it is likely that an online service will be billed to one location but be used in other locations – possibly

---

128   Tenn. Dept. of Revenue Ltr. Rules 00-29, 26 TAM pp 11- 46 (Sep 1, 2000) as cited in Hardesty (2001).

129   Hardesty, David (2001) Sales *Tax and E-Commerce,* (EcommerceTax.com 2001 Edition).

in states other than the state to which the service is billed. A mismatch in this case can cause serious problems for both the buyer and the seller and even for the states. The seller may collect too little or too much tax while the buyer may be subject to double taxation.

One possible approach to taxing e-commerce is to treat the state in which the predominant use of the service occurs as the state of *situs*. Services sold to locations outside the state would not be subject to sales tax. By analogy, most states treat the place where a telephone call originates or is received by the customer (and charged to the customer's address) as the *situs* of the call. A minority of states treat the location of the provider, not the customer, as the *situs* of the telephone call. In some cases, apportionment of sales tax may be appropriate if consumers use the services in multiple states. The difficulty with apportionment is that the sales tax (unlike the income tax) is concerned with one transaction, a taxable sale at retail. Apportioning income among states at year-end is common for multistate businesses, but apportioning sales tax is unusual for a tax that is determined by the transaction itself. Although making the apportionment calculation is possible, it is difficult and counterintuitive. Moreover, states may be able to impose a sales tax on the entire transaction even if only a part of the service occurred in state. With respect to telecommunications services, a state in which an interstate call originates or terminates may tax the customer's purchase of that call as long as the call is charged to a service address or paid by someone within the state that seeks to impose the sales tax.

However, it may not be difficult to determine the location of the buyer who uses a credit card to purchase a service or digital product. This is because almost all sellers demand complete address information from buyers to help combat credit card fraud. Identification of the location of buyers will become difficult if use of anonymous digital cash becomes widespread. Sellers are unlikely to need any information about buyers that make purchases using anonymous digital cash and buyers will not willingly provide that information. Without even a billing address, online sellers will have no certain way to determine in what state a sale takes place. The obvious solution is to have Congress enact a law authorizing state imposition of use tax collection obligations on out-of-state vendors selling to in-state customers over the internet or online. This is not very likely to happen. However, a discussion of how a state sales tax that is economically neutral and relatively easy to comply with would be structured is worthwhile and would indicate how extant sales taxes deviate from that system and the effects of those deviations. E-commerce can be a catalyst for long-overdue action by state and local governments applicable to sales by other types of remote (out-of-state) vendors. In Chapter 10, I shall revisit some of the issues discussed here with some alternative answers.

6.4   Conclusion

The avoidance of double taxation should be first and foremost among the general principles governing consumption taxation because the prospect of double taxation would do more to inhibit the development of electronic commerce than any other tax factor. Non-discrimination, neutrality and the avoidance of excessive compliance obligations should be recognized as guiding principles for indirect taxation. In particular, e-commerce, regardless of whether the method of delivery is online or offline, should not be subject to higher (or lower) tax rates or subject to greater compliance burdens than conventional commerce. Additionally, e-commerce imports should not be taxed at higher rates than domestic e-commerce. The guiding principles should include simplicity, encompassing the concepts of uniform classifications, clarity and consistency of rules and minimization of compliance burdens and costs and protection of the tax-base.

Chapter 7

E-Commerce: Loss of Revenue and Erosion of the Tax Base

Introduction

All taxes, direct and indirect, under whatever jurisdiction, must operate within a global economy. Where e-commerce presents its challenge to the established order is in the fact that it exists in a borderless virtual world whereas conventional wisdom regulates commerce and taxation through international treaties, which rely heavily on the establishment of the location of each of the transacting parties. The most fundamental threat to the international tax system posed by e-commerce is the erosion of the worldwide tax base and in consequence the damage to economic balances, economic efficiency and competitive fairness among vendors. The base of tax means the thing, transaction or the amount on which the tax is raised. All taxes have bases, which mean the precise boundary of what is taxed as distinct from what is not taxed. Each tax will have a limited tax base, the limits being of two kinds: the general limits on the kind of tax and specific exceptions. Clearly, the wider the tax base of a tax, the more revenue it will collect. The more exceptions that are allowed, the smaller the return from the tax. This chapter will look into the causes of the revenue loss but also will look into the potential disproportionate effect on developing countries. There is limited published work that attempts to evaluate the effect e-commerce would have on developing countries. The lack of systematic data sources means that on many occasions, the evidence is potentially suggestive. However, this chapter will not make quantitative estimates of the revenue losses from e-commerce; rather it will look into what would be the effect if e-commerce is treated differently from other trade in respect of income tax or consumption tax.

7.1   Tax Base

An important aspect of the tax system is the tax base. The base of a tax means the thing, transaction or amount on which the tax is raised. Identifying the *correct* tax base is the most important step in structuring a tax. The concept of a tax base refers to the specific measure to which a tax is applied. For direct taxes, which are levied on persons rather than commodities or transactions, the three main types of tax base are income, consumption and wealth. Among those who have considered the subject, each of these taxes has been suggested as a proxy for the benefits received from civil society.[1]

---

1   Duff, David G(2005) Private Property and Tax Policy in a Libertarian World: A Critical Review, 18 *The Canadian Journal of Law & Jurisprudence* 23.

Each tax will have a limited tax base, the limits being of two kinds: the general limits on that kind of tax and specific exceptions. Clearly, the wider the tax base of a tax, the more revenue it will collect. Hobbes suggested that the benefits that individuals enjoy under a commonwealth are best measured by what they consume.[2] In more recent times, consumption taxation has also been favoured on the basis that it is neutral between saving and spending and therefore affects individual choices less than most other kinds of tax. On this basis, some have argued that consumption taxation is most compatible with libertarian principles.[3]

Notwithstanding these arguments for consumption, wealth taxes, others regard income as the best measure of the benefits received from civil society.[4] According to Adam Smith, for example, 'the subjects of every state ought to contribute towards the support of the government ... in proportion to the revenue which they respectively enjoy under the protection of the state'.[5] Graeme Cooper makes a similar argument,[6] reasoning that 'the creation, maintenance and protection of a society within whose markets individuals can pursue and accumulate income and wealth, is a benefit derived from government',[7] that this benefit 'manifests itself in the income derived by individuals',[8] and therefore that 'income is an appropriate measure of the benefit'.[9] Although libertarians may question the extent to which the state is responsible for the creation and maintenance of income and wealth, many appear to accept these arguments in favour of personal income taxation.[10] Epstein, for example, endorses the idea of a broad-based or comprehensive income tax on the basis that 'everything of value protected by government is subject to taxation'.[11]

Westberg argues that the dynamic effects of e-commerce have been forgotten when it comes to taxation. Instead of worrying only about lost tax bases, we must also look for opportunities for new sources of revenue.[12] E-commerce generates new businesses, new products are being created and new markets are being opened.

---

2   Hobbes, Thomas *Leviathan* (1651), ed. by C.B. Macpherson (Harmondsworth, UK: Penguin, 1985).

3   Duff, David G (2005) Private Property and Tax Policy in a Libertarian World: A Critical Review, 18 *The Canadian Journal of Law & Jurisprudence* 23.

4   Duff, David G (2005) Private Property and Tax Policy in a Libertarian World: A Critical Review, 18 **The Canadian Journal of Law & Jurisprudence** 23.

5   Adam Smith, *An Inquiry into the Nature and Causes of The Wealth of Nations* (1776), ed. by Edwin Cannan (Chicago, IL: University of Chicago Press, 1977) Vol. 2.

6   Duff, David G (2005) Private Property and Tax Policy in a Libertarian World: A Critical Review, 18 *The Canadian Journal of Law & Jurisprudence* 23.

7   Cooper, Graeme S. (1994) 'The Benefit Theory of Taxation' 11 *Aus. Tax Forum* 397 at p 493.

8   Cooper, Graeme S. (1994) 'The Benefit Theory of Taxation' 11 Aus. Tax Forum 397 at p 493.

9   Cooper, Graeme S. (1994) 'The Benefit Theory of Taxation' 11 Aus. Tax Forum 397 at p 493.

10 Duff, David G(2005) Private Property and Tax Policy in a Libertarian World: A Critical Review, 18 *The Canadian Journal of Law & Jurisprudence* 23.

11 Epstein, Richard A.(1985) *Takings: Private Property and the Power of Eminent Domain* (Cambridge, MA: Harvard University Press, 1985) at p 60.

12 Westberg, Bjorn (2002) *Cross-border Taxation of E-Commerce*, IBFD p 225.

Traders who generate new business will increase the tax base for income tax purposes. The value of their supply of goods or services will be the basis for the taxation of consumption. If e-commerce is used for cross-border transactions, the tax base will be increased in the country where the business activity takes place as well as in the country of consumption. In the first country this will increase the base for income tax purposes and in the other the base for consumption taxation. For a given country this may result in a change from one form of taxation to another. From a global point of view, it means a further step in the direction of more consumption taxes and possibly fewer income taxes.[13]

7.2   Erosion of the Tax Base

The tax reforms implemented over the past several years were, at least in part, a response to the need to enhance economic performance. However, they can also be seen as a response to the perception that tax bases were being eroded due to high tax rates, increased avoidance and evasion and the migration of taxable income to low-tax jurisdictions.[14] Erosion of the tax base could take the form of legal avoidance or illegal evasion. If we begin with the assumption that government could, in principle, tax all income earned in the society, then choosing not to do so indicates some preferences being granted for some reason. The level of erosion of the tax base varies across countries. One type of tax base erosion that has attracted considerable attention and concern is the geographical mobility of tax bases. Table 7.1 offers a qualitative summary of mobility past, mobility present and mobility future, as it affects major elements of the tax structure.

E-commerce has increased the scope for tax avoidance and evasion through the choice of location of economic activity. The risk of tax base erosion in connection with e-commerce is seen in two different situations, one of which focuses on the changed pattern of doing international business and the other one relates to the ease of offshore establishment.[15] Business functions could be moved to low-tax jurisdictions and bank accounts and other financial assets could be held offshore. There are numerous examples of avoidance reducing tax revenues and, in some cases, tax rates have had to be reduced in order to stem the revenue losses. Empirical research also supports the view that taxation influences international investment flows, although some studies find little effect.[16] The inability to tax e-commerce, on the one hand, and non zero tariffs on physical cross-border trade, on the other, may hasten the pace of substitution of the mode of transactions to virtual commerce as it becomes technically feasible to do so. This in turn will further erode the tax base on tradable goods.

---

13 Westberg, Bjorn (2002) Cross-border Taxation of E-Commerce, IBFD pp 225-226.

14 OECD Economic Outlook (1998) 'Forces Shaping Tax Policy' Monday, June 1, 1998.

15 Westberg, Bjorn (2002) Cross-border Taxation of E-Commerce, IBFD p 234.

16 Leibfritz, W.J. Thornton and A. Bibbee (1997) 'Taxation and Economic Performance', OECD Economics Department Working Papers, No. 176.

Table 7.1   Qualitative Summary of Mobility of Tax Base

Tax Base Item	Mobility in 1970	Mobility in 2000	Mobility in 2030
Wage and salary income	Low	Low	Moderate
Consumption of goods	Low	Moderate	Moderate
Consumption of services	Low	Low	Moderate
Investment income	Low	Moderate	High
Corporate profits	Low	Moderate	High

The effect of geographical mobility on tax bases raises a number of concerns. The first is the extent to which the overall revenue-raising power of governments has been constrained. However, there is reason to believe that the pressures stemming from geographical mobility of tax bases would increase in the years ahead. As in this case, improvements in e-commerce would make the base for consumption taxes more geographically mobile and harder to trace. In general, the location of economic activity depends on many factors, of which taxation is one. An equilibrium taking account of these factors is established that, to date, has both constrained tax rates in many cases while still allowing substantial variability of tax rates across jurisdictions. However, this equilibrium is likely to shift as, *inter alia*, institutions and technologies develop. The challenge for tax policy would be to respond to these developments in order to fund needed government expenditures with a tax system that has minimal economic distortions. In view of the trend towards globalization and the threat posed by the geographical mobility of tax bases, a significant part of the response would necessarily involve greater international cooperation. It is increasingly difficult for individual countries to manage their tax bases in the face of these forces and, in particular, some tax practices have led to harmful and destructive cross-border 'tax competition'.[17]

Cockfield[18] argues that a narrow definition of a tax base creates problems for desired neutral tax treatment between traditional economic activity and activity involving digital goods. Consider the sale of a tangible good such as a print book; if a consumer purchases a particular copy of a book then nobody else has the right to buy that particular book.[19] In contrast, the sale of a digital book will not constrain the potential consumption of this product due to the ability to reproduce the digital book at a much much lower cost. The digital book is hence non-rival in consumption.[20]

---

17 OECD Economic Outlook (1998) 'Forces Shaping Tax Policy' Monday, June 1, 1998.

18 Cockfield, A.J. (2002) The Law and Economics of Digital Taxation: Challenges to Traditional Tax Laws and Principles, 56 *Bulletin for International Fiscal Documentation* 606.

19 Cockfield, A.J. (2002) The Law and Economics of Digital Taxation: Challenges to Traditional Tax Laws and Principles, 56 *Bulletin for International Fiscal Documentation* 606.

20 For discussion on rival versus non-rival goods, see Richard Musgrave, *Fiscal Functions of the Public Sector*, in 'Defining The Role Of Government: Economic Perspectives On The State' 1, 3 (Queen's University School of Policy Studies 1994) (noting that private goods are normally rival in consumption unlike public goods which are non-rival in consumption).

What are the tax implications that result from the fact that digital goods are non-rival goods? From a tax theory perspective, consumption is normally equated with using up economic resources. However, non-rival resources are not actually used up in any real sense if they can be replaced without cost. Still, this does not appear to pose any problems outside of theory because consumption tax systems generally only tax the purchase of goods and services in the market rather than actual consumption.[21] However, the way companies would price non-rival digital goods may present new tax policy challenges. Information economists assert that the non-rival nature of digital or information goods changes, at least to a certain extent, the way that companies should price their goods and services.[22] The potential near costless and infinite reproduction and supply of a digital good abolishes the supply side resource constraints that help to determine an appropriate equilibrium price. As a result, it is thought that they would appear to engage in selective pricing of their digital goods.[23] A digital product could be priced higher for commercial actors and lower for individual consumers. What happens when the price of a digital good drops to zero?[24] Under economic theory, companies would set the price of most goods at the marginal cost of production. Assuming the company cannot differentiate its product (for example, bundle the information good with a value-adding service) then, it has been noted, that price competition should eventually lead to a price of zero for many information goods.[25] However, companies would be able to generate a return on the digital goods through indirect means such as advertising. In these circumstances, the jurisdiction of consumption misses consumption tax revenues[26] (which are applied as a percentage of the sale price) because of its inability to tax and would further cause erosion of the tax base.

The discussion in Chapter 5 raises the question as to what effect these changes brought by e-commerce would have on direct taxation. As most commentators have suggested, there is serious concern on the part of the fiscal authorities in various countries that e-commerce has the potential for significantly eroding their income tax base. The potential sources for this erosion could be summarized as follows:

---

21 Warren, Alvin (1980) 'Would a Consumption Tax Be Fairer Than an Income Tax?' 89 *Yale Law Journal*, pp 1081-1084.

22 Hal R. Varian (1998) 'Markets For Information Goods' as cited in Cockfield, Arthur J (2002) The Law and Economics of Digital Taxation: Challenges to Traditional Tax Laws and Principles, 56 *Bulletin for International Fiscal Documentation* 606.

23 Cockfield, A.J. (2002) The Law and Economics of Digital Taxation: Challenges to Traditional Tax Laws and Principles, 56 *Bulletin for International Fiscal Documentation* 606.

24 Cockfield, A.J. (2002) The Law and Economics of Digital Taxation: Challenges to Traditional Tax Laws and Principles, 56 *Bulletin for International Fiscal Documentation* 606.

25 Hal Varian (1996) Differential Pricing and Efficiency, First Monday online journal available at http://www.firstmonday.dk/issues/issue2/different/.

26 Cockfield, A.J. (2002) The Law and Economics of Digital Taxation: Challenges to Traditional Tax Laws and Principles, 56 *Bulletin for International Fiscal Documentation* 606.

- Out-of-state businesses that in the past needed to have a PE to do business with their customer base within the taxing jurisdiction would no longer need to have one.
- It would be easier for domestic businesses to migrate to tax havens. This could be aggravated by tax competition from less developed nations seeking to attract capital by offering lower tax rates to businesses that migrate there.
- The general increase in cross-border trade would create increased opportunities for business to exploit the discontinuities between various national tax systems.
- The ability of financial institutions to create derivatives that can arbitrage tax discontinuities has been facilitated by the speed and flexibility supplied by the new technologies.
- The geographic flexibility of e-business may make it difficult to identify the residence of a particular business, particularly in those jurisdictions that base the residency of a business entity not on where it was formally organized, but where its 'seat of management' or 'principal place of business' is located. The cliché is that the global business may be resident everywhere and nowhere.
- To the extent that the internet permits business transactions to go forward without the intermediation of significant financial and commercial institutions, a major source of compliance and enforcement-related information reporting might be lost.
- The unprecedented nature of some forms of e-commerce and e-products creates definitional ambiguity. By blurring the distinctions between categories – tangible versus intangible, goods versus services, license versus sale – that have different tax rules, tax authorities feel compelled to draw finer and finer bright-line distinctions separating those categories. The result of this process is the creation of discontinuities in the system whereby transactions that differ in only minor details of form and not at all in substance have dramatically different tax consequences. Such discontinuities lead to uneconomic tax-motivated behaviour on the part of some taxpayers and a strong perception of general unfairness and arbitrariness in the system among the rest.

Tax avoidance and tax evasion have always been problems with which tax authorities have had to contend.[27] There have always been certain businesses that choose to locate their corporate headquarters or to conduct their business activities from states that offer low or no tax regulation. The cost of conducting offshore activities, however, can often outweigh the benefits of tax relief. For this reason, tax avoidance and evasion opportunities of this nature had been generally exploited by only a small number

---

27 A subtle, but conceptually useful distinction to make is that between tax *evasion* and tax *avoidance*. The latter is a situation in which the taxpayer makes use of all available loopholes and ambiguities in the statutes, including leaving the country altogether (if there is no control on capital flows). Tax avoidance is entirely legal (if not always moral), and is therefore also referred to as tax *planning*. Tax evasion is illegal and carries with it the possible imposition of penalties if caught. Thus, if there existed capital controls (on outflows) and capital flight were done through the parallel market, that would be tax evasion.

of businesses, as the majority were unable to support such schemes. Traditionally businesses had been deterred from locating in tax haven countries by other problems inherent to these countries. Although they could offer appealing tax rates, businesses also had to consider other characteristics that might not be conducive to maintaining a globally competitive business. Such characteristics include climate or geography that is not suitable to the particular business, high labour costs, low education levels, poor infrastructure, political instability or a small consumer base. However, a business operating through a commercial website would not be subject to the same physical constraints as a 'bricks and mortar' business. For example, a small- or medium-sized business in the UK could easily post its website with a host who operates from a tax haven country. In such a case, it would still be able to access profitable consumer bases while having its financial information hidden by the privacy protection that tax haven countries often provide.

The fact that an e-commerce business would not require any physical presence other than a server would also make the problems identified above irrelevant. It would not only be affordable for virtually any e-commerce business to locate in a tax haven but all of the incentives for doing so would remain while the disincentives would gradually disappear. Therefore, when business is conducted on the internet, the problem of tax competition reaches a new level of complexity. For some businesses, many of the physical constraints on tax evasion or avoidance remain. However, with digital goods and services that can be transacted entirely over the internet, states cannot rely on physical controls to prevent or deter tax avoidance and evasion. These and other tax issues have been the subject of discussion in a number of reports. Of particular importance in this respect are the reports produced by the US Treasury Department and by the OECD, not only because of the positions advocated in these reports but also because of the significance of the institutions behind them. What would the implications for tax revenues be of exempting e-commerce? Non-compliance with the payment of transactional taxes has real revenue implications for governmental entities. Since transactional taxes are a significant revenue source, an increase in non-payment would result either in an increase in other taxes or a contraction of government functions and/or programmes. Further, an increase in the ability to avoid or evade transactional taxes could adversely affect the local tax base. What will be the impact on the local tax base and economy of redirecting commerce from local bricks and mortar businesses to remote e-commerce businesses because of the perceived tax savings?[28]

7.2.1   *Erosion of the Tax Base: Reduction in Total Tax Income*

One of the main fears of policy-makers and tax collectors regarding e-commerce is the risk of losing tax revenue when trade is redirected from taxable commodities to – presumably – untaxable activities.[29] Much has been said about the importance of

---

28   Ward, Burke T and Sipior, Janice (2004) To Tax or Not To Tax e-Commerce: A United States Perspective, *Journal of Electronic Commerce Research*, Vol. 5, No. 3.

29   Rasmussen, Sandemann (2004) On the Possibility and Desirability of Taxing E-Commerce Working Paper No. 2004-08, Department of Economics, School Of Economics and Management - University of Aarhus.

e-commerce to state tax revenues, with particular attention to the effects that interstate sales have on the ability of states to impose and collect consumption taxes. To what extent should policy-makers and tax collectors fear substantial revenue losses from a growing proportion of consumption being made up of goods purchased through the internet? Estimates of the state and local government revenue losses for states, at least in general discussions, cover the spectrum from the expectation that state tax bases would be devastated to the contention that tax revenues would actually be increased by an economy that is invigorated by the internet. The differences depend on the perspective taken on issues such as the role that taxes play in allowing the development of e-commerce, the time analyzed and forecasts of how rapidly e-commerce will expand. Nearly everyone agrees that the revenue losses to date have been relatively limited because e-commerce is still in its infancy. The important question from a policy perspective, then, is how the losses would grow in the near and longer term, since it is future rather than current losses that would be affected by policy decisions and which should be a factor in structuring policy. As with most issues, the probable reality of the revenue implications lies between the purported extremes. In order to evaluate the relevance of such fears for loss of revenue at least three matters should be considered. First, loss of tax revenue requires that the trades now being conducted through the internet are actually untaxable which will only be the case for purely digitalized goods. Second, in the case of e-commerce substitutes for trade in commodities that are not taxed anyway, there are no tax revenues to be lost. Third, from a public finance point of view the required (or desired) tax revenue is not exogenously given but rather determined by the balance between the marginal benefits of public goods and the marginal costs of public funds, and, in principle, both the benefits and the costs may be affected by the emergence of e-commerce.[30]

If consumer transactions are taxed differently because of how commodities are obtained, efficiency losses are probable. Exempting business inputs purchased by e-commerce, while taxing many business inputs obtained in other forms, potentially at higher rates, could increase those efficiency losses. Goolsbee,[31] based on research in the US on the impact of taxation on e-commerce and consumer online purchasing patterns, concludes that consumers living in high sales tax areas are significantly more likely to buy online than those living in low sales tax areas. Hence, differentiated e-commerce taxation rules among countries could have a significant impact on consumers' purchasing behaviour, shifting from domestic to foreign suppliers.[32] Mazerov and Lav argue that a moratorium on taxation of internet sales would therefore benefit the affluent consumer able to shop around on the internet at the expense of those with

---

30 Rasmussen, Sandemann (2004) On the Possibility and Desirability of Taxing E-Commerce Working Paper No. 2004-08 Department of Economics, School Of Economics and Management - University of Aarhus.

31 Goolsbee, A. (1999). *In a World without Borders: The Impact of Taxes on Internet Commerce*, National Bureau of Economic Research (NBER) Working Paper No. 6863, Cambridge, MA.

32 Although, there are also barriers that could prevent this shift, such as other regulatory obstacles (besides taxation), delivery problems, or cultural and linguistic barriers. To circumvent these, some United States suppliers have started to buy local competitors in Europe (*The Economist*, 2000).

low and moderate incomes, with the resulting loss of tax revenue.[33] Revenue losses associated with international e-commerce transactions are difficult to estimate as there are currently no empirical studies that attempt to measure these losses.

The impact of such tax revenue losses would vary according to a countries' reliance on consumption tax as a proportion of their total tax revenue. Major differences exist between the EU and the United States; the EU countries derive a large proportion of government tax revenue from consumption taxes on domestic goods and services (mainly VAT).[34] In addition, VAT extra charges contribute 45 per cent to the EU Community budget (in addition to customs duties and GNP contributions).[35] The US government, on the other hand, derives most of its tax revenues from personal and corporate income tax and social security contributions.[36] The US is currently both a net exporter and the main exporter of e-commerce worldwide. Hence, it has a great interest in encouraging business (including e-commerce business) to locate in the US and pay direct taxes to US tax authorities. The EU, however, has considerable concerns over the increasing import of digital content and services from outside the EU, which would be exempted from VAT payments in the EU. It is not surprising, therefore, that the issue of consumption taxes has received most attention in the OECD and the EU. In particular, the EU feels very strongly about maintaining VAT duties and has modified tax rules in a way that will ensure a continuation of VAT contributions, rather than lowering or eliminating them.

Meijers[37] tried to quantify the magnitude of the effects of e-commerce on tax income. The analysis was carried out for the Netherlands, using a Dutch macro-economic model. Looking at the country of origin for online goods and services, he found that for the Netherlands, the imports from the US were much more important than the imports from other European countries. From survey data, it came out that about one-third of the goods and services purchased through the internet by Dutch inhabitants were sold by US firms. Based on these assumptions, the simulation experiments carried out on imported goods and services, which were purchased through the internet and other online services, showed that the online imports were taxed in a normal way. This implied that all goods were traced by the customs officers and that either there were no imported immaterial goods and services or that the buyers

---

33 Mazerov, Michael. Lav, Iris J. (1998) 'A Federal 'Moratorium' on Internet Commerce Taxes Would Erode State and Local Revenues and Shift Burdens to Lower-Income Households', *Centre on Budget and Policy Priorities, http://www.cbpp.org/index.html May 11, 1998*, www.cbpp.org/512webtax.htm#III.A Moratorium on Taxation.

34 29%.

35 The 45% contribution in 1997 was reduced to 35% in 1999 (projection) (European Commission, 1998).

36 Within the United States, individual states and local governments have autonomy over determining and collecting state and local sales tax, often their biggest source of revenue. Sales taxes differ substantially among states, ranging from 0 to 7%. United States-based online suppliers selling to out-of-state (including foreign) customers currently do not have to charge local sales tax. States are therefore becoming increasingly worried about how to secure their sales tax revenues in the light of e-commerce.

37 Meijers, Huub (1998) 'Fiscal Impacts of the Growing Use of Advanced Communication Technologies and Services: A Quantitative Analysis'.

or sellers paid the indirect taxes to the tax authorities. As discussed before, online services like computer software, video-on-demand, music-on-demand and tickets can be traded through the internet without being observed by the tax authorities.[38] Moreover, it is likely that the customs officers would not always be able to trace physical goods and consumers are often not aware of the fact that they should pay VAT on imported goods and services from outside the EU. As it stands, this implied that the indirect taxes on these imports from the US are not likely to be paid.

In order to investigate the effects of this tax evasion (or tax avoidance), Meijers[39] used both scenarios in which it was assumed that the VAT of 17.5 per cent, the current Dutch VAT percentage, was not levied on (about) 50 per cent of all online imports. This had two effects: first, the import prices were reduced, because of which the imports would increase. This would lower GDP and employment. Second, the government tax income would be reduced. In the first scenario, where there were very little online imports, the effects were not that drastic: in 2000 the deficit was increased by fl. 10 million (ECU 4.5 million), as compared to the first simulation run, whereas this figure increases to fl. 30 million in 2020 (ECU 13.5 million). However, for the high scenario, things become more serious. Online shopping as a percentage of total private expenditure was still low in 2000 (about 0.8 per cent) but would increase rapidly to almost 3 per cent in 2005 and would reach 5.5 per cent in 2020. So, whereas the effect was expected to be minor in 2000, it could become more important from 2005 and onwards. Indeed, the increase of the government deficit was only fl. 80 million (ECU 36 million) in 2000 due to tax avoidance (in nominal terms). The increase of the deficit would be about fl. 300 million in 2005 (ECU 135 million) whereas it would be more than fl. 1.4 billion in 2020 (ECU 0.63 billion). A reduction of the tax income by ECU 0.63 billion in 2020 due to the tax evasion, compared to the nominal value of the GDP in 1997 relative to the GDP in 2020, equal to about ECU 0.25 billion in 1997. This was about equal to the total budget of the Dutch Ministry of Finance in 1997 (excluding the rents on government debts), about equal to the total budget of the Ministry of Agriculture, one-third of the total budget of the Ministry of Defence and one-seventh of the budget of the Ministry of Education, the largest Dutch Ministry in terms of budgets.[40] However, the reliability of the data on which this assumption was based, for giving a decisive answer to the question as to what the effects of e-commerce on tax erosion could be, could be questioned, but then it was a step in the right direction ,emphasizing the magnitude of e-commerce and its effects on tax income. With regard to tax revenue losses from e-commerce in physical goods within the EU, the question is mainly one of redistribution of tax revenues, as it is likely that high tax countries will experience a deficit on the e-commerce trade balance due to the origin principle applying to at least part of the transactions. Hence, high tax countries will lose tax revenue and low tax countries will gain revenue.

---

38 For a detailed discussion on the EU Directive on Digital Sales refer to Chapter 8 of this book.

39 Meijers, Huub (1998) 'Fiscal Impacts of the Growing Use of Advanced Communication Technologies and Services: A Quantitative Analysis'.

40 Meijers, Huub (1998) 'Fiscal Impacts of the Growing Use of Advanced Communication Technologies and Services: A Quantitative Analysis'.

The lack of empirical evidence concerning revenue losses at the international level can be contrasted with the situation in the US sub-national context where several studies have shown that US state and local governments are suffering revenue losses in the billions of dollars as a result of increased remote consumer sales attributable to mail-order and e-commerce transactions.[41] In the US the state sales tax bases had been declining relative to state personal income for many years. For the average sales-taxing state, the tax base equalled 51.4 per cent of the state's personal income in 1979 but had fallen to 42.8 per cent in 1998.[42] The concerns of states and local governments about uncollected use tax revenue (from both B2C and B2B transactions) predate the rise of sales on the internet. Uncollected revenue from remote sales in 1994 reached $3.3 billion according to the Advisory Commission on Intergovernmental Relations, or 2.5 per cent of states' sales and use tax collections and 0.8 per cent of their total tax revenue.[43] One empirical study, however, does show that e-commerce developments may be facilitating international tax planning for US multinationals although, again, revenue losses associated with this planning remain uncertain.[44] Tax authorities have noted the rise of business models – 'black market' economic activity such as internet auctioning or bartering where capital gains often remain untaxed, along with gambling and pornographic websites located in offshore tax havens – that may be leading to revenue losses.

The most important factor responsible for the erosion of the tax base was the shift in consumption patterns towards greater consumption of services and less consumption of goods. Services are much less broadly taxed than goods, meaning the base shrinks relative to the economy as services become more prominent. There is evidence of a shift of consumption patterns towards greater consumption of services and less consumption of goods. Services are much less broadly taxed than goods, meaning the base shrinks relative to the economy as services become more prominent. The revenue losses from e-commerce generally arise because e-commerce significantly expanded the potential for remote sales causing a shift from collecting sales taxes at the point of sale to collecting use taxes for goods used, consumed or stored in the state. Compliance rates are much better for sales taxes than for use taxes. The revenue

---

41 Hellerstein, Walter (2003) Jurisdiction to Tax income and Consumption in the New Economy: A Theoretical and Comparative Perspective, 38 *Georgia Law Review* pp 1-70; Multistate Tax Commission, *Federalism at Risk*, 30 State Tax Notes 7 (2003). For revenue loss estimates, see U.S., General Accounting Office (2000) *Sales Taxes: Electronic Commerce Growth Presents Challenges: Revenue Losses Are Uncertain* (GAO/GGD/OCE-00-165); Donald Bruce & William Fox, State And Local Revenue Losses From E-Commerce: Estimates As Of July 2004 (Knoxville: University of Tennessee, Centre for Business and Economic Research, 2004) (estimating losses between U.S.$21.5 billion and U.S.$33.7 billion by 2008).

42 Bruce, Donald, and William E Fox (2000) 'E-Commerce in the Context of Declining State Sales Tax Bases' *National Tax Journal* 53 No. 4, Part 3 (December, 2000): pp 1373-1388.

43 Advisory Commission on Intergovernmental Relations (1994), *Taxation of Interstate Mail-Order Sales: 1994 Revenue Estimates.*

44 Carnaghan, Carla and Klassen, Kenneth J (2004) *E-Commerce and International Tax Planning* (Working Paper, June 2004).

losses described here are generally the result of tax evasion, not tax avoidance; since the use tax is due even if the sales tax cannot be collected.

Proposals to make the internet a tax-free zone could promise an end to sales and use tax revenue, going well beyond the problems of the current physical presence rule. The devastation to the sales and use tax results because virtually all business activity involves, at some stage in the purchase process, acquisition through e-commerce; every store-to-customer transaction would have been an internet transaction at some stage of the flow of commerce and hence not subject to taxation.[45] With strictest definition, the sales tax base falls to zero – not even the purchase of a motor vehicle would be taxable – and states and localities would have a major fiscal problem. At a minimum, the law would require massive interpretation to determine what is and what is not enough connection with the internet to make it tax free. Neither outcome would seem to be acceptable under normal ideas of sound tax policy.

Calculations of projected revenue losses from an increasing level of e-commerce – done mostly for the US – suggest that while only modest at the present stage they may turn out to become significant in the near future. Bruce and Fox's[46] study based on e-commerce sales drawn from Forrester Research Inc.'s annual forecasts for the years 2001 through 2011 showed that the incremental revenue loss from e-commerce sales is estimated to be 41 per cent more than the previous report of 2000 had indicated due to higher B2B transactions forecasted by Forrester.[47] In 2001, in the US, e-commerce caused a total state and local government revenue loss of \$13.3 billion. By 2006, this loss would have more than tripled to \$45.2 billion and in 2011, the loss would be \$54.8 billion; losses that would represent 5.6 per cent of state tax revenue in 2006 and 5.4 per cent in 2011.[48] Another set of estimates is considerably lower – \$3.2 billion in 2006 and \$4.5 billion in 2011, or less than 1 per cent of state and local tax revenue in both years.[49] The total e-commerce loss is the sales tax loss on all sales over the internet. Part of the loss would have occurred anyway, even without e-commerce on sales, for example, which might have otherwise been made by purchasers using the telephone and catalogues. The new e-commerce loss is from sales made through the internet both on goods that would have otherwise been purchased by the over-the-counter method and projected new goods that will be purchased over the internet. In 2001, the new e-commerce loss was \$7 billion. In 2006, it is expected grow up to \$24.2 billion and in 2011 it will be \$29.2 billion. Measuring the states' e-commerce revenue losses against their total state tax revenues also shows significant impact. In 2011, states would lose anywhere from 2.6 per cent to 9.92 per cent of their total state

45 Weiner, Stuart E (1999) 'Electronic Payments in the U. S. Economy: An Overview', *Federal Reserve Bank of Kansas City Economic Review* 84 No. 4 (Fourth Quarter, 1999) pp 53-64.

46 Bruce, Donald, and William E Fox (2001) 'State and Local Sales Tax Revenue Losses from E-Commerce: Updated Estimates', Centre for Business and Economic Research, The University of Tennessee, Sept. 2001.

47 Bruce, Donald, and William E Fox (2000) 'E-Commerce in the Context of Declining State Sales Tax Bases' *National Tax journal* 53 No. 4, Part 3 (December, 2000): pp 1373-1388.

48 Bruce and Fox, State and Local Sales Tax Revenue Losses from E-Commerce.

49 Johnson, A. Current Calculation of Uncollected Sales Tax Arising from Internet Growth.

tax collections to total e-commerce losses. A final measurement of the impact of e-commerce losses is the needed increase in the sales tax rate to replace the lost revenue. In 2011, rates would have to rise by between 0.83 and 1.72 percentage points to replace the total e-commerce losses.

The dominant role that B2B is expected to play in e-commerce sales means that the ability to collect revenues on B2B transactions is very important to the revenue loss for state and local governments. Indeed, B2B transactions represented 92.6 per cent of all e-commerce activity in 2001 according to the Forrester forecast, a share that would expand to 95.0 per cent by 2011.[50] The sales tax base erosion that was stimulated by e-commerce is part of a downward trend in the tax base that has been underway for many years. However, e-commerce has accelerated the trend that otherwise appeared to have been slowing in the mid 1990s. The revenue loss estimates provided here, totalling more than $16 billion in 2001 and nearly $45 billion in 2006, suggest that the combination of the trend decline and e-commerce would significantly alter state tax structures during the next several years.[51] The wide range of the estimates reflects the uncertainty arising from shortcomings in the data available to quantify uncollected revenue from remote sales. Factors that must be estimated include the rate of growth of e-commerce; the proportion of e-commerce that is not part of the sales tax base; the share of e-commerce that is part of the tax base that represents purchases by exempt entities; and the proportion of taxable e-commerce on which tax is already being collected and that replaces other forms of remote sales. A series of assumptions must be made to adjust for those factors in estimating total sales over the internet.

The overall revenue-raising power of governments has been constrained. Theory offers a wide range of possibilities, with the most pessimistic being that tax rates and tax revenues would be forced progressively downwards, even to the point where it becomes impossible to collect any revenues at all. The decline in the tax base in e-commerce would be caused by the loss of consumption-based taxes resulting from the difficulty in taxing purchases from outside the jurisdiction. This would be aggravated by the loss of tax revenue from workers displaced by new information technologies. To this 'double whammy' would be added the increase in tax avoidance (as explained in the previous section) made easier by the lack of paper trails on the internet.[52] Countries will be encouraged to move more towards indirect taxation, which will affect poorer families. Between countries, there will be considerable differential impacts due to the countries' ability to both shift to an indirect taxation system and to participate in the growth potential of e-commerce. It is my contention that developing countries would have greater difficulty on both these counts. To make reliable projections for future levels of the tax revenue losses

---

50 Bruce, Donald, and William E Fox (2001) 'State and Local Sales Tax Revenue Losses from E-Commerce: Updated Estimates', Centre for Business and Economic Research, The University of Tennessee, Sept. 2001.

51 New York City has even filed lawsuits against 4000 individual smokers for avoiding millions of dollars in use taxes on cigarettes purchased online. (See, www.cbsnews.com/stories/2005/02/11/eveningnews/consumer/main673628.shtml.)

52 Chan, Clayton W. (2000) Taxation of Global E-Commerce and the Internet: The Underlying Issues and Proposed Plans, *Minnesota Journal of Global Trade* 9: 233

it is not sufficient to obtain predictions on the future growth in e-commerce but also to obtain predictions of what part of the traditional trade this e-commerce is substituting. Predictions of future tax revenue losses should, therefore, not be based on aggregate estimates of the growth of e-commerce. A much more disaggregated framework is needed, concentrating on predicting the growth in demand for digital goods and tangible goods escaping use taxation by private consumers. However, part of these predictions amounts to predicting the demand for 'new' goods whose nature we may not know presently.

7.2.2   Erosion of the Tax Base: The Move from Fair Taxation

Tax regimes should be fair in both their horizontal and vertical dimensions. What is a 'fair' tax system? The definition of a 'fair' tax is, of course, at least partly a matter of opinion. However, as discussed in Chapter 4 some progress has been made using concepts such as horizontal equity and vertical equity. A tax system violates horizontal equity if taxpayers in similar situations pay markedly different amounts of tax. Vertical equity is commonly framed as ensuring a fair relationship between the tax burdens (usually defined as a fraction of income paid in tax) on households with different levels of income. These notions depend on one's own values and these values differ for different people, so there is not much that we can say in general about what is a 'fair' tax. Still, it seems obvious that one's notion of a fair tax will depend in some way on how taxes affect the distribution of income; that is, is the distribution of tax burdens progressive, proportional or regressive? A regressive tax extracts more tax, as a proportion of current income from lower-income taxpayers than from higher-income ones. A progressive tax takes more taxes, as a proportion of current income, as income rises. Both concepts represent value judgements about how taxes should be levied. As a result, one cannot evaluate the effect that the violation of those equity norms has on economic well-being as one can evaluate the effect of violating the efficiency standard.[53]

A mechanical application of the horizontal equity principle suggests that e-commerce sales should be treated the same way that non-internet sales are treated, either by eliminating the tax or by enforcing the tax. Otherwise, two consumers who purchase the same items, one online and one from bricks and mortar establishments are treated differently. Yet the proper measurement of horizontal equity is problematic. By definition, if both consumers have equal access to the internet, they are choosing to not purchase the same 'bundle' of goods and services. Presumably, each consumer has reasons for his or her choice of shopping arrangements, leading their equivalent situations to produce different outcomes. Whether horizontal equity, properly measured, is violated is not immediately obvious. Taxing online purchases may have another implication: consumers could be stimulated to avoid online taxation by shifting consumption towards untaxed activities, reducing the consumption tax base.

In order to recover from the revenue loss, state and local governments would be confronted with limited choices: they must cut expenditures, increase existing sales tax or VAT rates or shift to another tax source, such as the property or income tax. Each choice has important implications. The effects of the first option, shrinking

---

53 CBO (2003).

government, depend on the choices that are made. For example, reducing education and infrastructure spending could lower the economy's growth potential. If the size of government is not cut, the issue comes down to the way in which state and local governments are to finance themselves. With these decisions goes the full range of implications regarding taxation, including equity, administration and compliance, and behavioural incentives. From a public policy perspective, the issue is whether state and local governments are better financed with the triad of sales, property and income taxes, or whether the sales tax base should be allowed to continue shrinking and the focus increasingly shifted toward other broad-based taxes.[54] From an economic point of view, a uniform consumption tax is equivalent to a single-rated income tax, in which interest and other capital gains have been exempted.[55] However, if a tax rate is raised excessively, consumers will further attempt to take advantage of exempt online consumption. A vicious cycle leading to higher tax burdens on low income individuals could result. Tax rate increases could encourage more online consumption by high-income individuals, forcing further rounds of rate increases. As a consequence, low-income consumers limited to buying goods sold at bricks and mortar stores would be further burdened in absolute, as well as relative, terms. The same reasoning could apply to the hypothesis of non-uniform e-commerce taxation. Individuals searching across multiple online firms might avoid sales taxes by choosing one retailer over-intent on paying lower taxes or no taxes at all. Again, higher-income individuals, with easier access to online transactions, would have more opportunities to avoid taxation, as opposed to lower-income individuals.

Sales taxes, in the US particularly, currently finance approximately one-third of states' tax revenues and one-tenth of local tax receipts. As sales tax revenues decline, state and local governments will be forced to finance themselves through other means or to cut public services. This puts pressure on state governments to raise additional revenues through income taxes and on local governments through property taxes. Sales taxes not only help to diversify the overall revenue structure but surveys have often shown them to be the most acceptable tax.[56] Replacement of the lost local sales tax revenues with higher property taxes and the lost state revenues with higher income taxes would change the overall revenue mix. Bruce and Fox[57] estimated on the baseline scenario that the sales tax would fall from 25.1 per cent to 22.6 per cent of revenues between 1996 and 2003 if there were no rate hikes. In order to recover this loss in a revenue-neutral fashion, the personal income tax would have to rise from 21.2 to 23.2 per cent of total taxes and the property tax would have to rise from 30.2 per cent to 30.6

54 Bruce, Donald, and William E Fox (2001) 'State and Local Sales Tax Revenue Losses from E-Commerce: Updated Estimates', Centre for Business and Economic Research, The University of Tennessee, Sept. 2001.

55 Stiglitz, Joseph E (1988) *Economics of the Public Sector*, (W.W. Norton &Co, 2nd Edition, NY& London) pp 427-433.

56 William F. Fox. LeAnn Luna 'Taxing E-Commerce: Neutral Taxation is Best for the Industry and the Economy'.

57 Bruce, Donald, and William E Fox (2001) 'State and Local Sales Tax Revenue Losses from E-Commerce: Updated Estimates', Centre for Business and Economic Research, The University of Tennessee.

per cent. To replace only the new e-commerce losses in 2006 (based on 2001 estimation), sales tax rates will have to rise by between 0.44 and 0.91 percentage points.

People who make purchases through the internet are, on average, more affluent. Internet purchases generally require a personal computer with a modem, a connection to the internet through a service provider and a credit card with which to pay for the purchase. Income and education are key elements in the ownership of personal computers. Media Metrix[58] reports that internet users own the most powerful and expensive computers. Moreover, the internet is increasingly being used to make purchases of luxury items. The internet is especially well suited for consumers who want to customize their purchases of golf clubs and bicycles from hundreds of possible specifications.[59] On the other hand, lower-income households lack the equipment to access the internet, the training to use the equipment, and/or the financial stability and credit rating required for maintaining a credit card. If lower-income groups have limited access to those payment media, some vertical inequity from not taxing sales might persist unless cash on delivery became a generally available payment option.

As internet sales become a more significant share of consumption, states are likely to see taxable sales and consumption tax revenues diminish. The option would be to raise their consumption tax rates to maintain revenues, given that they would be unable to tax internet sales. However, indirect taxes are regressive; they absorb a larger share of the incomes of lower-income households. An increase in the consumption tax rate could set off a vicious cycle leading to ever more consumption taxes that are more regressive. As tax rates rise, higher-income households and businesses with internet access would have an ever greater incentive to make their purchases online to avoid taxes, while lower-income households without access to online services would remain liable for the taxes. Consumption tax liability would be increasingly concentrated among the lowest-income segments of the population. As already seen, in addition to this, states would be forced to reduce state funding programmes to compensate for diminished revenues, which causes a disproportionate cut of benefits for lower-income families and individuals.

Presumably, there is a concern about tax-induced distortions. If customers, for example, would prefer to buy from a local store but buy online only to avoid taxes, the tax is creating inefficiency. A major concern, then, is the extent to which taxpayers are discriminated against by the system, with reference to the fact that some individuals may not be able to avoid consumption taxes, while others may. This situation would impose burdens on consumers disproportionate to their amount of consumption, but according to their lack of ability to perform online purchases. The result is unfairness in both the horizontal and vertical aspects of the tax regime. There is evidence of such patterns of shifting tax liability from the use of mail order; upper-income households tending to use such systems more than low- to middle-income households.[60] The

---

58 Media Metrix (1998) 'Internet Users Spend More Time, Money on PCs' March 31st 1998 Internet News.com, Staff www.InternetNews.com/bus-news/1998/03/3102-mediametrix.html.

59 'Build It Yourself', http://www.internetworld.com/print/current/ecomm/19980302-build.html.

60 Statistics form *Direct Marketing* 1997.

argument of a regressive tax structure is not a new concept in the consumption tax debate. Critics have consistently shown consumption tax to be inherently regressive, while governments try to counteract these effects with exemptions and subsidies. There is no compelling policy reason why the governments should favour the wealthy and well-financed corporations and their equally wealthy customers at the expense of other businesses and other consumers. Community-based businesses and the cities and towns they serve are now endangered by unfair and ill-conceived economic distortions due to the tax breaks e-commerce companies enjoy. I accept that governments should be encouraging the growth of e-commerce but argue that the issue of unfairness in the tax regimes be considered in the light of such growth.

7.3   Revenue Loss for Developing Countries

The digital divide shows that the rich and educated have the best access to computers and the internet.[61] More high-income consumers shop online than low-income consumers. This is intuitive because they have a higher willingness to pay the fixed cost to shop online and their time is worth more to them (which makes conventional shopping less attractive). Therefore, if the online tax rate is lower than the conventional tax rate, the average affluent person will pay relatively less of their income in consumption taxes than the average poor person. Given a sufficient decrease in the fixed cost of shopping online, the electronic region can 'enter' and attract a tax base if they set relatively low tax rates. As the fixed cost of shopping online continues to decrease, increased use of e-commerce as a way of shopping is expected to rise. Conventional regions would see both lower tax bases and tax rates which would lead to lower tax revenues and this would make the developing countries more vulnerable because of their greater dependence on tariffs and taxes as revenue sources for their national budgets. In order to raise the lost revenue situation ideally calls for the rich to be taxed more heavily than the poor, but the economic and political power of rich taxpayers often allows them to prevent tax reforms that would increase their tax burdens. This practically explains why developing countries are more dependent on indirect taxes. In developing countries, tax policy is often the art of the possible rather than the pursuit of the optimal.[62] Tax exemption is at present a consistent policy justified to encourage the growth of e-commerce. Earlier discussion in Chapter 1 clearly indicates that e-commerce has achieved unparalleled growth not only in the developed countries but also in a large number of developing countries. It would appear that the success of e-commerce would depend not on tax exemption but on internet access, education levels and the propensity to consume imported products traded on the internet, side-stepping domestic alternatives and prices.

Hence, what would be the impact on the tax incomes of developing countries? Most of the developing countries rely heavily on consumption taxes. Data from

---

61 'Electronic Commerce and Tax Competition: When Consumers Can Shop across Borders and On-Line', Working paper No.00-13, November 2000, Department of Economics University of Colorado.

62 Jones, R and Basu, S (2002) 'Taxation of Electronic Commerce: A Developing Problem', *International Review of Law Computers & Technology*, Volume: 16 No.1 pp 38-42.

industrial and developing countries show that the ratio of income to consumption taxes in industrial countries has consistently remained more than double the ratio in developing countries, that is, compared with developing countries, industrial countries derive proportionally twice as much revenue from income tax than from consumption tax.[63] Developing countries are also importing countries, that is, its citizens and companies tend to buy from foreign countries more than foreign countries buy from its citizens and companies. In contrast, developed countries consist of relatively wealthy, exporting nations. While the size of these export-import trade deficits varies from year-to-year and from country-to-country, such deficits nevertheless overwhelmingly exist for developing countries. Within the WTO, developing countries have raised concerns about possible tariff revenue implications resulting from a ban on customs duties on electronic transmissions. However, they lack resources to provide evidence, which could support their concern. Many of them are still struggling to keep up with the rapid developments in the area of e-commerce recognizing that e-commerce has two sides and has the potential for substantial beneficial effects on their economies.[64]

The US accounts for almost 20 per cent of world exports of digitizable products followed by the UK, Germany, Ireland, Japan, France and the Netherlands, with a combined account of 66.5 per cent of total exports. Developed countries account for 88.5 per cent of exports, while the developing countries' share is only 11.5 per cent. Among the developing countries, the main exporters of digitizable products are Singapore, Hong Kong, China, Mexico, Korea, India, Honduras and Chile.[65] [66] On the import side, the US has again the largest share (16 per cent of all imports), followed by the UK and Canada. Main importers from the developing countries include Hong Kong, Mexico, Korea, China, Singapore, Brazil, South Africa, India and Argentina. The developed countries' share in total imports of digitizable products is 81.5 per cent. Growth rates for both exports and imports of digitized products are significantly higher than growth rates of total merchandise trade. In particular, developing countries' imports have grown considerably throughout the decade, although they slowed down in 1997 and 1998. The question here is how significant is this revenue loss for developing countries. The tariff rates of developing countries are higher than those of developed countries. Technological advancement affected the diverse nature of products.[67]

---

63 Jones, R and Basu, S (2002) 'Taxation of Electronic Commerce: A Developing Problem', *International Review of Law Computers & Technology*, Volume: 16 No.1 pp 38-42.

64 Jones, R and Basu, S (2002) 'Taxation of Electronic Commerce: A Developing Problem', *International Review of Law Computers & Technology*, Volume: 16 No.1 pp 38-42.

65 It may come as a surprise that India is not among the main developing country software exporters. This can be explained by the structure of the Indian software industry where software *services* account for 95 per cent of Indian exports whereas software *packages* (i.e. the products considered here) constitute only a small proportion of the Indian software industry output.

66 Teltscher, Susanne (2000), 'Tariffs, Taxes and Electronic Commerce: Revenue Implications for Developing Countries', UNCTAD Study Series on 'Policy Issues in International Trade and Commodities' No.5 UNCTAD/ITCD/TAB/5, Geneva.

67 Teltscher, Susanne (2000), 'Tariffs, Taxes and Electronic Commerce: Revenue Implications for Developing Countries', UNCTAD Study Series on 'Policy Issues in International Trade and Commodities' No.5 UNCTAD/ITCD/TAB/5, Geneva.

In order to calculate potential revenue losses resulting from a shift from the physical to electronic delivery of goods, these trade flows have to be linked to tariff rates currently imposed on the various products.[68] Data show that significant differences exist among the products. For example, while low tariffs (2–3 per cent) prevail on books and newspapers, high tariffs (up to 20 per cent) are imposed on postcards, calendars and commercial catalogues all of which comprise the 'printed matter' group. Higher tariffs also dominate most of the sound and media products as well as video games.[69] A disaggregating of the average MFN[70] tariff by a developed/ developing country would show that developing countries on average have higher tariffs on all product lines compared to developed countries. What fiscal losses would occur should physical delivery of products be replaced by electronic delivery and no tariffs imposed on the latter? The majority of countries that are mostly affected by tariff revenue losses come from the developing world. What is remarkable, however, is the magnitude: despite the developing countries' import share in digitizable products of only 18.5 per cent, their absolute tariff revenue (loss) is almost double that of the developed countries, amounting to 63 per cent of world tariff revenue losses for these products.[71]

This clearly shows that, as far as potential fiscal losses are concerned, developing countries would be much more impacted by the proposed ban. The top ten countries affected by fiscal loss are the EU, India, Canada, Mexico, Brazil, China, Russia,

---

68 This is useful for finding out which countries might be most affected by a ban on customs duties on these goods (in case of substitution of physical by electronic delivery); it doesn't offer much information on the tariff rates levied on different products. It also plays an important role considering that not all products are likely to be substituted immediately or in the near future, and some may always be distributed in physical or 'tangible' format.

69 Teltscher, Susanne (2000), 'Tariffs, Taxes and Electronic Commerce: Revenue Implications for Developing Countries', UNCTAD Study Series on 'Policy Issues in International Trade and Commodities' No.5 UNCTAD/ITCD/TAB/5, Geneva.

70 Within the WTO, there are important political and regulatory implications associated with the electronic delivery of goods and services. Depending on the classification, the trade is subject to different multilateral rules: goods are subject to the GATT, the Agreement on Technical Barriers to Trade, the Agreement on Customs Valuations, or rules of origin; while services would be subject to the GATS Agreement. In general, the multilateral rules for services are still far less elaborate than the multilateral rules for trade in goods, providing countries with substantially more leeway for national policy discretion in the services trade. One important difference between the GATT and the GATS relates to general obligations. While the GATT's general obligations include most-favoured-nation treatment (MFN), national treatment, and a general prohibition of quantitative restrictions, the GATS include the national treatment principle only in negotiated specific commitments and specific services. MFN treatment requires WTO members to apply the same duties and charges they apply to any Member of the WTO, immediately and unconditionally to all other Members. For example, if a country negotiates and agrees upon an import tariff rate with one country, the same tariff rate must be applied to all other member countries. GATT (1994), 'The Results of the Uruguay Round of Multilateral Trade Negotiations, The Legal Texts', Geneva.

71 Teltscher, Susanne (2000), 'Tariffs, Taxes and Electronic Commerce: Revenue Implications for Developing Countries', UNCTAD Study Series on 'Policy Issues in International Trade and Commodities' No.5 UNCTAD/ITCD/TAB/5, Geneva.

Poland, Argentina and Thailand.[72] Schuknecht[73] placed these losses in the context of total government revenues and compared tariff revenues from digitizable products to total revenues and revenues from import duties.[74] The percentages are relatively low for all countries, tariff revenues from these products account for only 0.16 per cent of total government revenues and 1.7 per cent of revenues from import duties. Nevertheless, some significant differences exist between countries, with shares ranging from 0 to 0.16 per cent of total revenue and from 0 to 2.7 per cent of revenues from import duties.[75] [76]

Apart from the applied tariffs, there are a number of additional duties and taxes levied on most imports by most countries. If imports of physical goods were replaced by electronic delivery that is exempted from customs duties, these additional duties would also be lost, besides the tariff duties. For most products, additional duties exceed tariff duties and hence could substantially change the revenue calculations presented before. There are two types of additional duties levied on imports: (i) customs surcharges that are only levied on imports,[77] and (ii) internal taxes that are levied on imports as well as on domestic goods.[78] Importers are normally obliged to cover all of them. Each country has its own regulation on how it levies and calculates import duties. Often, different types of products are subject to varying rates, for example food products could be subject to reduced rates while luxury goods, tobacco or alcohol are often subject to increased rates.

How important are these duties compared to the tariff? How do they differ among countries and between developed and developing countries, given what we know about the differing tariff rates? First, compared to the tariff rates, the rates for additional duties are significantly higher: they amount on average to 23 per cent, compared with only 6.9 per cent for the tariff. The final calculation of the duties levied on imports therefore increases from 6.9 per cent (tariff only) to 29.2 per cent (tariff, customs surcharges and taxes). Second, the size of additional duties differs substantially among countries, ranging from 0 to 120 per cent. In the case of tariffs,

---

72 Teltscher, Susanne (2000), 'Tariffs, Taxes and Electronic Commerce: Revenue Implications for Developing Countries', UNCTAD Study Series on 'Policy Issues in International Trade and Commodities' No.5 UNCTAD/ITCD/TAB/5, Geneva.

73 Schuknecht, L. (1999) 'A Quantitative Assessment of Electronic Commerce,' WTO Working Paper ERAD-99-01, September 1999, Geneva.

74 Schuknecht, L. (1999) 'A Quantitative Assessment of Electronic Commerce,' WTO Working Paper ERAD-99-01, September 1999, Geneva.

75 Furthermore, customs duties as a source of government revenue play a much more important role in a number of developing countries: while government revenues from import duties account for 2.6 per cent in developed countries, they account for 15.8 per cent in the developing countries.

76 Teltscher, Susanne (2000), 'Tariffs, Taxes and Electronic Commerce: Revenue Implications for Developing Countries', UNCTAD Study Series on 'Policy Issues in International Trade and Commodities' No.5 UNCTAD/ITCD/TAB/5, Geneva.

77 Customs surcharges usually consist of a mixture of duties, including undefined customs fees and uplifts or taxes such as statistical taxes, stamp taxes, or port taxes.

78 Internal taxes are usually value-added taxes, sales taxes, or other types of consumption taxes.

the developing countries were clearly the ones imposing (on average) higher rates than the developed countries. In the case of other duties, however, the rates between developed and developing countries do not differ considerably; averages calculated here amount to 23.1 per cent for the former and 22.9 per cent for the latter. This is largely due to the relatively high consumption taxes charged by many countries. They account for 15 per cent (all countries), 17.1 per cent (developed countries) and 14.3 per cent (developing countries).[79] Given the relatively high rates of additional duties on imports of digitizable products, significant revenue increases resulting from these duties ought to be expected.

The following can be observed: first, as far as absolute numbers are concerned, revenues have jumped from US$757 million (tariffs only) to US$6.9 billion (tariffs plus additional import duties), an increase of more than 800 per cent. Again, this is largely due to the high consumption tax rates levied on domestic goods and services: revenues from these taxes amount to US$ 5.1 billion or almost 75 per cent of the total (all countries). Second, while revenues from tariff duties were almost double in the developing countries compared with the developed countries, revenues from all duties (tariffs, customs surcharges, taxes) are now much higher in the developed countries than in the developing countries: US$5.3 billion compared to US$1.3 billion for the developing countries. This amounts to a 78 per cent share of the developed countries' import duties resulting from digitizable products, compared to a 22 per cent share for the developing countries. The developing countries' share is still significantly higher than their share in world imports of these products (16 per cent). Again, a major explanation for these numbers is the consumption tax levied by the developed countries combined with their much larger trade volumes. Third, revenues from import duties and taxes on digitizable products now account on average for 0.3 per cent of total government revenue, up from 0.06 per cent (tariffs only). Their share in tax revenues has increased from 0.08 per cent to 0.4 per cent. In both cases, this is an increase of 400 per cent. There is no major difference in these shares between developing and developed countries.[80]

To summarize, fiscal losses resulting from replacing physical by digital products go much beyond simple tariff revenue losses. Almost all countries levy some sort of additional duties and/or taxes on their imports, which normally exceed tariff duties. These revenues could potentially be lost if goods were delivered digitally. The importer normally pays the duties and taxes identified here. In the case of online delivery, these intermediaries are eliminated and the product delivered directly to the final consumer. This could raise major problems in the area of tariff and tax collection, in particular if consumers are not registered businesses.

The concern is of increasing numbers of small and medium-sized enterprises (SMEs) that would be drawn in by e-commerce from the developing countries, which have little experience in international taxation issues. Any solutions must have the

79 Teltscher, Susanne (2000), 'Tariffs, Taxes and Electronic Commerce: Revenue Implications for Developing Countries', UNCTAD Study Series on 'Policy Issues in International Trade and Commodities' No.5 UNCTAD/ITCD/TAB/5, Geneva.

80 Teltscher, Susanne (2000), 'Tariffs, Taxes and Electronic Commerce: Revenue Implications for Developing Countries', UNCTAD Study Series on 'Policy Issues in International Trade and Commodities' No.5 UNCTAD/ITCD/TAB/5, Geneva.

confidence of the developing world. 'Above all, what is needed is a recognition that globalization is not merely a matter of unrestricted market forces. It requires a strengthening of international standards and cooperative arrangements, to provide a basis of mutual confidence.'[81] With a few exceptions, developing countries would not be part of any OECD agreement on internet taxation. Nevertheless, they could use the principles and rules agreed upon as a basis for adjusting their own legislation. In addition, developing countries would attempt to use tax legislation, as they have in the past to attract private foreign direct investment (FDI). Multinationals increasingly operate in countries that have low taxes or are willing to negotiate favourable tax regimes to attract foreign business.[82] In fact, fiscal incentives are the most widely used type of FDI incentives.[83] Depending on the agreements adopted in the OECD, developing countries could negotiate specific bilateral treaties for e-commerce taxation, which would give them a competitive edge. For example, the transaction costs of setting up or moving a web server are low; hence, e-commerce allows companies to respond quickly to tax incentives by governments and move their web servers to a developing country. Any decisions, which developing countries may take on modifying their tax legislation to accommodate e-commerce, however, would have to take into account the significant role of tax and tariff revenues in their national budgets. Until new international agreements on e-commerce taxation have been defined, an increasing number of goods and services would be traded online, largely tax-free. This would have an effect on government revenue, especially if the goods and services have been subject to import duties in the past.

7.4 Conclusion

While e-commerce raises important issues that may seem to be new (for example, the continued viability of primary reliance on source-based taxation of income), in many cases it only accentuates problems that were there all along. Thus, some of the reforms needed are not only related to the taxation of e-commerce, *per se*, but with common sense reforms that have long been needed. I believe strongly that the commonly accepted goal of a level playing field for e-commerce cannot be achieved without addressing these more fundamental problems, especially in the state sales tax area. As emphasized by Tanzi (2000),[84] Alm, Holman and Neumann (2003)[85] and

81 Picciotto, S (2000) 'Lessons of the MAI: Towards a New Regulatory Framework for International Investment', 2000 (1) *Law, Social Justice and Global Development* (LGD). http://elj.warwick.ac.uk/global/issue/2000-1/picciotto.html.

82 *The Economist* (2000) A Survey of E-commerce, 26 February 2000.

83 UNCTAD (1996) Incentives and Foreign Direct Investment, UNCTAD/DTCI/28, Current Studies, Series A, No. 30, Geneva.

84 Tanzi, Vito (2000) 'Globalization, Technological Developments, and the Work of Fiscal Termites,' International Monetary Fund Working Paper 00/181. Washington, D.C.: International Monetary Fund.

85 Alm, James, Jill Ann Holman, and Rebecca M. Neumann (2003) 'Globalization and State/Local Government Finances' in David L. Sjoquist, ed., *State and Local Finance Under Pressure* Cheltenham, UK and Northampton, MA: Edward Elgar Publishing, 276-298.

others, fiscal systems face a wide range of new developments, most of which are related to a broad notion of 'globalization' and most of which reduce the ability of tax systems to generate tax revenues.[86] These 'fiscal termites' include such factors as:

- the growth of e-commerce and the corresponding decline in paper trails that allow transactions to be followed;
- the substitution of 'real' money by electronic money, which also makes it difficult to follow transactions, especially those involved in international transactions;
- the growth of transfer pricing within multinational companies, which can lead to grossly understated prices on transactions and which can also make it difficult to trace transactions;
- the increasing use of offshore financial centres and of new financial instruments;
- the difficulty (and/or the unwillingness) to tax highly mobile financial capital and highly mobile skilled individuals.

These kinds of developments make it increasingly difficult for all countries to tax income on a global basis. They pose a special challenge for countries without a sophisticated tax administration. In the face of these challenges, it seems likely that countries, especially developing countries, will need to find new technologies that can be applied to the ways in which taxes are collected. The ability to deliver the same goods and services in a variety of competing ways changes the nature of competition and places a high premium on economic neutrality and equity in tax policy. The costs of illuminating manuscripts were so much greater than those of printing them that taxation of printed matter would probably have had little impact on the choice of technology, unless truly confiscatory, but it seems reasonable to assert that substantial differences in taxation could have been tolerated without doing as much damage to neutrality or equity (or both) as in the case of competition between digital and pre-digital means of delivering information. The same is not true of competing ways of providing essentially identical goods and services (for example, software in 'canned' form or downloaded; books by mail order, downloading, or conventional retail sales) produced and distributed under market conditions that increasingly approach perfection. The problem for some of the developed and developing countries starts here; services are tax-free while goods are not, but how to distinguish them in the virtual world?

As a classical developing country situation, there is intense tax competition among the states to attract trade and industry to their respective jurisdictions. Generous concessions are offered to new industries, small industries and industrial units set up in backward areas through tax holidays and/or deferral tax payment by almost all the states to the detriment of revenue, as well as equity and causing problems for both enforcement and compliance. A website can reap all the benefits without contributing anything to the development of the local economy. The tax

---

86 Alm, James and Wallace, Sally (2004) Can Developing Countries Impose An Individual Income Tax? The Challenges of Tax Reform in a Global Economy' Andrew Young School of Policy Studies International Studies Program, Georgia State University, May 24-25, 2004.

base is itself quite narrow with the exclusion of services and concessions of various kinds, not to mention widespread evasion because of administrative weakness. In order to counterbalance the further loss of revenue due to e-commerce, the rates of tax have to be higher than would otherwise be necessary to collect the same amount of revenue, providing further impetus for evasion.

Tax policy considerations suggest that sales taxes should be imposed on a destination basis that tax should be collected by the jurisdiction where consumption occurs, not where production occurs. Yet, for technical reasons, sellers of electronic content may not know the destination of sales made over the internet. Thus, taxpayers may not even know the location of their customers. It is more difficult to monitor the transmittal of electronic signals than to monitor trade in tangible products, especially when the transmission network is becoming so widely decentralized and location plays such a small role. Secure methods of payment, which are needed for commerce to flourish, may impose significant impediments to tax administration. The 'audit trails' needed for tax administration may no longer exist (for example, where electronic cash or smart cards are used for payments). It may be possible to determine the total sales, revenues or income of a vendor, but impossible to know where some sales are made. It may not even be possible to know total revenues from sales, since it is not possible to utilize physical examinations (for example, of the movement of inventories) as a backstop to auditing of accounts, since electronic content (intangible products and services provided online) has no physical form. As *The Economist* noted, 'If a firm sells software on floppy disks then the number of blank disks purchased can be used to verify sales. But if the software is sold electronically, there is no corroborating evidence.'[87] European countries are having difficulties collecting VAT even on shipments of tangible products such as compact disks and 'policing products downloaded electronically – music and videos – will be even trickier.' In the past, pressure for revenue has impelled many states to go in for supplementary levies in the form of surcharges, additional sales tax and, in many cases, a turnover tax applicable at different stages of sale resulting in lack of transparency and uncertainty and, for several sectors, an unduly heavy burden of tax. That in turn generated pressures for further concessions for selected sectors and sections with the result that rates vary widely across commodities depending on their classification in the rate schedule which is based on distinctions that are often hair splitting, requiring judicial arbitration. Cases were taken to court to decide questions such as whether 'coconut' is fruit or oilseed.

As noted above, the property factor does not include intangible property. This is a major omission in industries where intangible assets are 'the franchise', as is the case in many aspects of electronic commerce in content (services and intangible products). Yet it is inherently difficult – indeed, perhaps impossible – to know the location of an intangible asset. For non-tax reasons (having to do partly with limitations of copyright laws), much of the intangible property that moves in electronic commerce, especially 'shrink-wrapped' (canned) software sold in mass markets, is licensed for use by the licensee, not sold. It could be argued that, where this is true, such property, in principle, should be included in the property factor of the seller/licensor, which

---

87 Taxes Slip Through the Net, *The Economist*, May 31, 1997, at p 22.

retains ownership of the underlying asset. Doing so would raise difficult compliance problems regarding where the asset is located, over and above the question of how to treat licence receipts in the sales factor. It seems far more practical to treat licences of canned software as sales. In that case, business buyers operating in multiple jurisdictions would face the issue of where these assets are located, whether they remain in use and their value.

Another source of problem and dispute is the exclusion of services from the tax base. As noted above, sales of intangible products commonly are attributed to the state where the greatest cost of performance occurs. This approach is fraught with conceptual and practical problems. Most obviously, attributing sales of services and intangible property to the state where economic activity/cost of performance occurs is quite inconsistent with the attribution of sales of tangible personal property to the state of destination. This difference can cause distortions. Thus, for example (leaving aside issues of nexus), the sale of content (for example, music, videos, information, software) is likely to have substantially different tax consequences, depending on whether the sale takes a tangible form (sales attributed to the purchaser's state) or an intangible form (attribution to the state or states where cost of performance occurs). The use of cost of performance in the sales factor for non-tangible sales can have perverse effects on the location of economic activity. As noted above, some states will increase the weight on the sales factor, presumably to reduce the weight on activities related to production. This is not an effective strategy in the case of sales of intangible products, including electronic commerce in content, unless the state also moves to adopt a market-related measure of the sales factor.

The access to the capital (both physical and human) needed to benefit from e-commerce is almost certainly more readily available to the affluent than to those of more modest means. This means that favouritism toward e-commerce is likely to imply vertical inequities: relatively higher taxes on the poor than on the affluent (*The Economist*, 1997). In a joint press release, the National Governors' Association, the National Conference of State Legislatures, the National Association of Counties, the National League of Cities and the United Conference of Mayors argue, 'individuals with the resources to purchase a high-speed personal computer enabling them to use the Internet to make purchases that most Americans make in local stores are not a class of taxpayers needing an exemption from state sales taxes'. In a developing country, the disparity in the level of income between rich and the poor is so extensive that any change in the indirect tax will have a profound and damaging influence over the economic condition of the poor.

Chapter 8

International Cooperation and Initiatives

Introduction

Tax policy experts, like Vito Tanzi, often lament the lack of international cooperation in taxation, but it does exist and it has a fairly long history.[1] As early as the nineteenth century, states began to conclude bilateral tax treaties, codifying common rules for sharing transnational tax bases. These helped the contracting parties to keep their tax systems separate even in cases where they participated in the same tax base. As long as transnational tax bases were few in number and fiscally unimportant, the number of tax treaties remained low: by the mid-1950s only about 100 treaties had been concluded worldwide. With the advent of globalization, however, the treaty network began to expand. Today, it connects virtually all OECD member states to each other and extends to almost all other countries worldwide, with the total number of treaties approaching 2300. Why the tax treaty regime is still organized bilaterally, when, as many argue, a multilateral regime would be much more efficient and effective, is in itself an interesting question.[2] Still, there can be no doubt that the spread of this regime is a reaction to the increased coordination needs of national tax administrations in a globalized economy.[3]

This chapter will deal with the question of how to reconcile national fiscal boundaries with the borderless world of e-commerce The focus is on consumption taxation as most of the cooperation has happened in that area. There is a growing environment of trust and cooperation between tax authorities and the business communities, which will prove useful in the drive to reach satisfactory tax solutions in e-commerce. For obvious reasons, much cooperation would be required from the governments around the world. Some say that cooperation is already in evidence. Attempts by the major economic powers have been underway for the last few years to address these e-commerce problems under the umbrella of the OECD, which, with the agreement of the majority trading nations, is developing a regulatory framework for e-commerce on a worldwide basis. This process was formalized at the Ottawa Ministerial Conference in October 1998 and its subsequent related review meetings, most notably in Paris, October 1999.

---

1 Tanzi, V (1999) Is there a need for a World Tax Organization? In E. Sadka (Ed) *The Economics of Globalization. Policy Perspectives from Public Economics* (Cambridge: Cambridge University Press): 173–186 as cited in Genschel, Philipp (2005) 'Globalization and the Transformation of the Tax State,' *European Review*, Vol. 13, Supp. No. 1, 53–71.

2 Rixen, T. and Rohlfing, I. (2004) Bilateralism and multilaterlism: institutional choice in international cooperation. Paper presented at the American Political Science Association Meeting, Chicago, 3–7 September 2004.

3 Genschel, Philipp (2005) 'Globalization and the Transformation of the Tax State,' *European Review*, Vol. 13, Supp. No. 1, pp 53–71.

These summit meetings produced five interim conclusions or guiding protocols for national governments and trading blocks for development of their tax policies in relation to the internet and e-commerce (under the title Electronic Commerce Taxation Framework). Similar constructive contributions have also been made by the US and by the EU. US initiatives, particularly in the field of consumption taxation, recognizes the great gulf of incompatibility between the US sales tax and EU VAT. The OECD purpose was to ensure that no unilateral moves took place on the part of individual state governments to regulate, inhibit or tax internet transactions or to discriminate against e-commerce by way of protectionist measures. However, as the chapter will show, such an effort by OECD has been confronted by major contradictions and limitations. Lastly, there is also the need to ensure the participation of developing countries so that they can also begin to influence the 'rules of the game'. However, what will it mean for the developing countries to have a meaningful voice at an international table on tax policies and standards? It will almost certainly have to mean that any dialogue on development of e-commerce tax principles should also protect their interest. Any solutions must have the confidence of the developing world. Above all, what is needed is a recognition that globalization is not merely a matter of unrestricted market forces. It requires a strengthening of international standards and cooperative arrangements to provide a basis of mutual confidence.

8.1　　WTO Response

The WTO has done a substantial amount of work with regard to e-commerce. But the crosscutting and rapidly evolving environment of e-commerce challenges the functional treatment of trade within the WTO (General Agreement on Tariffs and Trade (GATT) and General Agreement on Trade in Services (GATS)) as well as the future work programme of the WTO. At the 1998 Geneva Ministerial, WTO members agreed to a temporary moratorium on customs duties for all products delivered over the internet. A key motivation for the moratorium was the difficulty of distinguishing between the physical and electronic delivery of products purchased over the internet and the blurring of the traditional distinction between goods and services.[4] On the one hand, products purchased electronically but delivered physically would appear to be subject to existing WTO rules on trade in goods. On the other hand, a radiology scan delivered electronically would likely be a kind of service. Consider, though, software downloaded from the internet (and which may or may not exist on a hard medium such as a CD). Is this a good or service? Should these products fall under the purview of the GATS, GATT or neither?[5] To help clarify these issues, the Geneva Ministerial declaration mandated that the WTO General Council embark on a comprehensive analysis of all trade-related aspects of e-commerce. The General Council assigned

---

4　Mann, Catherine L. (2000) 'Electronic Commerce In Developing Countries Issues For Domestic Policy And WTO Negotiations', *Working Paper, Institute for International Economics*, March 2000.

5　Mann, Catherine L. (2000) 'Electronic Commerce In Developing Countries Issues For Domestic Policy and WTO Negotiations', *Working Paper, Institute for International Economics*, March 2000.

the work programme in parts to the Goods Council, the Services Council, the TRIPS Council and the Trade and Development Committee. In addition to examining the treatment of products delivered via the internet, the work programme more generally considered how the WTO should approach e-commerce relative to the scope of work of other organizations like WIPO, the OECD and regional trading groups.

One extreme possibility is to characterize all transmissions on the internet as goods with GATT discipline applied to them. Such a characterization accompanied by a ban on custom duties on the transmissions, currently in place, would amount to the WTO members committing themselves to complete free trade transactions routed by the internet. This is because national treatment and MFN status are general obligations under GATT. By accepting the GATT discipline, under national treatment, the member countries would give up their right to discriminate against internet imports as far as domestic taxes are concerned. In addition, the ban on customs duty would bind their tariffs on internet imports at zero.[6] However, a moratorium on customs duty, which was born as a result of US efforts in the Geneva Ministerial declaration, makes sense only if there is a consensus that digitized products are goods. Second, even if there were a consensus that digitized products are goods, it would be very difficult to administer customs duties on products invisible to customs officers.[7] At the opposite extreme stands the option of abandoning both GATT and GATS and developing an entirely new discipline for internet trade. Once again, virtually no one is advocating this position. For the search for a new discipline for e-commerce makes little sense. Internet services, which include internet service providers and phone lines on which transmissions flow, are already subject to GATS and the Agreement on Basic Telecommunications. All electronic transmissions that flow on the internet, on the other hand, have counterparts in either goods trade or services trade. As such, the rules necessary to regulate that trade can be found in GATT or GATS. Thus, the real choice is between applying GATS to all internet trade or GATT to that trade for which physical counterparts also exist and GATS to all other e-trade.

In my view, on balance, it makes more sense to define all electronic transmissions as services.[8] At one level, it may be argued that at the time internet transmissions cross the border between two countries, they do not have a physically traded counterpart. The eventual transformation of the transmission into a good such as a book or CD

---

6   Panagariya, Arvind (2001), 'E-commerce, WTO and Developing Countries,' *The World Economy* 23, 8, pp 959-78.

7   Mann, Catherine L., Sue E. Eckert, and Sarah C. Knight (2000), *Global Electronic Commerce: A Policy Primer* (Institute for International Economics, Washington D. C.) at pp 87-88; Cairncross, Frances (2001), *The Death of Distance* (Harvard Business School Press, Boston) at p 180.

8   The European Union strongly asserted that 'all electronic transmissions consist of services;' and, therefore, these products should fall under the purview of GATS. Most countries, including the US, agreed that services delivered over the internet are covered by GATS, but other products are more like a good or are a hybrid between a good and a service (electronic books are a popular example).The US argued that more time is needed to monitor the development of e-commerce before any final classification takes place. World Trade Organization, 'Communication from the European Communities and their Member States on the WTO Work Programme on Electronic Commerce', 9 August 1999.

does not negate the fact that at the border the transmission did not have a physically traded counterpart. Indeed, in many cases, the transmission may not be turned into the physically traded counterpart at all. For example, the recipient may continue to store it in the digital form with books read on the screen and music played directly on the computer. Nevertheless, the key advantage of adopting the across-the-board definition is that it is clean and minimizes possible disputes that may arise from countries wishing to have certain transmissions classified as intangible goods and others as services. Under a mixed definition, in any trade dispute involving internet trade, panels will have to first decide whether the object of dispute is a good or a service to determine whether the rules of GATT or GATS are to be applied in evaluating the dispute. The adoption of the across-the-board definition automatically resolves this issue.[9]

Now the question is if digitized products were services, which one of the four modes of service delivery would characterize digitized products. It is not clear whether digitized products should be construed as cross-border service trade (mode 1), from the territory of the supplier to the territory of the buyer, or as consumption abroad (mode 2) in the territory of the seller. Mode 1 commitments are more restrictive than mode 2 commitments because countries wanted to encourage foreign suppliers to set up commercial presence (mode 3). Mode 2 commitments were relatively liberal because it is not easy to check one's nationals from consuming services abroad.[10] If digitized products were viewed as cross-border trade, and, if governments could somehow control this trade, the illiberal commitments for cross border trade (mode 1) would restrict it. If, on the other hand, the same assumptions held for consumption abroad (mode 2), then countries may have overcommitted themselves in an era when they did not view digitized imports as being defined as consumption abroad. If a new mode 5 was created just to deal with digitized products within GATS, this would constrain global e-commerce and it would be tough to draw the boundary between mode 1 and 5.

Although much has been done, several significant questions remain. The US and the EU are approaching them in different ways and are arriving at different answers. The issues are whether to extend the moratorium, how to classify e-commerce trade and modalities for reconstituting the work programme. It is clear that the main thrust should be on how best to utilize e-commerce to promote continued liberalization of global trade, rather than spending scarce resources figuring out whether or not to liberalize it. However, that agenda making has shifted from the WTO, which was evident from the paper of Walter Hellerstein[11] submitted to the Committee on Trade and Development of the WTO. The author did not mention the developments within the WTO. The arena for decision-making has shifted to the US and the EU and to deliberations within the OECD. Nevertheless, keeping with its role as overseer and

---

9   Panagariya, Arvind (2001), 'E-commerce, WTO and Developing Countries,' *The World Economy* 23, 8, pp 959-78.

10   Drake, William J. and Kalypso Nicolaidis (2000), 'Global Electronic Commerce and GATS,' in Pierre Sauve and Robert M. Stern, Eds. *GATS 2000: New Directions in Services Trade Liberalization* (Brookings Institution, Washington D.C.) at pp 411-414.

11   Hellerstein, Walter (2002), 'Electronic Commerce and the Challenge for Tax Administration,' *Seminar on Revenue Implications of E-commerce on Development* (Geneva: Committee on Trade and Development – WTO).

arbiter of international trade, the WTO is particularly concerned with e-commerce's impact on developing countries. With the other e-commerce issues, however, the WTO appears currently to be taking a detached posture, only suggesting areas of concern for further consideration and study, waiting for member countries to develop their own policy responses before taking any firm positions of its own.

8.2   Policy Differences between US and EU

Historically, the EU and the US took different policy positions toward applying consumption taxation on e-commerce. Along a tax continuum, the US, at the federal level, has been more reluctant to permit the application of consumption taxes on electronic transactions than the EU. However, the states in the US have been divided into two groups about how aggressively they want to impose consumption taxes on e-commerce, whereas the EU member states held the position that consumption taxes should be applied on electronic transactions. A detailed analysis of why the EU and the US took different policy stances toward levying consumption taxes on e-commerce is beyond the scope of this chapter, which is more of political interest rather than economic benefit. But this is beyond any argument that e-commerce presented an unprecedented opportunity to examine, radically simplify and greatly improve the US states' current sales tax system.[12] Although appealing, exempting e-commerce from sales tax does not promote free trade. As Governor Leavitt stated, 'Free trade means level playing fields, not special advantages. The prohibitionist campaign is an effort to give an unfair competitive advantage to one group of sellers. It is protectionism cloaked as free trade'.[13] In addition, opposing tax on sales on the internet does nothing to remedy the overly complicated state sales tax systems currently in place. Finally, those who oppose the taxation of internet increase the appeal of their political rhetoric by characterizing the tax as a revenue protection measure when in fact it is not.

8.3   Development within the United States

8.3.1   Internet Tax Freedom Act

In the United States, Congress passed the Internet Tax Freedom Act (ITFA)[14] in 1998. In 1997, when state and local governments concerned with consumer migration to the internet were moving towards legislation that would impose 'use taxes' on digitized transactions, Representative Christopher Cox (R-California) and Senator Ron Wyden (D-Oregon) introduced the ITFA. The *Tech Law Journal* described the

---

12 I will discuss about the Streamline Sales tax project later in the next section.

13 Governor Michael O. Leavitt, Address to the National Press Club (November 16, 1999). As cited in McKeown, Rich (2000) 'Questioning The Viability of The Sales Tax: Can It Be Simplified To Create A Level Playing Field?', Brigham Young University Law Review, Symposium Transcripts.

14 The act is mislabelled because it does not 'free' internet commerce from any tax that applies to comparable sales.

ITFA as 'perhaps the most important issue in the 105th Congress', and many at that time believed that it banned all internet taxes on e-commerce. The ITFA put a three-year moratorium of multiple or discriminatory taxes on e-commerce and taxes on internet access fees for the period of 1 October 1998 to 21 October 2001 and extended it until November 2003. The first exception to this moratorium is on internet access taxes 'generally imposed and actually enforced' before 1 October 1998 (H.R. 4328 1998, 1782–3).[15] The second exception involves the tax on B2B communication services between a telephone company and an ISA, unlike those between a customer and ISP. The purpose of this legislation is to prevent a single state or municipality from passing legislation that would adversely impact interstate commerce.

It also created a temporary 19 member Advisory Commission on Electronic Commerce (ACEC) 'a thorough study of Federal, State and Local, and international taxation and tariff treatment of transactions using the internet and internet access and other comparable intrastate, interstate, or international sales activities'. Its members represented federal, state and local governments, consumers and businesses. On 3 April 2000, the ACEC presented to Congress the results of its ten-month study of the issues of taxes and the internet. Although the commission was unable to generate the two-thirds majority vote required by the act to send a 'formal' recommendation to Congress on the subject of taxing electronic commerce, a simple majority of its 19 members did agree on a fairly comprehensive plan that addresses many internet and telecommunications tax policy issues.[16]

One of the most fundamental issues before the Commission concerned the application of state and local sales and use taxes to internet and other remote retail sales.[17] Most, if not all, of the Commissioners expressed the view that fundamental

---

15 It requires that the states which originally imposed internet access tax to phase out the tax by November 1st 2006.

16 Wagner (2000), p659. The proposal includes:
- A five-year exemption for digitized content downloaded from the Internet and 'their non-digitized counterparts.' This proposal would effectively exempt music, videos, books and magazines, games, and software from taxation.
- Codification of the *Quill* decision regarding nexus for use tax purposes and provision of safe-harbours that would prevent corporate affiliation, repairs, and returns from being construed as evidence of a physical presence in the state.
- Application of the physical presence test of *Quill*, extended as described above, to nexus for business activities taxes.
- A suggestion that the National Conference of Commissioners on Uniform State Laws (NCCUSL) be asked to draft a uniform sales and use tax act that would include: (a) uniform tax base definitions; (b) uniform vendor discount, (c) uniform and simple sourcing rules; (d) one sales and use tax rate per state and uniform limitations on state rate changes; (e) uniform audit procedures; (f) uniform tax returns/forms; (g) uniform electronic filing and remittance methods; (h) uniform exemption administration rules (including a database of all exempt entities); (i) a methodology for approving software that sellers may rely on to determine state sales tax rates; (j) a methodology for maintaining revenue neutrality in overall sales and use tax collections within each state.

17 Sales taxes are 'consumption-type' taxes designed to generate revenue. In general, these taxes are calculated and collected by businesses at the point of sale and remitted to the

uniformity and simplification of the existing system are essential. The need for nationwide consistency and certainty for sellers as well as the need to alleviate the financial and logistical tax collection burdens and liability of sellers were common themes throughout discussions. Commissioners also identified issues raised by sales of digitized goods over the internet. They discussed the challenge of determining the identity and location of the consumer of digitized goods and the need to protect consumer privacy rights. The Commission's proceedings helped widen public awareness of the issue and provided an exceptional framework for debating complex tax issues.

On 7 December 2004, the ITFA was amended and extended for four more years until 1 November 2007. The amendment basically reaffirmed the tax-exempt status of internet access, and at the same time, due to the rapid progress in internet technology, expanded the definition of 'internet access'. Ordinary telecommunication services are subject to federal excise tax and state and local sales tax, while internet access is not. The amended ITFA now mandates that the ISP make a clear distinction of the two, but the distinction may become less clear in future. The legislation also gives states more time to create a unified position, although history would tell us that this might prove to be a challenging effort.[18] Therefore, what is the essence of the new definition of internet access? The ITFA states that internet access:

> means a service that enables users to access content, information, electronic mail, or other services offered over the internet, and may also include access to proprietary content, information, and other services as part of a package of services provided to consumers. The internet access does not include telecommunication services, except to the extent such services are purchased, used or sold by a provider of internet access to provide internet access.[19]

This definition clearly indicates that regular telecommunication service is taxable, while internet access connection to the ISP, that in turn provides access to the world wide web, is tax free.[20]

The amended ITFA further provides that 'the term "tax on internet access" means a tax on internet access, regardless of whether such tax is imposed on a provider of internet access or a buyer of internet access and regardless of the terminology used to describe the tax'.[21] This means state and local governments cannot impose internet access tax on either the individual consumer or the internet access

---

appropriate taxing authorities. While the exact impact of e-commerce on sales tax revenues may be uncertain, clearly the need for substantial sales tax simplification is necessary in this emerging digital economy. In the course of the Commission's examination of the impact of e-commerce on sales and use tax collections, there was general agreement among the Commissioners that the current sales and use tax system is complex and burdensome.

18 Brooks, Barrett (2005) E-Commerce and State Sales Tax, *Journal of State Taxation*, 24, 2 pp 47-49.

19 Internet Tax Freedom Act (P.L. 105-277) Oct. 21, 1998 as amended.

20 Yang, J.G.S, Chang, C and Xing, R (2005) Current Status of Internet Commerce Taxation, *Journal of State Taxation*, 23, 3 pp 56-661.

21 Internet Tax Freedom Act (P.L. 105-277) Oct. 21, 1998 as amended.

provider.[22] Further, 'the term tax on internet net access does not include a tax levied upon or measured by net income, capital stock, net worth, or property value'.[23] This implies that the internet access tax is a consumption tax rather than a tax on income or property.[24] Yang, Chang and Xing argue that it is possible for ISPs to package internet access that includes a regular communication service and charge a higher fee. If internet access is tax-exempted, the regular communication service may become tax-free altogether. As a consequence, state and local government stands to lose US$12 billion a year.[25] In order to prevent the possible great escape of tax through the internet, the amended ITFA requires that the internet access provider separate the taxable communication services from the tax exempt internet access connection. If not, all telecommunications, including internet access, will be taxable.[26] However, the language of the ITFA is so loose that it may not be able to prevent the bundling of unforeseen internet products in the future. The second important issue arising from e-commerce concerns the purchase of goods online. The amended ITFA does not address this issue; instead it is still governed by the provisions of the original ITFA. It continues to affirm the state and local governments' taxing authorities on sales tax and use tax. The third important element of e-commerce is downloaded software and information. In this area, the original and amended ITFA did not deny or alter the state's taxing authority on sales tax or use tax.[27] In fact '19 states currently tax information and software purchased and downloaded from internet. Nine states exempt paid information downloads, but tax paid software downloads. The rest of the states either exempt these types of paid downloads or have no sales tax'.[28]

8.3.2   Streamlined Sales and Use Tax Agreement

On 12 November 2002 representatives of over 30 states voted to approve the Streamlined Sales and Use Tax Agreement,[29] an agreement between states aimed at simplifying taxation for all retailers and increasing the collection of taxes by mail-order and online companies. The Agreement will become effective when a sufficient number of individual states amend their tax laws to comply with its model tax laws.

---

22 Yang, J.G.S, Chang, C and Xing, R (2005) Current Status of Internet Commerce Taxation, *Journal of State Taxation*, 23, 3 pp 56-661.

23 Internet Tax Freedom Act (P.L. 105-277) Oct. 21, 1998 as amended.

24 Yang, J.G.S, Chang, C and Xing, R (2005) Current Status of Internet Commerce Taxation, *Journal of State Taxation*, 23, 3 pp 56-661.

25 Cline, Robert (2002) Telecommunication Taxes: 50 State Estimates of Excess State and Local Tax Burden, *State Tax Notes*, at pp 931-947.

26 Yang, J.G.S, Chang, C and Xing, R (2005) Current Status of Internet Commerce Taxation, *Journal of State Taxation*, 23, 3 pp 56-661.

27 Yang, J.G.S, Chang, C and Xing, R (2005) Current Status of Internet Commerce Taxation, *Journal of State Taxation*, 23, 3 pp 56-661.

28 Kee, Charles, E (2001) Taxing the Internet: The State's Next Frontier, *Journal of State Taxation*, at pp 1-14.

29 www.streamlinedsalestax.org/index.html. See Reese, J. Michael (2003) 'Does the Streamlined Agreement Signal the End of Quill In the Area of E-Commerce?' *State Tax Notes* (September 1): 639.

So far, representatives of 36 states and the District of Columbia voted to approve the agreement. Eventually, this document could affect the way tax is collected on over US$3.5 trillion in annual retail sales in the US. The Agreement, which supporters claim will greatly reduce the tax compliance burdens of retailers, is the culmination of over two years' work by the Streamlined Sales Tax Project.

The passage of the Agreement is only the beginning. To be effective, at least ten states, comprising at least 20 per cent of the total population of states with a sales tax, must become members in the Agreement. In order to do so, they must first amend their own tax laws to comply with the terms of the Agreement. It takes effect after the tenth state is found in compliance but could not take effect before 1 July 2003.[30] The Agreement is between individual member states, which are described as 'cooperating sovereigns'. It provides a mechanism through which member states will maintain a 'cooperative, simplified system for the application and administration of sales and use taxes under the duty adopted law of each member state'.[31] The Agreement does not invalidate, amend or supersede any provision of state law. Instead, member states must bring their own sales and use tax laws into compliance with the Agreement, as a condition of becoming members in the Agreement.[32] Only member states are bound by the Agreement. Individual taxpayers are not directly affected. Individual taxpayers are affected only when member states amend their own laws in order to comply with the Agreement. It is intended, under the Agreement, that no person will have a course of action under the Agreement and that no person can bring action related to a state's non-compliance with the Agreement.[33] To simplify the administration of sales and use tax, the Agreement provides model tax rules in a number of areas, which all member states must adopt. By applying a consistent set of rules, the tax compliance burden for multi-state retailers is lessened.[34] The provisions of the Agreement offer existing taxpayers a more modern tax collection system that provides more simplification and uniformity, coupled with a greater use of technology. The provisions provide a simple voluntary solution for sellers not collecting today that wish to expand their business into areas where they are not currently required to collect tax.[35] For businesses

---

30 SSUTA 701.

31 SSUTA 1101.

32 SSUTA 1102.

33 SSUTA 1103.

34 SSUTA would radically simplify the collection of sales tax through two key reforms: First, states that adopt the SSTP rules would use consistent sales tax definitions – for all sales, not just those in e-commerce. No longer would an item untaxed in one state be taxable across the border under a different classification. In addition, the SSTP would increase tax collections, through a simple, national seller registration that would try to capture currently untaxed sales.

35 The main concern of the majority in *Quill* was that inter-state commerce would be inhibited if state and local governments were permitted to impose collection obligations on out-of-state businesses. This concern is being addressed by the SSUTA, it is proposed that online vendors (or any remote vendors) will register online once with a central registration system (remote vendors must currently register with each state through a paper registration system). The states will maintain an online database with all relevant tax rates (assigned to zip codes) that can be accessed by the software programs employed by the remote vendors.

concerned about the cost of compliance, a seller that volunteers can receive a tax collection function at no cost, by choosing the Certified Service Provider (CSP) model, or at a low cost, by selecting the Certified Automated System (CAS) model.[36] When implemented, the proposed technological solution could represent a practical solution to the daunting compliance issues for many remote retailers by automating the tax collection process.[37] The growing use of 'Automated Tax Collection Systems', however, in turn creates concerns surrounding other interests such as consumer privacy and anonymity.[38] The SSUTA combines features of the destination-based registration and the technology fix. It is a step in the right direction but it falls short of a fundamental reform of the sales and use tax system. The Agreement will help states in their push for congressional action on the e-commerce issue.

There is a probability that some people would oppose this Agreement, particularly those who would be hurt by the simplification.[39] For example, under the Agreement, each member state would provide for state level administration of sales and use tax. This means that both state and local tax would be administered by the same state agency. This would take away the power to administer local tax from local authorities where it currently exists. Some people will attack the Agreement on Constitutional grounds. They would argue that, by agreeing to cooperate in the administration of sales tax, states are overstepping their authority and attempting to regulate interstate commerce. However, under the Agreement, as under current law, online sellers that do not have physical presence in a state cannot be compelled to collect tax, though Agreement supporters are hoping these sellers will come forward voluntarily to collect the tax. Further, some supporters are hoping that a simplified sales tax system will help the states in their effort to win Congressional or Supreme Court approval of the power to compel remote sellers to collect tax.[40] Whatever the federal system does in future regarding taxing remote sales, this had been a step in the right direction.[41]

---

36 Collins, Charles (2003) The Streamlined Sales Tax Agreement, What it means for Business, *Tax Executive.*

37 It will use of computer software to simplify the calculation, (in real time), remittance, and auditing of sales and use taxes. The state tax authority would administer all local sales taxes. Uniform sourcing rules would apply, allowing for origin taxation if the purchaser's location–that is, the destination of the good–cannot be determined. If a vendor agrees to comply with the SSUTA, it will be required to collect sales and use tax in any state that is a party to the agreement, and it will receive compensation for compliance. The SSUTA does not specify how closely the compensation will match the actual compliance costs. To lower the compliance costs of vendors, the SSUTA proposes a number of reforms.

38 Cockfield, A.J. (2001) 'Transforming the Internet into a Taxable Forum: A Case Study in E-Commerce Taxation' 85 *Minn. Law Review* p 1171.

39 SSTP planning must also still cross the Rubicon of privacy issues that have bedevilled e-commerce for years. Despite the SSTP agreement's strong privacy protections, 50 state legislatures may be sceptical of centralizing sensitive tax and financial data in today's world of identity theft and privacy breaches.

40 'Collection by sellers of sales and use taxes on remote sales remains voluntary under the Agreement until either Congress or the Supreme Court acts to make this collection mandatory.' SSUTA.

41 Hardesty, David (2002) 'Streamlined Sales and Use Tax Agreement – Part 1', www. ecommercetax.com/SSTP.htm December 1, 2002.

8.4   Development within the EU[42]

In the Lisbon European Council meeting in March 2000, the 15 member states agreed that concrete measures were to be taken to allow e-commerce to reach its full potential in the EU. The Council decided that this could only be achieved through the furtherance of rules that would make the regulation of e-commerce inside the EU as predictable as possible, while at the same time inspire business and consumer confidence. Informally, the Council approved the efforts that were already being made since 1997 to draft a proposal for a Council Directive to amend the Sixth Directive in the light of the new fiscal challenges. In 1997, the European Commission made one of the first official statements on the future of the EU's VAT system when the Commission started to examine the tax implications of e-commerce. This approach was inspired by the fact that the internet as a novel way to trade internationally was posing questions on whether the existing fiscal principles and mechanisms would be able to collect the potential tax revenue created by e-commerce. During 1997, the Commission launched a series of informal meetings with representatives of the 15 national tax administrations who examined the ways in which the growth of e-commerce was likely to affect the EU's VAT structure and attempted to shortlist the problems that could be encountered and the practical ways to overcome them.

By April of the following year, the Directorate General for VAT and Customs (XXI) was able to produce an 'Interim Report'.[43] Following a review of the ways in which e-commerce was marked to influence the ways in which people and businesses buy and sell things, and therefore how they consume goods and services for the purposes of VAT, the report concluded that the existing system of indirect taxation was the best way to approach the fiscal challenges of e-commerce. However, the Interim Report also pointed out that the administration would need to be mindful of the likely impact of changes in the pattern and in the volume of transactions. At this time, therefore, the Commission committed itself to not introducing any new mechanisms of taxation or amending the legal base of the Sixth Directive and recommended that the existing system would be sufficient to ensure collection of taxes.

The Interim Report also outlined some of the immediate hurdles. This was, in particular, applied to physical goods that are purchased by private consumers over the internet but are then delivered by traditional means. For VAT purposes, these are treated in the same way as any other form of distance sales, either in the member state of the seller or the buyer (dependent largely on the volume of such trade carried out by the other seller). There are well-established channels for taxing these transactions – goods purchased from third countries are taxed at import, exported goods are zero-rated and intra community sales of goods are taxed under a special regime for distance sales. While the report said that no changes were necessary it,

---

42 This section is adopted from the paper Basu, Subhajit (2002) 'European VAT on Digital Sales' *The Journal of Information, Law and Technology* (JILT) 2002(3) website: www.elj.warwick.ac.uk/jilt/02-3/basu.html.

43 DG XXI, Interim Report 98/0359 of the 3rd April 1998 available at http://europa.cu.int/comm/dgs/taxation_customs/.

however, called for a simplification of the rules on the customs clearance of small volume imports and at the same time did not exclude that, as more and more people would be ordering goods from internet stores, some fine-tuning of the EU distance selling rules would become necessary. Meanwhile, the Commission had anticipated that a simplification of the customs clearance procedures could be included in the framework of the next VAT strategy drawn up by the EU.

The Interim Report further recommended that a revision of the VAT rules was urgently necessary to protect the tax base for direct e-commerce transactions. The possibility that products could be delivered electronically was something unheard of when the Sixth Directive was first put into place. The Directorate General warned as early as 1998 that there was a possibility of revenue loss that could give rise to serious long-term problems for tax administrations. It was decided, therefore, that amendments to the Sixth Directive were to be made as quickly as possible to prepare the European VAT system for the inevitable explosion of e-commerce and particularly the possibility of new products being delivered digitally. It was proposed that the VAT legislative base be amended to take into account new principles and review the models of compliance, control, and enforcement. It also recognized that a level of concerted effort based on international collaboration was necessary in streamlining principles, avoiding double taxation or unintentional non-taxation.

Hence, to achieve international consensus, the European community worked with the OECD to provide a wide international forum bringing around the same table the major countries that both adopted a system of indirect taxation compatible with that of the EU and which are major trading partners of the EU. To this end, the Commission adopted a set of guidelines[44] published in June 1998, drafted on the principles which regulate VAT in the EU. These guidelines gave due recognition to the need for international accord. The starting point for the achievement of this harmonization, the guidelines suggested, was an international recognition of neutrality as the most important principle in any fiscal treatment of e-commerce.

This principle of neutrality was also included among the five principles[45] contained in the Taxation Framework Conditions approved by the participating ministers in the Ottawa conference of the OECD[46] and during the ensuing work by the various working parties of the Committee on Fiscal Affairs and particularly the talks with representatives of business; it emerged as the most important principle. In its guidelines,[47] the Commission described the principle of neutrality as the basic

---

44 Commission of The European Community, 'E-Commerce and Indirect Taxation', Communication to The Council of Ministers, The European Parliament and to The Economic And Social Committee (COM (98) 374) June 1998, Website: http://europa.eu.int/comm/dgs/taxation_customs/.

45 The five principles identified in the Taxation Framework Conditions are (i) Neutrality, (ii) Efficiency, (iii) Certainty and Simplicity, (iv) Effectiveness and Fairness and (v) Flexibility, OECD (1998) 'Electronic Commerce: Taxation Framework Conditions', A report by the Committee on Fiscal Affairs, October.

46 OECD (1998) 'Electronic Commerce: Taxation Framework Conditions', A report by the Committee on Fiscal Affairs, October.

47 Commission of The European Community, 'E-Commerce and Indirect Taxation', Communication to The Council of Ministers, The European Parliament and to The Economic

condition that would link the trading between the EU and the rest of the world and ensure that all electronic supplies for consumption in the Community would be subject to EU VAT while supplies to other jurisdictions would not be. This approach, which in effect tried to make non-EU based suppliers charge VAT on the products delivered to the customers within the EU, would eventually lie at the basis of the proposal for the Directive amending the Sixth Directive in an attempt to level the competitive advantage enjoyed by non-EU vendors over EU vendors.

The Commission's communication was considered by the ECOFIN council at its meeting on 6 July 1998 which welcomed it as the basis of a consistent Community input to the forthcoming OECD Ottawa conference and the political foundation on which changes to the VAT system made necessary by e-commerce should be made. The ECOFIN summarized this political framework in three points: (i) the existing system of VAT should be used for the indirect taxation of e-commerce and new forms of taxes should be excluded. This requirement follows from the principles of neutrality and simplicity. Neutrality in this context means that the method of commerce used to effect transactions should not influence the consequences of taxation. The principle of simplicity aims at keeping the compliance burden of the tax system to a minimum; (ii) electronic deliveries warranted a revision of the interpretation of the distinction between goods and services, which is fundamental in the workings of VAT, and recommended that products that are delivered through digital means should not be considered as goods but services through a specific provision to that effect in the Sixth Directive. Due to the lack of tangibility in the case of electronic transmissions, this classification is the only way to catch these transactions for VAT purposes. By clearing up the uncertainty surrounding the interpretation of digital deliveries now, this guideline also serves the purposes of legal certainty, which is essential for reducing the risks of unforeseen tax liabilities; (iii) that the jurisdiction of the EU to charge VAT on indirect e-commerce should be limited only to those products consumed within the territory of the Union and therefore making necessary a revision of the interpretation of the principle of consumption.

The ECOFIN also recommended that effective ways for the control and enforcement of e-commerce should be explored. It highlighted the need to adopt a legislative framework through which electronic invoicing would be allowed throughout the EU without the need for the supplier to also issue paper invoices, and simplifying as much as possible the rules with which non-EU operators have to comply, most notably the requirements of registration for VAT purposes. Finally, the ECOFIN also considered the importance of automating all the fiscal obligations of operators by enabling them to discharge them through electronic VAT declarations and accounting. The Council further said that once a mechanism enabling the returns to be filed and declarations to be made electronically was in place, there should be no reason why this should be limited only to e-commerce businesses, thus simplifying the entire VAT system by modernizing and computerizing it.

At the Ottawa conference of the OECD in October 1998, the Taxation Framework Conditions confirmed the Commission's approach, which generally repeated the

---

And Social Committee (COM (98) 374) June 1998, Website: http://europa.eu.int/comm/dgs/ taxation_customs/.

principles which had been advocated in the EU in its first initiatives on the subject a year earlier. The Commission further recognized that answers to the questions posed by the fiscal treatment of e-commerce should be pursued in close association with the business community, who, together with the national tax administrations, would be directly affected by any potential changes to the Sixth Directive. For this reason, in January 1999, the Commission organized a round table conference in Brussels on the options available to the EU VAT system and e-commerce. The meeting provided the Commission with the ideal opportunity not only to explain to the business sector its initiatives on the issue but also to encourage comments from the participants. This initiated a process of dialogue and led to the creation of an informal contact group bringing together representatives of the Commission and of European business, which would continue meeting regularly to assess together any developments. The willingness with which businesses participated in meetings and discussions that characterized the consultation process can easily be explained through their concern to protect their commercial interests, above all, by ensuring that any new rules that would be introduced by the EU would be clear enough to ease compliance and guarantee certainty.

The Commission's Taxation and Customs Union Directorate General issued a Working Paper[48] in June of 1999. This was a significant step towards arriving at the level of certainty sought by the business community by proposing a set of options as to how the principles developed since then should be implemented through legislative amendments within the framework of the EU's VAT system. This duality followed from the fact that even though Europe wishes to take advantage of the great economic opportunity brought about by e-commerce, it also has an interest in protecting the revenues and competitiveness of its member states.[49] The paper outlined an approach that would be taken up by the Commission as one of the major concerns that should be addressed by legislative reform. It also argued that since international trade was fast being dominated by the delivery of services in intangible form, the reverse charge mechanism[50] was not adequate to comprehensively take into

---

48 European Commission's Taxation and Customs Union Directorate General (DG XXI), 'Indirect Taxes and E-Commerce', 1201/99.

49 Commission Of The European Community, DG XXI, Interim Report on the Implications of Electronic Commerce for VAT and Customs, XXI/98/0359-EN, April 3, 1998 (Working Paper – 1998). See Commission of the European Community, Harmonization of Turnover Taxes, Working Paper of see Directorate General XXI, June 8, 1999 ('Working Paper 1999'). See Commission of the European Community, Explanatory Memorandum to the Proposal for a Council Directive amending the Sixth Directive as regards the value added tax arrangements applicable to certain services supplied by electronic means (COM (2000) 349 final) June 7, 2000 ('the Explanatory Memorandum').

50 Verification of the taxable status bears outstanding importance in cases of cross-border supplies to businesses, where the Sixth Directive assigns tax liability to the business recipient of certain services under the 'reverse charge' method. The rationale behind the reverse charge or self-assessment system is the wish to ensure taxation at destination. However, application of reverse charge is merely viable in case of business recipients, who have the sufficient means to fulfil such obligation and are motivated for compliance by the right to deduct the input credits. Final consumers lack both; moreover, the lack of audit-trail would render enforcement impossible. Consumption Tax Aspects of Electronic Commerce, A Report from

account the wide array of services that, with constant technological developments were capable of electronic delivery.

The efficiency of any tax system largely depends on the voluntary compliance of the taxpayers.[51] One of the core objectives of the VAT system, therefore, was the *minimization of the compliance burden*. Further, to develop such administrative rules it should take into account the diversified, decentralized and evolving nature of the electronic market. For the sake of such requirements, the Commission proposed to facilitate electronic invoicing and the discharge of fiscal obligations by means of electronic VAT declarations and accounting. When voluntary compliance fails, tax systems should be ready to enforce fiscal obligations.[52] As will be seen below, *enforceability* is the Achilles heel of the prospective VAT system. Enforcement causes problems owing to the difficulties in identifying suppliers and customers in general within the digital world. However, the problem is more acute with respect to foreign suppliers. On what grounds and by which means can the European system oblige third country enterprises to comply with Community rules?[53] The Proposal of the Commission tried to find the answers to these questions.

8.4.1 Proposal for a Council Directive Amending the Sixth Directive

The EU Commission proposed amendments to the Sixth VAT Directive. The proposed amendment addresses a very narrow field of e-commerce,[54] *direct e-commerce*, focusing on the issue of cross-border supply of digitized products, with special regard to those destined to final consumers in the Community. The Proposal of 7 June 2000 was the first attempt to give a black-on-white solution to the problems which were examined since 1997. It also put doubt on previous statements of the Commission that there would be no need to effect any radical changes to the European VAT system and that e-commerce could be taxed using the same VAT platform, save some minor amendments such as the Proposal itself. The explanatory memorandum[55] spoke in brief of how e-commerce was poised to change the way in which people buy and sell things, in other words the world of trade. The Commission predicted

---

Working Party No. 9 on Consumption Taxes to the Committee on Fiscal Affairs, OECD, 15 (2001).

51 Tait, Alain A. (1998) *Value Added Tax*, 3 (International Monetary Fund ed., Washington, D.C. p 270.

52 Tait, Alain A. (1998) *Value Added Tax*, 3 (International Monetary Fund ed., Washington, D.C. p 270.

53 This question constitutes one dimension of the conflict between the US and European approaches to taxing e-commerce. Namely, the Supreme Court of the United States decided in the Quill-case that businesses are not responsible for collecting a use tax unless they have a physical presence (nexus) in the customer's home state. *Quill Corp. v. North Dakota* (91-0194) 504 U.S. 298 (1992).

54 Preamble of the Proposal, Explanatory Memorandum, at pp 11-12.

55 Commission of the European Community, Explanatory Memorandum to the Proposal for a Council Directive amending the Sixth Directive as regards the value added tax arrangements applicable to certain services supplied by electronic means (COM (2000) 349 final) June 7, 2000 ('the Explanatory Memorandum').

that at some point 'a full scale review of the exiting VAT' would be necessary. The 7 June Proposal failed to capture enough support, as a result of which the Commission placed the 7 May 2002 Proposal. In the following section, I will discuss the 7 June Proposal. The basic objective that was laid down in the June Proposal also remained the same in the May 2002 Proposal. Hence, the following discussion will provide a comprehensive outline with some criticisms. Specific issue-based criticism will be provided with the May 2002 Proposal.

8.4.2   7 June 2000 Proposal

On 7 June 2000, the European Commission presented a Proposal for a Directive to modify the rules for applying VAT to certain services supplied by electronic means as well as subscription-based and pay-per-view radio and television broadcasting. The Commission proposed[56] to change the EU VAT regime for e-commerce operators by proposing amendments to sections 9, 12, 24, 28g and 28h of the Sixth Directive. 'The Commission's intention is that the Proposal should give e-commerce operators a clear framework in which to charge, collect and remit VAT on electronic deliveries.'[57] The direction taken by the Proposal is to: (i) clarify the provisions regulating VAT chargeability; (ii) simplify the procedures for the collection and remittance of VAT; and (iii) remove the competitive advantage enjoyed by non-EU e-commerce operators.

Under current rules, goods imported into the EU are subject to import VAT, which is collected when the goods enter the EU. Non-EU sellers of goods are not required to register for or collect VAT. The lack of an obligation to register did not hinder the collection of the tax due because the VAT was collected at import and paid directly by the private customer. The importation of goods requires the same to be physically transported from outside the EU to a member state where they would have to go through the post or customs. Such shipments can presently be easily checked to determine whether the VAT has been paid. If VAT is still due, authorities would not release the goods until the buyer comes forward to settle the tax outstanding.

Whether a transaction should be subject to VAT, or at what rate such transaction should be charged, is determined by processing a set of information. The determination of whether a transaction is subject to VAT, and according to what jurisdiction and rate should be easy enough to allow business themselves, although not without resource to tax professionals, to do it. For a person to be able to decide on the VAT chargeability of a transaction he must be aware of: (i) the tax status of the customer; (ii) under which jurisdiction the transaction falls; and (iii) which VAT rate should apply. On the other hand, for VAT purposes a supplier should know the tax status

---

56 European Commission, 'Proposal for a Council Directive amending Directive 77/388/ EEC as regards the value added tax arrangements applicable to certain services supplied by electronic mean', 7th June 2000, 500PC0349(02).

57 Commission of the European Community, Explanatory Memorandum to the Proposal for a Council Directive amending the Sixth Directive as regards the value added tax arrangements applicable to certain services supplied by electronic means (COM (2000) 349 final) June 7, 2000 ('the Explanatory Memorandum').

of his customer and therefore whether he is either registered for VAT or otherwise a private consumer. Under the general VAT rules, the supply of goods or services to a VAT-registered business by a supplier established in the same member state should be charged tax according to the prescribed rates; no tax would be charged by the supplier if the customer is a business registered for VAT in another member state. In that case, the customer would be able to account for tax through the reverse charge mechanism. The above is already the case for the application of VAT to non-electronic transactions where the verification of the VAT registration number of a customer normally occurs through information made available by the national VAT authorities of the country of the supplier.

In the case of e-commerce, where the transaction would occur instantly, the supplier would need to be able to make the verification in real time, and for this reason the Proposal recommended that a structure should be put in place, augmented by the necessary tools and technical measures, to provide EU-registered VAT numbers online. Clearly, the inability of the VIES system to provide online, real time verification prevents the suppliers from fully exploiting the comfort and speed offered by electronic trade and, therefore, potentially hampers the pursuance of such activity.[58] At the time of with confirming the tax status of the customer's location should also be verified. With regard to business purchasers, if the verification process through the VIES system is successful, the location of the business can be inferred from the registration number.[59] In the case of final consumers, there is no such supplementary system. In traditional circumstances, the consumer either paid on the spot or was required to let the supplier know of his address for the purposes of delivery and payment. When ordering online, consumers use electronic mail for communicating with the seller but e-mail addresses tell little about the real, physical residence of its user.[60] The most evident means of finding out their location is to ask the customers to self-declare this information.[61] However, unless underlining this practice with reliable verification, buyers might feel tempted by the anonymity of online trade to disclose falsehoods.[62] Despite the diverse efforts to solve this problem, there is still no reliable and feasible means of identifying and locating consumers in lack of voluntary compliance.[63] For the time being, suppliers might verify disclosed

---

58 Commission of the European Community, Explanatory Memorandum to the Proposal for a Council Directive amending the Sixth Directive as regards the value added tax arrangements applicable to certain services supplied by electronic means (COM (2000) 349 final) June 7, 2000 ('the Explanatory Memorandum').

59 Subsection (d) section (1) of Article 22 of the Sixth Directive.

60 Working Paper - 1998, Eriksen, Nils and Hulsebos, Kevin (2000) Electronic Commerce and VAT – An Odyssey towards 2001 in VAT Monitor July/August.

61 Consumption Tax Aspects of Electronic Commerce, A Report from Working Party No. 9 on Consumption Taxes to the Committee on Fiscal Affairs, OECD, 15 (2001) at p 13.

62 By disclosing false information as to their location, consumers can save significant VAT costs because of the differences in the VAT rates of the Member States and third countries.

63 OECD (2000) Technology Technical Advisory Group (TAG), 'Report on Tax and e-Commerce', December 2000. Report on the technological questions of tax collection, The conclusion of the Report is that work should be continued in the field of defining reliable technology for jurisdictional identification.

data by using the credit card information requested from the purchaser previous to the conclusion of the contract.[64] They might also rely on the currency of payment in determining the taxing jurisdiction.[65] Evidently, neither of these examples is a guaranteed solution.[66] Moreover, the Commission also hoped it could rely on the modernization of the VAT Information Exchange System (VIES).[67]

The Proposal has been the subject of severe criticism by non-Europeans who would have to collect VAT on sales to customers in the EU and remit the tax to a VAT authority in the member state of registration. The majority of critics come from the US. Ken Wasch, President of the American Software and Information Industry Association, considered a notable lobby in the US Congress, was reported to have said that, 'US vendors should not be tax collectors for European governments. It is also doubtful, under public international law, whether the EU has any authority to impose such a legal obligation on US entities'.[68] It also appears that online taxes for downloaded items would be higher than the taxes which were being applied to the same products delivered through traditional ways. During the first week of July 2000, an American delegation led by Under-Secretary of Commerce Robert LaRussa was in Brussels for a series of meetings with Commission officials on how taxation and data protection were being affected by e-commerce. Speaking after one of the meetings LaRussa said: 'we need to set up some kind of process where the US and the EU with our business communities can address these issues. There are peculiar US-EU issues, and you really do need an early warning system or you are going to address them too late'.[69]

The European Commissioner for Taxation, Frits Bolkestein acknowledged that although VAT revenue losses because of B2C transactions were still small, they were bound to grow and the sooner amendments were put in place the better. Bolkestein described the present situation and the need for change thus:

---

64 Commission of the European Community, Explanatory Memorandum to the Proposal for a Council Directive amending the Sixth Directive as regards the value added tax arrangements applicable to certain services supplied by electronic means (COM (2000) 349 final) June 7, 2000 at p 8.

65 Commission of the European Community, Explanatory Memorandum to the Proposal for a Council Directive amending the Sixth Directive as regards the value added tax arrangements applicable to certain services supplied by electronic means (COM (2000) 349 final) June 7, 2000 ('the Explanatory Memorandum').

66 According to the report of the Technology TAG of the OECD, credit cards are likely to remain the dominant form of payment in the majority of countries for consumer transactions over the Internet. However credit cards are not reliable sources of data on consumer jurisdiction. While the concept of matching a credit card number to the country of residence was originally thought to have promise, further investigation demonstrated that there was no numerical PIN correlation to geography. Technology TAG Report, supra note 32.

67 DN IP/02/864 'VAT: New Commission OnLine Validation Service Saves Time And Costs For Businesses', Brussels, 14th June 2002.

68 DN IP/02/864 'VAT: New Commission On-Line Validation Service Saves Time And Costs For Businesses', Brussels, 14th June 2002.

69 DN IP/02/864 'VAT: New Commission On-Line Validation Service Saves Time And Costs For Businesses', Brussels, 14th June 2002.

Today European producers of digital products, such as computer games and software, are at a competitive disadvantage compared with non-European producers because they have to apply VAT to their products within Europe. US competitors, by contrast, can export to Europe free of VAT. Similarly, European exporters to the US are now obliged to pay European VAT, whereas US producers are not faced with the same obligation. I propose to put European producers of digital products on an equal footing with Japanese competitors and US by applying VAT to digital imports into the EU and exempting digital exports from the EU. This would create a global level playing field for European and non-European companies.

However, the Proposal sought to achieve this 'global level playing field' where, however the US businesses would be unwilling to play. Yet, for Hardesty,[70] one of the critics to the Proposal, the EU disregarded one of the fundamental conclusions of the OECD conference. The participating ministers at the conference had agreed that for solutions on the indirect taxation of e-commerce to be truly effective these must be the result of an international consensus. He felt the Commission overlooked this agreement and pursued its own individual solutions without waiting for what might be internationally acceptable avenues for the indirect taxation of e-commerce.

The most controversial point that had been criticized in the Proposal was the suggested introduction of a new single-place registration for VAT. This would have enabled companies to apply for a VAT registration under one of the 15 national tax authorities and be able to trade with customers in the entire Community. Since the registration would have the effect of creating a place of establishment in the country of registration, all transactions of that company would be taxed according to the rates applicable in that tax jurisdiction. It is understandable that companies might prefer to seek registration in countries such as Luxembourg, which apply a 15 per cent VAT rate, instead of in countries with a higher rate of up to 25 per cent, such as Sweden or Denmark. It is also understandable why countries such as Sweden and Denmark raised opposition to the amendments as they predicted a plummeting of their VAT revenues from tech-companies. Not only would VAT revenues decrease but the amendments would also create an unfavourable situation for the traditional bricks and mortar businesses[71] as these businesses would be selling their products at a price which could be at least 10 per cent more expensive than online retailers simply because the latter have a VAT registration in another Member State with lower VAT rates. On these grounds, Snel[72] criticized the Proposal as running counter to the principles of neutrality and discrimination, which had earlier been identified by the ECOFIN Council, and later also by the OECD, as two of the pillars on which any future taxation of e-commerce should be constructed. Snel further argued that the success of ideas such as a single point registration would depend on the

---

70 Hardestey, David (2000), 'Europe Proposes New Taxes on Non-EU Sellers'.

71 Snel, Jan L.N. (2000) 'European Union reaches out across borders: EU proposes to tax US-based e-commerce companies with Value Added Tax in the EU', Baker & McKenzie, Palo Alto, San Francisco.

72 Snel, Jan L.N. (2000) 'European Union reaches out across borders: EU proposes to tax US-based e-commerce companies with Value Added Tax in the EU', Baker & McKenzie, Palo Alto, San Francisco.

willingness of operators to comply with such regulations. The only way to bring back an equilibrium between traditional retailers in high VAT member states and their online competitors would be to apply the same lower VAT rates that apply for those type of services delivered by electronic means to services of the same class delivered offline by the bricks and mortar stores in the country with high VAT rates. However, such a task would be monumental and would be defying the Commission's philosophy that e-commerce should be taxed using the existing VAT platform. This is perhaps one of the first instances which confirm the Commission's concern that sooner or later the indirect taxation of e-commerce would call for a wider revision of the existing VAT system. In the late November 2000 meeting, the ECOFIN Council recommended to the Commission to rework the Proposals and present an amended version. Shortly after the ECOFIN meeting, on 28 November 2000, a detailed report on the Proposal, drawn up by the European Parliament's Committee on Economic and Monetary Affairs, chaired by Jose Manuel Garcia-Margalloy Marfil, was tabled to Parliament.[73] On 14 December 2001, the Parliament voted to endorse the report as its official opinion suggesting a series of amendments to the Commission's Proposal. In practice, this had the effect that the Proposal was blocked and although not formally withdrawn, shelved for the moment.

The Parliament stipulated that in order to ensure a fair sharing of VAT revenues resulting from transactions between non-EU suppliers registered in one member state and non-taxable persons in another member state, a system of refunds between member states should be introduced. The Parliament further recommended that a structure should be created to provide for permanent monitoring by the Commission of the state of play as regards the implementation of the Proposal in the member states to ensure no distortion of the market. The original Commission Proposal foresees that non-EU suppliers with annual sales above EUR100,000 operating in the EU will have to register in at least one member state, which would then be the tax jurisdiction responsible for applying the tax. The Parliament felt that to counter the risk, already mentioned above, of companies choosing to register in a low tax country such as Luxembourg, the Commission should draft another proposal to address the question of VAT revenue distribution among member states. Moreover, the Parliament proposed the threshold for registration be lowered from EUR100,000 to EUR40,000.

In the explanatory statement to the report, the Committee on Economic and Monetary Affairs also spoke about the future convergence between internet and mobile phone technology. The Committee outlined its position clearly concerning this and dismissed any problems because of a fundamental distinction, which was illustrated by means of an example. The report said that in relation to a customer who

---

73 European Parliament, 'Report on the proposal for a European Parliament and Council regulation amending regulation (EEC) No 218/92 on administrative cooperation in the field of indirect taxation (VAT) (COM(2000) 349 – C5-0298/2000 – 2000/0147(COD)) and the proposal for a Council directive amending directive 77/388 EEC as regards the value added tax arrangements applicable to certain services supplied by electronic means (COM(2000) 349 – C5-0467/2000 – 2000/0148(CNS))', 28th November 2000, Committee on Economic and Monetary Affairs, Manuel Garcia-Margallo y Marfil.

was able to download information through a mobile phone, the charge for connection and airtime would fall under the heading of telecommunications, while the charge for the information would fall under the heading of e-commerce.

The Parliament's opinion broadly supported the Commission Proposal in spite of some shortcomings. The report suggested that these shortcomings mainly result from uncertainties on future developments and advised that these should be overcome in time before entry into force of the proposed Directive. 'The creation of a level playing field in electronic services is a matter of urgency, but it is essential that a system of distribution of tax revenues be put in place to compensate the advantage of those Member States with the lowest VAT rates.'[74] Moreover, Parliament defended the Proposal against criticism that it might be pre-empting the work that was still being undertaken by the OECD. The Committee mentioned how the main opposition to the Proposal came from across the Atlantic with the intention of preserving the competitive advantage that US companies currently enjoy. This advantage was further strengthened by the US Congress's approval to extend the moratorium on the taxation of electronic services at least until 2006.

While drafting its report, the Committee sought the assistance of the Parliament's Committee on Industry, External Trade, Research and Energy chaired by Carlos Westendorp y Cabeza and the Committee on Legal Affairs and the Internal Market chaired by Ana Palacio Vallelersundi. In its opinion the Committee on Legal Affairs and the Internal Market recommended that Parliament should request the Commission to withdraw its Proposal for a Directive until such time as: (i) a thorough review has been carried out on the VAT charged on goods and services supplied by non-electronic means; (ii) the ongoing discussions in the OECD and other international fora have been brought to a conclusion; and (iii) a complete package of measures can be proposed. Finally, during the 5 June 2001 meeting of the ECOFIN Council, the British Chancellor of the Exchequer made known that his country would not support the Proposal despite the fact that the other 14 member states expressed their willingness for plans to implement the Proposal to proceed.

However, the UK's blocking of the Proposal led to the formulation of the May 2002 Proposal. The UK believed that the draft Directive published in 2000 was unworkable on the grounds that there were no effective means of forcing such vendors to register and there was a danger of the system losing all credibility. The alternative proposed by the UK was radically different; namely removing tax from digitized sales within the EU altogether, which in policy terms mirrored the prevailing view in the US.[75] A level playing field would have been created in terms of pricing, but inevitably at the cost of VAT revenues. Yet it never occurred to the Commission

---

74 European Parliament, 'Report on the proposal for a European Parliament and Council regulation amending regulation (EEC) No 218/92 on administrative cooperation in the field of indirect taxation (VAT) (COM(2000) 349 – C5-0298/2000 – 2000/0147(COD)) and the proposal for a Council directive amending directive 77/388 EEC as regards the value added tax arrangements applicable to certain services supplied by electronic means (COM(2000) 349 – C5-0467/2000 – 2000/0148(CNS))', 28th November 2000, Committee on Economic and Monetary Affairs, Manuel Garcia-Margallo y Marfil.

75 Ivinson, Jonathan (2003) Why the EU VAT and E-commerce Directive Does not Work, *International Tax Review* (London).

to consider the positive fiscal impact of increased inter-EU trade flows, increased direct tax revenues, and to set these against the negative VAT consequences. This may be explained by the fact that VAT provides the EU with half of its resources.[76] The UK did not, however, use its veto to block the Proposals altogether but accepted the compromise proposed by Sweden, which substantially forms the basis of the Directive as it stands today. The reasons for the UK's change of policy probably have more to do with the rough and tumble of real politics than any intellectual conversion to the majority point of view.[77]

The UK's opposition was consistent with its approach to e-commerce in the context of direct tax. In its submissions to the OECD technical advisory group, the UK took a robust stance on the question of whether a website or a server could constitute a PE.[78] In their view, neither in itself was sufficient to give rise to the taxable nexus sufficient to constitute a PE. The domestic law of certain other EU member states has taken a very different view in analogous situations in order to try stake a claim to a proportion of the profits of cross-border oil and gas supplies or transport services. The UK's concern was that if a website or server could in itself constitute a PE, the corollary would be that it would be difficult to establish a claim to tax the profits of an enterprise that located a server in a tax haven and paid a UK management services company a cost plus fee for back-office services.[79] The requirement of substance in order to assert a taxable presence was seen by the UK as a more valuable tool in its armoury than a theoretical right to tax a share of the profits derived from unmanned items of computer equipment that happened to be situated in the UK. That was not a view universally shared by other member states. Although the OECD discussions were in the context of direct tax, the approach of some continental European countries to taxable nexus in that context is illustrative of an approach to the indirect taxation of e-commerce that asserts tax competence on the basis of trading with a state rather than trading in it.[80]

8.4.3 Verification of VAT Numbers for Electronic Supplies

The Proposal of June 2000 brought attention to the fact that the present regulation of the confirmation of the validity of a VAT registration number of a person by the member state needed to be changed because this would not allow national VAT authorities to give confirmation of the validity of a customer's VAT identification number to a person supplying services by electronic means. The procedure for the verification of VAT numbers is controlled by section 6 of Regulation (EEC)

---

76 Ivinson, Jonathan (2003) Why the EU VAT and E-commerce Directive Does not Work *International Tax Review* (London).

77 Ivinson, Jonathan (2003) Why the EU VAT and E-commerce Directive Does not Work *International Tax Review* (London).

78 Ivinson, Jonathan (2004) Overstepping The Boundary - How The EU Got It Wrong On E-Commerce, *Computer and Telecommunications Law Review*, 10(1), pp 1-4.

79 Ivinson, Jonathan (2003) Why the EU VAT and E-commerce Directive Does not Work *International Tax Review* (London).

80 Ivinson, Jonathan (2003) Why the EU VAT and E-commerce Directive Does not Work *International Tax Review* (London).

No. 218/92, which limits the confirmation only to 'persons involved in the intra-Community supplies of goods or of services'. The Proposal stressed that the confirmation of validity of VAT identification numbers by electronic means was one of the ways through which trade could be facilitated and therefore described its plans to amend the legal base to make such thing possible. On 14 June 2002, the Commission introduced the online validation service.[81] The online service, which any member of the public can now access free of charge, allows checking of the databases of VAT registration numbers which each member state maintains as part of the VIES. The database of VAT identification numbers is only one aspect of the VIES. Members of the public logging on to the site will not be able to see any of the other VIES information which is used by member states' taxation authorities for VAT control purposes and which should, in the interests of taxpayer confidentiality, remain reserved for the use of taxation authorities only.

Under the current VAT system, all intra-EU supplies between traders subject to VAT are exempted from VAT in the country of sale, the tax being declared at destination by the receiving trader. Normally the customer provides her VAT identification number to the supplier when she orders the goods. But it is the responsibility of the supplier to confirm that his customer is indeed VAT registered in another member state before he sends the goods free of VAT. Otherwise, the supplier may be obliged to pay the VAT himself. Up to now, a supplier wishing to confirm the validity of the VAT identification number provided by its customer generally had to contact its own tax administration which would check the VIES and confirm that the number quoted was valid. By cutting out the intermediary, this new service speeds up this verification procedure, thus saving time and money for both businesses and tax administrations. The overall aim is to facilitate legitimate commercial transactions within the Internal Market while improving controls against fraud.[82]

8.4.4   May 2002 Proposal (Council Directive 2002/38/EC)

On 7 May 2002, the European Council adopted Directive 2002/38/EC and Regulation No. 792/2002.[83] The new Directive will come into effect on 1 July 2003 and shall remain in effect for three years, after which time it may be extended or revised.[84] By the adoption of this Directive, digital service providers located outside of the EU would be required to register with European tax authorities by July 2003 and have to collect VAT on sales of digitally delivered products. While the rules do, indeed, place new burdens on some foreign firms, the European Commissioner for Taxation, Frits Bolkestein, believes that, ultimately, everyone's interest will be served by the legislation. 'I welcome the decision of the council to adopt these rules on applying

---

81 DN IP/02/864 'VAT: New Commission On-Line Validation Service Saves Time And Costs For Businesses', Brussels, 14th June 2002.

82 The online service can be accessed at the following address: http://europa.eu.int/vies.

83 Full text of the Directive is available at http://europe.eu.int/comm/taxation_customs/whatsnew.htm.

84 Taxation and Customs Union, VAT on electronic commerce (June 3, 2002), http://europa.eu.int/comm/taxation_customs/taxation/ecommerce/vat_en.htm.

VAT to digital products. They will remove the serious competitive handicap which EU firms currently face in comparison with non-EU suppliers of digital services, both when exporting to world markets and when selling to European consumers.'[85] The Directive applied to electronically delivered services as well as radio and television broadcasting services.[86] The first category included digital products that are distributed over the internet such as software. The EU treats all products that are distributed electronically as services. An annex to the proposed legislation sets out an illustrative list of the types of services that are targeted by the new framework: (i) website supply, web hosting, distance maintenance of programs and equipment; (ii) supply of software and updating thereof; (iii) supply of images, text, information and making databases available; (iv) supply of music, films and games, including games of chance and gambling games, and of political, cultural, artistic, sporting, scientific and entertainment broadcasts and events; (v) supply of distance teaching.

The Proposal contained two separate sets of provisions. The re-definition of the place of supply rules for electronic deliveries and the amendment of connected administrative provisions necessary for the implementation of the redefined rules, along with a set of provisions under a special scheme to facilitate the compliance with fiscal obligations by operators providing electronically supplied services who were neither established nor required to be identified for tax purposes within the Community, form the heart of the Proposal. The other key point of the document was the set of provisions facilitating the discharge of VAT obligations by electronic means. The Proposal sets forth two distinct places of supply for digital deliveries in accordance with the varying tax status and location of the recipient. The first place of supply rule determined the place of transactions to final consumers within the Community. It deems the location of the supplier's business or fixed establishment as the place of supply. This resulted in the practical extension of the general place of supply rule of the Sixth Directive to B2C digital transmissions.[87] While if a customer located outside the Community is supplied by a business established in the EU, that transaction would not fall under the tax jurisdiction of any member state and would thus not be subject to VAT. Section 9(3) enabled EU members to implement special tax rules to avoid 'double-taxation, non-taxation or the distortion of competition'.[88] In practice, this section would allow member states to treat the place of supply that

---

85 Reuters (2002) 'Europe Approves Net Tax Law', May 7, www.wired.com/news/print/0,1294,52351,00.html.

86 Hardesty, David (2002) European VAT on Digital Sales, March 3, www.ecommercetax.com/doc/030302.htm.

87 Sub-paragraph 1(b) of the Directive proposes that: (1) In Article 9(2), the following point (f) is added: '(f)...the place where services referred to in the last indent of subparagraph (e) are supplied; when performed for non-taxable persons who are established, have their permanent address or usually reside in a Member State, by a taxable person who has established his business or has a fixed establishment from which the service is supplied outside the Community or, in the absence of such a place of business or fixed establishment, has his permanent address or usually resides outside the Community, shall be the place where the non-taxable person is established, has his permanent address or usually resides.'

88 Lambert, Howard (1998) 'VAT and Electronic Commerce: European Union Insights into the Challenges Ahead', 17 Tax Notes International Nov. 23.

under section 9(2) would fall within the territory of a member country as being situated outside the Community, 'where the effective use and enjoyment of the services take place outside the Community', and treat the place of supply that would normally fall outside the Community as actually being within the member state 'where the effective use and enjoyment of the services take place within the territory of the country'.

The place of supply in the case of a transaction between an EU operator and a taxable person inside another member state would be deemed the country where the recipient to the transaction was established. This envisages B2B transactions because the supply would be made to a taxable person and not to a private consumer. If, on the other hand, the recipient of such a transaction was a private individual but also a taxable person located in the same member state of the supplier, the place of supply would now be the place where the supplier was located. Article 9, paragraph 4 is amended as follows:

> In the case of telecommunications services and radio and television broadcasting services referred to in paragraph 2(e) when performed for non-taxable persons who are established, have their permanent address or usually reside in a Member State, by a taxable person who has established his business or has a fixed establishment from which the service is supplied outside the Community, or in the absence of such a place of business or fixed establishment, has his permanent address or usually resides outside the Community, Member States shall make use of paragraph 3(b).

By means of the new section 9(4), EU members could change the determination of the place of supply by virtue of section 9(3b) in the case of services to non-taxable persons in the EU by non-EU ISPs when such services are 'effectively used or enjoyed' in Community territory. Section 9(3b), however, can only be applied in the case when the services were supplied to 'non-taxable persons established'[89] and not necessarily to EU residents only. This presents a much wider net for VAT taxation including non-Europeans using or enjoying ISP services of non-EU providers while passing through Community territory. It was argued that this could potentially have double-taxation implications.[90] In practice, therefore, this allowed member states to tax intangible services supplied from non-EU member states to non-taxable customers using or enjoying such services within their country.

The Commission proposed to amend the basic rule of the Directive to allow the place of supply for the supply of such services, not to apply to the place where the services are physically carried out, but to the place where the customer either (i) has established his business, or (ii) has his or one of his fixed establishments to where the given service is actually supplied or in the absence of either (i) or (ii), where the customer (iii) has his permanent address or usually resides. There would be no tax to collect on free downloads, free information or free access to the internet as VAT is not generally a consideration when no charge is made. The Commission also pointed

---

89 Sec. 9 (4) Sixth VAT Directive.

90 Lejeune Ine, Vanham Bart, Verlinden Isabelle, Verbeken Alain (1988) 'Does Cyber-Commerce Necessitate a Revision of International Tax Concepts?' Part I, *European Taxation*, 1998, volume 38.

out in an accompanying note to its original Proposal that nothing will change in respect of services where the internet was only used as a channel of communication between the supplier and the customer.

The Proposal added Article 26c for non-established taxable persons supplying electronic services to non-taxable persons; the Article provided definitions[91] and a special scheme for services supplied electronically. The Proposal permitted a non-established taxable person supplying electronic services to a non-taxable person who was established or had his permanent address or usually resides in a member state to use the special scheme in accordance with the provisions laid down in the Proposal. Non-EU suppliers were allowed to register in a single member state under the 'special scheme', but they would have to be able to account for VAT in all of the EU member states in which they had 'final' consumers, and further they would be required to levy VAT on those transactions with EU consumers if their revenues exceeded a certain threshold amount.[92]

In addition, tax administrators would provide operators with the means to distinguish easily the status of their customers (whether the customer is a VAT registered business or a private customer), and this would provide a means whereby any supplier acting in good faith would be able to determine whether or not a transaction should be charged with VAT. In order to facilitate the introduction of the new system, non-EU suppliers would be offered a simplified online registration and compliance mechanism that would allow them to fulfil their VAT duties without establishing a physical presence or 'fiscal representative' within the EU.[93] However, they must register with the chosen authority by providing information including name, postal and electronic addresses, websites, national tax number and a statement that the company was not already identified for VAT purposes in the EU. The chosen tax authority would then provide the supplier with a dedicated number by email after which the supplier must submit a quarterly VAT return that includes details of the total value of sales and tax collected in each member state. The suppliers then have

---

91 For the purposes of this chapter:

'Non-established taxable person' means a taxable person who neither has established his business nor has a fixed establishment within the territory of the Community and who is not otherwise required to be identified for tax purposes under Article 22.

'Electronic services' and 'services supplied electronically' means those services referred to in the last indent of Article 9 (2) (e).

'Member State of identification' means the member state which the non-established taxable person chooses to contact to state when his activity as a taxable person within the territory of the Community commences in accordance with the provisions of this Article.

'Member State of consumption' means the member state in which the supply of the electronic services is deemed to take place according to Article 9 (2) (f).

'Value added tax return' means the statement containing the information necessary to establish the amount of tax that has become chargeable in each member state.

92 The initial proposal contained a 'minimum turnover threshold' of Euro 100,000. At present, it is not clear whether this threshold will be dropped entirely so that a non-EU supplier would have to register with a EU member state even though there are only occasional sales to EU consumers.

93 Art. 26c VAT Directive as amended.

to remit tax collected to the tax authority that is then responsible for reallocating the VAT revenues among the other member states.

The application of VAT for electronic services supplied from one member state to consumers in another member state within the EU would be charged at the applicable rate in the member state where the supplier is registered.[94] For Non-EU suppliers the directive, in its current form, does not address the issue of tax rates specifically, but the Commission would undertake a general review of all aspects of these tax rates shortly as part of its quest to modernize VAT. It is clear that a 'standard' tax rate will be established for each country within the EU and non-EU suppliers will levy VAT according to the 'standard' tax rate of the member state within which they are registered. Under the scheme for supplies made to third countries, VAT would be levied at a rate applicable in the member state where the customer is a resident and revenue will be re-allocated to that state after a purchase is made. The suppliers would also have to make tax records available to the member state of where they register and those member states where their consumers reside. They should keep such records for ten years after the sale. Member states have agreed that this system should be applied for three years following implementation of the Directive and then be extended or revised. According to the European Commission: 'the single registration model offers a streamlined set of obligations, which can be easily completed, online without the need for a fiscal representative or for any physical presence. This special registration scheme will be easier to operate and more business friendly than rules for non-resident businesses generally.'[95]

8.4.5   Council Directive 2006/58/EC

By Council Directive 2006/58/EC adopted on 27 June 2006 these[96] VAT arrangements were extended by a further six months up to 31 December 2006.[97] On 15 May 2006,

---

94 This is applicable so long as the seller's sales do not exceed the 'distance selling' thresholds defined for each country. Thus, taxation at the place of supply would remain in effect for all member states with the EU. For example a UK Company A, selling software and delivering it over the internet to consumer B in Germany will be charged VAT at the rate applicable in the UK.

95 Taxation and Customs Union, 'VAT on electronic commerce' (June 3, 2002) http://europa.eu.int/comm/taxation_customs/taxation/ecommerce/vat_en.htm.

96 Council Regulation issued in October 2005, and generally effective July 1, 2006, includes place of supply rules governing electronically supplied services covered by the Sixth Directive, Article 9(2)(e). For services to customers outside the EU or for taxable persons established in another country within the EU, the services covered in the Regulation generally take place where the customer has established his business or has a fixed establishment to which the service is supplied or, in the absence of such a place, the place where he has his permanent address or where he usually resides. Article 11 of the Regulation covers services delivered over the Internet or over electronic network. See Alan Schenk and Oliver Oldman (2006) *Value Added Tax: A Comparative Approach*, (Cambridge University Press) pp 215-216.

97 Council Directive 2006/58/EC of 27 June 2006 amending Council Directive 2002/38/EC as regards the period of application of the value added tax arrangements applicable to radio and television broadcasting services and certain electronically supplied services.

the Commission adopted a report to the Council on the operation of this Directive as well as a proposal to extend the period of its application to the end of 2008.[98] Taxation Commissioner László Kovács urged 'the EU Council of Ministers to rapidly reach an agreement on this extension as I cannot imagine we would revert to the rules prevailing before the e-commerce Directive was introduced'. 'I also request support from the EU Council to adopt as soon as possible the two Proposals on the place of taxation of services and on the One Stop VAT Shop scheme,[99] which will in essence give permanent effect to the measures in the e-commerce VAT Directive.' The report[100] of the European Commission to the EU Council concludes that the e-commerce VAT Directive has operated in a satisfactory manner and has achieved its objective of creating a level playing field for the taxation of electronic services. It recommends extending the period of application of this Directive until more permanent wider measures are in place. Without this extension in time, the VAT rules would revert to those prevailing before the e-commerce Directive was introduced.[101]

8.4.6 Criticism and Defence

So how will the EU enforce its laws against suppliers with no establishment in the EU? Suggested solutions so far have included a withdrawal of intellectual property protection for offenders and reliance upon the fact that companies would have difficulty raising capital in the public markets with substantial tax debts in the EU.[102] Such threats may work in respect of the larger players, many of whom established themselves in low VAT territories such as Madeira or Luxembourg prior to the Directive taking effect. It must be very doubtful that compliance will be widespread among the smaller players. The Proposal had been the subject of severe criticism by non-Europeans who will have to collect VAT on sales to customers in the EU and remit the tax to a VAT authority in the member state of registration. As has already been mentioned earlier,

---

98 A report to the Council for operation of COUNCIL DIRECTIVE 2006/58/EC of 27 June 2006 amending Council Directive 2002/38/EC as regards the period of application of the value added tax arrangements applicable to radio and television broadcasting services and certain electronically supplied services.

99 The One Stop VAT Shop scheme would allow traders to carry out their VAT obligations for all EU wide activities in the member state where they are established. Traders could use a single VAT number for all supplies throughout the EU and make their VAT declarations via a single electronic portal.

100 A report to the Council for operation of COUNCIL DIRECTIVE 2006/58/EC of 27 June 2006 amending Council Directive 2002/38/EC as regards the period of application of the value added tax arrangements applicable to radio and television broadcasting services and certain electronically supplied services.

101 The temporary provisions contained in the Directive will be given permanent effect when the EU Council of Ministers adopts the proposals from the Commission on the place of taxation of services (COM (2005) 334; see IP/05/997) and on the simplification of VAT obligations (the proposal for 'One Stop VAT Shop'; COM (2004) 728; see IP/04/1331). The extension proposed should allow sufficient time for the adoption of these proposals.

102 Ivinson, Jonathan (2003) Why the EU VAT and E-commerce Directive Does not Work *International Tax Review* (London).

the majority of critics hail from the US. While this Proposal sounds unassuming at first, there are several potential concerns. Since VAT rates differ according to EU member states, the accounting could become a bit tricky. The standard VAT rates currently range between 15 per cent in Luxembourg to 25 per cent in Denmark or Sweden. Thus, any non-EU firm providing services to EU residents must keep track of their customers' locations in order to properly assign taxes. Thus, if a non-EU operator decides to register in Great Britain and makes sales to individuals in France, Germany and Sweden, the operator will need to know that the rates to be applied at the customer location are 19 per cent, 16 per cent and 25 per cent, respectively. Further, it also means that a book delivered online will be subject to the standard tax rate while, the same book delivered in physical form may be subject to a lesser rate, or even a zero rate.[103] It is unclear whether this discrepancy would be remedied. If no steps are taken to remedy it, a situation may arise in which the rate applicable to certain electronic media will differ greatly from the rate applicable to the same product when it is physically delivered.[104] In this simple example, a single product yields three possible tax rates depending on the form and geography of the transaction – hardly the OECD goal of 'neutrality, efficiency, certainty and simplicity, effectiveness and fairness, and flexibility'. The problem, as the US sees it, is that while EU companies charge tax based on where their headquarters are located, non- EU companies would be required to charge tax based on where the buyer lives. That means European companies could charge a flat tax rate for all purchases made by European customers, while US and other non-EU companies would have to determine where each buyer resides before calculating tax. Such a process would place a significant administrative and technological burden on US e-tailers.[105] The Proposal could be 'a significant problem' for US and other non-EU e-tailers, Gartner analyst French Caldwell told the *E-Commerce Times*. It could also cause international conflict. Gartner previously

---

103   While one objective of the directive is to apply the tax rate, equally to electronic and traditional media for directly equivalent products, reduced or 'zero' rates are currently in effect printed materials such as books, newspapers, and periodicals. (Taxation and Customs Union, *VAT on electronic commerce* (June 3, 2002)). http://europa.eu.int/comm/taxation_customs/taxation/ecommerce/vat_en.htm.

104   For example: Consumer A purchases a book online. It is subject to the 'standard rate' VAT depending upon his country of residence. Consumer B purchases the same book, and it is delivered in physical form. It may be subject to a lesser rate, or even a 'zero' rate VAT.

105   A letter from the US Council for International Business to Commissioner Bolkestein on February 7 2002 effectively summaries the concerns expressed on behalf of businesses:
- Proving a customer's location is difficult and may result in greater business costs for businesses;
- Services are not being treated equally to goods since they are standard-rated, and, in many jurisdictions, the equivalent goods enjoy a reduction in the applicable rate;
- Rate discrimination results from the fact that non-EU operators' tax burdens will be greater than that of EU operators who can charge a lower rate of VAT to EU customers if they are tax-registered in a low-tax jurisdiction (such as Luxembourg);
- Non-EU operators will face administrative burdens that are not sufficiently spelled out yet and may result in significant costs.

predicted that differences between EU and US tax laws will become a major source of friction in international trade by 2003. A report released by the research firm said, 'The EU's decision to move forward with its proposals raises the probability.'

The Bush administration has 'serious concerns' about the Proposal and indicated that the plan may violate existing treaties and rules set out by the WTO. US Deputy Treasury Secretary Kenneth Dam called for 'further efforts to achieve a more global consensus that reflects a consideration of all the issues raised'. He pointed to current discussions on e-commerce tax issues being held at the OECD. He further added 'the proposal may potentially be inconsistent with international trade obligations in the WTO, in particular the commitment to accord national treatment to foreign goods and services'. The concept of one set of countries imposing a consumption tax regime on other nations is perhaps most troublesome of all. Unilateral proposals such as this may encourage others to take unilateral measures, rather than waiting for the global consensus that can be developed through a deliberative and inclusive process, such as the OECD's. Hardesty[106] expressed similar concern that the unilateral impetus in the EU to tax electronically-delivered products might trigger a worldwide reaction with many countries following in the steps of the Commission and enacting laws that will allow them to levy indirect taxes on all electronic deliveries that are finally consumed within their territory, regardless of their country of origin. This would make e-businesses wrestle with tens of different VAT regimes worldwide and the burdens of compliance would be so immense that non-compliance would be the order of the day. The EU argues, however, that the new Directive simply removes a competitive handicap by not levying the VAT outside the EU and by subjecting non-EU suppliers to the same VAT rules as EU suppliers when providing electronic services to EU customers.[107]

Caldwell[108] on the other hand pointed out that even if the policy were approved, it would be unenforceable because it will be impossible to determine whether an EU consumer has downloaded digital goods from a server based outside the EU. 'And how are you going to charge VAT on Web services? That is the next thing', Caldwell added. There may even be legal trouble. The US Supreme Court has ruled that companies cannot be forced to collect taxes on interstate sales when they do not have a physical presence in the consumer's state. According to the Gartner report, if that ruling is extended to international sales, US companies could be legally barred from collecting value added tax on behalf of EU countries. In the end, the EU's proposed policy may come back to haunt it. 'The bigger problem is not for the U.S. companies, it's a problem for EU companies potentially locked out of the U.S. market if the U.S. decides to retaliate.' Further, this would likely add to a series of disagreements between the US and the EU over trade, including the dispute over new US steel import duties.[109]

---

106   Hardesty, David (2000) 'EU Continues Efforts to Tax Digital Products'.

107   Taxation and Customs Union, 'VAT on electronic commerce' (June 3, 2002) http://europa.eu.int/comm/taxation_customs/taxation/ecommerce/vat_en.htm.

108   On Feb. 23, 2006, the OECD launched a new project to provide guidance to governments in this area. IBFD Tax News Service, 'OECD project on clarifying VAT/GST application in cross-border trade,' Feb. 27, 2006.

109   Reuters (2002) 'EU Taxes U.S. E-Commerce', May 6 www.wired.com/news/print/0,1294,52325,00.html.

The Proposal has not provided a comprehensive definition of what digital goods and services are covered. The list seems to be unsatisfactory in respect of the novel types of service as well.[110] Due to the dynamic evolution of the internet and e-commerce, there are already some services which would fall outside the scope of subsection (2e).[111] The taxation of these services, therefore, would also happen according to the general place of supply rule. The next issue of concern is the over-complication of the place of supply rules that would follow from the adoption of the proposed amendments to Article 9 of the Sixth Directive. Furthermore, the Proposal is salient on the issue of how the consumer's jurisdiction can be accurately identified. To assess which member state rate is applicable to the sale, the non-EU suppliers are going to have to be able to verify their customers' identity (business or final consumer) and jurisdiction in a real-time, online environment. Many companies have stressed that the technology is not yet available to achieve this with 100 per cent accuracy.

The compliance regime for non-EU suppliers will be more onerous than their EU based counterparts. The US Treasury has argued that while a European company will be able to charge the same tax rate to every European customer, US businesses will have to calculate the tax rate for each European customer who buys a download, based on the country they live in. Industry groups argue the new Directive will cost large companies business and make it difficult for smaller firms to sell digital products in Europe.[112] The EU has argued that the special scheme is its best effort at lightening the compliance regime. It should be noted that the process of registration for non-EU suppliers applies only to 'a non-established taxable person', and not to anyone who is already established or has a fixed establishment for VAT purposes in any EU state. Some businesses may find it advantageous to make sure their activities are within the new registration regime, though others may find it an advantage to create an establishment in the EU and account for VAT under the existing regime. The preferred course of action will depend on the individual circumstances of each business.

Hardesty[113] also highlighted another shortcoming in the Proposal. In its explanatory memorandum to the June 2000 Proposal, the Commission briefly explained the ways in which it was planning to ensure compliance with the suggested amendments. The key to the EU's enforcement of these new rules is online identification of consumers. As of now, technology would not allow the online seller to verify the location of a consumer or whether the consumer is VAT registered. The Directive assumes that this technology would become available, but if it is not the entire Directive becomes unenforceable. The Proposal itself is

---

110   It can generally be stated that the list-approach is flawed with respect to electronic transactions considering the rapid development of technology offering newer and newer opportunities for e-commerce transactions. See Eriksen, Nils and Hulsebos, Kevin (2000) Electronic Commerce and VAT – An Odyssey towards 2001 in VAT Monitor July/August.

111   Such as, e.g., *co-location services* and *registration of domain names see* ibid.

112   Glasner, Joanna (2002) 'U.S. Not Happy about EU Tax', May 8 Website: http://www.wired.com/news/print/0,1294,52378,00.html.

113   Hardesty, David (2000) 'EU Proposes New Taxes on Non-EU *Sellers*', *E-Commerce Tax News*, June 18, 2000 Website: http://www.ecommercetax.com.

absolutely silent on how compliance is to be ensured and therefore leads one to deduce that the mechanisms for compliance would be constructed on those already used for traditional commerce. However, the intangible nature of e-commerce gives rise to new problems of compliance peculiar to this new way of buying and selling things electronically. The Proposal provides no detail as to how the EU national VAT authorities will be able to trace non-compliant businesses. Hardesty, however, predicted that the EU competitors of offending non-EU companies would have an interest in reporting them and tip off tax authorities on where to look for non-compliance. This is not a practical solution that can offer any degree of predictability. Even if the national VAT authorities, following tip-offs or some other system, identify non-EU companies which are not compliant with the requirements of the suggested amendments, there would also be problems of enforcement and, in particular, collecting the unpaid VAT due. Once again, although the explanatory memorandum hints at what might be the tools used for the enforcement of VAT rules on non-EU sellers, the Proposal itself contains nothing on the matter. The Commission suggested that non-EU companies would have an interest in collecting VAT on sale to EU customers because the EU Framework would already be protecting their intellectual property rights within Community territory. In other words, this is a form of give and take situation. Nevertheless, give and take situations are not law, and it is not unheard of that people with an interest to make a profit take as much as they can and do not give. Various other solutions have been suggested, although not by the Commission itself.

The Directive also represents something of a landmark in fiscal policy as the EU is attempting to enforce its sales tax laws way beyond its physical boundaries, rather like California's assertion of worldwide taxing rights but on a grander scale. Somewhat surprisingly, it either did so without fully considering the implications of such an assertion of taxing competence, or was cavalier about those consequences. The lack of an agreed methodology between trading nations also presents a major risk of double taxation.[114] The EU may have been attempting to seize control of the agenda by forcing through the Directive, yet nobody will relish duplicating an assertion of taxing competence that requires no taxable nexus, that is impossible to enforce and which violates some of the fundamental principles of world trade and international taxation.[115] One unexplored solution to the problem may be a multilateral agreement between the EU and third countries, establishing a commonly agreed method of taxing electronic services and, perhaps most important, agreement to exchange information in order to increase the chances of successful enforcement. In the event that the EU shifts to the origin principle of taxation in the future, such treaties will be necessary with third countries in order to prevent double or indeed no taxation of exports from countries operating different systems.[116]

114　Ivinson, Jonathan (2003) Why the EU VAT and E-commerce Directive Does not Work *International Tax Review* (London).

115　Ivinson, Jonathan (2003) Why the EU VAT and E-commerce Directive Does not Work *International Tax Review* (London).

116　Ivinson, Jonathan (2003) Why the EU VAT and E-commerce Directive Does not Work *International Tax Review* (London).

8.5   OECD Response

During the past few years, the OECD had been the most important forum for discussion on the fiscal implications of e-commerce, bringing together governments and key business players. The work of the OECD's Committee on Fiscal Affairs produced the Taxation Framework Conditions, which were adopted by the Finance Ministers of the OECD member countries meeting at Ottawa in October 1998.[117] The Taxation Framework Conditions is regarded as a document which has served both as starting point and point of reference for governments from all over the globe rising to the fiscal challenges of e-commerce. The fundamental guiding principle in the conclusions of Ottawa was that the tenets of taxation that guide governments in relation to conventional commerce should also guide them in relation to e-commerce. The participating ministers in the conference had unanimously agreed that rather than trying to develop a new system of taxation,[118] the existing systems of VAT and GST should be modernized. The Taxation Framework Conditions proposed that taxation of e-commerce should occur in the jurisdiction where the consumption of the good or service takes place. It supports the view that the supply of digital products should not be treated as a supply of goods even though this might initially appear to be running counter to the general rules of traditional consumption taxes.[119]

One of the major works done by the OECD was highlighting the ever-widening gap that exists between the European and US approach to the taxation of online trade. OECD initiatives in the past years have proved to be central in the effort in the possible worldwide harmonization of basic taxation principles which probably in future can dismantle existing barriers and lead to a fiscal climate where e-commerce can flourish. OECD member countries are concerned not only to ensure that the consumption tax systems they use are efficient but also to guarantee the preservation of the tax base that is threatened to be eroded in direct and less direct ways. The OECD embarked on a broad revision of consumption tax principles, and work of how the consumption tax systems should be updated was entrusted to Working Party No. 9 on Consumption Taxes. The Working Party No. 9 acted as a forum to discuss policy, administrative and technical issues. Working Party No. 9 has been actively involved in areas such as financial services, international cooperation, taxation and the environment and in the field of e-commerce, ensuring that 'VAT systems remain a robust mechanism concerning the taxation of consumption in the light of the development of electronic commerce'.[120]

The major achievement of this Working Party's work had undoubtedly been the drafting of the Ottawa document. Following the Ministerial conference, the Working Party No. 9 later embarked on a period of meetings and discussions, examining reactions and comments to the Tax Framework Conditions, with special emphasis on

---

117   OECD (1998) Electronic Commerce: Taxation Framework Conditions, A Report by the Committee on Fiscal Affairs of the OECD.

118   The controversial Bit tax.

119   OECD Commission on Fiscal Affairs, *Electronic Commerce: Taxation Framework Conditions*, at 5, Pt V, para.11(v).

120   OECD, 'Taxing Consumption', available at http://www.oecd.org/daf/fa/c_tax/consum.htm.

the international character of online trade. This process of studying in further detail the possible ways in which the principles laid down in Ottawa could be put into practice was planned to be concluded by March 2001, and in February 2001 the Working Party presented its latest report. This document, however, failed to take into account the concurrent developments in Europe. In its report, the Working Party designated clear areas of reference and issues that were to be discussed during international meetings of experts. The Working Party No. 9 planned to undertake intensive work in trying to address questions such as whether a website or a server could constitute a PE for the purposes of giving a country power to exercise its tax jurisdiction, to examine and suggest new ways in which the payment for electronically delivered products should be categorized under the existing tax treaties, and, most important within the ambit of consumption taxes, to build a consensus among OECD member countries but also non-members as regards two separate definitions, that of the place of supply and a workable definition of services and intangible property. This agenda was set out in the Taxation Framework Conditions itself, which commissioned the Working Party No. 9 to draw up the various implementation options that were listed with respect to the areas covered in the Ottawa document. The document itself had emphasized the importance of working hand in hand with businesses, which will ultimately generate the taxes paid to their respective governments. Moreover, the OECD recognized the fact that it would be unable to bring forward truly global solutions to the consumption tax of e-commerce unless it would be able to rally widespread international support to its initiatives from among non-member countries. To make this work easier for the Working Party, a number of technical advisory groups (TAGs) where created to focus on specialized key areas relying on the expertise provided by governments and businesses.

Several non-OECD countries were involved in the Turku tax round-table on e-commerce in 1997 and participated in the dialogue on tax and e-commerce in the run-up to the OECD Ministerial conference in Ottawa in October 1998[121] during which the participating delegations set out the general principles that should underlie solutions to problems confronting e-commerce. Various approaches to problems were discussed and organizations were identified that were considered able to develop and implement any future solutions. The Turku conference stated for the first time that 'the communication poses challenges for the traditional concepts underlying VAT systems'[122] and called for an international effort to address these challenges. Among other taxation issues, the conference discussed the present state of application of VAT in its member states and of GST in Canada and New Zealand, agreed that the VAT concept of 'place of supply' should be re-studied and amended according to the new needs of e-commerce, recommended a clearer distinction of goods and services for the purposes of taxing digital trade, examined the distinctions that should be drawn between different types of services, suggested a study on the impact of VAT and customs procedures on e-commerce, and also reviewed the US proposals

---

121 OECD 1998 Conference.

122 OECD, 'Electronic Commerce: The Challenges to Tax Authorities and Taxpayers', An Informal Round Table Discussion between Business and Government, November 1997.

for the internet to be declared a tariff-free environment whenever it is used to deliver products or services.

In late 1997, the first OECD efforts started taking shape, namely under the Committee on Fiscal Affairs, to put forward solutions for the many issues outlined in the Turku report. Within a few months, the various Working Parties and Technical Advisory Groups started to identify the options that governments could consider individually or collectively. Turku laid the foundations for what was to be agreed upon less than a year later in Ottawa. All 29 OECD member countries, 12 non-member countries, 12 international organizations and representatives from business, trade unions, consumer groups and other non-governmental organizations attended the ministerial conference.[123]

In October 1998, the OECD succeeded not only in persuading its members that there was a need for urgent debate, but above all agreement, on the rising questions on the taxation aspects of e-commerce, but managed to attract unanimous support from the finance ministers of the member countries who signed a document that would lay the foundations for all the future work that the organization would do in this field. As was already stated above, the Ottawa Taxation Framework Conditions are concerned with how e-commerce is challenging not only the traditional systems of consumption taxes but also income taxes and the existing tax treaties. The Committee on Fiscal Affairs managed to secure a number of ground rules that were posed to guide the future treatment of the fiscal issues of e-commerce. Rather than proposing strict rules, at this early stage it was felt that the best approach would be to establish basic principles to which all the participating countries at the Ottawa conference would have no problem ageeing to. The most basic principle was that the existing taxation principles that already guide governments in relation to conventional commerce should also guide them in relation to e-commerce. The Committee explained, however, that this approach was not to be interpreted strictly and that therefore it did not preclude new administrative or legislative measures or changes to the traditional tax principles provided these new measures were intended to assist in the application of the old tax systems. The Committee had stressed that these new measures should in no case be allowed to give rise to a discriminatory tax treatment of e-commerce transactions.

The Ottawa document further provides that whatever these measures to tune the existing tax systems to the new needs created by a worldwide e-commerce might be, their application should be structured in such a way as to safeguard the fiscal sovereignty of a country, to achieve a fair sharing between countries of the tax base from e-commerce and to continue to avoid double taxation or unintentional non-taxation even in the ambit of digital sales. The most important part of the Ottawa document was the recognition of five fundamental principles that should apply in any fiscal treatment of e-commerce, and particularly in any future specific regulating documents that the OECD might pursue in the future. In fact, the Ottawa document can safely be described as an exercise in the identification of guiding principles. In

---

123 OECD (1998) Report on the OECD Ministerial Conference, 'A Borderless World: Realising the Potential of Global Electronic Commerce', 7-9th October 1998, Ottawa, Canada.

1998, it was widely agreed that it was too early to try seeking more permanent and formal solutions, but rather to clear the ground to be tackled and the problems that should be avoided.[124]

Talks since the Ottawa conference have shown (as can be seen in the February 2001 report on the *Consumption Tax Aspects of Electronic Commerce by the Committee on Fiscal Affairs)* how much experts are worried about the business community trend to place particular focus on the principle of neutrality. Sometimes these principles may be in competition with one another, and the achievement of a balance between them could be proved more complicated than predicted. Moreover, governments and businesses might have different views on how such a balance should be achieved or on what principle should be given priority while being applied in particular circumstances. This highlights why the OECD insisted on the importance of a close dialogue between governments and businesses, something that was achieved with a certain degree of success in the conferences that have followed Ottawa. In the latest report from the Working Party No. 9 on consumption taxes, it was stated that neutrality is the most important principle, which is given priority in almost all cases. 'The Working Party, while mindful of that particular business focus and determined to foster consensus wherever possible, nonetheless believes it important to give due weight to all the principles, recognising that they form a package.'[125] Such a statement should not, however, be considered as a final settlement on the competition in which the principles are put by the often opposing sides of government and business.

More specifically on consumption taxes, the Ottawa document developed another set of minor principles further identifying the ground for the future initiatives of the OECD. In fact, the Taxation Framework Conditions states that the rules for the consumption taxation of cross-border trade should result in taxation in the jurisdiction where the effective consumption takes place, and that effort should be made to achieve an international consensus on the circumstances under which supplies should be held to be consumed in a jurisdiction.[126] The importance of reverse charge, self-assessment

---

124   The five Ottawa principles are goals that should be achieved in the drafting of international agreements on the tax treatment of e-commerce, and the document itself set in motion a process of further meetings and consultations between experts coordinated by a number of Working Parties. The five principles identified in the Taxation Framework Conditions are (i) Neutrality, (ii) Efficiency, (iii) Certainty and Simplicity, (iv) Effectiveness and Fairness and (v) Flexibility. I have discussed these principles while discussing the EU's effort in the previous section. OECD, 'Electronic Commerce: Taxation Framework Conditions', A report by the Committee on Fiscal Affairs, October 1998.

125   OECD (2001)Consumption Tax Aspects of Electronic Commerce: A Report from Working Party No. 9 on Consumption Taxes to the Committee on Fiscal Affairs (OECD February 21).

126   According to the (2005) OECD report 'The Application of Consumption Taxes to the International Trade in Services and Intangibles: Progress Report and Draft Principles' consumption taxes should impose tax where goods or services are consumed, but for administrative reasons, countries may rely on proxies to determine where goods and services are consumed. On the basis of the principle that final consumers should bear the economic costs of VAT, the report included the principle that taxable businesses should not bear, as an economic cost, the VAT on goods and services used in making taxable supplies.

or other equivalent mechanisms was also acknowledged. These systems, according to Ottawa, would, in the case of businesses and other organizations acquiring services and intangible property from outside their country of establishment, allow tax jurisdictions immediate protection of their tax base while ensuring the competitiveness of their domestic suppliers. The document also called on countries to ensure that appropriate systems are developed in cooperation with the World Customs Organization and in consultation with carriers and other interested parties to collect tax on the importation of physical goods, and that such systems do not unduly impede revenue collection and the efficient delivery of products to consumers. On 12 February 2001, the OECD's Committee on Fiscal Affairs commented on achievements since the Ottawa conference.[127] Gabriel Makhlouf, the chair of the Committee, was reported to have greeted some of the recommendations, which his Committee forwarded to the OECD since Ottawa, as a 'significant step forward in international efforts coordinated by the OECD to address the tax implications of e-commerce'. The Committee continued that with respect to consumption taxes, OECD member countries 'have made significant progress towards identifying pragmatic ways of achieving the desired result of effective taxation in the place of consumption'.[128]

The Committee reviewed the conclusions of a report that was presented in February 2001 for public comment by its Working Party on Consumption Taxes which stressed the importance for a clearer definition on the principle of taxation in the place of consumption and the need to identify the collection mechanisms that could best support the operation of the principle of taxation at the place of consumption. The Committee also approved and encouraged the publication of the report inviting the public and businesses in general to comment on the Proposal. The Working Party's report also proposed the drawing up of a set of guidelines that would assist in the definition of the place of taxation for cross-border services and intangible property. Particular emphasis was placed on how the place of establishment of the recipient business in the case of B2B e-commerce and to the place of establishment, and therefore the jurisdiction of the more common B2C transactions, would be allowed to affect the determination of the place of taxation in the case of cross-border services and intangible goods. The report also delved into the possible development of the collection mechanisms of indirect taxes. The report recommended that for B2B transactions, the tax should be collected through a reverse charge or self assessment mechanism, and for B2C transactions, the tax should be collected through a registration-based mechanism.

The Working Party concluded that in the case of B2B transactions the most viable solution was to employ self-assessment mechanisms, while in the case of B2C transactions the most viable options would inevitably be those facilitated by the latest digital technology, although for the time being it would still be easier and safer to rely

---

127   OECD (2001) progresses towards achieving an international consensus on the tax treatment of e-commerce, news release, 12th February 2001 at http://www.oecde.org/media/release/nw01-15a.htm.

128   OECD (2001) progresses towards achieving an international consensus on the tax treatment of e-commerce, news release, 12th February 2001 at http://www.oecde.org/media/release/nw01-15a.htm.

on the older registration-based systems. It should be mentioned that annexed to the report were two very important documents which sought to summarize and clarify the proposals of the working party with regards to the guidelines on the definition of the place of consumption, with particular emphasis on B2B transactions, and more specifically recommending approaches to the practical application of such guidelines.[129] This annex could be viewed as the basis for the drafting of a final document that would be presented for formal approval by the Committee on Fiscal Affairs and thus reaching the last stage before a wider international agreement on the definition of the place of consumption of intangible property in the context of e-commerce through the OECD itself. The Working Party stressed the need that further work was required to comprehensively address the issues, old and new, arising from its months of examination. For this reason the report identified eight areas that should be 'pursued actively in 2001' by the Working Party. These are (i) the verification of the declared jurisdiction of residence of the consumer in respect of B2C online transactions in order to identify practical and effective methods which appropriately balance the needs of revenue authorities with those of the businesses and consumers alike, (ii) the verification of the status of the customer in order to earmark ways of distinguishing between business and private consumers, which provide sufficient assurance to revenue authorities while minimizing specific demands upon business, (iii) the registration of thresholds with the purpose of further clarifying the role that definite registration parameters can play in reducing the compliance requirements for non-resident suppliers, (iv) technology-based and technology-facilitated collection mechanisms and in particular to examine their feasibility, the time frames in which these could be implemented and also the role that other related standards and tools can play in supporting tax-related functions, (v) encourage and support international administrative cooperation and identify more clearly practical steps regarding how this can realistically be achieved, (vi) strive to develop ways in which the taxation of e-commerce can be simplified, and thus to evaluate rigorously relative priorities taking into account the feelings of the business community, (vii) address compliance-related questions identifying areas of risk in relation to effective assurance and compliance and to study the possible solutions, and finally (viii) developing longer-term strategies for exploiting the potential of technology-based mechanisms. The Committee on Fiscal Affairs welcomed this report and mandated the Working Party to proceed with its sterling work. Moreover, the Committee requested the Working Party to submit a summary and review of the reactions to the report, to draft guidelines and associated recommended approaches for their application to be formally approved by the Committee and to present a comprehensive status report on the progress of the further work that was envisaged in the February report. Meanwhile, 'there is much that tax administrations can and should do to share their experience and expertise internationally. It is important that we maintain our efforts to strengthen the emerging international consensus, so as to provide governments and business with the certainty that they need about how taxation rules should apply to e-commerce', Makhlouf added.

---

129   The report suggested that for B2B transactions, to the jurisdiction in which the recipient has located its business presence, and, for B2C transactions, by reference to the recipient's usual jurisdiction of residence.

In December 2000, the Technical Advisory Group on consumption tax set up by the Working Party under the framework of the Committee on Fiscal Affairs published its latest report, in which it suggested the adoption of a '*Simplified Interim Approach*'. The report maintains that a simplified tax compliance system, particularly about the tax collection mechanisms that could be implemented by the OECD, would, at least until the approval of long-term solutions with the necessary international support, encourage vendors which have not yet established themselves in any particular country to collect and remit tax just the same. Although the report itself fails to explain in detail how such an approach could be achieved, in practice the TAG said this solution would focus on the need to simplify all aspects of tax compliance for non-established sellers, thus including their registration, identification of turnover and calculation of tax, electronic submission of returns and audit processes. More simply, 'the thrust of the simplified interim approach is that VAT compliance should be so simple that non-established vendors would be thereby encouraged to register'.[130]

Although it might be still too early to measure the implications of this approach, the simplified interim approach could eventually become a major backbone in all the work that the OECD is doing in the field of consumption tax of e-commerce. All the sub-groups entrusted with formulating a clear policy for the OECD that would be acceptable for both governments and businesses can in fact use this approach as their guiding principle. Success for governments on the one hand by collecting revenues and success for businesses on the other by limiting as much as possible the burdens of compliance to national and international rules lies undoubtedly in simple but efficient rules. The OECD has to work hard towards the conciliation of these two requirements of simplicity and efficiency to be able to steer a common international approach to the consumption taxes of e-commerce. However, this would be a monumental task, most notably because of the ever-widening views advocated across the Atlantic. Although the OECD itself might develop a final document on the taxation of online commerce, its success in practice would depend solely on whether the EU and the US support it. And while the US continues to develop its own ways to deal with the fiscal questions of e-commerce by ensuring one tax moratorium after another, the EU has already experienced how it cannot propose its own solutions if these do not concur with the American approach. One would be tempted to ask whether the OECD's initiatives could also be blocked by opposition raised in the US as happened in the case of the proposed EU Directive on the VAT treatment of e-commerce. In this way, simplicity on its own might not be enough and once again, this could be another case confirming the saying that 'money talks'. Both the EU and the OECD seem to try to appease the US in matters of taxation of online trade because they can in no way compete with the American giant where hundreds of internet retail operations are being opened every day. In a document drawn up by the business members of the TAG,[131] annexed to the TAG's report, experts have agreed

---

130   OECD (2000) Report by the Consumption Tax Technical Advisory Group (TAG), December 2000, at p 6.

131   Including PricewaterHouse Coopers, America Online, UBS AG, Keidanren, Electronic Data Systems Corporation, Microsoft Corporation, Nortel Networks, KPMG, Swisscom AG, AT&T, ABN AMO Bank and Philips.

that the simplified interim approach should be adopted to implement the framework conditions of Ottawa in the near term. This document unequivocally states that in view of the present state of development of technology and the inherent limitations of technology to provide more robust technical methods to collect consumption taxes, a simplified approach should be one based on the supplier-registration model.

This option has been analyzed in much more detail by another of the technical advisory groups established by the Working Party as will be seen shortly below. The same document continues that, 'for governments, the primary concern with consumption tax and e-commerce relates to B2C transactions that involve digitally-delivered services and intangible goods'.[132] The TAG's business members' key concerns with respect to the application of existing consumption tax systems to B2C e-commerce can be summarized in four points: (i) countries do not yet allow vendors to transmit a fiscal invoice solely in an electronic matter, thus hindering the opportunities for businesses to reduce their costs by rendering transactions completely paperless, (ii) technology still cannot offer a totally comprehensive e-commerce tax solution since an element of human judgement is still needed to determine, among others, the tax jurisdiction of the rate of tax for each individual transaction, (iii) in an online transaction, businesses are currently unable to verify user-provided information against external data sources because authorities do not make such data available or otherwise this data cannot be accessed instantaneously, or rather, contemporaneously to the transaction, and (iv) compliance procedures are still complicated and lack standardization, and therefore require a lot of manual work which frustrates the development of system-based and completely automated solutions. Although the business members said that the amount of consumption taxes generated by B2C transactions involving digitally-delivered intangible goods and services is still relatively low, the increase of this form of trade will not necessarily mean that there will also be an increase in the potential for revenue leakage. The business members predicted that in the near term, most supplies of intangible goods and services crossing borders would be made by larger and more sophisticated companies who are capable of dealing with at least some of the complexities of cross-border trade. Moreover, large companies are better equipped and more inclined to be tax compliant because they would want to keep up their corporate image and amidst strong competition protect the operations they have in different countries. The businesses warned the OECD that 'simplification remains the tax authorities' single greatest tool to encourage compliance'.[133]

Government officials from over 100 countries met in Montreal to discuss how to develop and implement such a taxation framework. The Montreal Conference was held from 4 June to 6 June 2001 and was hosted by the Canada Customs and Revenue

---

132   Report by the Consumption Tax Technical Advisory Group (TAG), Annex V, 'Outline of the Consumption Tax TAG Business Members' Recommendations for a Simplified Interim Approach, as submitted to the WP9 Sub-group on Electronic Commerce', November 2000, at p 37.

133   On Feb. 23, 2006, the OECD launched a new project to provide guidance to governments in this area. IBFD Tax News Service, 'OECD project on clarifying VAT/GST application in cross-border trade,' Feb. 27, 2006.

Agency (CCRA) Conference Tax Administrations in an Electronic World by the conference's five co-sponsoring organizations, the Commonwealth Association of Tax Administrators (CATA), the Inter-American Centre of Tax Administrations (CIAT), le Centre de Rencontres et d'Etudes des Dirigeants des Administrations Fiscales (CRÉDAF), the Intra-European Organization of Tax Administrations (IOTA) and the OECD. Representatives of the IMF, UN, World Bank, Regional Development Bank and the EU also participated. The co-sponsors of the meeting set themselves ambitious objectives at the outset. Participants agreed that these objectives had been fully met. 'There was general agreement that the conference should be the start of an ongoing process by which governments work together to improve their tax systems, to exploit the opportunities offered by the new technologies to improve taxpayer service and to enable governments to raise revenues in an effective and equitable way', said Mr Etcheberry, the President of CIAT.[134] The presidents and chairs of the other sponsoring organizations also shared the same view. *The ongoing dialogue would focus on four related areas:* identifying best practices in the area of taxpayer service; improving the capacity of tax administrations to identify taxpayers engaged in e-commerce and to assess and collect tax due; the implication of consumption taxes to cross-border e-commerce transactions; and direct taxation with exchange of information. The footnote below provides an outline of the strategy that would be followed to take forward these discussions.[135] In 2005, the OECD issued draft

---

134   Tax Administrations in an Electronic World, Montreal, 4-6 June 2001, www.oecd. org/EN/document/0,,EN-document-101-nodirectorate-no-20-2829-29,00.html.

135   To follow up the Montreal discussions the co-sponsoring organizations would:
- Continue to discuss the key tax administrative issues raised by e-commerce with a view to developing a taxation framework that can accommodate established taxation principles that operate across a wide range of countries;
- Encourage governments to identify the opportunities provided by the new technologies to improve taxpayer service and to reduce compliance costs for taxpayers and administrative costs for tax administrations;
- Assist governments to identify taxpayers engaged in e-commerce and to audit, assess and collect tax due.

More generally, the sponsoring organizations will:
- Identify outstanding e-commerce issues which require joint work;
- Strengthen the ties between them thereby improving the level and quality of communications and assist in the development of a framework for improved co-operation including areas that go beyond e-commerce.

To achieve these aims the sponsoring organizations will:
- Maintain the informal steering group, which has contributed to the success of the Montreal conference;
- Develop links between the websites of each of the participating organizations;
- Develop joint papers on issues of concern to tax administrations where common guidelines and best practices could emerge;
- Develop further the joint training programmes, which already exist between the organizations;
- Explore the hosting of further conferences on topics of mutual interest to their member countries.

principles[136] governing the place of supply for the international trade in services and intangibles.[137]

The OECD[138] has summarized the key issues of e-commerce and the internet for tax authorities as follows: a) to review existing taxation arrangements, including concepts of sources, residency, permanent establishment and place of supply, and to modify the existing arrangements or develop fair alternatives, if required; b) to ensure that e-commerce technologies, including electronic payment systems, are not used to undermine the ability of tax authorities to properly administer tax law; c) to provide a clear and equitable taxation environment for businesses engaged in both physical and e-commerce; and d) to examine how these new technologies can be exploited to provide a better service to taxpayers. Developing countries must take the lead of the OECD in undertaking analyses of how e-commerce will impact the tax base and tax regulations, administration and compliance for specific taxes such as VAT, and plan for a coordinated approach to tackle the challenges posed by the internet.[139]

---

136   OECD (2005) The Application of Consumption Taxes to the International Trade in Services and Intangibles: Progress Report and Draft Principles, Informal Working Group of Working Party 9 of the Committee of Fiscal Affairs (OECD Centre for Tax Policy and Administration 11 February 2005).

137   Consumption taxes should impose tax where goods or services are consumed, but for administrative reasons, countries may rely on proxies to determine where goods and services are consumed. On the basis of the principle that final consumers should bear the economic costs of VAT, the report included the principle that taxable businesses should not bear, as an economic cost, the VAT on goods and services used in making taxable supplies.

138   OECD (1997) Electronic Commerce: The Challenges to Tax Authorities and Taxpayers, (Paris: OECD) p 9.

139   For a list of other OECD reports on trade in international services and intangibles, see http://www.oecd.org/.

Chapter 9

Emerging Tax Policy

Introduction

It is no coincidence that some of the oldest documents in existence are tax returns.[1] So how are tax questions researched? It is important that I explore this. The tax system should be clear so that the taxpayer can see in advance how much tax must be paid. Second, enforcement should be consistent and universal. There is nothing more destructive of a taxpayer's morality than the suspicion that others are not paying. This means that people should be able to understand the rules. This thought leads to another of the paradoxes of tax. The simpler the rules are, the less fair they are. But the fairer they are, the more complex they are. The more complex they are, the harder they are to understand and to put into effect. There is another matter; although the effectiveness of a tax system depends upon its enforcement, it also relates to cost-effectiveness. This chapter states in broad terms the economic objectives and principles that should guide the taxation of e-commerce. It presents different proposals and options for reforming the taxation of e-commerce derived from those objectives and principles. In these circumstances, it seems an imperative for the taxing authorities to examine their approach and policies towards the taxation of e-commerce more comprehensively than they have to date. I am of the view that the attention of the taxing authorities should not simply focus upon the location and function of servers, characterization of income and the place of consumption. Instead, the analysis should extend more broadly to ensure a deeper understanding of the nature of e-commerce as it is today and as it will develop tomorrow.

9.1   The Nature of the Debate: New Taxes or No Taxes?

Tax systems should be designed to yield the needed revenue in an equitable and efficient fashion. Most people will agree with these basic goals but they will differ once they take a closer look. As taxes are imposed, taxpayers respond by adjusting their behaviour. Consumption, work, saving and investment will be affected, as will the distribution of the tax burden and the economy's overall performance. Moreover, administrative constraints limit what can be done, as there may be diverged interests of fiscal politics. No wonder then that tax design has long been a difficult and controversial issue.[2] In the past, the study of taxation had been largely a parochial

---

1   Morse, Geoffrey and Williams David (2004) *Davis: Principle of Tax Law*, (London: Sweet and Maxwell) Fifth Edition.

2   Musgrave, Peggy B. (2002) Combining Fiscal Sovereignty and Coordination National Taxation In A Globalizing World, *The New Public Finance*.

issue. It focused, mainly, on national concerns. Globalization, however, initiated international cooperation and the development of 'international taxation'. However, even when an international perspective had been necessary, such as the taxation of truly multinational enterprises, it is still usually approached as an aggregation of national perspectives rather than by adopting a truly international one. How should tax bases be divided? Which jurisdictions should be entitled to tax what part of the base and at what rate? How is inter-nation equity to be determined? Should these issues be resolved through the policy choices of single jurisdictions, should they be settled by tax competition or will coordinating measures secured through cooperative agreements be needed to attain equitable and efficient results?

The issue of taxation of e-commerce is not about desirability; it is more about the possibility. Kobrin argues that in discussions of e-commerce taxation issues, four assumptions should work. First, taxation should be economically neutral, that is, it should not influence the location or form of economic activity. Second, there should not be double taxation, neither should taxation be avoided. Third, there should be an equitable distribution of tax revenue. Fourth, fiscal sovereignty based on geographically defined nation states should be maintained.[3] As the question of PE indicates, however, it will be difficult to satisfy all four of these principles simultaneously. Indeed, given the non-geographic nature of e-commerce transactions,[4] 'it may be impossible to resolve jurisdictional issues, distribute revenue, or even collect sufficient revenues to sustain governmental activities while maintaining the practice or principle of mutually exclusive jurisdiction- political and economic control exercised through control over geography'.[5]

The basic incompatibility of the sales tax system[6] with the VAT system[7] is the major unsolved tax problem. So far, the post-Ottawa process has shied away from a radical solution to this problem as being impractical to implement. It may be that with the continuing growth in e-commerce, this cautious position will have to be reconsidered by the OECD and the international community. However, OECD member states have already developed guiding principles for a framework to tax international e-commerce transactions, including a desire to use traditional international tax principles that promote neutral treatment between physical commerce and e-commerce, low compliance costs and flexible rules to keep pace with technological developments.[8] Indeed, developments in technology would be indispensable at least for the collection of consumption taxes on e-commerce to provide an automated tax charging and collection mechanism. A system for collecting

---

3 Kobrin, Stephen J. (2000) Taxing Internet Transactions, 21 *U. PA Journal of International Econ L* 666, 671.

4 Berman, Paul S (2002) The Globalisation of Jurisdiction, Uni. of Connecticut School of Law Working Paper Series, paper 13 p 335.

5 Kobrin, Stephen J. (2000) Taxing Internet Transactions, 21 *U. PA Journal of International Econ L* pp 666, 672.

6 Imposed individually by the bulk of the states in the US and a number of other major trading nations.

7 Applied by EU and certain other jurisdictions.

8 OECD (2000) Committee on Fiscal Affairs, Implementing The Ottawa Taxation Framework Conditions 2.

taxes must be technically feasible, efficient and cost-effective. The focus of this book specifically has been on the issue of taxing intangible products and has been based around three broad questions: what should be taxed? Who should be entitled to tax? How should tax operate for e-commerce?

In response to the debate, a few scholars have addressed the equity issues associated with taxing e-commerce, mainly in theoretical terms, supported by arguments from traditional public finance economics. Charles McLure, who compared e-commerce events to the history of mail-order catalogues, stated that e-commerce should be taxed.[9] McLure[10] claimed that policies, based on the argument that there should be a moratorium on internet taxation until e-commerce is 'mature' enough would inevitably keep favoured industries from ever 'growing up'. The question of whether e-commerce should be taxed to level the playing field between e-commerce and conventional commerce had been addressed in several other studies, but with mixed results.[11] Those who favour taxation argue that exemptions for e-commerce, combined with current taxation systems, would lead to significant distortions that would put conventional retailers at a great disadvantage. Others claimed that the tax differential would merely inspire conventional retailers to migrate to the internet, and that if state governments are genuinely concerned about equity, they should consider 'harmonizing tax rates downward for local retailers', rather than imposing new taxes on the e-commerce to eliminate the tax differences.

Those making the 'infant industry' argument favour no taxes whatsoever on e-commerce, justifying preferential treatment as a way to stimulate development of e-commerce.[12] They suggested that taxing e-commerce would throw sand in the gears of economic progress. To support their position they cited the empirical work of Austan Goolsbee on the possible effects of imposing sales taxes and compliance costs on the internet. Goolsbee[13] attempted to determine the price elasticity of demand associated with e-commerce sales and the sales and consumption choices that would follow from such tax, drawing upon the data from a survey conducted by Forrester

---

9   McLure, Charles E. Jr (1999) 'The Taxation of Electronic Commerce: Background and Proposal', Hoover Institution Stanford University. Prepared for discussion at a Hoover conference on 'Public Policy and the Internet: Taxation and Privacy,' October 12, 1999; in Nicholas Imparato, editor, *Public Policy and the Internet: Taxation and Privacy* (Stanford: Hoover Press.

10 McLure, Charles E. Jr (1999) 'The Taxation of Electronic Commerce: Background and Proposal', Hoover Institution Stanford University. Prepared for discussion at a Hoover conference on 'Public Policy and the Internet: Taxation and Privacy,' October 12, 1999; in Nicholas Imparato, editor, *Public Policy and the Internet: Taxation and Privacy* (Stanford: Hoover Press).

11 Lukas, Aaron (1999) Tax Bytes: A Primer on the Taxation of Electronic Commerce, Cato Institute, *Trade Policy Analysis*, no.9, December 17, 1999. (028.2/C29).

12 James S. Gilmore, III, 'No Internet Tax: A Proposal Submitted to the 'Policies & Options' Paper Of the Advisory Commission on Electronic Commerce,' available at www. ecommercecommission.org.

13 Goolsbee, A. (2000) 'In a World without Borders: The Impact of Taxes on Internet Commerce', *National Bureau of Economic Research (NBER) Working Paper No. 6863*, Cambridge, MA.

Research in late 1997. Forrester examined the purchasing decisions of 25,000 users as a function of their demographic traits and their residential characteristics, including local sales tax rate. His primary objectives were to determine how the local sales tax rate affected an individual's choice to purchase something online and how it affected the advantage amount of money spent online by the typical consumer. Goolsbee[14] found that the coefficient on local tax rate was positive and significant, which implied that the higher the local sales tax rate, the greater the amount of money the average consumer would spend online. However, Goolsbee's findings were not without limitation, because the growth of e-commerce has exploded since 1997. It is conceivable that Goolsbee's study suffered from a selection bias in that a majority of the consumers in the sample were more technologically sophisticated and more tax sensitive than typical offline consumers.[15] According to Hellerstein,[16] the principle question here would be: what kind of taxing regime would allow participants in e-commerce to pay and collect taxes in an administratively feasible fashion to those states with a legitimate claim on tax revenues? The objective behind any tax policy would be to find an answer to this question. The literature does, however, point to the factors that should be considered in making tax policy decisions regarding e-commerce and emphasizes that the question is relative, not absolute.[17]

9.2   Principles for Cross-Border Taxation of E-Commerce

A possible policy approach to accommodate the taxation of e-commerce transactions is to leave the existing international jurisdictional rules and concepts as they are currently in the OECD Model Convention.[18] The existing international tax regime has enjoyed a long history and has been the product of many years of development.[19] Against this background, countries would be reluctant to move from a system that is both familiar to them and that has taken many years to develop. It is also arguable that the present system, though far from perfect, has served the international community well by forging a workable compromise between the competing fiscal interests of countries that engage in international trade. Therefore, from a traditional

---

14 Goolsbee, A. (2000) 'In a World without Borders: The Impact of Taxes on Internet Commerce', *National Bureau of Economic Research (NBER) Working Paper No. 6863*, Cambridge, MA.

15 Goolsbee, A. (2000) 'In a World without Borders: The Impact of Taxes on Internet Commerce', *National Bureau of Economic Research (NBER) Working Paper No. 6863*, Cambridge, MA.

16 Hellerstein, Walter (2001) 'Electronic Commerce and The Challenge For Tax Administration' Paper presented to the *United Nations Ad Hoc Group of Experts on International Cooperation in Tax Matters in Geneva, Switzerland*, on September 12, 2001 pp 16-18.

17 Bruce, Donald, William E Fox and Murray, Matthew (2003) To Tax or Not to Tax? The Case of Electronic Commerce, Contemporary Economic Policy, Vol.21 No.1 pp 25-40.

18 OECD Model Tax Convention on Income and Capital (Paris, 2003).

19 Pinto, Dale (2005) 'Conservative' And 'Radical' Alternatives For Taxing E-Commerce (Part 1) Journal of International Taxation.

or historical perspective, there may be merit in leaving the current rules as they presently stand.[20]

It is, therefore, important to question what (if anything) has changed because of e-commerce that presents new challenges requiring changes to the existing international tax regime.[21] According to Pinto, if e-commerce transactions are considered analogous to their mail-order counterparts, it can be argued that the principle of neutrality would require that the same (existing) tax rules should apply in both situations. If an e-commerce transaction would be subject to a tax that would not be incurred in a mail-order purchase, that taxation would be discriminatory. On the other hand, if e-commerce transactions are not considered analogous to mail-order transactions, the argument is seriously weakened and changes could be warranted. It is, therefore, both instructive and necessary to give further consideration to the nature of the analogy between mail-order and e-commerce transactions.[22] From a tax perspective, the problem may be similarly stated in both situations: income flows from the jurisdiction of the consumer to that of the vendor in circumstances where the vendor need not establish any physical presence in the country of the consumer.[23] However, Pinto argues[24] that with e-commerce, while the type of challenge in establishing physical presence is the same as in a mail-order business, there are important differences between the two types of transactions, which challenge the validity of the analogy, and therefore the assertion, that existing tax rules that apply to mail-order transactions should also apply to e-commerce transactions. First, the lack of a local physical presence in the consumer's country is more acute for a mail-order vendor as compared with an e-commerce vendor. Second, it is often argued that as e-commerce is simply a communication and advertising medium not unlike a mail-order catalogue, it represents merely another channel for retailers to sell their products and services rather than a new mode of commerce.[25] Third, while mail-order transactions are confined to the purchase of tangible products, e-commerce transactions can involve not only the purchase of tangible products, but can also extend to the consumption of intangible goods and services, including for example,

---

20 Pinto, Dale (2005) 'Conservative' And 'Radical' Alternatives For Taxing E-Commerce (Part 1) *Journal of International Taxation.*

21 Pinto, Dale (2005) 'Conservative' And 'Radical' Alternatives For Taxing E-Commerce (Part 1) *Journal of International Taxation.*

22 Pinto, Dale (2005) 'Conservative' And 'Radical' Alternatives For Taxing E-Commerce (Part 1) *Journal of International Taxation.*

23 Hellerstein points out that the physical location of businesses is a less reliable indicator of the source of income in today's economy than in the past. See Hellerstein, Walter (2003) *Jurisdiction to Tax income and Consumption in the New Economy: A Theoretical and Comparative Perspective*, 38 Georgia Law Review pp 1-70.

24 Pinto, Dale (2005) 'Conservative' And 'Radical' Alternatives For Taxing E-Commerce (Part 1) *Journal of International Taxation.*

25 However, this proposition can be challenged, as e-commerce is not just a communication channel or advertising medium, but constitutes a means of interaction and distribution. Indeed, it is the interactivity of e-commerce that most prominently distinguishes it from a mail-order purchase.

software, photographs, stock trading and gambling.[26] Fourth, the speed of an electronic communication is a distinguishing feature of e-commerce compared with a mail-order transaction.[27] Finally, the ability to effect payment online differentiates an e-commerce transaction from a mail-order purchase.[28] In the light of the above analysis, it is argued that e-commerce transactions are not completely analogous to mail-order transactions and therefore the case for extending to e-commerce transactions the present rules that apply to mail-order transactions on the ground of neutrality is not compelling.[29]

9.3   Direct Taxation: Implications for Tax Policy and Tax Administration

Even though governments and international organizations appear concerned about the potential challenges posed by e-commerce and its digital appurtenances, many industrialized nations feel that existing taxation principles can be extended to include e-commerce transactions. In order to bring e-commerce within the scope of prevailing tax rules and norms, tax authorities have to invoke inadequate definitions and inappropriate analogies. The debate surrounding the desirability of residence-based taxation as opposed to source-based taxation preceded the advent of e-commerce. It has been argued that in order to address tax avoidance concerns, residence countries should be granted primary authority to tax e-commerce business profits.[30] Effective enforcement of tax laws, as with other laws, requires accurate identification of a party and evidence that can be linked to the party. In fiscal matters, this equates to identifying a taxpayer, obtaining evidence of income and linking the income to the taxpayer.

There are two major ways tax authorities seek to verify disclosed income tax liabilities. The first, the specifics method, examines transactions which have been disclosed to the revenue authorities and seeks to establish by an examination of the relevant facts and law whether or not a particular item is taxable or is a legitimate tax deduction. This method is unlikely to change under the e-commerce environment, but the techniques used to apply this method must be adapted to take into account

---

26 This has implications not only because of the broader range of goods and services that can be traded via e-commerce, but also for tax purposes in terms of the characterization of a transaction, which may become more difficult to ascertain than in a mail-order purchase. Apart from characterization issues arising from the intangible nature of many e-commerce transactions is the determination of a purchaser's identity and location.

27 Only the physical shipping of products slows the process down, but for the growing range of products and services that can be delivered electronically, this impediment is gradually being removed.

28 This feature also adds to the speed of e-commerce transactions, reduces the credit risk for vendors, and makes it possible to charge for small amounts, which may be insignificant individually but important in the aggregate. That e-commerce makes it possible to pay anonymously online using electronic cash, rather than by credit card, may create tax administration concerns with no reliable audit trail as evidence for such transactions.

29 Pinto, Dale (2005) 'Conservative' and 'Radical' Alternatives For Taxing E-Commerce (Part 1) *Journal of International Taxation.*

30 Ine Lejeune (1998) Does Cyber-Commerce Necessitate a Revision of International Tax Concepts? 38 Eur. Tax notes 50, at p 58.

technological developments. The second method is not a single method as such; it is a collection of non-specific methods relating to measurement of assets or spending and funds over time frequently supplemented by inspection of particular matters. The growth in unaccounted electronic payment systems and e-commerce create problems in the application of this method. Non-specific methods depend critically on the tax authorities' ability, under powers conferred by law, to obtain information and evidence compulsorily, both from taxpayers and third parties. E-commerce also poses a number of practical evidentiary problems for both taxpayers and tax administrators in the area of identity and transaction verification. This is particularly relevant as it could preclude enforcing tax in respect of business activities by residents and even between residents. Identification and registration requirements will have limited success because of the growing ease with which websites can be offshore. While revenue authorities typically have extensive powers to compel disclosure of information and production of documents, their writ usually runs only within their own jurisdiction and they must rely on cooperation under applicable treaty provisions with other jurisdictions. However, even where such cooperation is forthcoming, difficulties arise while attempting to obtain information and evidence in respect of documents or payments in encrypted digital form. However, new technologies create solutions to some of these problems. For example, digital certificates can make it possible to verify the identity of an online entity, and digital notarization can make it possible to verify that electronic records have not been altered.

There are substantive issues of law involved in the area of taxation of e-commerce. Current tax concepts, PE and source of income concepts were developed in a different technological era. However, the principle of neutrality between physical; and e-commerce requires that existing principles of taxation are adapted to e-commerce, taking into account the borderlessness of the internet. Different tax rates or other distinctions related to income taxation require legal definitions of different sources, different allowances. If these definitions do not correspond to basic economic thinking, there are clear incentives to avoidance. Another advantage of an approach based on existing principles in addition to neutrality is that such an approach is suitable for adoption as an international standard. Exiting principles are, in broad outline, common to most countries' tax laws. However, Cockfield has argued that digital technology completely destroys the economic and legal basis for the existing rules of international taxation, implying the necessity of a complete overhaul. Extending the existing rules into the digital era, as suggested by developed countries, will increase the revenue share of developed countries at the loss of developing countries, and despite this foreseeable outcome, developing countries do not have much choice but to suffer.[31]

9.3.1   Analysis of Options for Direct Taxation

May taxation take place at source or not? Does a certain use of a server pass the threshold for a PE? This is the main problem to be solved when determining the

---

31 Cockfield, A. (2002) *Designing Tax Policy for the Digital Biosphere: How the Internet is Changing Tax Laws*, 34 Conn. Law Review. p 333.

applicable jurisdiction in respect of income taxation. The following discussion reviews a number of potential reform alternatives for income generated by e-commerce transactions. A detailed discussion of each and every potential reform is beyond the scope of this book, however some of them require to be dealt with in detail, although it is accepted that some of the reforms may not be practical. Nevertheless, an approach which is dismissed by one country as impractical may be seen by another country as necessary in order to fairly allocate profits generated through e-commerce.[32]

In order to defend the existing concepts of international taxation, Cockfield divides disputants on this issue into three camps: Doubting Thomases, Purists and Pragmatists. Doubting Thomases take the view that the problems created by e-commerce are not serious enough to justify changes in the traditional conceptual basis of international taxation.[33] 'The dire prediction that e-commerce will allow companies to earn significant revenues from states of consumption without having a local physical presence have not come true. Simply put, those advocating change have not offered compelling enough reasons to justify deviating from a conceptual basis of international taxation that has had overwhelming acceptance for over 80 years.'[34]

Purists, such as Jinyan Li, seek solutions to the problems posed by e-commerce by replacing existing international tax concepts with concepts that are more conceptually pure.[35] Pragmatists, a label Cockfield applies to himself, concede that the proposals advocated by the Purists are 'both sound and theoretically attractive', but doubt that these solutions could be effectively implemented.[36] In addition to noting a number of technical issues that would have to be resolved in developing a formulary approach, he points out that the adoption of some kind of a system for apportioning the worldwide tax base of a group of related corporations on the basis of a formula would require an implausible degree of cooperation between nations and, since the method would require a substantial degree of harmonization of the tax base, would require them to surrender a considerable amount of sovereignty over their own tax rules. He observes that 'the path of international law is directed by three main drivers: tax sovereignty concerns, practical administrative concerns,

---

32 Doernberg, Richard L. and Hinnekens, Luc (1999) Electronic Commerce and International Taxation Kluwer Law International, p 302.

33 Cockfield, A.J. (2004) 'Formulary Taxation Versus the Arm's Length Principle: The Battle Among Doubting Thomases, Purists, and Pragmatists, *Canadian Tax Journal* Vol 52, pp 114-123.

34 Sprague, Gary D. and Hersey, Rachel (2003) 'Permanent Establishments and Internet-Enabled Enterprises: The Physical Presence and Contract Concluding Dependent Agent Tests,' February 27-28, 2003, 1 (available online at http://www.bmck.com/ecommerce/tax-art1.doc).

35 Cockfield, A.J. (2004) 'Formulary Taxation Versus the Arm's Length Principle: The Battle Among Doubting Thomases, Purists, and Pragmatists, *Canadian Tax Journal* Vol 52, pp 114-123.

36 Cockfield, A.J. (2004) 'Formulary Taxation Versus the Arm's Length Principle: The Battle Among Doubting Thomases, Purists, and Pragmatists, *Canadian Tax Journal* Vol 52, pp 114-123.

and guiding international tax principles'.[37] It may be preferable to adopt a reform approach that protects tax sovereignty and is technically feasible.'[38]

9.3.2   Enhanced Residence-Based Taxation

Perhaps the central international tax issue arising out of e-commerce is the allocation of business profits between the residence and source countries and leakage to tax havens.[39] It has been argued that in order to address tax avoidance concerns, residence countries should be granted primary authority to tax e-commerce business profits.[40] If countries are permitted to exclusively tax a resident company's worldwide business profits, then multinational enterprises will arguably be discouraged from shifting their profit-making activities to lower tax jurisdictions since the residence country will continue to tax these profits. It is being seen that capital exporting nations tend to support residence-based taxation under the principle of capital export neutrality, which is achieved if a taxpayer's choice between investing at home or in a foreign country is not affected by taxes. The greatest proponent of a move towards a residence-based system for the taxation of international income is the US, which also happens to be the world leader in the production and export of e-commerce goods and services. Proponents of a strict residence-based system for taxation of e-commerce profits believe that electronic transactions may escape taxation altogether unless the resident vendor is taxed on its net income. The reality is that the strict application of residence rules would lead to greater tax avoidance due to the increasingly malleable nature of corporate residency. Under a pure residence-based system of taxation, multinational enterprises have considerable incentive to incorporate entities in tax havens and low-tax jurisdictions. Existing companies will be driven by the impetus to relocate their e-commerce and other profitable operations through isolated corporate entities. Start-up technology companies will be encouraged to establish the income-producing aspects of their operations within tax havens in order to avoid paying taxes. A company that is incorporated or deemed to be a resident of a tax haven country may never pay any income tax whatsoever on its e-commerce profits under a pure residence-based approach.[41]

A move towards residence-based taxation of all forms of business income would entail radical shifts in the international distribution of tax revenues. The existing

---

37 Cockfield, A.J. (2004) 'Formulary Taxation Versus the Arm's Length Principle: The Battle Among Doubting Thomases, Purists, and Pragmatists, *Canadian Tax Journal* Vol 52, pp 114-123.

38 Cockfield, A.J. (2004) 'Formulary Taxation Versus the Arm's Length Principle: The Battle Among Doubting Thomases, Purists, and Pragmatists, *Canadian Tax Journal* Vol 52, pp 114-123.

39 Doernberg, Richard L. and Hinnekens, Luc (1999)Electronic Commerce and International Taxation Kluwer Law International, p 302.

40 Lejeune Ine, Vanham Bart, Verlinden Isabelle, Verbeken Alain (1988) 'Does Cyber-Commerce Necessitate a Revision of International Tax Concepts?' Part I, *European Taxation*, 1998, volume 38, p 58.

41 Cockfield, A.J. (1992) Balancing National Interests In The Taxation of Electronic Commerce Business Profits 74 *Tulane Law Review* at p 172.

regime of jurisdictional allocation as embodied within most bilateral tax treaties assigns the taxpayer's country of residence the exclusive right to tax foreign source business income in the absence of a PE in the foreign jurisdiction. Based on current economic trading patterns, the abandonment of source-based taxation of business profits would dramatically increase the flows of tax revenues from the treasuries of developing countries to the coffers of developed countries. Any further shift in the tenuous equilibrium of inter-nation revenue distribution in favour of the treasuries of the wealthy nations would have profound international economic consequences. Since the adoption of a pure residence-based system of taxation for e-commerce or traditional commerce transactions would exacerbate distributive disparities among nations, it is unlikely that such a proposal would obtain the requisite international support.

9.3.3   Expansion of Source-Country Tax Base

It is often presumed that the tax revenues in the source country are declining and that, consequently, an enlargement of the tax attributes in the source country as well as taxation according to the source principle is necessary in order to guarantee inter-nation equity. Expansion of taxation by the source country is based on the argument that a nation should have the primary claim to tax all business income derived within the borders of the country. Developed countries as well as developing countries have expressed their inclination to favour source-based tax rules for business income.[42] The principle of tax neutrality requires that all business income, whether arising out of e-commerce transactions or through more traditional means, be taxed in a similar manner. Effective source-country taxation would involve modifications of traditional international tax norms, such as those dealing with transfer pricing, PE and the characterization of income. Proposals to expand the jurisdiction of the source country to tax business income arising within its boundaries include: (i) the restricted force of attraction principle; (ii) withholding taxes on e-commerce payments; and (iii) unrestricted domestic taxation of all business income generated within the country.

Observers have noted that international tax policy analysis suffers from a certain degree of arbitrariness because analysts and tax authorities generally cannot come to an agreement on the ways that accepted general principles such as the need for inter-nation fairness should guide actual reform efforts. The problem in part is that a particular nation's international tax interests may vary depending on its economic circumstances. As a result, capital importing nations tend to support source-based taxation under the principle of capital import neutrality, which maintains that

---

42 Developing countries have long favoured an expansion of the source country jurisdiction to tax cross-border business income. Some wealthy nations, such as Canada, are also net capital importers. Compared with countries like the United States, Canada has a strong commitment to source taxation because of its history as a capital importer: Brian J. and Arnold, A (1996) The Canadian International Tax System: Review and Reform 43 *Can. Tax. J.* 1792, at 1807. See also Susan M. Lyons, A International Consensus Needed in Taxation of Electronic Commerce (1997) 14 Tax Notes Int'l 1199, at p 1203.

companies operating abroad should be placed in the same tax position as their local competitors. However, there may be a number of practical and administrative problems associated with taxing e-commerce profits on the basis of the source of the consumer. As with other approaches, the identification of the taxpayer would be a prerequisite to the imposition of an income tax. The ability of internet users to prevent identification of their e-commerce transactions may present challenges for tax authorities. The vendor is obligated to remit income tax to the consumers' jurisdiction because it is the vendor's income that is being taxed. Without appropriate identification mechanisms, it would be difficult for governments to trace the productive processes of international business transactions through to the ultimate taxpayer. Where tax authorities are able to identify and audit prospective taxpayers, it is likely that some source-based withholding tax rules would be established to protect the interests of the treasury against foreign resident taxpayers with nominal assets in the market country. In such cases, the source country may establish a regime that could treat foreign companies less favourably than domestic enterprises. To respond to reasonable equity concerns, most countries should permit foreign businesses to file as a net-basis taxpayer.

According to Doernberg, it is useful to adopt the 'base erosion' approach in taxation of income streams in source countries. The proposal requires taxation of any payment to a foreign enterprise if it is tax deductible in the hands of a taxpayer in the source country. The implementation of the tax would be in the form of a low withholding tax, with the option for being taxed on net income. This proposal implies that the concept of PE continues to exist. In this context, it is further suggested that the 'base erosion' approach offers a possible solution for equitable tax sharing between residence and source countries when:

- the concept is applied to all commerce and not just e-commerce;
- the tax is implemented through a low withholding tax on all tax-deductible payments to the foreign enterprise; and
- the withholding tax is final, without the option of tax on net income being given to the taxpayer or the tax administration.

Before considering a solution on these lines, trade data needs to be studied carefully to ascertain if, and to what extent, there will be erosion of the tax base. However, it is recommended that a thorough study must be undertaken:

- to examine the practicality of taxing all imports; and
- to assess the erosion of the tax base as a result of credit for taxes levied by other countries on exports.

It is, however, felt that the base of 'erosion approach' is contrary to the international consensus that withholding taxes are appropriate only in certain limited cases. This approach is a radical departure from this consensus and is in conflict with the internationally accepted standards on when a jurisdiction has the right to impose an income tax on a non-resident enterprise.

9.3.4   Permanent Establishment an Outdated Concept?

Proponents of change would argue that the fundamental concept underlying current OECD nexus and income attribution rules that income should be attributed to the location where value is created is obsolete. For internet-enabled enterprises, nexus should not be based solely on the location of manufacturing, research, marketing and other wealth-creating activities. Rather, the place of consumption should also give rise in some way to a direct tax nexus. Some argue that change is required as a matter of tax policy, while others argue that change is required as economic development policy vis-à-vis developing countries.[43] In many cases, the demands for change are made in quite strident terms. Due to this weakening connection between physical and economic presence, the current definition of a PE which largely relies on physical manifestations of an economic presence might give rise to anomalous results and to a violation of the tax principles outlined above.

A comprehensive study of the PE principle conducted before the emergence of e-commerce concluded that modern commercial practices had already eroded the PE concept to a large extent.[44] The PE concept does not envision or encompass the existence of a nexus between intangible business activities and foreign markets. Support for the 1920s compromise that sacrificed tax revenues in favour of administrative simplicity has deteriorated. Nonetheless, while the PE concept may be a relic of early trade practices, it continues to be the prevailing standard for determination of tax jurisdiction for international business income. One author advocated that the US relax its PE rules (at least temporarily) and allow software programs to be treated as dependent agents for PE purposes to allow 'capital importing, developing source countries to tax foreign e-commerce income' made within their borders.[45] Otherwise, only a few countries would be able to collect income tax revenue from the internet, which would be an 'unjust e-commerce income tax' policy.[46]

Various suggestions have been made on how to overhaul the PE-based system of taxation. One suggestion is that Article 5 incorporates the concept of a 'virtual' PE. Under this system, once a foreign enterprise's sales into a jurisdiction have reached a certain level, the foreign enterprise would be *deemed* to have a PE in the jurisdiction and the enterprise's profits attributable to that virtual PE could be taxed by the source jurisdiction. The conceptual basis for taxation under such a system holds providing a healthy customer base is enough to entitle a source state the right to tax profits

---

43 Sprague, Gary D. and Hersey, Rachel (2003) 'Permanent Establishments and Internet-Enabled Enterprises: The Physical Presence and Contract Concluding Dependent Agent Tests,' February 27-28, 2003, 1 (available online at http://www.bmck.com/ecommerce/tax-art1.doc.

44 Skaar, Arvid A. (1991) *Permanent Establishment: Erosion of a Tax Treaty Principle* 78, pp 573-574.

45 Schaefer, B. (1999) *International Taxation of Electronic Commerce Income: A Proposal to Utilize Software Agents for Source-Based Taxation*, 16 Computer & High Tec. L.J. at p 211.

46 Schaefer, B. (1999) *International Taxation of Electronic Commerce Income: A Proposal to Utilize Software Agents for Source-Based Taxation*, 16 Computer & High Tec. L.J. p 111.

arising in (or from) that state.[47] Some proposals would attempt to isolate 'e-commerce' transactions and subject them to a different tax regime. The most widely discussed proposal, however, is the suggestion that direct tax nexus would exist whenever a foreign enterprise receives a payment from an in-country payor. As first introduced by Doernberg,[48] cross-border payments from a payor who is entitled to deduct the payment for its local tax purposes would be subject to a withholding tax regime. This approach is referred to generally as the *base erosion approach.* According to Doernberg, such a regime would supplement, rather than replace, the traditional PE nexus rules.[49] States would retain the right to tax all non-resident enterprises with a PE in the jurisdiction.[50] The report of India's high-powered Commission also recommended the abandonment of the PE concept on the basis that the application of the PE standard to e-commerce creates considerable uncertainty and disturbs the equilibrium in sharing of tax revenues between countries of residence and source.[51] India's E-Commerce Report declared that an alternative to the concept of PE must be developed, but the report fell short of promoting any particular set of alternate treaty rules.[52]

Advocates of retaining a PE nexus-based system of international taxation argue that the existing OECD principle that income tax revenue should be attributed to the location where an enterprise is engaged in value-creating activities remains the appropriate basis for the imposition of an *income* tax. The conceptual framework remains correct from a policy standpoint. Those advocating change have not offered compelling enough reasons to justify deviating from a conceptual basis of international taxation that has had overwhelming acceptance. The 'digital' economy, just as much as the 'traditional' economy, requires an enterprise to utilize capital, labour and other property in core income producing activities to produce and market its products and services.[53] Even if the nature of those inputs and outputs may differ somewhat under the digital economy, the essential fact remains the same: physical presence and activity as reflected by an entrepreneur's labour inputs, property

---

47 Sprague, Gary D. and Hersey, Rachel (2003) 'Permanent Establishments and Internet-Enabled Enterprises: The Physical Presence and Contract Concluding Dependent Agent Tests,' February 27-28, 2003, 1 (available online at http://www.bmck.com/ecommerce/tax-art1.doc.

48 Doernberg, R (1998) *Electronic Commerce and International Tax Sharing*, 16 Tax Notes Int'l p 1013.

49 Doernberg, R (1998) *Electronic Commerce and International Tax Sharing*, 16 Tax Notes Int'l p 1013.

50 Sprague, Gary D. and Hersey, Rachel (2003) 'Permanent Establishments and Internet-Enabled Enterprises: The Physical Presence and Contract Concluding Dependent Agent Tests,' February 27-28, 2003, 1 (available online at http://www.bmck.com/ecommerce/tax-art1.doc.

51 Ministry of Finance (India) (2001) Report of the High Powered Committee on E-Commerce and Taxation pp11-12.

52 Doernberg, R (1998) *Electronic Commerce and International Tax Sharing*, 16 Tax Notes Int'l 1013 at pp 11-12.

53 Sprague, Gary D. and Hersey, Rachel (2003) 'Permanent Establishments and Internet-Enabled Enterprises: The Physical Presence and Contract Concluding Dependent Agent Tests,' February 27-28, 2003, 1 (available online at http://www.bmck.com/ecommerce/tax-art1.doc.

investments and risk assumption remain necessary components to an enterprise's creation of products and services.[54]

There is thus no basis arising from digital economy business models to change a state's justification to share in an enterprise's tax base. There is no basis for utilizing different attribution algorithms for the digital and 'traditional' economies. The nexus rules appropriate for the taxation of internet-utilizing businesses are the same as those which over the years have proven acceptable and effective for more 'traditional' businesses models. The current rules do not allow a jurisdiction to tax a foreign enterprise's business profits *unless* the enterprise itself conducts core income-generating activities in the jurisdiction. If one agrees that these rules are appropriate for non-internet based enterprises, then it is only fair that these same rules be applied to internet-based enterprises. To not do so would be unfair to those jurisdictions in which the income generating activities were, in fact, being performed.[55]

Moreover, there is no logical distinction between 'traditional' businesses and those utilizing advanced communications technology (that is, the internet) in their business models. E-commerce continues to infiltrate and be incorporated into the most 'traditional' of business enterprises (for example, the automotive and airline industries, bricks and mortar retail store outlets). While e-commerce has created new business models, opportunities, products and services, it has also changed the way 'traditional' business activities are being conducted by 'traditional' business enterprises.[56] The origin of wealth for these enterprises remains where it has always been at the place where the cost and risk to develop, produce and distribute product is borne.[57]

From a pragmatic viewpoint, the current system remains appropriate as well. Given the expansive treaty network based on the current PE rules, and e-commerce's permeation into all facets of current business affairs, designing one set of nexus rules for e-commerce companies and another for non-e-commerce companies makes no logical sense and would be practically impossible to implement.[58] The PE provision was also designed with administrative practicality and convenience in mind. It is generally acknowledged that a country's jurisdiction to tax should not extend beyond its power to impose a tax. Therefore, if a taxpayer is not physically present in a country, tax should not be imposed upon the income of the taxpayer

54 Sprague, Gary D. and Hersey, Rachel (2003) 'Permanent Establishments and Internet-Enabled Enterprises: The Physical Presence and Contract Concluding Dependent Agent Tests,' February 27-28, 2003, 1 (available online at http://www.bmck.com/ecommerce/tax-art1.doc.

55 Sprague, Gary D. and Hersey, Rachel (2003) 'Permanent Establishments and Internet-Enabled Enterprises: The Physical Presence and Contract Concluding Dependent Agent Tests,' February 27-28, 2003, 1 (available online at http://www.bmck.com/ecommerce/tax-art1.doc.

56 E.g., the means by which existing business have introduced efficiencies into their procurement of materials and components; collaborative R&D efforts; means of delivering products and services to customers; back-office functions such as accounting and finance, etc.

57 Sprague, Gary D. and Hersey, Rachel (2003) 'Permanent Establishments and Internet-Enabled Enterprises: The Physical Presence and Contract Concluding Dependent Agent Tests,' February 27-28, 2003, 1 (available online at http://www.bmck.com/ecommerce/tax-art1.doc.

58 Sprague, Gary D. and Hersey, Rachel (2003) 'Permanent Establishments and Internet-Enabled Enterprises: The Physical Presence and Contract Concluding Dependent Agent Tests,' February 27-28, 2003, 1 (available online at http://www.bmck.com/ecommerce/tax-art1.doc.

by that country. The reasons for this conclusion are twofold. First, as a matter of principle it is generally inappropriate for a country to assert jurisdiction over persons or matters beyond its actual power of enforcement. Second, as a practical matter, a country should not seek to impose taxes that it cannot collect. A system of taxation is only perceived to be fair if it can be applied in accordance with its terms. If there is a class of taxpayers (for example., foreigners with no physical connection to the jurisdiction) that are technically subject to a tax, but as a matter of practical reality are never required to pay the tax, then the taxpaying public will perceive that the system of tax is unfair and discriminatory.[59] Therefore, the requirement of a fixed place of business serves the interests of fairness and administrability as well.[60]

9.3.5   Issue Relating to Income Characterization

In terms of income characterization, e-commerce has pushed the principles and rules of international taxation to their logical limits and beyond.[61] The distinction between business profits (including income from services) and royalties is important. Li proposed[62] that the characterization of income into two classes may go a long way toward addressing many acute problems created by the current system of international taxation and the characterization of income into numerous classes producing different tax results. If it is recognized that the distinction between royalties and business profits is highly problematic, and if enforcement issues make it difficult to give effect to that recognition, then the focus should be on enforcement, not on an artificial distinction between two classes of income. Basically, Li suggested reforms involve dividing all income into two broad categories: portfolio income and business profits. Portfolio income would be subject to a uniform withholding tax in the country in which it had its source; profits of integrated businesses would be apportioned among countries on the basis of a formula. Thus, under her proposals, the present number of categories of income would be greatly reduced; the concept of residence would be significant only for portfolio income; and the concepts of PE and the arm's length standard that are at present used for allocating business income would be thrown away. Although these proposed reforms might seem to be a radical break from the OECD consensus, Li argues that they in fact represent evolutionary changes dictated by pragmatic considerations.[63] She concedes that there would be numerous administrative difficulties in implementing them, including the need to continue to distinguish between royalties and business profits, but thinks these difficulties

---

59 See Adams (1932) T.S., *Interstate and International Double Taxation*, Lectures in Taxation 101, 112 (1932).

60 Sprague, Gary D. and Hersey, Rachel (2003) 'Permanent Establishments and Internet-Enabled Enterprises: The Physical Presence and Contract Concluding Dependent Agent Tests,' February 27-28, 2003, 1 (available online at http://www.bmck.com/ecommerce/tax-art1.doc.

61 Tadmore, Niv (2004) Further Discussion on Income Characterization, *Canadian Tax Journal*, Vol 52, No 1.

62 Li, Jinyan (2003) International Taxation in the Age of Electronic Commerce: A Comparative Study (Toronto: Canadian Tax Foundation).

63 Li, Jinyan (2003) International Taxation in the Age of Electronic Commerce: A Comparative Study (Toronto: Canadian Tax Foundation).

are no greater, and probably considerably less, than the difficulties confronted in administrating the present rules. She deals at some length with the objection that her proposals would require countries to relinquish a considerable amount of sovereignty over the formulation of their own tax rules. She notes that even under the present rules, several factors have caused countries to more closely align their tax rules. She concludes by observing that 'the growing convergence or coordination of national tax rules gives tax "purists", such as myself, reason to hope that the sovereignty hurdle to international tax reform could be removed in the near future'.[64]

Niv Tadmore argues that although this distinction has always been difficult to make, in the context of e-commerce it has become impossible. In the course of thoroughly reviewing the OECD guidelines,[65] Tadmore demonstrates that they in fact do not provide reliable bright-line tests for distinguishing between business profits and royalties in all sorts of increasingly common transactions. He then reviews the historical reasons for distinguishing between business profits and royalties and concludes that although the distinction never had a strong rationale, in the context of e-commerce the same reasons that justify the source-based taxation of business profits also justify the source-based taxation of royalties.[66] In both cases, 'the source state provides the communications infrastructure that facilitates the trade online; it offers the market where demand exists; and most important, it provides the protections that shield the value of the digital supplies by the non-resident'.[67] He concludes by summarizing other adverse implications and the enforcement problems entailed in retaining a distinction between royalties and business profits in taxing income from e-commerce.[68]

9.3.6   Formulary Taxation[69]

An alternative form of international taxation of global business profits requires the apportionment of income among related companies based on a stipulated formula.[70] The main argument in favour of formulary taxation is that the system does a better job of addressing the economic reality of multinational firm behaviour. The main deficiency, in turn, of the transactional arm's length principle is that the system

---

64 Li, Jinyan (2003) International Taxation in the Age of Electronic Commerce: A Comparative Study (Toronto: Canadian Tax Foundation).

65 Tadmore, Niv (2004) Further Discussion on Income Characterization, *Canadian Tax Journal*, Vol 52, No 1.

66 Tadmore, Niv (2004) Further Discussion on Income Characterization, *Canadian Tax Journal*, Vol 52, No 1.

67 Tadmore, Niv (2004) Further Discussion on Income Characterization, *Canadian Tax Journal*, Vol 52, No 1.

68 Tadmore, Niv (2004) Further Discussion on Income Characterization, *Canadian Tax Journal*, Vol 52, No 1.

69 The analysis made here is based on arguments made by Arthur J. Cockfield in his article Cockfield, A.J. (2004) 'Formulary Taxation Versus the Arm's Length Principle: The Battle Among Doubting Thomases, Purists, and Pragmatists, Canadian Tax Journal Vol 52, pp 114-123.

70 Li, Jinyan (2002) 'Global Profit Split: An Evolutionary Approach to International Income Allocation' 50 Can. Tax J. p 823.

artificially attempts to draw lines between related aspects of a firm where no line truly exists. In particular, multinational firms are becoming more highly integrated with each other's operations located in different regions: it is often not possible to find comparable transactions with unrelated parties. Formulary taxation, on the other hand, accepts the reality of firm integration and tries to come up with a workable solution that matches each jurisdiction with tax revenues related to the value-adding economic activity that takes place within the jurisdiction. Finally, formulary taxation could be used to address the problem of source-state base erosion by employing factors such as sales in the jurisdiction of consumption.

These arguments in favour of formulary taxation are quite powerful. The conceptual legitimacy of the formulary approach for income taxation is widely acknowledged. In fact, the shortcomings of the current transfer-pricing regime are becoming more prevalent and prominent as the process of globalization encourages enhanced regional and global economic integration. Perhaps for this reason, Li's views on formulary taxation are often supported by prominent tax economists and others as the way to fix the current system. Formulary taxation does seem more conceptually pure than the current arm's length system, which is supported by international consensus among national tax authorities. In reality, at least below the surface, there is much disagreement concerning arm's length principles on issues such as the allocation of profits among the different PEs within a single legal entity.

However, formulary apportionment presents a variety of seemingly insurmountable practical difficulties. The multiplicity of tax bases in the world ensures that a formulary approach would be administratively unfeasible. The most obvious barrier to wholesale adoption of formulary taxation is that it would require a degree of cooperation among tax authorities that may not be possible in the current political environment. OECD rejects formulary taxation in part because it 'would present enormous political and administrative complexity and require a level of international cooperation that is unrealistic to expect in the field of international taxation'.[71] Moreover, the system would intrude to an unacceptable extent on a nation's tax sovereignty: countries would need to reach agreement on a set of common rules at the supranational level that would determine how much revenue each state would collect from cross-border transactions. By doing so, each state would have to cede fiscal sovereignty with respect to aspects of its international income tax laws. Even proponents of formulary taxation suspect that effective formulary taxation will require an even greater sovereignty sacrifice because it will require the harmonization of corporate tax bases and possibly even tax rates.[72] In short, fiscal sovereignty concerns continue to play a critical part in a nation's decision to reform its international tax system.[73]

---

71 Organization for Economic Co-operation and Development, Transfer Pricing Guidelines for Multinational Enterprises and Tax Administrations (Paris: OECD) paragraph 3.66.

72 McDaniel, Paul R.(1994) 'Formulary Taxation in the North American Free Trade Zone' vol. 49, no. 4 *Tax Law Review* pp 691-744.

73 Cockfield, A.J. (1998) 'Tax Integration Under NAFTA: Resolving the Conflict Between Economic and Sovereignty Concerns' vol. 34, no. 1 *Stanford Journal of International Law* pp 39-73.

The reality is that the OECD and its member states seem wedded, at least for the foreseeable future, to the maintenance of the transactional arm's length standard, despite its many deficiencies. Comparative review of the responses by national tax authorities suggests that these authorities have for the most part approached taxation of e-commerce issues in a tepid and conservative manner, relying on traditional principles. Moreover, in two documents signed at the OECD conference on global e-commerce held in Ottawa in October 1998, the OECD and the business community set out the view that traditional tax laws and principles should guide the formulation of reform efforts directed at international e-commerce.[74] This slavish following of traditional principles has led to some misguided reform efforts, such as the enshrining of a new server/PE rule in the commentary on the OECD model convention.[75] Still, the nations that, for good or ill, design the international tax rules have signalled that great leaps forward will not be tolerated. Richard Bird points out, 'Changes in tax policy and tax structure reflect changes in administrative realities as much [as] or more than they do changes in policy objectives.'[76] It may be preferable to adopt a reform approach that protects tax sovereignty, and is technically feasible. Pragmatic concerns have shaped the current international tax system and they will undoubtedly influence its development in the future.[77]

9.4   Indirect Taxation: Implication for Tax Policy and Tax Administration

The principal difficulty in developing an e-commerce taxing regime is that the internet is still a new medium whose full ramifications are not close to being understood. However, with regards to tax policy it is believed that while it would be necessary to modify tax systems of both states and local governments to accommodate e-commerce, the basic contours of taxation are not likely to be changed dramatically, neither the composition nor the nature of taxation would likely change fundamentally. OECD's work on consumption taxes, which was firmly based on the Taxation Framework Conditions, expressed similar views. In this context, it would be worth recalling the most relevant emerging conclusions of these conditions:

1. the taxation principles that guide governments in relation to conventional commerce should also guide them in relation to e-commerce. In other words, no new taxes should be introduced exclusively for e-commerce;

---

74 Organization for Economic Co-operation and Development, Electronic Commerce: Taxation Framework Conditions (Paris: OECD, 1998); and 'Joint Declaration of Business and Government Representatives: Government/Business Dialogue on Taxation and Electronic Commerce,' Hull, Quebec, October 7, 1998.

75 Cockfield, A.J. (2000) 'Should We Really Tax Profits from Computer Servers? A Case Study in E-Commerce Taxation' vol. 21, no. 21 Tax Notes International pp 2407-15.

76 Bird, Richard (2003) Taxing Electronic Commerce: A Revolution in the Making, C.D. Howe Institute Commentary no. 187 (Toronto: C.D. Howe Institute), p 15.

77 Jinyan Li (2003) *International Taxation in the Age of Electronic Commerce: A Comparative Study* (Toronto: Canadian Tax Foundation) p 591.

2. existing taxation rules must be used to implement these principles;
3. the process of implementing these principles should involve an intensified dialogue with business and with non-member economies.

Next to these Conditions, the OECD identified a number of Taxation Principles. The most relevant for collecting consumption taxes were:

1. *efficiency*: compliance costs for taxpayers and administrative costs for the tax authorities should be minimized as far as possible;
2. *neutrality, certainty and simplicity*: the tax rules should be clear and simple to understand so that taxpayers can anticipate the tax consequences in advance of a transaction. This includes knowing when, where and how the tax is to be accounted. Simplicity often conflicts with other important objectives of tax policy; where this is true, it is necessary to make trade-offs between simplicity and other objectives.

What are the consequences of these Conditions and Principles for the collection of consumption taxes? By endorsing these Conditions and Principles, the member states of OECD have made it very clear that they want to tax the new, digital supplies that e-commerce brought and that they want to do so in the same way as traditional commerce is taxed. McLure[78] identified the principles which should guide deliberations in this area of tax policy. First, and most obviously, it is important to avoid distorting choices of how to satisfy a given need. Taxation rates should not differ depending on the technology and commercial channels used to satisfy needs. It should treat all commerce equally. It should not discriminate in favour of or against e-commerce; nor should it distinguish between types of products (tangible, intangible or services) or income thereon. As for example, taxation should not distort the choice of how to provide the following products: music (tapes or compact discs v downloads from the internet), movies (video cassettes v downloads), and reading materials (printed books, magazines and newspapers v downloads). Second, it is important not to distort the choice of technology used to provide particular intangible products and services: for example, the provision of television signals over the air using traditional broadcast technology, via cable using wires (provided by either cable companies or public utilities) and fibre optic cables, or via direct transmission to satellite dishes. Third, taxation should not affect the choices of whether and how to 'bundle' various goods and services for the purposes of pricing. This means that there should be neutrality towards bundling. For example, whether to include software on compact discs sold with books and whether to use lump sum prices or itemized charges for basic and enhanced telecommunications and for the services of ISPs and OSPs, including, especially, the bundling of content and internet access. Fourth, taxation should not distort location decisions or trade between jurisdictions and should neither favour nor penalize local producers and distributors. This has several dimensions, including

---

78 McLure, Charles E Jr (1997) 'Taxation of Electronic Commerce: Economic Objectives, Technological Constraints, and Tax Laws', *Tax Law Review*, Symposium on Taxation and Electronic Commerce.

avoidance of tax-induced distortions of competition in the provision of tangible products, intangible products and services. Location distortions may have either interstate or international dimensions. Administration of (and compliance with) any taxing scheme should be relatively easy. Nexus should be predicated on the presence of taxable activity in the taxing jurisdiction. The possibility of nexus by affiliation, as well as nexus by agency, should be recognized. Jurisdictions at a given level (nations and in case of sub-national authorities) should adopt essentially uniform nexus rules, definitions of tax bases and administrative practices (but not necessarily uniform tax rates). Nevertheless, work should be done in order to reduce the number of taxing jurisdictions and blending of rates. Taxpayers should not be expected to comply with a multitude of locally differentiated rates. Given the difficulty of determining the physical location of customers buying electronic content, vendors should be allowed to assume that the billing address is the destination of such content, though this approach is potentially vulnerable to abuse.

There is need for international cooperation, and this cooperation must extend beyond bilateral treaties and even beyond multilateral agreements between signatories, to 'play by the rules'. It must include the possibility of sanctions against nations that provide a hospitable setting for those who desire to operate in a sheltered environment in order to avoid taxes on their sales and income. The challenge for policy makers would be to respond according to these principles to ensure that needed government expenditures could be funded and that tax distortions are minimized, a significant part of the response would necessarily involve greater international co-operation. It is increasingly difficult for individual countries to manage their tax bases in the face of these forces, and, in particular, some tax practices have been harmful and distort cross-border 'tax competition'. It should be noted here that this is not an attempt to stall the economic progress by protecting the prior technology from the onslaught of new technology. It is also not a plea to penalize the prior technology by giving the new technology tax breaks. An example should help to clarify this point. It may turn out that, for non-tax reasons, video rental stores would be unable to compete with companies offering to download videos electronically over the internet.[79] However, being forced to pay taxes that their cybernetic competitors do not pay should not hamstring video stores. More generally, there is no reason tax law should favour out-of-state vendors or differentiate between tangible products, intangible products, and services, as it does now.[80]

The principle objective in designing taxation for e-commerce would be to achieve neutrality. Neutrality avoids distortion in choices involving consumption, production, location or methods of finance.[81] Neutrality would be especially

---

79 Professor Negroponte predicts that 'videocassette-rental stores will go out of business in less than ten years.' Similarly, Ray Hammond writes, '... I wouldn't buy shares in Blockbuster until I heard about the company's plans for Net delivery).' Hammond (1996), at 201.

80 McLure, Charles E Jr (1997) 'Electronic Commerce, State Sales Taxation and Intergovernmental Fiscal Relations', *National Tax Journal*, Volume: 50 no 4, pp 731-49 at p 383.

81 Slemrod, Joel (1990) Optimal Taxation and Optimal Tax Systems, 4 J. *Econ. Persp.* 157.

important in the taxation of e-commerce, because of the ease with which transactions can be diverted in response to differential taxation, for example, to seemingly different products that satisfy the same underlying needs, to quite similar products that are delivered through different distribution channels or to sources located elsewhere. How to achieve economic neutrality in VAT and sales tax involving cross-border sales? An economically neutral sales tax would apply at a single rate to all consumption occurring within a given jurisdiction but not to business purchases or to exports.[82] This would be true whether a given product is tangible or intangible or a service and whether it is produced domestically or imported. In principle, VAT produces this result automatically, since both imports and domestically produced products are subject to tax, exports are zero-rated, and business taxpayers are allowed a credit against tax liability on sales for VAT paid on purchases. While full competitive neutrality was achieved with respect to the supply of services by EU suppliers to non-EU customers, non-EU suppliers were not required to charge VAT when they supply services to EU customers and thereby caused competitive disadvantage. However, in response to this, as discussed in Chapter 8, the EU Commission amended the VAT Directive by which EU suppliers would not be required to charge VAT on online transactions involving non-EU customers so that competitive neutrality with respect to EU exports to non-EU countries is achieved and VAT treatment of non-EU suppliers with EU taxable persons would be taxed at the location of the EU customer following a destination based taxation.[83]

McLure[84] argued it would be much more difficult, even in theory, to achieve a neutral sales tax than to achieve a neutral VAT. It would not be difficult to eliminate two of the most glaring defects of state sales taxes – the 'bright-line physical presence' test for use tax nexus and the exemption (or differential treatment) of intangible products and many services – though changes have long been high on

---

82 Due, John F. and Mikesell, John L (1994) *Sales Taxation: State and Local Structure and Administration* 1-4 (2d ed.) p 49,

83 As discussed in Chapter 8 EU suppliers would not be required to charge VAT on online transactions involving non-EU customers so that competitive neutrality with respect to EU exports to the US is achieved. The rules for supplies by EU suppliers to EU customers remain unchanged, i.e.

- Supplies to taxable persons remain subject to the reverse charge procedure, and
- Supplies to consumers are taxed where the supplier has established his business.

The VAT treatment of non-EU suppliers, however, would change completely: B2B-transactions with EU taxable persons will be taxed at the location of the EU customer; the tax would be levied via the reverse charge mechanism which requires EU taxable persons to withhold, remit and account for VAT.

Non-EU suppliers who sell their products to EU consumers would have to register with the VAT authorities of a member state of their choice. They would be required to levy VAT on their transactions with EU consumers if their revenues exceed a certain threshold amount. VAT would have to be levied at the rate that is applicable in the member state where the consumer lives.

84 McLure, Charles E Jr (1997) 'Electronic Commerce, State Sales Taxation and Intergovernmental Fiscal Relations', *National Tax Journal*, Volume: 50 no 4, pp 731-49.

the agenda of tax reform in this area. But in order to do so, greater uniformity of state laws (as it is applicable to different states of the US), simplified administrative procedures, and rationalizing nexus rules, as well as and unifying the tax treatment of tangible and intangible products and services, will be required. Otherwise, it would create an unacceptable burden of compliance, especially on small business firms making interstate sales, and aggravate the problem of pyramiding the collection of tax on both business inputs and sales to final consumers.

In order to implement the solution in the context of the sales tax, it would be necessary to distinguish between sales to businesses and sales to households; the former should be exempted, even if the latter is taxed. This problem is ordinarily addressed by exempting certain goods (essentially those that are unlikely to be bought by households) and by allowing firms to buy on a tax-exempt basis. It is useful to ask here whether households or business firms derive most benefits from government services. To the extent that public services are provided primarily to households and are complementary to private consumption, it is appropriate to levy a tax on consumption (as under a destination-based VAT or an ideal sales tax) as a quasi-benefit tax; to the extent they are provided primarily to business and are complementary to production, a production-based tax (such as an origin-based VAT) would be more appropriate. While there is no easy answer to this question, a consumption-based tax levied under the destination principle would be more appropriate. If this is true, tax should be applied to all sales to consumers in a given state; mail-order sales and their tangible and intangible counterparts in e-commerce should not be exempt just because vendors lack a physical presence in the state.

9.4.1   Analysis of Options for Indirect Taxation

While it is generally appropriate that existing taxes should be applied to e-commerce, they would have to be done so based on four objectives. First, it might not be easy to achieve this objective. It might be necessary to rethink how some laws could be applied to make them suitable for the world of e-commerce. Second, some current tax laws, especially at the state level, made no sense; such features include 'nexus' rules, especially as applied to mail-order sales, failure to tax sales of tangible products, intangible products and services equally, application of sales taxes to many purchases by business. Defects that were already troubling would become increasingly untenable and fundamental restructuring would be needed. Third, to solve either of these problems would require substantial cooperation between jurisdictions, be they states or nations; unilateral solutions are not likely to be satisfactory. Fourth, it is possible that 'no new taxes' would not be the right answer and would require further research and analysis. Hence, taxation should seek to be neutral and equitable between forms of e-commerce and between conventional and e-commerce. Taxpayers in similar situations carrying out similar transactions should be subject to similar levels of taxation. It requires a consistent tax policy with, as a matter of principle, no exemptions.[85] For cross-border business, the principles determining jurisdiction must correspond. There should be no distinctions based on

---

85 Westberg, Bjorn (2002) *Cross-border Taxation of E-Commerce,* IBFD p 61.

the method of delivery and place of taxation for supply of goods compared to a similar supply of information in digitized form. The application of different taxes to different services can influence the neutrality of competition. State and local transaction taxes on telecommunications are considered more onerous and burdensome than the general US sales and use taxes. The increasing difficulties in distinguishing between services supplied by traditional telecommunications operators and providers of internet services make all distinctions of that kind questionable.[86]

Proposals to make the internet a 'consumption tax-free zone' would be attractive but would have potentially devastating economic, tax and social consequences. It would distort several dimensions of consumer and business choices: in favour of content delivered online, instead of in tangible forms, and in favour of products that could be delivered online as electronic content, relative to products that could not be (notably tangible products and services that cannot be delivered in this manner). It would avoid some problems otherwise created by bundling, but would pose formidable problems of classification, especially the need to distinguish between telecommunications (presumably taxable) and internet access. Moreover, it would be grossly unfair, both horizontally and vertically. Particularly pernicious is the effect it would have in undermining local retail stores. By exempting a large and growing fraction of consumer purchases, this policy would require higher tax rates to raise a given amount of revenue. Finally, it would do nothing to remedy the problems of the existing system.

The discussion earlier in Chapter 7 showed the incredible growth in e-commerce. This growth has been accompanied by the creation of a small number of brands which have become global leaders in the marketing and distribution of their products through the internet. The world's most popular e-tailer is Amazon.com. Though largely associated with its beginnings as a pure online bookseller, its success and business model have expanded considerably. The market leadership and consumer acceptance of Amazon.com is also evident in other market segments by e-tailers such as 'CDnow' (for music) and 'eBay' (for auctions). What has now become evident is that these internet companies were using their high market values to eliminate their competitors and to take over other companies with high market shares?[87]. During 1999, eBay acquired Butterfield & Butterfield (the 134 year old San Francisco auction house) and Kruse International (the upscale car auctioneer).[88] Similar alliances and acquisitions had also been identified by the OECD as prevalent in international markets.[89] In 2000, a survey by Ernst and Young showed that only 10 per cent of e-tailers indicated that acquisition of other businesses was part of their

---

86 Westberg, Bjorn (2002) *Cross-border Taxation of E-Commerce*, IBFD p 62.

87 Although the current trend in Dotcom companies in past one year was not encouraging but it is believed by most commentators that this downward trend would be temporary and was result of the much of wider economic stagnation. In any case for the past two years major world economies were slowing down. It would appear in coming years that 'bust' of e-commerce companies during this period was exception rather than rule.

88 The January 2000 announcements of the mergers of 'America Online', 'Time Warner and EMI, was another example of such acquisition.

89 OECD (1998) 'The Economic and Social Impact of Electronic Commerce: Preliminary Findings and Research Agenda', 24 August 1998, DSTI/ICCP (98) 15/PART5, p 12. Available at www.oecd.org/subject/e_commerce/summary.htm.

growth strategy.[90] However, if this 10 per cent was the top end of the market, backed with the enormous buying power their share prices gave them, their size would continue to grow as they worked towards reducing competition and competitors in their chosen markets. Of even more concern for traditional retailers was the research by Jupiter Communications, which indicated that the growth in e-commerce would be at the expense of traditional sales.[91] Jupiter found that only 6 per cent of B2C internet sales in 1999 were incremental sales; it was suggested that this figure would increase to 6.5 per cent for internet sales in 2002. This data indicated that 94 per cent of internet sales were sales that traditional retailers would have expected to make. While some proportion of these sales would be facilitated by the internet operations of traditional retailers, the fact remains that most of the sales of the pure internet e-tailers were sales poached from traditional retailers.

The continuation of the preferential taxation treatment of e-commerce will continue to exacerbate the sales losses of traditional businesses as the e-tailers exploit their unfair advantage. It could be expected that this may result in the forced closure of many traditional businesses offering services to local and remote communities. How would the local bookstore compete against the purchasing power of companies such as Amazon. com and Barnes and Noble when this is also backed by a tax-advantaged position for their internet sales? Bruce and Fox's study based on e-commerce sales drawn from Forrester Research Inc.'s annual forecasts for the years 2001 through 2011 showed that the incremental revenue loss from e-commerce sales was estimated to be 41 per cent more than the previous report of 2000 had indicated due to higher B2B transactions forecast by Forrester. In 2001, e-commerce caused a total state and local government revenue loss of US$13.3 billion. By 2006, this loss would be more than triple to US$45.2 billion and in 2011 the loss would be US$54.8 billion. Ernst & Young's survey leading to their 'Third Annual Online Retailing Report' asked respondents why they shopped online.[92] While the convenience factor was important, 'because items cost less' was the response from 16 per cent of those surveyed while 12 per cent noted that it was because they did not incur sales tax. Both responses indicate that consumers were price sensitive on the products they purchase online. Similar findings had also been reported by Goolsbee.[93] However, the price benefits that online purchases are facilitating are not available to all. After analyzing several surveys across a number of countries, the OECD concluded that: 'One consistent finding across many countries is that there is a strong positive correlation between the use of information technology (PC ownership, access to the Internet) and household income: for every $10 000 increase in household income, the percentage of homes owning a computer increases by seven points.'[94]

90　Ernst & Young (2000) 'Global Online Retailing', January 2000, p 47.

91　Jupiter Communications (1999) Press release, 'Digital Commerce Growth Will Be at Expense of Off-line Dollars', 4 August 1999. www.jupitercommunications.com/company/pressrelease.jsp? doc=pr990804.

92　As reported by CyberAtlas, 'Online Holiday Shoppers to Triple' 9 November 1999, available at www.cyberatlas.internet.com.

93　Goolsbee, Austan (1998) 'In a world without borders: the impact of taxes on Internet commerce, November, p 5.

94　OECD (1998) 'The Economic and Social Impact of Electronic Commerce: Preliminary Findings and Research Agenda. Executive Summary', 19 August 1998, p 14.

The US demographic figures from the Ernst and Young[95] report indicated that while 53 per cent of households have PCs, only 34 per cent were online and only 17 per cent had shopped online. These online buyers had a weighted average annual income of US$59,000. Clearly, this indicates that online shopping is not available to all. This situation is unlikely to change while many families cannot afford computers. This demographic figure is not only applicable for the US but it is representative for all countries that have been part of or have experienced the growth of e-commerce. If similar studies were carried out in developing countries, the disparity would be more striking. If preferential tax treatment continued with e-commerce, the possibility of running into the risk of widening the gap of the digital divide would also increase. It would cause a societal inequity where higher income earners would be able to benefit from buying goods cheaper online through a distribution network not available to many lower income families. It is hard to justify why this inequity should be further subsidized by the non-application of sales/use taxes and VAT to e-commerce. It is also enlightening in this regard to look at what consumers are buying online. In order of most popular internet purchases, consumers are buying computers, books, CDs, electronics and toys. Given the demographics of online buyers as outlined above, these consumer items are not those that inherently need government subsidization. Use of the internet and e-commerce are facilitating growth quickly amongst those in society who can afford access and have the purchasing power to enjoy the benefits it is providing. To minimize the adverse effects of this growth on society, it is believed that the current inequity in treatment between the distribution method of goods and services purchased from traditional sources and those purchased over the internet should be removed. In summary, taxing all e-commerce would perpetuate or aggravate compliance and administrative problems. However, exempting it would create inequities and distortions and would aggravate existing problems of classification and compound discrimination.

9.4.2 Destination- or Origin-Based Taxation

The destination principle is almost universally employed for the sales taxation of international trade in tangible products, and the EU is moving toward the destination-based taxation of intangibles and services.[96] The question is which of these competing alternatives is preferred on efficiency grounds. Conceptually, the answer hinges on the relative mobility of factors versus sales (or consumers) across jurisdictions, as well as costs of administration and compliance.[97] Most proposals put forward in the formal and informal literature prefer tax collection on a destination basis; a minority favours taxation at source. Destination-based taxation has several conceptual advantages. First, destination-based taxation is much less likely to distort the location of economic activity than origin-based taxation. Second, taxation

---

95 Ernst & Young (2000) 'Global Online Retailing', January 2000.

96 European Union Directive (2002/38/EC) and Regulation No.792/2002 amending the Sixth VAT Directive (77/388/EEC) known as EU Directive VAT on Digital Sales.

97 Fox, William F, Murray, Matthew N and Luna, LeAnn (2005) How Should a Subnational Corporate Income Tax on Multistate Businesses Be Structured? *National Tax Journal*, Vol. LVIII, No. 1.

of consumption is probably a better proxy for the benefits of public services than taxation of production.[98] However, the application of destination-based registration at a global level would impose an insurmountable compliance burden on globally operating firms in a world of more than 100 different VAT systems.[99] To facilitate the process of destination-based registration, as Doernberg and Hinnekens argue,[100] a real-time online system should be provided whereby the non-resident vendor could check the validity of purchasers' VAT registration numbers. Substantial international cooperation is required to prevent blocs of countries from implementing mutually inconsistent tax policies – potentially giving rise to double or no taxation of trade flows and to provide for the mutual enforcement of tax debts.[101]

Perhaps most important is the political attraction of the destination principle. It is not difficult to understand why those producing for the domestic market would not quietly accept origin-based taxation, as it would imply that they would have to pay taxes while their foreign competition would not. Under the destination principle, market jurisdictions will collect the same tax on domestic and foreign production. Similarly, exporters are not likely to take kindly to a suggestion that exports should be taxed. It is relatively easy, ignoring legal obstacles for the moment, to collect destination-based taxes on tangible products. Where there are fiscal borders, as between nations that are not members of a common market, tax can be collected at the border. Within a common market, it may be possible for vendors to collect the tax, because they know where they ship goods. However, increasingly important technological shifts from the production and sale of physical to digital products would make destination-based taxation difficult to implement. In contrast to products traditionally sold in shops and in a format that gave them some physical content, digital goods do not have physical characteristics. Consequently, it would be difficult to determine the location of purchasers. By comparison, origin-based taxation would be relatively easy to implement in this case. So far, the VAT and sales tax systems have concluded that the destination model should apply whereby the tax system and tax rate of the destination jurisdiction should apply. The idea being that if consumption is the appropriate subject of taxation, then the country in which goods are received for consumption receives the revenue generated by that consumption. This however creates a tax problem, which is also economically disruptive in two particular ways:

---

98 Defenders of destination-based taxation argue that the principle is essential to the purpose of taxing *consumption*. An origin principle, they say, would 'conceptually' transform a consumption tax into a tax on production.

99 Ligthart, Jenny E. (2004) 'Consumption Taxation in a Digital World: A Primer' (September) CentER Discussion Paper No. 2004-102. Available at SSRN: http://ssrn.com/abstract=625044.

100 Doernberg, Richard L. and Hinnekens, Luc (1999) *Electronic Commerce and International Taxation* (The Hague: Kluwer Law International).

101 Ligthart, Jenny E. (2004) 'Consumption Taxation in a Digital World: A Primer' (September) CentER Discussion Paper No. 2004-102. Available at SSRN: http://ssrn.com/abstract=625044.

- the source country has the ability to enforce compliance but no revenue interest in doing so, while the destination country has a revenue interest in doing so, yet the destination country has a revenue interest in compliance but has difficulty with enforcement, especially in relation to non-corporeal goods such as digital products purchased over the internet;
- the source country saves money on enforcement and potentially gains other revenues; gains occur in areas such as income taxes from jobs and property taxes on centres of production, and thus business within such jurisdictions can enjoy a competitive tax advantage.

Would origin-based taxation solve these problems? In view of the administrative complexities associated with taxation on a destination basis, a number of commentators[102] have proposed to tax e-commerce at origin. While no solution is perfect and each solution creates new issues, origin-based taxation would seem to answer the major problems posed by a destination-based tax and would be relatively easy for the states to implement. By this system, sales tax or VAT would be collected by the seller only at the point of origin of the e-commerce sale which would be defined as the seller's physical location. This would eliminate sellers' concerns over nexus uncertainties, analysis of whether items were taxable or exempt in the various jurisdictions, privacy concerns and the costs of collection and remittance to hundreds, if not thousands of jurisdictions. Effectively, the major concerns raised by a destination-based tax would be answered. Particularly, some scholars in the USA have suggested an origin-based consumption taxation system as a solution. Origin-based taxation appears to solve most compliance complexities of US sale/use tax. The e-commerce seller would be required to collect all the state and local taxes in the jurisdiction where the 'principal place of business' of the e-commerce seller would be located, regardless of where the product would be shipped or the service performed. The seller's sales would be subject to one tax rate and one jurisdiction's tax laws and regulations. The tax revenue thus generated would be allocated according to the laws of the state where the vendor's principal place of business is located. Under an origin-based system, the e-commerce seller would have to collect at only one rate of tax, on only one tax base (that is, one set of tax laws and regulations – that of the state of their principal place of business). This would minimize the burden on the seller in a number of ways.

Another positive aspect would be the statutorily extinguished 'use tax' liability of the buyer even if the customer's home state imposed tax at a higher tax rate. Because the e-commerce vendor would be physically located in the state asserting taxing jurisdiction, there would be no question that nexus exists. Actual physical presence would satisfy due process nexus concerns as well as the substantial nexus requirements of the US Supreme Court. Another potential positive impact of origin-based taxing would be maximizing the revenue collected. As nexus considerations

---

102   See Terry Ryan and Eric Miethke (1998) 'The Seller-State Option: Solving the Electronic Commerce Dilemma' (October 5) State Tax Notes 881-92, Andrew Wagner and Wade Anderson (1999) 'Origin-Based Taxation of Internet Commerce' (July 19) State Tax Notes 187-92.

would be eliminated, it is reasonable to assume that many transactions that currently escape taxation would now be taxed. In addition, because it would be easy to administer and enforce by the taxing officials of the state in which the seller is located, non-compliance would be greatly reduced. Finally, because the sales would be taking place in one location, local taxes imposed in that jurisdiction would also be collected, eliminating the need for a uniform state tax rate, which many states might be legally or politically precluded from providing.

However, some could view this as a serious invasion of the purchaser's privacy, which would require the seller to obtain information from the purchaser and deliver that information directly to tax officials. It would be an intrusion that would be unique to e-commerce purchasers because such information is generally not taken from traditional 'bricks and mortar' buyers. As under an origin-based proposal, the purchaser would be treated the same for tax purposes as a customer who walked into the vendor's store, there would be no need for inquiry into the identity or location of the buyer. Further, origin-based taxation would maintain the autonomy of local governments and other local taxing jurisdictions that are strongly opposed to the one-tax-rate-per state idea (this is particularly important for US state and local governments). This would be both politically realistic and would respect the notion of federalism, that is, that the federal government should not overly intervene in the taxing prerogatives of the states.[103]

Under a destination-based VAT, tax is applied to goods imported into the taxing jurisdiction and exports from the jurisdiction occur tax-free. Under an origin-based VAT, exports are subject to tax, and tax is applied only to the value that is added after importation. Under this proposal, as with bricks and mortar retailers, the buyer is viewed as visiting the sellers' location, rather than the seller visiting the buyers' location. For example, if an online software company in the UK uploaded a game to a customer in the USA (say Oregon), the software company would be liable for the VAT. The same would be true if the software were uploaded to a customer in London, Moscow or an aeroplane crossing the Atlantic. Under an origin-based tax system, taxes would be collected on all sales out of the relevant tax jurisdiction and no businesses would be expected to collect taxes for a government from which they derive no benefits. Whether or not the digitized sale is taxable is to be determined by the seller's state, just as when a buyer physically enters a state to make a purchase. As the GIIC has noted, 'an origin based system, universally applied, would simplify indirect taxation, would result in more effective enforcement, would reduce opportunities for avoidance, and would eliminate double taxation'.[104] Since businesses are subject to audit, the expected compliance rate with origin-based tax rules is also very high. Mechanisms to enforce compliance with domestic consumption tax collection responsibilities are already in place, so a move to origin-based taxation would place no additional burdens on businesses and little (if any) new burdens on national tax

---

103   Hence an origin-based taxation promises to minimize enforcement and compliance difficulties. Even its opponents have conceded its theoretical elegance and practical advantages. see Charles E. McLure (1997) 'Taxation of Electronic Commerce: Economic Objectives, Technological Constraints, and Tax Laws,' 52 *Tax Law Review* 269.

104   Global Information Infrastructure Commission (2000).

administrations. A final benefit of origin-based taxation, although most governments do not see it that way, is that such a system fosters robust tax competition between states. Critics of origin-based taxation often warn that such tax competition will not be healthy, but rather be a 'race to the bottom' for nations, undermining their ability to raise revenue.[105]

It has also been argued that origin-based taxation would disadvantage domestic producers on their export sales. Although the design of a nation's tax system can affect export competitiveness, the true burden facing domestic producers is the overall level of taxation. Thus, businesses subject to VAT collection responsibilities may not suffer any competitive disadvantages under an origin-based system if tax rates are kept at reasonable levels. A Deloitte & Touche paper puts it this way:

> A consumption tax without border tax adjustments (an origin-principle consumption tax) … at first appears to create a disadvantage for domestic producers relative to foreign producers in overseas markets. Border tax adjustments, though, may not be the only mechanism operating to maintain neutrality. Other self-executing adjustments by the markets, such as reductions in wage rates or in the value of the domestic currency, could offset wholly any potentially detrimental trade effects of origin-based taxation on exported goods.[106]

The European Commission has recognized the inherent benefits of origin-based consumption taxes, albeit only on an internal basis. In 1996, in its work programme for the gradual introduction of a new common VAT system, the Commission announced its intention to advocate a switch from taxation at destination to taxation at origin for sales within Europe. The changes being contemplated are minor. 'All transactions giving rise to consumption in the EU', a Commission paper states, 'would be taxed from their point of origin so that the existing remission/taxation mechanism for trade between Member States would be abolished.'[107] However, switching to origin-based taxation would shift substantial amounts of tax base from developing countries to developed countries where digital contents originate, particularly to the US. (In essence, for B2B transactions, the origin principle is tantamount to exempting the tax free imported component of final products from tax.) There is also a further argument that countries of origin are quite likely to tax digital content preferentially in order to prevent its providers from locating elsewhere. This implies that digital content would have a substantial competitive advantage over non-digital equivalents, which would be taxed under the destination principle. This would create further downward pressure on the tax base of developing countries.

---

105   Charles E. McLure used this phrase to describe the consequences of taxing sales at their origin during testimony before Advisory Commission on E-Commerce on June 22, 1999.

106   Deloitte & Touche LLP (1996) 'Consumption Tax Issues Briefs,' *Fundamental Tax Reform*, available at http://www.dtonline.com/TAXREF/trissue.htm.

107   Eggermont, Tino (1998) 'The Commission's work programme for the gradual introduction of the new common VAT system,' European Commission, 1998, available at http://www.ecu-activities.be/1998_2/eggermont.html.

9.4.3   BIT Tax

A number of alternative approaches have been canvassed, with some attention being paid to the notion of a 'bit tax'. 'Bit tax' was radical or even revolutionary because it did not fit into the framework of income or consumption taxation. In essence, this would involve charges being levied upon internet users dependent on the volume of data transmitted to or from their equipment. Arthur Cordell and Thomas Ide first proposed the notion of such a tax in 1994. Cordell and Ide argued that existing tax bases were no longer appropriate in an environment where the major economic activity was represented by the transmission of data. The report 'Building the Information Society for US All'[108] produced by a group of independent experts appointed by the European Commission, suggested in 1996 that the Commission investigate:

> Appropriate ways in which the benefits of the Information Society (IS) can be more equally distributed between those who benefit and those who lose. Such research should focus on practicable, implementable policies at the European level which do not jeopardise the emergence of the IS. More specifically, the expert group would like the commission to undertake research to find out whether a 'bit tax' might be a feasible tool in achieving such redistribution aims.

Cordell[109] argued that a tax on gasoline did not slow down the development of the automobile industry. However, this happened because of an implicit assumption of the inelastic demand for cars. Whether the demand for accessing the internet and, more important, the demand for using the internet is inelastic remains an open question.

In the report 'Globalization with a Human Face', the United Nations also argued in favour of 'bit tax'.[110] This report advocated levying a tax on data sent over the internet, with the findings used to support the development of a telecommunications infrastructure in the least developed countries of the world. Statistics produced by NUA surveys indicate a massive variation in access to and use of the internet between the various regions of the world. Some 304.6 million people are estimated to use the internet. A tax of 1 per cent per 100 e-mails, it was estimated, would yield annual income of US$70 billion. The UN proposal did not receive a warm welcome in the developed world, where it was described as 'an unnecessary and burdensome tax on the internet'. The bit tax was heavily criticized by the OECD's 1998 Ottawa ministerial meeting of the WTO. To this end, the EU also rejected the proposal of 'bit tax':

> In order to allow electronic commerce operators to reap the full benefits of the Single Market (i.e. the European Market), it is essential to avoid regulatory inconsistencies and to ensure a coherent legal and regulatory framework for electronic commerce at EU level... In parallel, a number of key horizontal issues affecting the entire electronic commerce activity need to be addressed. These include data security, protection of intellectual

---

108   Available from www.meritbbs.unimaas.nl/publications/2-hleg.pdf.

109   Cordell, A and Ide, J (1994) 'The New Wealth of Nations-Taxing Cyberspace', Buenos Aires, Argentina: Between the Lines Publishers, paper prepared for annual Meeting of the Club of Rome, November.

110   Available from www.undp.org/hdro/99.htm, published in July 1999.

property rights and conditional access services, privacy, as well as a clear and neutral tax environment.[111]

The main appeal of the bit tax was its ostensible simplicity. A specified tax rate was applied to the volume of interactive cyberspace 'traffic' travelling over lines run by telecommunications carrier companies, and the resulting tax revenues would then flow directly to national governments. However, such simplicity may be more apparent than real, for the bit tax presents vexing problems of how to accurately measure the volume of data flow and how to precisely separate which data would be taxable and which would not. Consequently, tax collections could either be inflated or deflated, bringing unintended distortions in the tax base and instabilities in the tax system. Additionally, taxing business transactions in a different manner specifically because they were conducted by means of e-commerce violates the principle of tax neutrality.

A distinguishing characteristic of the bit tax was that the entire burden of collecting and remitting the tax was borne by the carrier company. While it could be argued that carrier companies possess the necessary technical and labour resources to effectively perform such a function, it would be uncertain as to who, in the final analysis, would shoulder the bulk of the tax burden or incidence. Would carrier companies absorb the cost or would they pass it on to consumers? If carriers choose to pass the costs on to consumers (a reasonable assumption, it appears), they would have to do so in a non-neutral manner, because carriers lack the means to accurately separate e-commerce from non-e-commerce data flows. With a bit tax, there could also be problems with enforcing compliance on the part of carrier companies. Without a central international regulatory agency to oversee the carriers, there would be difficulties in ensuring that companies collect the correct amount of tax and accurately allocate the funds to the designated governments. The bit tax is a specific tax; it does not take into account the value of the good that is being taxed, as an *ad valorem* tax does. Accordingly, high-bit-volume, low-value transactions are taxed disproportionately: for example, the downloading of a new computer manual would trigger less tax than the transmission of a personal photograph, thus creating distortions. Per-unit taxation is common practice for phone companies, however, which typically price and tax phone calls on the basis of distance and usage time. Moreover, the value-added that is generated by internet access is difficult to measure and thus difficult to tax on an *ad valorem* basis.

The arguments put forward for the 'bit tax' were not grounded in free market based economic principles, but rather in moral and sociological reasoning. With limited exceptions, a free market operates most efficiently when taxes are designed to minimize interference with the production processes. Thus, the burden of taxation is limited to the revenue raised and there is no additional cost to lower economic output. A 'bit tax' failed this basic principle of taxation because it would discourage electronic transmission of information. Economic resources would be wasted through

---

111   A European Initiative in Electronic Commerce (1997) Communication to the European Parliament, the Council, the Economic and Social Committee and the Committee of the Regions, COM(97) 157,.May 1997,.<http://www.cordis.lu/esprit/src/ecomcomx.htm>.

efforts to minimize the 'bit tax'. Further, it would also be counterproductive in that it burdens e-commerce and its productivity. For example, software companies might continue to ship magnetic tapes and cartridges rather than to use the more efficient method of transmitting the data electronically.

Electronic transmission of information is highly efficient and thus extremely low in cost. Proponents of the 'bit tax' further argued that the price of electronic transmission does not reflect true value. They argue for taxing electronic transmission according to bits rather than value, as is the case under a value-added tax. Experience has shown that when prices are set by social planners rather than by the operation of the free market, the loss of economic efficiency can be enormous. There was no reason to believe that the market place could not adjust pricing systems to better align prices with resource availability. With regard to the discouraging effect of the 'bit tax' in freeing up internet resources, while congestion on the existing internet is a valid issue today, discouraging use of the internet would not be a desirable goal. It would be premature to conclude that existing taxes could not be successfully adjusted to accommodate technological innovations. The solution to these problems lay not in new taxes but rather in technology itself. What would be required is a matter of clearly defining tax compliance requirements and making reasonable adaptations to existing tax rules and then a matter of taxpayers adapting the technologies to satisfy those compliance requirements.

9.4.4   Share of Tax Base

To nullify this distortion and improve overall cross-frontier compliance, a solution must aim for ease of administration, revenue neutrality and a fairer allocation of the tax revenues between source country and destination country. Taylor, in his paper 'An Ideal E-Commerce Consumption Tax in a Global Economy' proposed a solution which is feasible and beneficial to both the developed and developing countries. It was based on the principle of sharing the consumption tax base between the origination and destination countries. By sharing revenue, the destination country gives the origination country an interest in insuring that the consumption tax is collected and paid. The destination country should determine the rate of the tax or the exemption from the tax and this ensures tax neutrality along with safeguarding the interest of developing countries (as they have the more consumers). As I have said earlier, the economic impact of loss of revenue over the developing countries will be more. According to the proposal, the origination country would receive an amount of tax equal to half of its VAT or sales tax rate or half of the VAT or sales tax of the destination country; whichever of the two is less. For origination countries, which do not have applicable consumption taxes, the proposal provides an incentive of 3 per cent or half of the destination jurisdiction's consumption tax, in the form of an export tax.

In order that the system works, it would need a universal product coding system, which would determine which product is subject to what tax. The coding system would also help the taxing jurisdictions to modify the rates of tax for different products or to make certain products exempted from tax. In order to avoid the pyramiding of consumption taxes, a business will be allowed to register in each country where it actively conducts its business through one or more physical establishments. Sales to registered businesses will be exempted from consumption taxes on the theory that the goods are being used as inputs for subsequent taxable sales. The collection and payment of the tax would be entrusted upon a 'Trusted Third Party', which could be the credit card companies or the banking institutions and they would receive a fee for their administration of the system. Universal software would be developed in order to determine the tax due on each transaction. The primary audit function would fall on the destination country. As so many taxing jurisdictions will be involved, safeguards should exist for protecting the privacy of businesses and consumers.

By sharing the tax revenue, the system should work as it creates interest for both jurisdictions. Neutrality is preserved within the jurisdictions because the consumption rate does not vary based on the origin of sale. The proposal is quite attractive for the EU as it solves the problem of designating the point of sale within the EU and preserves most of the VAT tax base for sales outside the EU. However, it had not been written with the EU Directive on Digital Sales in mind, which would make the proposal not adaptable in principle. Most of the state and local governments would support the proposal as it solves the problem of nexus in the light of the *Quill* decision. One of the main drawbacks of the proposal is that there is a possibility that businesses and other entities would claim the exemption when they are not entitled to it. There is also a possibility that the consumers would claim to reside in low or no tax jurisdictions but actually reside somewhere else. The approach offered in this paper may not be conceptually pure. The option works with burdens imposed on the destination country. The rate of tax or exemption would be determined by the destination country; even the primary audit function would fall on the destination country; however, by providing a share in tax to the origin country when their responsibility would be limited only to monitoring would provide them undue favouritism. The basic problem for e-commerce in the case of consumption taxes is how to determine the location of the consumer, which has not fully been explored in the proposal.

9.4.5   OECD TAG Proposals

During the past few years, the OECD Working Party on Consumption Taxes working together with business and non-member countries has focused on five possible mechanisms for the collection of consumption taxes, which were:

- self-assessment;
- registration of non-resident suppliers;
- tax at source and transfer;
- collection by trusted third parties; and
- technology-based solutions.

The Working Party identified the merits of each of the collection mechanisms and those which may be suitable and workable in different circumstances. To see which mechanism was the most preferable, a simple test could be used. These mechanisms have been judged by the test used by the Working Party, which contained three criteria. The first criterion was the *feasibility of implementation*. Does the mechanism have a chance of implementation? The second criterion was the *compliance burden*. The costs for business of implementing and applying the mechanism should not be so high that it would prevent compliance and encourage avoidance and evasion. The third and final criterion was the *administrative burden*. If perception costs were too high, levying consumption taxes becomes inefficient.

The first collection mechanism the Working Party examined was self-assessment, also referred to as reverse charge. Under a self-assessment system, recipients would be required to determine the tax owing on the imports of digital supplies, and to remit this amount to their domestic tax authority. While this mechanism is very suitable for transactions where the recipient is a business, it is impractical for transactions where the recipient is a private consumer. This mechanism to a lesser or greater extent is in use for B2B transactions in most OECD countries. It had proven feasible and effective and carries a low compliance and administrative burden. For transactions involving private customers however, it is highly ineffective. Taxing a private customer for the digital supplies he had received would be very burdensome on both the consumer and the tax authority in terms of compliance and control. Taxing private individuals using this mechanism delivered high compliance and administrative costs. Asking consumers to keep books and to control those books was too costly and burdensome on both taxpayers and tax administrators. This means that the risks of evasion and avoidance would be high. Therefore, self-assessment could only be considered as an option for B2B transactions.

The second collection mechanism the Working Party worked on was registration of non-resident suppliers. A registration system obliges a non-resident seller of digital supplies to register in a jurisdiction in which he had made sales. After registration the seller would have to charge, collect and remit the consumption tax to the country in which the consumption took place. For example, a French seller of digital music, selling music to customers in Canada, would have to register in Canada. She would have to charge and collect Canadian consumption tax and remit the tax to the Canadian tax authorities. From an administrative point of view, registration of non-resident suppliers would, for the most part, be feasible and effective. Since the registration of non-residents would not directly require bilateral or multilateral arrangements, this mechanism was relatively easy to implement.[112] Difficulties arise in terms of identifying non-resident suppliers as well as in imposing registration requirements and enforcing obligations on non-residents. This mechanism could therefore increase the costs for tax administrations and for businesses. This would be particularly true for businesses making supplies in multiple jurisdictions. Without international cooperation, there would also be a risk that businesses would not comply. In the absence of international co-operation, this mechanism depended on the voluntary compliance of non-resident suppliers. To encourage voluntary compliance, the registration and remitting of tax should be as simple as possible.

The third collection mechanism the Working Party examined was the tax at source and transfer system. Under this system, a business would collect consumption

---

112   The EU is applying VAT on digital sales using the principle of this system, as discussed in Chapter 8.

tax on sales made to non-resident consumers and remit the tax due to its domestic revenue authority. In turn, the domestic revenue authority would forward the tax revenue to the revenue authority of the country of consumption. This system shares some features with the registration system. A major difference of course being that under a system of tax at source and transfer, suppliers of digital supplies would not have to register abroad. Businesses can handle their foreign consumption tax responsibilities with their national tax authorities. However, this mechanism requires tax revenue to be transferred from one tax jurisdiction to another. This means that considerable international agreement would be needed, which would make this mechanism difficult to implement. The significant compliance cost associated with the registration mechanism would be largely avoided by the tax at source and transfer mechanism. This, however, would be replaced by significant administrative costs that come with the required international cooperation.

The fourth option the Working Party considered was an entirely new system where third parties would be enlisted to collect consumption taxes on transactions between recipients and suppliers of digital supplies. A trusted third party would monitor the transactions between buyers and sellers and would charge the buyers consumption taxes and remit these taxes to the tax authorities of the countries where consumption took place. If a trusted third party were to take on the levying and recovery of certain taxes, both compliance and administrative costs could be kept to a minimum, making this mechanism appealing in this respect. The feasibility of this mechanism, however, is a point of concern. Shifting the onus of collection onto a commercial organization is troublesome. Today, many consumption taxes are collected by businesses that do not receive compensation for this imposed task. Granting a fee for the collection of consumption taxes in the field of e-commerce makes it difficult to deny an allowance in other fields. Ideally, tax collection would be part of a package of services for which the supplier would be willing to pay. Otherwise, if there were no business opportunity, paying the tax collection bill would not be easy.

The fifth and final mechanisms for collecting consumption taxes the Working Party studied were technology driven options. Various technology-based and technology-facilitated options had been debated. One approach would involve the use of tamper-proof software, which would automatically calculate the tax due on a transaction and remit (through a financial intermediary) the tax to the jurisdiction of consumption. Bilateral agreements would provide for verification by the tax authority in the jurisdiction from which the supply was made. It would do so on behalf of the tax authorities in the jurisdiction where the consumption takes place and would also monitor the installation and operation of the software. Technology based or technology-facilitated options offer a broad range of possible mechanisms. As these mechanisms were still to be developed, it was possible to incorporate requirements for feasibility and effectiveness into the development programmes. Doing this by definition will produce mechanisms that can easily be implemented and carry low administrative and compliance costs. Now such technology driven collection mechanisms are being developed. They would probably be available in the medium term. However, none of these methods was perfect but several of them could be used together to provide a reasonable level of assurance. The need for simplicity provided some guidance on who should be registered for tax and with which authorities. The need for automation made it clear that any feasible solution must be technological to a high degree. The WP9 paper argued that technology could support any part of the overall compliance model.[113] However, one can go further and say that technology-based solutions should not be seen as a separate class of solution at all. They simply provide ways to make it easy for taxpayers to account for tax and to give tax authorities the confidence that they are collecting the right amounts of tax given the legal relationships between taxpayers and authorities that have been selected.

9.5   A Global Tax System

> When there is no longer a territorial imperative, when the place of residence and the investment are no longer a given but a choice, when added value is generated in too abstract a fashion for its creation to be assigned a precise location, taxation is no longer a sovereign decision. (Jean-Marie Guehenno, 1995)

Adam Smith, economist and philosopher, in his book *Wealth of Nations* (1776) said that all should contribute to taxation as a sign of citizenship of a state. He based his principles on the propositions: ability to pay, certainty of payment, convenience and minimal cost. The relationship between taxation and emergence of the modern state, in short, was one of 'mutual constitution': 'taxes made the state and the state made taxes'.[114] Put differently, the modern state grew and flourished in part because it made fiscal sense at the time: it was a form of political organization that was particularly good at collecting taxes. Given this history, it is not surprising that taxation was, and continues to be, viewed as a central function and prerogative of the state. However, this history now raises intriguing questions for the present day. Territorial states are not particularly well-suited to the task of taxing non-territorial e-commerce. As e-commerce would grow in volume, states would experience a corresponding decline in their ability to tax global e-commerce. More precisely, states would experience a decline in their '*autonomous*' taxing abilities. Does this unprecedented phenomenon of e-commerce necessarily argue for the creation of a new tax system? The current international tax scene is rich in initiatives and programmes, however it lacks:

- clear and transparent mechanisms for the coordination of these programmes; and
- a real input from developing countries in the way programmes are constructed and international tax issues debated.

There are very few forums where developing countries can speak and raise their concern. The development of e-commerce has not brought any fundamental change to this apart from participation of some developing countries in OECD. However,

---

113   OECD (1999).

114   Hoffman, Philip T and Kathryn Norberg (1994) *Fiscal Crises, Liberty and Representative Government* (Stanford: Stanford University Press) at p 303.

as most commentators would agree, developing countries must be able to raise the revenue concern, which is required to finance the services, demanded by their citizens and the infrastructure (physical and social) that would enable them to move out of poverty, and taxation plays the key role in this revenue mobilization. Merilee Grindle, Professor of International Development and author of *Ready or Not: The Developing World and Globalisation* admitted that 'many developing countries are at a competitive disadvantage in the context of rapid globalisation ... in fact, the gap between the wealthy North and much of the poor South is likely to increase in the years ahead, despite some development success stories.' In almost all developing countries, it would be the elites who benefit significantly from e-commerce and to a broad extent globalization. However, they stand in great contrast to most of the population in their countries, whose low levels of education, health and economic security put them at a particular disadvantage in the knowledge-driven era of globalization. If these are the challenges faced by developing nations, one can well imagine the impact on impoverished countries, which suffer from weak economic, legal and political institutions, making them unattractive for domestic or foreign investment.

Some commentators argue that the stage is set for a global fiscal showdown. With the increased frequency of e-commerce, it is conceivable that until international consensus is achieved on the taxation of global trade, less developed countries would find themselves at the losing end in terms of revenue collection from business conducted within their own territories. On the other hand, developed nations with the technological infrastructure to carry on business in a borderless world would have the edge. Potentially, a redistribution of billions of tax dollars is at stake. The issue is not just about shifting of tax revenue from less developed to more developed countries, but more important, the potential leakage from state treasury coffers arising from the use of offshore centres and tax havens. It may be timely to think 'outside the box' with the view to develop a new mechanism to deal with the new challenges of a new era. One possible measure perhaps is to move towards some form of global tax system. As Owens noted, 'if governments are to meet successfully the challenges posed by internet tax systems, a coordinated approach is required'.[115] Global taxes are not a new idea. Legal scholar James Lorimer referred to the idea in his 1884 book *Ultimate Problems of International Jurisprudence*. Many of the most famous economists of the earlier twentieth century likewise considered it, including Alfred Marshall, John Maynard Keynes and James Meade.[116] Around the time of the United Nations' founding in 1945, economists and policy makers often spoke of the need for robust international economic policy to avoid the dangers of renewed depression and war. To them, global economic management and even global wealth redistribution seemed not only desirable but a logical necessity. In order for a global tax system to work it would require overlying and extending the national tax system beyond

---

115   Owens, Jeffrey (1997) The Tax Man Cometh to Cyberspace (presented at the Symposium on Multi-jurisdictional Taxation of Electronic Commerce, Harvard Law School).

116   Frankman, Myron J. (1996) 'International Taxation - The Trajectory of an Idea from Lorimer to Brandt,' *World Development*, vol. 24 (May).

traditional frontiers. Ideally all the national tax systems would be harmonized by a combination of standardized administrative procedure and technology to achieve some degree of consistency, and it is envisaged that such a tax would be administered by a world-nominated agency, collected based on international transactions and/ or consumption, and the funds applied towards approved global causes such as eradication of poverty, health and social development.

Those who advocate for a global tax system argue that, whether the taxation of international e-commerce is pursued through an enhanced source based system, an enhanced residence-based system or formulae apportionment system, whether consumption taxes for the cross-border e-commerce follow origin-based, destination-based or share of tax base, a considerable broadening and strengthening of the international tax regime would almost certainly be necessary. It is difficult to imagine any such arrangement that would not involve the creation of some from of permanent international tax institution. Some day, an international political authority would levy global taxes. However, at present, a robust authority of this kind, with sufficient accountability *and* enforcement powers, does not exist. No one would argue the moral case for having a global tax system. However, a relatively simple moral argument requires substantial political will and motivation for implementation. Hence, one of the most strenuous criticisms of proposals for global taxation concerns its feasibility. An examination of the actions that must be taken if a system of global taxation is to be adopted and implemented indicated that although it is feasible from a technical, legal and administrative point of view. The biggest obstacle would be political. The creation of an international fiscal leviathan to swallow up the world's tax base and divide it among participating countries carries with it the risk of authoritarian misuse, as do lesser moves in the same direction to harmonize and unify tax systems across jurisdictional boundaries.

Keat[117] expressed that in order for a global tax system to be successfully implemented, there must be consensual acceptance by all countries, particularly the richer and more developed nations, which are likely to bear the heaviest burden. There must also be general agreement by these nations that the funds collected be used for approved global priorities, judiciously determined based on prescribed qualifying criteria. The global tax system must also reflect fair principles of taxation but, most important, the richer and more developed nations must have the political will to support such an initiative, otherwise it would be an exercise in futility. However, the supposed reluctance of individual states to commit to an international effort could be explained, at least in part, by the prisoners' dilemma analysis of international cooperation. In the classic prisoners' dilemma, when two people are suspected of a crime. If neither person confesses, there would not be enough evidence to convict either one of them. At the same time, however, when there is an offer that whoever confesses first would receive a reduced sentence, each prisoner knows that the optimum outcome for both of them could be accomplished if both prisoners agree not to confess. However, neither one of the prisoners could be sure what the other would

---

117   Keat, Khoo Chuan (2001) 'Towards a Global Tax System' *available at* www. pwcglobal.com/servlet, *visited 10th November 2001*, Prof Khoo Chuan Keat is Executive Director and Tax Leader, Pricewaterhouse Coopers Malaysia.

do. Consequently, both confess, giving the authorities all the information they would need to convict both the prisoners.[118] The same scenario could be applied loosely to international efforts for an agreement to a global tax system. Even if each state may recognize that it would be in the general interest of the international community to agree to such a system. This outcome would only be optimal if a sufficient number of states comply. If this does not occur, states that would be party to the agreement would suffer a competitive disadvantage in comparison to those states that chose to remain outside the agreement. Therefore, without sufficient international consensus, no state would feel confident in entering into a binding agreement. Any global tax system would also violate the accepted principles of taxation:

- administrative simplicity: this is not possible because of both the likely governing structure and the need to coordinate tax collection across some 200 jurisdictions;
- flexibility: the governing structure makes it unlikely that a global tax system could respond appropriately to changing economic conditions and, in fact, makes it likely that the system would respond perversely;
- transparency: the complications of a global tax would make it difficult to impossible to determine where true tax incidence fell, particularly given the tax would be on international movements, not end-users;
- fairness: for the preceding reasons, both vertical and horizontal fairness could not be ensured and would likely be deliberately violated.

The growth of e-commerce has made the differences between the tax systems of the world quite apparent. If the objective is to maintain the tax base and protect the revenue loss, then what would be required is to develop tax rules that make compliance simple and inexpensive. Any solution that would meet these requirements would have to be based on simple and consistent tax rules across all jurisdictions. Would this require developing a global tax system? Perhaps not in the way many of the proponents of the global tax system would like to see. The best method in the short term may not be the best method in the long term: new technology may change our preferences. However, guiding principles must be kept simple and must be realistic. Complexity puts businesses off, and would lead to their withdrawing cooperation. In addition, human beings are too precious a resource to spend on the routine administration of amounts of tax which are individually small.

---

118   Fudenberg, D and Tirole, J. (1999) *Game Theory* (Cambridge Mass: MIT Press).

Chapter 10

The Future Direction of Taxing E-Commerce

Introduction

Structural and policy adjustments are as old as humanity. Every time socio-economic changes take place, it requires structural adjustments and adoption or amendment of policy. However, there is always the distinction and disagreement between the *descriptive* and *prescriptive* study of policy making. Policy making requires both 'knowledge of' and 'knowledge in' policy making. Despite the danger of sacrificing 'policy analysis' to 'policy advocacy', it is important to state up front that the focus of this thesis is to provide a balance between the *prescriptive* (how policies ought to be made or should be made in future) and the *descriptive* (how policies are being made or are in existence), with the rider that it should be viewed as an analysis of the prescriptions or options and would end with the recommendation of a fixed approach.

The borderline between tax policy and tax administration is rarely clear. Policy reforms are, in part, driven by what is administratively feasible. And, in practice, the tax administration is engaged in day-to-day reform of the tax system. By far the greatest concern on the part of the tax authorities is with regard to the actual collection of taxes. The resources used in the collection of taxes are a dead-weight loss unless the benefit flowing from the expenditure policy exceeds the dead-weight loss. Hence, it is necessary to use minimum resources in the collection of taxes. Tax collection and enforcement is also in the interest of fair taxation and competitive neutrality.[1] However, tax collection in the digital environment poses a number of problems including:[2]

- determining the type of tax to be collected;
- the ability of the vendor to collect the tax;
- determining the jurisdiction in which tax should apply;
- verifying the place of consumption;
- determining the correct tax treatment of bundled products;
- retaining data;
- complying with audit requirements.

---

1 Owens, Jeffrey (1997) Emerging Issues in Tax Reform: The Perspective of an International Bureaucrat, *Tax Notes International*, Issue 22 pp 2035.

2 Basu, Subhajit (2004) 'Implementing E-Commerce Tax Policy', *British Tax Review*, 1 p 46.

McLure argued that 'both income and sales taxes contain rules that can be understood in historical context but have little economic rationale'.[3] 'There is no quick fix', he said, 'that leaves these irrational systems essentially intact and reforms only the tax treatment of electronic commerce. The appropriate response is radical reform of the current system.[4]' The final section of this chapter of the book will propose a particular analytical framework within which taxation of e-commerce is possible. Unless there is some mechanism for forcing action, there is a chance that nothing would happen. The focus is on consumption taxation as it is more of an immediate cause for concern.

In the area of tax administration and compliance, e-commerce creates new variations on old issues as well as new categories of issues. These developments require that practical techniques be developed to deal with these technological innovations. These technological developments touch on a wide range of issues affecting the administration of our tax laws. Private sector and international cooperation is likely to be necessary to develop and implement appropriate software and hardware technologies. In the first instance, what is needed is a dependable and verifiable mechanism. E-commerce is still developing and electronic money has yet to achieve widespread usage. However, it is important that these issues are considered now, while e-commerce is still under development.

In any future solution for taxation of e-commerce, the national governments should play a decisive function, since taxation is a prerogative of the sovereign governments. This chapter in the light of a proposed solution will also discuss the role of the governments. Trade, whether conducted via the medium of the internet or any other, is very simply trade. Therefore, the taxation of it is a legal issue, not a technological one. However, if the technology makes it impossible to extract tax, society has a problem. In my view, the technology will provide a solution. Most would agree that the ability to effect transactions through electronic means has dramatically altered the way we conduct business, but not all would agree that such change necessitates a total re-evaluation and re-examination of current fundamental tax principles.[5] The framework is directed at answering two questions: who will bear the tax and compliance burden? How will the resulting taxes be collected? It includes a glimpse at innovations in the fields of technology and taxation that are in the offing and, perhaps, represents a preview of the e-commerce dynamic. It is the very existence and character of this dynamic that makes advancement on these questions so important and mandates a solution that is neither a patchwork calibration nor a reengineering that is too tightly structured. The proposal outlines a system for collection of e-commerce taxes that is sufficiently flexible and is even cable of adapting to future technological advancement. However, I am not fully certain that my proposal will bring an end to the confusion and contradictions; but I am convinced that it would be a beginning.

---

3   McLure, Charles E., Jr. (1997) 'Taxation of Electronic Commerce: Economic Objectives, Technological Constraints, and Tax Laws.' *Tax Law Review* 52 (3): pp 269–423.

4   McLure, Charles E., Jr. (1997) 'Taxation of Electronic Commerce: Economic Objectives, Technological Constraints, and Tax Laws.' *Tax Law Review* 52 (3):pp 269–423.

5   Greve, Michael S (2003) Sell Globally, Tax Locally: Sales Tax Reform for the New Economy, The AEI Press (Washington DC).

10.1   Law and Technology: A Solution to the Problem?

Legal rules and principles have an interactive, dynamic and complex relationship with technological developments. There is nothing new about technology affecting taxation.[6] Digital fiscal pessimists contend that the digital revolution has overthrown the administrative and informational underpinnings of the present system. The implications of the apparent temporal gap between technological innovation and legal change in time promotes legal uncertainty where affected parties cannot fully understand 'What may be a sound rule from a tax policy perspective may be totally unworkable in light of available technology, for example, the ability to make anonymous, untraceable electronic cash payments or the ability to locate a server anywhere'.[7]

In what circumstances should regulators seek more explicit control over technological developments? For the most part, it is accepted that law should only indirectly influence technological innovations by providing a legal framework for these developments to take place: capitalist democracies accept that law enables private property regimes under the values of liberalism, or in an attempt to promote wealth creation, by protecting the interests of innovators.[8] Markets in turn determine whether technologies persist or become obsolete. In certain circumstances, however, regulators should take more direct steps to mandate the use of technologies to protect interests and values. The 'code is law'[9] approach can be considered to assist state and local governments in protecting interests such as the need to collect tax revenues. Cockfield[10] further argues 'that to determine the relationship between law and technology is to ask how law should adjust to a given and expected technological environment, an approach that may ultimately prove to be more successful at promoting desired behaviour and policy objectives their legal rights and obligations'. At the same time technologies should be adopted as long as they promote an instrumental purpose that enhances efficiency.

Tax authorities may need to promote the use of internet technologies to perform functions that protect these objectives. For example, technological solutions could: (a) identify the location where the purchaser of information good resides; (b) automatically charge, assess and remit taxes on information good transactions to lower compliance costs; and (c) employ online extranets to enhance information exchange among sub-federal and federal tax authorities.[11] The more taxing authorities

---

6   Bird, Richard M (2003) 'Taxing Electronic Commerce: A Revolution in the Making', *C.D. Howe Institute, Commentary, No 187.*

7   McLure, Charles E., Jr. (1997) 'Taxation of Electronic Commerce: Economic Objectives, Technological Constraints, and Tax Laws.' *Tax Law Review* 52 (3): 269–423.

8   Cockfield, A.J. (2004) 'Towards a Law and Technology Theory'. *Manitoba Law Journal*, Vol. 30, p 404.

9   Lessig, Lawrence (1999) *Code and Other Laws of Cyberspace* (New York: Basic Books) at p 6.

10   Cockfield, A.J. (2004) 'Towards a Law and Technology Theory'. *Manitoba Law Journal*, Vol. 30, p 383.

11   Cockfield, A.J. (2002) The Law and Economics of Digital Taxation: Challenges to Traditional Tax Laws and Principles, *Bulletin for International Fiscal Documentation*, Vol. 56, p 606.

are driven to share information and to promote identification technology that reveals the jurisdiction of buyers and sellers, the more effective will become the taxation not just of e-commerce but of all international and inter-jurisdictional transactions.

10.2   A Possible Solution for Income Taxation: Agreement in Principle?

Consumption and income taxation share the same problem in respect of cross-border e-commerce: the supposed difficulties in securing tax compliance. 'It is an understatement to write that it is complicated and difficult to secure compliance related to the taxation of income and consumption in connection with cross-border e-commerce.'[12] 'Tax should not be assigned to a jurisdiction which cannot effectively administer and collect the tax.'[13] If 'tax administration is tax policy', as is widely recognized, it is imperative to identify the role of the tax administration, so that responsibility and accountability is clearly established. In this interrelationship, however, tax policy formulation is generally seen to precede tax administration. This is because only when a tax structure is legislated does tax administration come to play its role in the implementation of the law. Effective tax administration must include the power and means to enforce the substantive tax rules, the ability to obtain information and to protect the tax base from businesses which locate in tax havens and to collect taxes generally is essential. It is a fine balancing act to legislate on the basis of an intellectual and equitable framework on the one hand and to take proper consideration of enforcement barriers and administrative practicalities on the other. Inaction on the part of taxation authorities in today's e-commerce environment is simply not an option.

The internet infrastructure revolution, also offers some benefits to tax administration. These include: possibilities of more accurate and efficient record-keeping, faster and easier compliance with tax requirements, including through the electronic filing of returns and automated deductions of certain taxes such as payroll and social security taxes and the provision of information to taxpayers. It is also possible to use the internet for the exchange of information among the tax administrators of different countries. However, the advantages of the internet revolution for tax administrators, particularly those in developing countries, will not definitely be automatic. Tax administration systems would need to be revamped, requiring substantial investments in IT hardware, the development of specialized software, intensive high quality training for existing tax officials and modifications in personnel policies to secure requisite manpower comfortable with new technologies. The governments would need transparent, consistent and realistic policies for taxing e-commerce.

Broadly, two lines of approach to the income tax problems arising from e-commerce can be considered at each level of government: independent action or coordinated action. In the previous chapter considerable attention has thus been paid to the problem of how to source income from e-commerce. As I have discussed in the previous chapter, most of the commentators felt the necessity to revisit some of the principles of international direct taxation. Some tax authorities have attempted

---

12 Westberg, Bjorn (2002) Cross-border Taxation of E-Commerce, IBFD p 242.

13 Adams, Thomas S (1932) 'Interstate and International Double Taxation', in Ross Magill, ed, Lectures on Taxation (Chicago: CCH) at p 112.

to reformulate source rules to capture digital income, while countries like the US have attempted to extend residence rules for the same purpose. Some have focused on the PE concept currently used to establish 'nexus', the legal basis for imposing tax, and argued that it can be altered to accommodate the new realities. Still others have argued for formulary apportionment approaches. Finally, some believe that the only solution lies in the creation of some new international tax organization with worldwide authority. However, it seems unlikely that the divergent views on this, presumably held in accordance with national interests, can easily be reconciled at the international level. It is also possible that in the foreseeable future perhaps technology will also provide a solution for income taxation; as Randler sees it 'income taxation may be rather simple: most of the information needed is already contained in the central computer and will be correspondingly processed. The taxpayer has only to check whether the information provided by the computer is correct.'[14] To a considerable extent, this already is the case in Singapore, where the tax authority has taken tax withholding to its logical limit and transfers funds directly from personal bank accounts to the treasury.[15] However, it is my submission that there is no real alternative to the concept of 'place of effective management' and that this should continue to be used. While in the case of a globally integrated enterprise there might be no unique solution available through the concept of 'place of effective management', a solution can be found in the 'source based' taxation. Applying the existing principles and rules to e-commerce does not ensure certainty of tax burden and maintenance of the existing equilibrium in the sharing of tax revenues between countries of residence and source.

Each option has some positive and some negative aspects embedded within. Given the complex structure and significant ramifications of our tax system today, the apparent need is for simplification. Bird argues[16] that 'the real tax policy issue... is how governments agree to allocate tax revenues from cross-border transactions'.[17] Revenue may not be the main issue for economists, who focus more on the impact of taxes regardless of who they are paid to, but it certainly matters to policy makers. Developed countries unsurprisingly favour extensions of the residence concept as they would stand to gain from it. Countries that would gain from more source-based rules tend, equally unsurprisingly, to favour such rules. Bird and Wilkie[18] have argued, however, that what is at issue is not really whether source or residence countries should, in principle, have first claim on income but the more basic issue of who can best identify, measure, assess and effectively tax income. From this perspective,

---

14 Radler, Albert J. (2000) 'The Future of Exchange of Information.' In Victor Uckmar, ed., *L'evoluzione dell'ordinamento tributario italiano.* Milan: CEDAM.

15 Bird, Richard M., and Oldman, Oliver (2000) 'Improving Taxpayer Service and Facilitating Compliance in Singapore.' PREM Note 48. Washington, DC: World Bank.

16 Bird, Richard M (2003) 'Taxing Electronic Commerce: A Revolution in the Making', *C.D. Howe Institute, Commentary, No 187.*

17 Goulder, Robert (2001) 'American Bar Association Section of Taxation Panel Eyes OECD Conclusions on Taxation of E-Commerce. *Tax Notes International* 22 at p 360.

18 Bird, Richard M., and J. Scott Wilkie (2000) 'Source- vs. Residence-Based Taxation in the European Union: The Wrong Question?' In S. Cnossen, ed., *Taxing Capital Income in the European Union*, Oxford: Oxford University Press.

what seems most important is not so much to establish the correct principles but to determine what can be done and then, within the limits set by feasibility, to determine how it should be done, by whom and in what way.[19] The emphasis on rules rather than principle implies that a gradualist approach rather than a holistic approach should be adopted. It is in my view that more attention should be paid to the process by resolution to international (e-commerce) tax issues are reached and less to the alleged and often disputable normative principles.

'No area of the law is closer to the subject of sovereignty than taxation.' In legal theory, countries are totally able to determine their own internal tax policies; in reality these same internal polices have an impact far beyond the countries 'borders and are a legitimate concern of other sovereign nations. As the e-commerce process unfolds further with the introduction on m-commerce, it may be increasingly difficult to sustain the current methods of taxing e-commerce companies operating in different tax jurisdictions. In the absence of true international tax law, in the sense of a multilateral tax convention or legislation of an international tax organization, national tax sovereignty will result in divergent policies and principles governing the taxation of international income. However instead of taking each jurisdiction as a separate entity, consideration may need to be given to the adoption of the unitary or worldwide tax base for the corporate income tax, with an internationally agreed system of tax credits or allocation procedures to prevent double taxation and to maintain international competitiveness. McLure's conclusion can be generalized to the international setting: 'There are no good answers to many issues investigated in the paper. The best that can be achieved may be a set of arbitrary rules that are reasonable and mutually consistent.'[20]

10.3   Tax Collection: Proposal for Consumption Taxation

Consumption and income taxation share the same problem in respect of cross-border e-commerce: the supposed difficulties in securing tax compliance.[21] It is not that the internet eliminates borders but rather it creates a world where everyone lives on a border, where crossing into another 'jurisdiction' to transact is effortless and unconstrained.[22] Collection, enforcement and administrative adjudication are the responsibilities of the tax administration.[23] The tax collection mechanism is in fact the most significant issue affecting consumption taxes in an e-commerce environment both from the point of view of tax administrators and businesses which are concerned about requirements to register, collect and remit the tax.

---

19 Bird, Richard M (2003) 'Taxing Electronic Commerce: A Revolution in the Making', *C.D. Howe Institute, Commentary, No 187.*

20 McLure, Charles 'Implementing State Corporate Income Taxes in the Digital Age.' *National Tax Journal*53 (4): pp 1287–1306.

21 Westberg, Bjorn (2002) Cross-border Taxation of E-Commerce, IBFD p 239.

22 Goolsbee, Austin (2000) 'In a World Without Borders: The Impact of Taxes on Electronic Commerce,' *Quarterly Journal of Economics*, 115 (May) 561-76.

23 Bruce, Donald, Fox, William and Murray, Matthew (2003) 'To Tax or Not to Tax? The Case of Electronic Commerce,' *Contemporary Economic Policy*, 21, 1 p 25.

10.3.1 Elimination of Intermediaries and the Threat to Tax Collection

Historically, tax treatment of cross-border sales is uniformly decried as terribly complex, burdensome and inefficient.[24] To effectively tax a consumption transaction under traditional taxation principles, tax collectors need to know where the transaction takes place and whether the transaction involves a good or a service.[25] Incidentally, the intangible nature of e-commerce eliminates the paper trail which is a fundamental component of international tax audit and verification practices of most self-reporting systems.[26] Vendors of intangibles often do not know – and usually do not need to know – the physical location of their customers. The relative anonymity of the internet makes it easy for customers to hide their identity and their physical location, either for privacy reasons or to avoid the payment of tax. The nature of e-commerce also makes it difficult for the tax authorities to determine the locations of the vendors, which normally collect consumption taxes.[27]

Tax authorities all over the world have found intermediaries to be excellent compliance sentinels, and transactions dealt with by intermediaries to be administratively convenient points of collection and assessment, this is particularly so in relation to indirect taxes. The digital revolution has changed the nature of global business. Retailers and financial institutions have historically acted as audit and collection points for national governments. In many sectors private businesses have been conscripted to collect sales taxes from consumers on behalf of the state. Tax authorities rely upon various audit points as sources of information in respect of taxpayers and transactions. These 'bricks and mortar' organizations serve as important intermediaries for the collection of transaction taxes. The state's collection of value-added taxes and other sales taxes becomes problematic when traditional retailers are replaced with e-tailers. The lack of an audit trail in the channels of e-commerce is particularly troublesome in a self-reporting tax system.[28] The absence of traditional intermediaries in the electronic world constitutes a serious problem for tax authorities because governments have been unable to devise an efficient administrative system for the due and timely collection of e-commerce tax revenues. Theoretically, the elimination of intermediaries should not affect the fundamental results of a commercial transaction: the methodology of taxing the sale of software or downloaded music from the internet should not differ from that of the sale of the same products in a physical environment. However, in the e-commerce environment

---

24 Greve, Michael S. (2003) *Sell Globally, Tax Locally: Sales Tax Reform for the New Economy*, The AEI Press (Washington DC).

25 Ligthart, Jenny E. (2004) 'Consumption Taxation in a Digital World: A Primer,' CentER Discussion Paper No. 2004-12, Tilburg University.

26 Forgione, Aldo (2004) Taxing Obscene Profits: Removing Government Incentives for Internet Porn Centre for Innovation Law and Policy.

27 Ligthart, Jenny E.(2004) 'Consumption Taxation in a Digital World: A Primer,' CentER Discussion Paper No. 2004-12, Tilburg University.

28 The use of electronic cash presents even greater concern to tax authorities. The absence of financial reporting from intermediaries presents one of the principal challenges to the tax system arising out of e-cash transactions. E-cash potentially removes another audit point and important source of information.

the two most obvious tax collection requirements are a mechanism which requires the supplier to register and collect the tax and a system which requires the recipient of supply to 'self assess' the tax due and remit it voluntarily to the tax collector. The fact that it is highly unlikely that individual customers will be sending cheques to the government after having downloaded digital property or services over the internet in the privacy of their own home indicates the potential for tax leakage.

The laws of most jurisdictions conscript traditional retailers to collect and remit taxes on behalf of the national treasury. It is difficult to apply collection obligations to the digital forum due to inconsistencies in the tax base and the absence of verification controls. Discrepancies in the tax treatment of e-commerce goods and traditional products also unduly influence the market behaviour. In the absence of any effective regulatory controls on the internet, the ability of tax authorities to monitor taxable transactions is also severely restricted. E-tailers and other e-commerce vendors manage to bypass tax collection mechanisms with relative impunity because of the absence of a governmental verification mechanism. Ironically, by eliminating the traditional intermediaries, e-commerce manages to expose deficiencies in a self-reporting tax system. Pitfalls in existing collection, administration and enforcement mechanisms will result in reduced tax revenues.

10.3.2 Some Further Issues: US Sales Tax

Can the US sales tax be 'saved' or is it structurally incompatible with the twenty-first-century economy? It is clear from Supreme Court rulings and legislative initiatives that, if states are ever going to collect taxes from remote sales, they must minimize or eliminate the 'undue burden' of collection by simplifying state and local sales taxes. The threshold issues in deciding whether a particular seller of goods or services is subject to sales tax in 'State A' are, first, does State A have the authority to require the seller to pay the tax,[29] and secondly, is the sale one that is subject to tax under the particular regime'. In the US, the principal limitations on the states' ability to tax derive from the Commerce Clause and Due Process Clause of the Federal Constitution. The distinction between Commerce Clause limitations and due process limitations is important in that Congress has the power to overrule the first, but not the second. Over the past several decades, a substantial body of law has developed defining the constitutional limits on a state's ability to tax remote vendors, principally in the mail-order context. The current US sales/use tax system is governed by the nexus standard as clarified by the Supreme Court in *Quill*.[30] In *Quill*, the Supreme Court held that the Commerce Clause of the Constitution bars a state from burdening interstate commerce by imposing a sales or use tax collection responsibility on a vendor unless that vendor has a physical presence within the state. Accordingly, out-of-state vendors who do not have a physical presence within a state may make sales to an in-state consumer without incurring a responsibility

---

29 Note that even if the seller is not required to pay the tax, the transaction may still be, at least in theory, taxable. If the product purchased is consumed in the state levying the tax, the consumer may be required to pay a use tax on the value or cost of that product. Most states and localities make no effort to enforce their use tax laws on consumer purchases of this type.

30 *Quill Corp. v. North Dakota* [1992] 504 U.S. 298, 112 S.Ct. 1904.

to collect and remit sales or use taxes to the taxing jurisdiction. The US Supreme Court ruled that physical presence is not required for Due Process Clause 'minimum contacts' analysis, but retained the *Bellas Hess*[31] bright-line rule requiring physical presence for Commerce Clause purposes based on the value of certainty and *stare decisis* in fostering business investment. However, the *Quill* court implicitly questioned whether the physical presence test was in fact the right test and explicitly invited Congress to overrule its holding if it deemed it desirable. It is the responsibility of the consumer to self-assess and remit use tax with the appropriate jurisdiction. However, there is virtually no compliance or enforcement of this system. This also may be in part due to the complexity that is inherent in the sales and use tax system. There are more than 6,000 overlapping state and local jurisdictions, which may impose sales/use taxes. Each jurisdiction is constitutionally empowered to determine both the sales/use tax rate that will apply within its borders, and which transactions it will tax. As noted by the Supreme Court in *Quill*, this has led to an increasingly complicated 'quagmire' of multiple sales/use tax rates, multiple characterizations of the same transaction and multiple audits of the same transaction by multiple authorities.[32]

Unless Congress acts, the *Quill* decision may mean that states simply cannot constitutionally obtain jurisdiction over remote e-commerce. Congress, recognizing the special nature of e-commerce sales, could reverse *Quill* and eliminate the requirement for physical presence to establish substantial nexus under the Commerce Clause. The question would then be how to articulate and interpret the new standard. The most obvious would be to preserve the overall *Complete Auto*[33] analysis, but to declare that the substantial nexus prong of that analysis would be satisfied if the Due Process Clause is satisfied, that is, that for purposes of requiring a remote vendor to collect sales tax on a sale into a state, there would be substantial nexus if the vendor purposefully directed its activity toward that state. That approach, although appealing in its simplicity, has significant problems. From the state's point of view, this would give them the right to require a much larger category of remote sellers to collect their sales tax but in the absence of other tools, it would give them no practical way to enforce that right. From the e-commerce seller's point of view, this would cause greater compliance problems. Having the obligation to collect sales tax from almost any purchaser, it would require that the seller would have to determine how much to collect and where to send it to among thousands of different taxing authorities. However, nexus issues are inherently intractable, involving as they do fundamental fairness concerns and deep constitutional principles. It would require more political will rather than legal to make any changes. Many commentators also believe that the current system of sales/use taxation must be radically simplified if the current nexus

---

31 [1967] 386 U.S. 753.

32 Ibid.

33 Under the Commerce Clause, a state tax on interstate commerce must meet four criteria in order to be upheld as valid: (1) the tax must be applied to an activity that has substantial nexus with the state; (2) the tax must be fairly apportioned to activities carried on by the taxpayer in the state; (3) the tax must not discriminate against interstate commerce; and (4) the tax must be fairly related to services provided by the state. *Complete Auto Transit v. Brady* [1977] 430 US 274.

standard is to be altered.[34] A system, which is radically simplified, would potentially lead to better compliance and an increased revenue flow to state and local government as a result. Additionally, a radically simplified system would reduce the cost to state and local governments of administration and enforcement. Further, a simplified system would benefit all vendors because it would reduce their cost of compliance.[35]

Development of such a uniform process of classification would not be too difficult as there have already been steps taken through the Streamlined Sales Tax System (SSTS). The goal of SSTS is to develop a more simple, uniform and fair system of state sales and use taxation that reduces significantly the burden imposed on retailers, preserves state and local sovereignty, and enhances the ability of US firms to compete in the global and information economy. Although the proposal is voluntary, and retains current law with regard to 'nexus', however the SSTS is step in the right direction. Radical simplification is, only the beginning to dealing with all of the issues regarding the sales and use tax system. If radical simplification could be achieved, then there could be standardization and clarification of the nexus rules, that is; all taxable transactions could be treated equally regardless of the medium used for purchase. Currently the nexus standard, as upheld by the Supreme Court, requires that a vendor must have 'substantial nexus' with a state before the state can impose the obligation of the collection of sales tax. The definition of substantial nexus and what level of activity within a state rises to the level of substantial nexus is the subject of much controversy and had been widely litigated. The nexus rules should be rationalized into a standardized set of rules where all taxable transactions would be treated equally. There appears to be a consensus that it would be necessary to give the states the ability to require a broader group of remote sellers to participate in the collection and/or enforcement of the existing system of sales and use taxes if we are to deal effectively with the issues of base erosion and discrimination. It is clear that, in reality, any effort to give the state and local tax authorities the power to require more remote sellers to join their tax system must be coupled with efforts to significantly simplify the process and lighten the compliance burden on those sellers. This would require the cooperation of Congress, the state and local tax authorities and industry groups representing the various business interests involved, electronic and otherwise.[36]

---

34 Proposals Submitted to the Advisory Commission on Electronic Commerce. See 'Establishing a Framework to Evaluate E-Commerce Tax Policy Options' by Rich Prem of Deloitte & Touche, San Francisco; Hal Varian and Alan Auerbach of the University of California-Berkeley; Austan Goolsbee, the University of Chicago; Annette Nellen, San Jose State University; Scot Grierson, Deloitte & Touche; Costa Mesa; Ed Jajeh and Tara Bradford of Deloitte & Touche, San Francisco. The report was based on issues and ideas raised in an 'E-Commerce Taxation Roundtable' on October 1, 1999 at UC-Berkeley.

35 For a simplified system to work effectively states must also adopt a common set of definitions of products and services subject to the sales and use tax. Right now, the same product may be defined differently depending on the state. A common set of definitions would allow the development of a database that would tell retailers whether the product they are selling is taxable or exempt in each state. States would also need to agree on standardized filing, treatment of exempt organizations, and simplified audit and record keeping procedures.

36 For a simplified system to work effectively states must also adopt a common set of definitions of products and services subject to the sales and use tax. Right now, the same

10.3.3   Tax Collection by Digital Intermediaries: The Proposal

It has often been stated that tax should be neutral; that is, it should not serve as either an incentive or a disincentive in determining the manner in which sales are conducted. This principle of neutrality, by itself, as applied to e-commerce respects the idea that e-commerce sales should be taxed in the same manner as its conventional equivalent. In theory, the burden of the sales/use tax or VAT is passed on to the consumer. In practice, it depends on the particular good or service that is sold. If demand is highly inelastic or if the reach of the tax is sufficiently broad to apply to the consumer's alternatives, it would be passed on. On the other hand, where the consumer is able to purchase the same good or service through other means that avoid the tax, then the seller who is subject to the tax would almost certainly have to absorb the cost. The assumption that the tax is passed on to the consumer is critical to understanding the jurisdictional issues that arise from sales into a state from a remote source and, in particular, to understanding why it important to achieve neutrality.

As is mentioned earlier in this chapter, virtually all concerned parties agree that state taxes on e-commerce should maintain competitive equality between similarly situated economic actors. The principle of tax competitive equality suggests that those who provide goods or services in e-commerce should be taxed no differently than those who provide goods or services in conventional commerce. It is a principle of consumption tax that state taxes on e-commerce should be uniform, including uniform standards and definitions. Simultaneously the taxes on e-commerce should also be administrable, so that compliance burdens are not excessive and the costs of administration are reasonable. The basic economic activities of governments are to raise and re-distribute revenues and to provide public services. If these activities are considered as the 'business of government', then just as private businesses are reaping efficiency gains from the internet and e-commerce, so too could governments increase the efficiency of what the internet does as a business. The governments should also think about how to use e-commerce to improve services to citizens. The OECD back in 1998 recognized that e-commerce technologies could also be used for administering tax laws, and collecting tax revenues. It identified some opportunities offered by the technologies, including:

- revolutionizing communications between tax authorities and taxpayers and enhancing access to information for taxpayers to help them in complying with their tax obligations;
- simplifying tax registration and filing requirements;
- electronic assessment and collection of tax becoming the norm rather than the exception; and
- finding easier, quicker and more secure ways of paying taxes and of obtaining tax and facilitating refunds.

---

product may be defined differently depending on the state. A common set of definitions would allow the development of a database that would tell retailers whether the product they are selling is taxable or exempt in each state. States would also need to agree on standardized filing, treatment of exempt organizations, and simplified audit and record keeping procedures.

Governments were urged to seize the opportunities offered by the new communication technologies to improve the service they provide to taxpayers, to reduce the cost of complying with tax rules and to use more effectively the resources devoted to the collection of taxes. Though it did not provide any guidelines as to what part of the internet or what technology could be used, it was effectively recognized that it would ultimately be a combination of technology and principles, which would provide the answer to tax collection complexities. Hence, what must a solution provide?

- Identification of the parties to the transaction (the status of the customer as a business or a consumer).
- Identification of the jurisdiction in which tax should be applied: this would be the state, which has the appropriate connection with the customer, probably the state where the customer resides, but ideally the state where consumption takes place.
- Categorization of products including intangible products and services, so that the correct tax rate can be applied.[37]
- Tax calculation product classification and rate determination.
- Reporting and remitting of taxes to the appropriate government authority.
- Compliance verification – proving to an auditor that taxes were paid.

The system should also provide individuals and businesses an 'architecture of trust' between them, which could comprise:[38]

- authentication to confirm the identity of individuals;
- authorization to ensure an individual is permitted to conduct a particular function;
- privacy, to ensure others cannot discern what exchanges are taking place;
- integrity, to ensure the transmission is not corrupted; and
- non-repudiation, to ensure the liability and accountability of the sender.

As a matter of pure tax policy, the state has a legitimate interest in administering a tax system that:

- is fair to those who are subject to it;
- minimizes any distortion of economic decision-making within the economy;
- does not require undue effort by either the tax collector or the taxpayer to interpret and administer; and
- raises a sufficient amount of revenue to carry out the legitimate functions of government.

---

37 Categorization will have an impact in some cases on both the place of supply and manner of tax collection and hence overlaps both of the prior issues. It also affects the timing of the liability for the tax and in some cases, the rate of tax applicable.

38 Gail L. Grant *Understanding Digital Signatures*, at p 14, as excerpted in Lessig, at p 40.

Generally, all four of these goals are best met through a tax system that has as broad a base as possible and that has effective but socially acceptable methods of enforcement. The focus of the proposal is on VAT and EU Digital VAT as the EU has already committed itself to tax digital transaction without effectively describing the possible mode of collection. Assuming the worst-case scenario from a VAT collection and enforcement perspective, a private consumer within the EU downloads a virtual good, for example a software program, from a server located in a Caribbean low-tax jurisdiction. Payment is made using a non-accounted payment system, such as the customer sends credit card details by fax.

Before implementing any solution for such cases, it is necessary to define what the tax authorities need to ensure before taxation in the related EU member state. The answer is quite simple: it is the properly calculated tax paid to the member state where the transaction is taxable. The other three requirements are:

- to learn that a (taxable) transaction has taken place; and
- to obtain the information necessary to determine the appropriate tax rate in which the transaction is taxable; and
- to gather the information to properly calculate the tax due.

The required information depends to a great deal on the implementation of the places of supply principle. However, the EU Directive on Digital Sales provided that there are two distinct places of supply for digital deliveries in accordance with the varying tax status and location of the recipient. Accordingly, this has created the necessity for identifying the location of supplier. There is a difference between taxation of digital transactions originating either from outside or within the EU. Based on the above-mentioned elements of indirect taxation, further issues particularly relevant for imposing EU VAT on digital sales are added below:

- EU resident: currently it is not technologically possible to identify with certainty the geographical location of the buyers.
- Registration status of the customer for VAT purposes: the tax status of the customer to determine whether the recipient is registered for VAT purposes or is a private consumer. This, however, could be solved by modernization of the VIES system, which the EU Commission has already initiated and is now available to the traders at the time and place required. However, this does not ensure that the buyer is who she claims to be.
- Other VAT exceptions: sellers will not be required to collect VAT under these rules if their only activity in the EU is the supply of these services and if the annual sales in the EU are below the threshold. If a non-EU seller sells only to VAT-registered businesses, the seller will not be required to register for VAT.
- The tax rate: there is a potential issue to be addressed concerning the possibilities of different tax rates applying to ostensibly similar goods and services.

In the example scenario mentioned before, only two parties are involved in the transaction: the vendor, or rather his server, and the customer and the ISP of the customer. There is a lack of intermediaries such as wholesalers and middlemen. The central element in the proposed new system is re-creation of 'intermediaries' which in this scenario is the ISP. Connections to an ISP are typically made through a local point of presence (POP), commonly through a local or toll-free call utilizing telecommunications facilities acquired from other companies. Since ISPs know the identity of the user and the characteristic nature of the internet requires the ISP to copy all internet communications, including e-commerce transactions, for subsequent transmission to the user, it is possible they could take the responsibility of keeping track of all financial transactions a particular user makes and act as tax collector.

In order for the proposal to work effectively, all participating states and local governments are required to enter into contracts with one or more ISPs to operate the tax administration system. As the seller and his access provider reside outside a particular jurisdiction (in the above example, outside the EU), they will not be subject to public duties such as the collection of taxes. Again, it is not feasible to enter into contracts with the sellers' ISPs, as theoretically there can be 'n' number of ISPs and concluding mutual agreements with them is not even a theoretical solution. This leaves only the buyers' ISP who can be made liable for the collection of taxes. Primarily the proposal is aimed to be as simple as possible. The proposal is coherent with the conditions and principles laid down by the OECD Ottawa Taxation Framework Conditions. The system is simple to administer. It will not require any fundamental change to the tax principles and neither does it contradict any established tax principles. The proposal is consistent with the view that tax policies should be respectful of the fiscal sovereignty of a nation state. The system only applies the 'applicable tax' for the 'appropriate' jurisdiction. It is consistent with the beliefs that governments should keep the tax and administrative burden on consumers and businesses as low as possible. Hence, the proposal utilizes the available technology at its disposal, based primarily on four basic elements: an ISP, a digital certificate, a database of universal product classification and software for calculation of the tax. It provides a structure, which facilitates the collection and remittance of sales tax or VAT that is due but currently goes uncollected.[39] [40] ISPs would not impose taxes; they only execute the collection procedure based upon a set of rules and guidelines outlined by revenue agencies.

It is the EU Directive that provides the law and rules to collect the tax on digital sales. The proposal only provides the method and the means to collect the

---

39 In 2001, the new e-commerce loss was $7 billion, in 2006, it grows to $24.2 billion and in 2011, and it is $29.2 billion. Measuring the states' e-commerce revenue losses against their total state tax revenues also shows significant impact. In 2011, states would lose anywhere from 2.6% to 9.92% of their total state tax collections to total e-commerce losses. A final measurement of the impact of e-commerce losses is the needed increase in the sales tax rate to replace the lost revenue. In 2011, rates would have to rise by between 0.83 and 1.72 percentage points to replace the total e-commerce losses. See Donald Bruce, and William E Fox 'State and Local Sales Tax Revenue Losses from E-Commerce: Updated Estimates' *Centre for Business and Economic Research, The University of Tennessee*, Sept. 2001.

40 Bruce, Donald and Fox, William E (2001) 'State and Local Sales Tax Revenue Losses from E-Commerce: Updated Estimates' *Centre for Business and Economic Research, The University of Tennessee*, Sept. 2001.

taxes. E-commerce changed the paradigm under which consumption taxes had been established; selling of intangible goods over the internet is a relatively new phenomenon for traditional consumption tax structures. Hence, it is more out of necessity that the governments should re-define the tax bases and provide a uniform categorization of goods and services that could facilitate a process of coordination. That is, because the e-commerce marketplace is so integrated, the policy toward handling one issue, even within the national context, has implications for the policy set that is available to policy makers on other issues.

The proposal, keeping in mind the global reach of e-commerce, will implement the uniform product classification not only within boundaries but also across boundaries. Further, such an activity should also be carried out under the auspices of a world trade organization. The benefit of involving a world organization will be first, to provide consistency, and second, to encourage the much-needed involvement of developing countries in the dialogue in order to protect erosion of their tax base. Such an effort could also initiate cooperation between the developed and developing countries in the broader area of tax policies. The process of uniform product classification will ultimately provide 'tax neutrality'. The system will levy applicable taxes to purchases regardless of the domain of the seller. In effect, due to the uniform product classification, the system will have a universal acceptance. Hence, purchases from the local shop will receive similar tax treatment to purchases made through a catalogue or by e-commerce. From a sales tax or VAT perspective, this means certain socio-economic groups will not receive unfavourable treatment since they do not have internet access or they live in a certain geographic location.

Why should ISPs, and not the financial intermediaries like credit card companies themselves, be responsible for the collection of taxes? Financial intermediaries do play an important role not only in e-commerce transactions but also in all other forms of remote selling. It has been proposed 'as a way out'. The OECD Consumption Tax TAG and the WP 9 sub-group have suggested that credit card companies could be enlisted to collect the consumption taxes. One of the reasons for this suggestion was that financial institutions already facilitate the financial transaction between the business and the consumer. There are advantages to this view.

- In the long run, it is expected that most of the financial intermediation on the internet would be in the hands of institutions that are of sufficient size and sophistication to handle the complexities of offering credit/debit services in what must be the most complex market place in history. Hence administering a system for the collection of sales tax or VAT could fit fairly naturally into their systems.
- Reliability, respectability and creditworthiness would be a *sine qua non* for any successful participant in financial intermediation on the internet. Thus, a system in which they play a leading role would be more stable and predictable with comparatively lower compliance costs for the tax authorities.
- There is likely to be sufficient nexus between such institutions and the states whose tax they assist to collect; an institution that extends credit to residents of a state will undoubtedly use the resources, including the courts, of that state as part of its own collection and dispute resolution processes, which

predictably should work quite adequately for a destination based consumption tax system.

However, there are also disadvantages. A number of financial institutions or credit card companies have already indicated that they do not collect the necessary data to perform the tax collection task.[41] Although financial institutions are in a better position than the seller to know the place of consumption or purchase data that is relevant to collecting the tax on a particular transaction, they are in an inferior position with respect to knowing what taxable category the product being sold falls into. They will have to be in a position to rely on data given to them by either the buyer or seller in determining whether a particular sale is entitled to exemption or a lower rate of tax in the relevant jurisdiction. In fact, financial institutions claim that they are not engaged in the business of selling goods and taxable services and therefore are not equipped to collect and remit consumption taxes. Putting the financial intermediary in the position of tax collector in a credit extension context increases their credit risk with respect to the taxes collected. Compensating them for that risk will be another cost of such a system.[42] Without any form of financial compensation, this system is not commercially viable; banks would have to bear the fixed costs of setting up the system and the variable costs associated with each transaction. Currently, banks and other financial institutions are technically not well equipped to deal with the transmission of massive amounts of data. In sum, allocating the collection task to financial institutions would only be legitimate if banks are allowed to charge a fair fee for services provided.

There is also further concern about privacy.[43] A customer's expectation that a financial institution will respect the privacy and confidentiality of their business relationship is fundamental to the relationship between an institution and its customer. To the extent that a card issuer provides or verifies personal information, such as a residential address to a merchant or to anyone else for a purpose unrelated to approval or disapproval of the credit card transaction, raises privacy and confidentiality

---

41 Some commentators have suggested that consumption tax on digital products be withheld through credit card companies at the time of the sale, depending on the applicable tax rate in the location of the purchaser and the type of purchaser (household or exempt business). Such a real-time system would require the financial institution to maintain a database of the tax bases and rates of each state and local jurisdiction. In addition, vendors would have to submit essential information on the sale and the parties (that is, the account numbers of the vendor and purchaser, the value of the sales, the amount of tax due and the billing address of the purchaser). Typically, the billing address on file with the credit card company would determine the location of the purchaser. To streamline the tallying and remitting of tax to the jurisdiction of consumption, it has been proposed that the financial institutions employ a clearing-house system.

42 The involvement of financial institutions in consumption tax collection raises the issue of anonymity. To avoid taxation, online shoppers might establish a mailing address in a low-tax jurisdiction by using a post office box, a friend's mailing address or mail-forwarding service.

43 A purchaser's identity cannot be ascertained if the credit card used for payment is issued by a country with bank-secrecy laws.

concerns. A cardholder has a reasonable expectation of privacy in the information that it furnishes to card issuers for obtaining credit. Privacy protections of cardholders' personal information are contained in privacy laws in the US, the EU and in other major jurisdictions around the world. The privacy provisions differ considerably from country to country and there are restrictions on transferring personal data from the European Union to other countries. A card issuer's access of its records to obtain personal information about a cardholder in order to disclose or verify such information with a merchant could potentially expose the card issuer to liability. An important component of the card issuer-cardholder relationship is the reassurance given to the cardholder that the institution will safeguard personal information in strict confidence. This confidentiality promise is written into many card agreements and policy statements published on the internet and elsewhere to inform customers of the institution's policy. Such assurances are essential to customer confidence, particularly in the case of online transactions, where customers' concerns about privacy are especially acute. Credit card issuers are sensitive to consumer fears about revealing their personal and confidential information over the internet. The public perception that financial institutions would release to online merchants personal information such as a cardholder's place of residence raises industry concerns that this could seriously erode consumer confidence, compromise confidentiality and could potentially expose them to legal liabilities.

However, even if all the issuers could be drafted as tax collectors, there is always the possibility that credit cards would be replaced by unaccounted digital cash in the future as the principal means of financial transaction, which would progressively diminish their usefulness in establishing the location of consumers. Digital cash systems are more than a hypothetical possibility. MasterCard and Mondex, for example, have been testing 'smart cards' for several years and in Denmark, a consortium of banking, utility and transport companies has announced a card that would replace coins and small bills.[44] A tax system based on credit cards would only exacerbate the trend towards digital cash: the anonymity it offers would become immediately more attractive if governments seek to monitor consumers through their credit transactions. Finally, there is always a psychological barrier particularly in consumers accepting credit card companies and tax agencies working together for collecting taxes.

It is worth considering that these alternate intermediaries have no obligation to serve as tax collectors or even transaction reporters. While seeking a centralized pressure point on which to impose collection or reporting obligations is attractive to the taxing agencies, it seems unlikely that financial intermediaries would cooperate. For example, rewriting the entire credit card industry's software and billing systems to support a tax reporting, collecting and remittance system would be far too costly to implement. Further, making use of credit card companies would not provide any collateral benefit for the growth of the internet and, hence, e-commerce. The growth of the internet is directly proportional to the cost of development of its infrastructure and cost of accessing. In fact, the more central the player is in the e-

---

44 Solomon, Elinor Harris (1997) *Virtual Money* (New York: Oxford University Press), at p 70.

commerce arena, the more attractive as a collection point they would appear to tax agencies. It would therefore be entirely logical to utilize the ISPs as they perform a more central function than their financial counterpart. Working out the system that works well from a compliance point of view, while not giving the ISPs an overly burdensome duty of inquiry into the bona fides of the information provided to them, will be a delicate task.

10.3.4   The Proposal: Analysis

The system as proposed is to work in two stages. The first stage would involve identification of the parties to the transaction. The ISP's seller's website and identification technologies would act in combination in order to:

- verify the location of the consumer by utilizing the digital certificate;
- identify if it is a taxable sale to a consumer or an exempt sale to business (or to a non-profit organization or government);
- utilize supportive infrastructure allowing controlled access to the information relevant to taxation, like a tax calculation software agent. This software would determine tax rates by customer and product type. However, reasons of economy, custom and convenience argue for the participation of a financial intermediary (depending upon the payment system) who would also be involved.

In the second stage, the ISP would be responsible for receiving required information on transactions from a seller and would provide software for determining the taxability of a transaction, the appropriate state and local tax rate and the tax due. The system would be supported by a universal product classification database and all states and local governments would utilize the same definitions of tangible and digital products and services based on that classification. The sellers would be made aware of tax information at the time of the sale, so that the information on tax due would be available to the customer before completion of the transaction. The credit card companies and other electronic payment processors would transfer the tax due to the ISPs for transmittal to the respective governments.

10.3.4.1 Identifying the Location of Consumption for Tax Purposes   Digital certificates   A prerequisite to any tax is identifying the taxpayers who are participating in an international transaction as well the geographic location of these parties. However, the decentralized nature of the internet frustrates attempts by e-commerce businesses to identify the location of these parties. A similar problem would be faced by the ISPs when acting as tax collectors. Although they would be aware of the location of the consumer, they would, however, require verifying it beyond any reasonable doubt. As well as finding out which jurisdiction the customer should be linked to, it would be important to find out whether a customer is a business or a consumer. Digital certificates are suggested as one such mechanism that would assist in this process. Digital certificates (also known as electronic credentials or digital IDs) are digital documents attesting to the binding of a public key to an individual or entity. They allow verification of the claim that a given public key does in fact belong to a

given individual or entity.[45] Although this technology has been in existence for some time now, it is not in widespread use. Such technology is mainly used on 'commerce servers'. These server IDs allow websites to identify themselves to users and to encrypt transactions with their visitors. This kind of digital certificate helps the host server's users know that they are communicating with a particular host and not an impostor.

Digital certificates go hand in hand with digital signatures. Digital signatures work on key pairs, one of which is public and the other private. The private key is used to encrypt a document while the public key is used to decipher it. The private key needs to be protected to preserve its value. The private key can be stored in various ways. For example, it can be stored on the user's hard disk, on removable media (such as a floppy disk) or on a smart card or other 'smart device'. These digital signatures are usually used with digital certificates to authenticate the attestation in a certificate. They could also be used to digitally sign a VAT invoice so that a business purchaser has an electronic invoice that could form the basis of claiming an input tax credit for VAT paid. The digital certificate could be registered with a so-called 'trusted third party' that could be a government agency or even a private company; the trusted third party would act as a kind of bonding agency to ensure the veracity and accuracy of information given out by the digital certificates.[46] [47]

For the proposal to work effectively it would be required to identify whether their customers were consumers or businesses. This is because VAT would need to be applied by suppliers to sales to consumers but not to sales to businesses. Business customers would operate the reverse charge as they do now. Under the reverse charge system, a business buying certain services and digitized products from abroad pretends that it is selling these items as well as buying them. It then charges VAT on those notional sales, accounts for that VAT and pretends that it had suffered the same VAT on its purchases. The overall effect is the same as if the business had paid VAT on the purchases in the first place.

Some commentators have argued that it would be quite straightforward for suppliers to identify the difference between business customers and consumers but, in fact, it would not. So long as business customers are left to apply VAT to their own purchases, consumers would have a financial incentive to pretend that they were businesses so that suppliers did not impose VAT on them. It would therefore be of no use to include a question on an order form such as 'Are you a business?' If

---

45 A more elaborate definition indicates: 'A digital certificate is an electronic "credit card" that establishes your credentials when doing business or other transactions on the Web. It is issued by a certification authority (CA). It contains your name, a serial number, expiration dates, a copy of the certificate holder's public key (used for encrypting and decrypting messages and digital signatures), and the digital signature of the certificate-issuing authority so that a recipient can verify that the certificate is real. Some digital certificates conform to a standard, X.509. Digital certificates can be kept in registries so that authenticated users can look up other users' public keys.' Whatis.com, located at <http://www.whatis.com/digitace.htm>.

46 Smith, Brian W. and Tufaro, Paul S (1998) *To Certify or Not to Certify? The OCC Opens the Door to Digital Signature Certification*, 24 Ohio North. University Law Review p 813.

47 Note that certification authorities are 'essential to the development of electronic commerce and electronic banking'.

more subtle questions were designed to check the answer, it would be likely to put consumers off: people are not used to being quizzed when they go into shops and they resent being quizzed when shopping on the internet.[48]

The distinction between consumers and businesses is not something inherent to internet technology. However, digital certificates have the potential to deliver this feature. A certificate includes the following information: identity of certificate service provider; name and details of signatory; validity period; unique certificate number; limitations/exclusion on third party use; details of how key was generated; system for protecting signatory private key; details of revocation provisions; details of service hardware and software; and the certificate service provider's own digital signature. The digital signature on the other hand provides the following features: (i) it is uniquely linked to the signatory; (ii) it was created under the control of the signatory; (iii) its integrity is clear; and (iv) the integrity of the message is clear from the signature.

It should be noted, however, that in some legal systems, only natural persons might hold certificates and the person in their corporate function may only be distinguishable from the private person using an attribute field. However, such a situation could be avoided if the revenue authority in a country, or a trusted third party, certifies businesses as being registered in a particular country or countries for VAT purposes by issuing them with digital certificates. If the purchaser presents a digital certificate, the transaction would be relieved from tax. If the purchaser does not present a digital certificate, it would be treated as a consumer and VAT would apply using the identification techniques under a fallback sitution which I am going to discuss below. In my view, the adoption of the use of digital signatures in conjunction with a digital certificate would assist the identification process and would be able to provide information such as the location of the user beyond any reasonable doubt.[49] It would also help to determine accountability of a particular transaction, integrity of the documents and records used, along with identification of the sale to a consumer or a business.

IP Address and Credit Card   In a fallback situation where ISPs are unable to utilize a digital certificate, alternative means to rely on include: IP address, credit card number, credit card billing address and self-declaration. According to the OECD

---

48 This was recognised in the Consumption Taxation TAG paper, annex II, paragraph 11.

49 Electronic Signatures in Global and National Commerce Act, S. 761, 106th Congress (June 30, 2000) (effective October 1, 2000). The legislation permits individuals to use binding electronic signatures for interstate or foreign commerce. A digital signature has been defined as follows: 'A digital signature (not to be confused with a digital certificate) is an electronic rather than a written signature that can be used by someone to authenticate the identity of the sender of a message or of the signer of a document. It can also be used to ensure that the original content of the message or document that has been conveyed is unchanged. Additional benefits to the use of a digital signature are that it is easily transportable, cannot be easily repudiated, cannot be imitated by someone else, and can be automatically time-stamped. A digital signature can be used with any kind of message, whether it is encrypted or not, simply so that the receiver can be sure of the sender's identity and that the message arrived intact. A digital certificate contains the digital signature of the certificate-issuing authority so that anyone can verify that the certificate is real.' Whatis.com, located at http://www.whatis.com/digitasi.htm.

Consumption TAG, all of these identifiers have some, if not significant, limitations. Internet Protocol (IP) addresses offer potential in that they are an essential part of every access point to the internet. However, IP systems would seem to offer limited possibilities in terms of securely identifying a consumer with a taxing jurisdiction at the time a transaction takes place. While credit cards are currently the dominant method of payment for goods purchased over the internet, it is important to note that there have been significant developments towards other payment mechanisms, including digital cash and stored value cards. Alternative payment mechanisms such as digital cash and stored value cards are the second-generation payment systems for many internet accessible jurisdictions around the world. These payment systems are becoming more widely accepted for e-commerce transactions as new and innovative solutions come to the market place. Credit card systems as currently designed are not much help in identifying jurisdiction. Although as a part of the marketing purposes, the credit card issuers are likely to be interested in whether cards were held for business or personal use, providing such would cause serious customer privacy concern. This would not be a practical option for three reasons.

- Only minimal information about cardholders is passed to suppliers, both in order to reduce the scope for fraud by learning enough about cardholders to impersonate them and because of cardholders' concerns about privacy.
- The status of a cardholder is not computable from the card number. Thus, an additional stage of looking up the status and transmitting it to the supplier would be necessary. While the concept of matching a credit card number to the country of residence was originally thought to have promise, further investigation demonstrated that there was no correlation between numerical Bank Identification Number and geography.
- The determined evader of VAT would simply apply for a new card, telling the card issuer that it was for business use, even if it was in fact for personal use.

It would further raise some troubling privacy issues. Currently, governments generally do not have access to credit card company data unless a particular cardholder is suspected of committing a crime. The use of such data for tax collection purposes would potentially put a detailed record of a person's buying habits in the hands of government authorities on a regular basis without the normal judicial protections. The possible abuses of that information are enormous and it is doubtful whether many individuals would easily accept the unprecedented invasion of their privacy. None of the two foregoing would deal with every conceivable scenario and they would be susceptible to some manipulation. What they do have going for them is they are (potentially) readily accessible – the question is how to be sure of the information at that point when it is required. It is evident that neither of the two systems of 'IP address' and 'credit card' would individually be capable of providing all the requisite information. However, if they were used collectively and applied by a method of 'tests and check', it would be able to provide a definitive answer. A rule could be made that the jurisdiction given by two tests out of three would be accepted or any other rule of the form 'x out of y', if enough tests were available. However, the closer x gets to y, the more often these automatic tests would fail to be decisive. Hence, on balance, digital certificates would provide much more accurate information which could also be applied automatically. It would be much easier and reliable to use one decisive method instead of a combination, thereby making limited efforts to establish jurisdiction and determine the tax status of the customer.[50]

10.3.4.2 Tax Rates and Product Classification   The key to getting tax calculated correctly is not to make the calculations simple but to make the required inputs simple. Once the tax jurisdiction and status of the purchaser is determined, the rate of tax for that jurisdiction must be determined. This rate is often dependent on subtle classifications in the domestic tax code. There is no international consensus as to classification and treatment. Therefore, the proposed system would need to eliminate multiple definitions of the same products or services. It is widely recognized that the current system allows for multiple characterizations of the same product or service when delivered to different jurisdictions, and making the task of compliance for e-commerce businesses extremely cumbersome and unwieldy. This burden would be correspondingly greater for small web-related businesses who do not have the financial or human resources to track changes in these characterizations on an international basis. In the proposed system, all the countries and local governments would utilize the same definitions of tangible and digital products and services. Uniform product and service definitions would significantly ease the compliance burden of both traditional and e-commerce businesses. This corrective step would require that states along with their constituent local jurisdictions work together, possibly in some organization such as the WTO or the OECD, to develop the uniform definitions.[51] What is called for is to develop concise, well-formulated definitions, which would be acceptable for all parties. On the other hand, collaboration to develop

---

50   It also possible to use geolocation technology, a fairly recent innovation, to determine the location of customers. Geo-location products match IP addresses associated with online customers with outside sources of data to pinpoint the geographic location of the online customer at the point where the customer's computer signal enters the internet. Because of a shortage of IP addresses for all possible internet users, this dynamic numbering system was designed to overcome this problem by assigning to an Internet user for the duration of any given visit to the Internet a specific IP address drawn from a fixed pool of addresses 'assigned' to each geographical area. Various geolocation software providers claim that they can identify the customer's physical location within 50 miles of where they are actually located, under the very best of circumstances. Because most software deployed to locate an individual internet user is non-invasive and does not utilize cookies, web beacons, registration information or click-stream data, it is possible only to isolate the user's location to a level of precision that reflects the point where the customer joins the internet. Various geolocation software providers claim that they can identify the customer's physical location within 50 miles of where they are actually located, under the very best of circumstances. Because most software deployed to locate an individual internet user is non-invasive and does not utilize cookies, web beacons, registration information or click-stream data, it is possible only to isolate the user's location to a level of precision that reflects the point where the customer joins the internet. However, due to the fluid nature of the IP addressing system, geolocation software databases must be constantly monitored and updated, it also has other drawbacks.

51   A similar type of product classification system is already in use: United Nations Central Products Classification System (available at www.un.org/depts/unsd/class/cpcprof.htm).

uniform definitions would motivate certain definitional clarifications, e.g. 'services' v 'digitized products', that would simplify the task of compliance and administration on the parts of both the states and businesses.

Once the jurisdiction and the kind of product is known, the next step will be a universal product coding database 'lookup' which can provide the appropriate tax rate to apply to the value of the sale. Clearly, the ability to harmonize systems and methods as well as the ability to change tax amounts are factors solely within the competence of the governments of the world. It would thus be the primary responsibility of the governments to create such a database for each taxing jurisdiction. This database would be used to determine which products are to be taxed and which are to be exempted. The countries would be able to change the tax rates. This would also reduce the cost of maintenance of the database and the calculating software.

The design of the database would be kept simple. Each jurisdiction would use one tax computation formula and one set of parameters, applicable to all sales of digitized products. Different classifications for different digitized products would be eliminated, because otherwise each product would need to be coded as 'category 1 if sold to jurisdiction A, category 4 if sold to jurisdiction B, category 2 if sold to jurisdiction C' and so on. In such a situation, people categorizing products would probably make mistakes and changes in categories would be overlooked or misinterpreted. Countries would not be able to unilaterally make changes in the product classification, exemption definition or sourcing rules. Instead, an organization like the OECD or the WTO would look out for changes that would be necessary from time-to-time. Countries would be able make changes to the database as and when such requirement would arise, and all the participating countries would have to adopt those changes. This database would also be maintained by the same world organization responsible for coordinating such an effort and would be publicly available free of charge on a website, so businesses would always have access to the correct information and that format would allow easy downloading into tax computation programs.

For some commentators, development of such a database would be a difficult task, apparently because of the magnitude of the task and the number of parties involved. In my view there are precedents of such compilations. The World Customs Organization publishes a Harmonized Tariff, in which all goods (not services) are capable of being classified for customs purposes under thousands of six-digit categories. The Harmonized Tariff is designed to ensure that a particular good is classified under the same Tariff item regardless of the country of export and import. Each country attaches *its* duty rates to the six digit numbers and the duty rates can and do vary by country. Most of the more than 150 major trading nations use the Harmonized Tariff as the basis for applying customs duties to imports.

10.3.4.3 Tax Compliance Software   The next step for the proposal would be to calculate the consumption tax due on each sale. A world organization like the OECD or WTO, which would be responsible for the development of product classification, would also contract out to develop the software that would list the state and local sales tax and VAT rates on all categories of items for all the countries and some local governments. It would be a technologically neutral system designed to be incorporated easily into commercial websites running on any computing platform.

Both e-commerce sellers and ISPs would use this software, which would be free 'shareware'. This would reduce network delays before the consumer committed to the purchase, thus enhancing the purchasing experience. When a consumer makes an online purchase, the software would check the tax rate in the area according to the information about the jurisdiction provided in the digital certificate. If the consumer were not using a digital certificate then the software would calculate the tax rate according to the IP address or credit card details, as appropriate.

All tax calculations in real time would be performed by the software assuming that it would receive the required data to make the calculation. The software would display the tax rate along with all other incidental charges. When the consumer makes the purchase, he or she would simply pay the full amount (cost of the product, sales tax or VAT, shipping and handling, and so on). In addition to a formal acknowledgement of the tax due, it would also provide a reference number that would be used for audit purposes. Some commentators have suggested that the indirect tax system is too complex to be modelled even with current computer and internet capacity. This is easily disproved, as these aspects of this model are already available in existing commercial products, which offer sales/use tax calculations for approximately 6,400 jurisdictions in the US. Several tax software packages such as 'TAXWARE', 'Certitax' and 'CORPTax' are available to internet vendors in order to determine their taxability of sales. 'Taxware' International already employs an online service that tracks all of the sales tax rates of all US state and local tax jurisdictions, as well as most VAT jurisdictions, and calculates the relevant tax payments (although online vendors must provide customer location information). Combined with IBM WebSphere® Commerce Suite, TAXWARE provides a comprehensive solution for automatically calculating and managing US and international taxes correctly for each transaction from the order information entered into WebSphere Commerce Suite. The new E-Commerce Tax System for IBM makes it possible to calculate sales, use and consumers' use taxes for both the US and Canada, manage exemption certificates, verify addresses and calculate VAT, goods and services tax (GST) and consumption taxes for all of the European Union and most of Asia Pacific and South America.[52]

10.3.4.4 Cost of Collection Ultimately, even feasibility becomes a question of cost.[53] What is technologically unfeasible may be viewed as feasible but with unacceptably high adoption costs. Hence who pays for the cost of collection? Little hard evidence exists about compliance costs of various taxes. The studies that do exist tend to examine existing technologies rather than offer a useful methodology for extrapolating various proposed systems. Hence, there is no fixed parameter to

---

52 TAXWARE International, Inc. 'TAXWARE's E-Commerce Tax System for IBM', http://www.taxware.com/ See www.taxware.com/Zproducts/salesuse/sutaxsys.htm).

53 Every tax system must be administered; tax laws must be enforced, and taxpayers – both individuals and businesses – must spend time and money to comply with those laws. Administrative costs can be thought of as the expenses incurred by the tax authorities, the state and local agencies charged with collecting taxes. Compliance costs are borne by others, typically those who pay a tax.

judge whether the cost collection would be unreasonable.[54] Tax authorities should also be prepared to pay for the work that would need to be done in the private sector. Normally, tax authorities expect the private sector to bear the cost of compliance with new laws and they can use the force of the law to make companies comply.[55] However, here, authorities would have to deal with companies which would be outside their jurisdictions. Hence, it would therefore be reasonable to expect authorities to pay for the work that would require to be done. The objective always remains the same: the cost of compliance should be proportional to the revenue.

Currently, the supplier who holds the liability for tax collection enjoys the benefits of this positive cash flow. Under this system, the ISP would share in the benefit received by suppliers depending on their relative contributions to the process or could remit funds to the government immediately. The cost of development of the software and creation of the database would be shared between the different countries, calculated in proportion to the internet usage of the population. Similarly, the deployment and maintenance costs would be apportioned to revenue agencies according to usage. The cost of obtaining a digital certificate would also be competitive as it would create a huge new business potential for this sector. It is currently not clear what type of pricing structure would prevail, for example, fixed initial price + annual charge based on number of users, fixed initial price + percentage annual cost or other pricing arrangement. The cost of integrating the system with the respective vendor websites would be borne by the vendor. The states or local governments would pay the ISP on a 'per transaction' basis based on negotiated rates so that burdens of tax compliance would fall on the general revenue system, not vendors alone (based on Forester Research's current B2C e-commerce sales forecast by category in the US, a 5 per cent commission on the estimated tax collected could generate between US\$500 and US\$600 million). This would act as a source of revenue for the ISPs and hence in the long term it is possible to think of a much-reduced cost of internet access, which will be quite beneficial for growth of e-commerce in developing countries. In addition, vendors could also pay a fee to the ISP for the service, which they would be receiving as part of an end-to-end business system. In such a system, the tax module is generally small relative to the other business modules such as order processing, inventory management systems, and so on, which are being utilized by the vendor.

10.3.4.5 Audit Function   The key elements of an auditable system are the detail of the transactions that is available and how easily and in what format the data may be accessed. E-commerce transactions present the following difficulties for the determination of audit trails:

- the ability to locate and access records that are kept in electronic formats;
- the ability to encrypt electronic records with encryption key technology;
- the lack of authenticity, integrity and, ultimately, reliability of an electronic record.

---

54   It is desirable to minimize the costs of administering and complying with a tax.

55   Sometimes the consumers bear the compliance costs indirectly in their role as taxpayers if tax authorities compensate retailers for those costs out of collected revenue.

The primary audit function would fall on the destination country as the proposal is modelled around the destination principle. Hence, it is the destination country which will be most interested in compliance. ISPs will act as the principal intermediary in any audit programme, thereby alleviating a majority of the burden from businesses. It would fall on the respective states to decide on the guidelines. The countries should preferably conduct sales audits in the manner that is customary in law within their state. However, the proposal would favour uniform audit procedures, including uniform record-keeping and retention requirements and a uniform statute of limitations and appeals process. Transaction detail would be retained such that an individual seller can be identified but not an individual buyer. The buyer detail would be retained by the seller. A unique number would identify each transaction by the system. Any transaction reports provided to the seller would also contain this number. This improvement would ease the burden on companies by clarifying and simplifying their audit-related responsibilities. As the system would be capable of providing periodic information on taxable sales and tax receipts collected, it is suggested that such procedure is undertaken at regular time intervals. Since this system is electronic and since it interfaces at the time of the purchase transaction, revenue officials would have an audit trail that is more comprehensive. It is also suggested that the states should allow the filing of tax returns and the submission of annual reports on the taxable activity by electronic means.

10.4   Conclusion: The Way Forward

The technological revolution thus brings with it not just problems but also the possibility of technological solutions.[56] The burden of tax compliance and the question of administrability have been central to the debate over taxation of e-commerce.[57] It is possible to find the solution to the consumption tax problem in the technology that makes e-commerce possible in the first place. E-commerce businesses only need help to determine the amount of consumption tax chargeable on each transaction and automatically remit the tax to the relevant tax authorities. However, as Li argues in contrast, 'the solution to international income tax problems is more conceptual and fundamental. Even with the appropriate technology for tax collection, international tax principles and concepts must be reformed to allow such technology to be effective'.[58] I believe that in this chapter I have identified a number of specific issues and addressed them in order to create a definitive consumption tax compliance system. The potential solution to the international consumption tax problem may offer the potential to plug leaks in the shrinking tax base that income taxation faces as a result of the e-commerce challenges. A blanket exemption from the taxation of e-commerce is not necessarily consistent with 'optimal tax policy'.

---

56 Doernberg, Richard L., et al. (2001) *Electronic Commerce and Multijurisdictional Taxation* (London: Kluwer Law International).

57 Bruce, Donald, Fox, William and Murray, Matthew (2003) 'To Tax or Not to Tax? The Case of Electronic Commerce, *Contemporary Economic Policy*; 21, 1 p 25.

58 Li, Jinyan (2003) *International Taxation in the Age of Electronic Commerce: A Comparative Study (*Toronto: Canadian Tax Foundation).

The proposal is aimed at providing a long-term solution. Its focus is on the basic problem that e-commerce exists in a borderless virtual world which de-emphasizes the significance of the place in which economic activity is carried out and provides the solution by involving the very technology that made internet and e-commerce possible. However, this has led to the question of state sovereignty; there would be arguments that some of these proposed measures (the proposal for a uniform tax base) would be an unwelcome intrusion on state fiscal sovereignty. That view loses sight of the larger picture. The argument is about the relevance of the above question. The time is right for what might be a turning point in the history of taxation.

Until now, national governments have designed and administered their tax polices in near-splendid isolation from one another. Apart from the minimalist and voluntary constraints of the OECD Model Tax Convention and a network of bilateral treaties to prevent double taxation, states have remained largely autonomous agents of taxation, even as the globalization of production and commerce and to a lesser extent the globalization of business regulations have gathered momentum. The state sovereignty that was possible when local merchants sold primarily tangible products almost exclusively to local customers is no longer possible, or at least not a realistic alternative, as it implies enormous complexity for remote vendors and thus the legal inability to tax remote sales, including those in e-commerce. The most likely result of these developments would be a shift in the relative balance of *de facto* taxing authority from the domestic to the international level, in short, a globalization of taxation, as states come to realize that technological changes in the nature of commerce require considerably higher levels of international coordination in the field of taxation. Countries should be persuaded to coordinate their tax policies and cooperate in tax administration through negotiation, accommodation or policy emulation. Recognizing that states could no longer formulate and enforce tax policy independently, however, did not indicate that the status of the state as an international actor is in decline. Nor did it suggest that sovereignty is no longer a central concern in international relations. States have always faced situations in which they must cooperate with both internal and external actors. It is in my view that the digital economy will eventually strengthen the government's role as a tax collector, 'as tax inspectors remain chained to the borders of each country. International cooperation will help nations preserve national control over tax policy and thus strengthen their fiscal sovereignty'.[59]

Tax authorities therefore need to work out their approaches now. And what is more, their chosen approaches should be ones which will last. Businesses never really like to spend money on tax compliance. They certainly do not want to spend money on installing compliance systems which will become redundant within a few years because tax authorities change their minds. With consumption taxes on e-commerce, the cost of such changes could be very high. This is because the nature of the problem means that solutions are likely to involve software changes deep inside e-commerce systems. Tax compliance software will not be a separate module that can be bolted on to the outside of a company's system and changed quickly and easily.

---

59 Li, Jinyan (2003) *International Taxation in the Age of Electronic Commerce: A Comparative Study* (Toronto: Canadian Tax Foundation) at p 590.

Bibliography

Abrams, Howard E. and Richard L. Doernberg (1997) 'How Electronic Commerce Works', *State Tax Notes*, 13.

Adams, Sally (1997) 'Danger: Internet Taxes Ahead', *Taxes*, September.

Adams, Thomas S. (1932) 'Interstate and International Double Taxation', in Ross Magill (ed.), *Lectures on Taxation* (Chicago, IL: CCH) pp. 101–27.

Advisory Commission on Intergovernmental Relations (1994) 'Taxation of Interstate Mail-Order Sales: 1994 Revenue Estimates'.

Alm, James, Jill Ann Holman and Rebecca M. Neumann (2003) 'Globalization and State/Local Government Finances', in David L. Sjoquist (ed.), *State and Local Finance Under Pressure* (Cheltenham, UK and Northampton, MA: Edward Elgar), pp. 276–98.

Alm, James and Sally Wallace (2004) 'Can Developing Countries Impose an Individual Income Tax? The Challenges of Tax Reform in a Global Economy', Andrew Young School of Policy Studies International Studies Program, Georgia State University, 24–25 May 2004.

Anderson, James (1986) 'The Modernity of States', in James Anderson (ed.), *The Rise of the Modern State* (Atlantic Highlands, NJ: Humanities Press International).

Arnold, Brian J. and M.J. McIntyre (1995) *International Tax Primer* (The Hague: Kluwer Law International).

Ault, Hugh (1997) *Comparative Income Taxation: A Structural Analysis* (New York: Springer).

Australian Taxation Office (1999) *Tax and the Internet: Second Report December 1999* (Canberra: Government Printing Service).

Avi-Yonah, Reuven S. (1996) 'The Structure of International Taxation: A Proposal for Simplification', *Texas Law Review*, 74: 1301–59.

Avi-Yonah, Reuven S. (1997) 'International Taxation of Electronic Commerce', *Tax Law Review*, 52: 507–55.

Avi-Yonah, Reuven S. (2000) 'Commentary to International Tax Arbitrage and the International Tax System', *Tax Law Review*, 53: 167–75.

Avi-Yonah, Reuven S. (2005) 'The Three Goals of Taxation', available at SSRN: <ssrn.com/t=796776>.

Avi-Yonah, Reuven S. and Joel Slemrod (2001) '(How) Should Trade Agreements Deal with Income Tax Issues?', University of Michigan, Working Paper #01-008.

Bankman, Joseph and David A. Weisbach (2005) 'The Superiority of an Ideal Consumption Tax over an Ideal Income Tax', working paper.

Basu, Subhajit (2002) 'European VAT on Digital Sales', *The Journal of Information, Law and Technology (JILT)*, <www.elj.warwick.ac.uk/jilt/02-3/basu.html>.

Basu, Subhajit (2003) 'Relevance of E-Commerce for Taxation: An Overview', *Global Jurist Topics*, 3(3), article 2, <http://www.bepress.com/gj/topics/vol3/iss3/art2>.

Basu, Subhajit (2004a) 'Implementing E-Commerce Tax Policy', *British Tax Review*, 1: 46–69.

Basu, Subhajit (2004b) 'To Tax or Not to Tax? That is the Question: Overview of Options in Consumption Taxation of E-Commerce', *The Journal of Information, Law and Technology (JILT)*, <http://www2.warwick.ac.uk/fac/soc/law/elj/jilt/2004_1/basu/>.

Begun, Dov (2004) 'The Scope and Focus of Jinyan Li's Book', *Canadian Tax Journal*, 52(1): 109–13.

Berman, Paul S. (2002) 'The Globalisation of Jurisdiction', University of Connecticut School of Law Working Paper Series, 13: 335.

Bernstein, Jack (2000) 'Canadian Taxation Issues for Electronic Commerce', *Tax Notes International*, 21 (July 17): 263–71.

Bird, Richard (1986) 'The Inter-jurisdictional Allocation of Income', *Australian Tax Forum*, 3: 333–54.

Bird, Richard (2003) 'Taxing Electronic Commerce: A Revolution in the Making', C.D. Howe Institute Commentary, no. 187.

Bird, Richard M. (2005) 'Taxing Electronic Commerce: The End of the Beginning', ITP Paper 0502, International Tax Program, Institute of International Business.

Bird, Richard M. and Jack M. Mintz (2003) 'Sharing the International Tax Base in a Changing World', in Sijbern Cnossen and Hans Werner Sinn (eds), *Public Finance and Public Policy in the New Century* (Cambridge, MA: MIT Press).

Bird, Richard M. and Oliver Oldman (2000) 'Improving Taxpayer Service and Facilitating Compliance in Singapore', PREM Note 48 (Washington, DC: World Bank).

Bird, Richard M. and J. Scott Wilkie (2000) 'Source- vs. Residence-Based Taxation in the European Union: The Wrong Question?', in S. Cnossen (ed.), *Taxing Capital Income in the European Union* (Oxford: Oxford University Press).

Bird, Richard M. and Eric M. Zolt (2005) 'Redistribution via Taxation: The Limited Role of Personal Income Tax in Developing Countries', *UCLA Law Review*, 52(6): 1627–95.

Bittker, Boris I. and Lawrence Lokken (1997) *Fundamentals of International Taxation: U.S. Taxation of Foreign Income and Foreign Taxpayer* (2nd edn, Boston, MA: Warren, Gorham & Lamont), pp. 66–97.

Bolkestein, Frits (2001) 'Harmful Tax Competition, VAT on Digital Deliveries, Taxation of Savings', address to the European American Business Council, Washington DC, May.

Bourgeois, Pierre J. (2000) 'Income_Taxes.Ca.Com: An Update', *Canadian Tax Journal*, 48(4): 1274–98.

Bracewell-Milnes, Barry (1980) *The Economics of International Tax Avoidance* (Rotterdam: Kluwer).

Brian J. Arnold (1996) 'The Canadian International Tax System: Review and Reform', *Canadian Tax Journal*, 43: 1792–1818.

Brooks, Barrett (2005) 'E-Commerce and State Sales Tax', *Journal of State Taxation*, 24(2): 47–9.

Bruce, Donald and William E. Fox (2000) 'E-Commerce in the Context of Declining State Sales Tax Bases', *National Tax Journal*, 53(4), part 3 (December): 1373–88.

Bruce, Donald and William E. Fox (2001) 'State and Local Sales Tax Revenue Losses from E-Commerce: Updated Estimates', Centre for Business and Economic Research, The University of Tennessee, September.

Bruce, Donald and William E. Fox (2004) *State and Local Revenue Losses from E-Commerce: Estimates as of July 2004* (Knoxville, TN: University of Tennessee, Centre for Business and Economic Research).

Bruce, Donald, William Fox and Matthew Murray (2003) 'To Tax or Not to Tax? The Case of Electronic Commerce', *Contemporary Economic Policy*, 21(1): 25–40.

Cairncross, Frances (2001) *The Death of Distance* (Boston, MA: Harvard Business School Press).

Cameron, Angus (2006) 'Turning Point? The Volatile Geographies of Taxation', *Antipode*, 38(2): 236–58.

Carnaghan, Carla and Kenneth J. Klassen (2004) 'E-Commerce and International Tax Planning', working paper, June 2004.

CBO (2003) 'Economic Issues in Taxing Internet and Mail-Order Sales', paper of The Congress of the United States, Congressional Budget Office, <http://www.cbo.gov/ftpdoc.cfm?index=4638&type=0>.

Central Board of Direct Taxes (2001) *Report of the High Powered Committee on Electronic Commerce and Taxation* (New Delhi: Ministry of Finance).

Chan, Clayton W. (2000) 'Taxation of Global E-Commerce and the Internet: The Underlying Issues and Proposed Plans', *Minnesota Journal of Global Trade*, 9: 233.

Cigler, James D. (1997) 'International Taxation of Electronic Commerce: An Evolution Requiring Planning and Action', unpublished paper presented to the International Tax Reform Forum, Tax Policy Group, Silicon Valley Joint Venture, 4 December 1997.

Cigler, James D. and Susan E. Stinnett (1997) 'Treasury Seeks Cybertax Answers with Electronic Commerce', *Journal of International Taxation*, 8.

Cline, Robert (2002) 'Telecommunication Taxes: 50 State Estimates of Excess State and Local Tax Burden', *State Tax Notes*, pp. 931–47.

Cline, Robert J. and Thomas S. Neubig (1999) *Masters of Complexity and Bearers of Great Burden: The Sales Tax System and Compliance Costs for Multistate Retailers* (Ernst & Young).

Cockfield, A.J. (1998) 'Tax Integration under NAFTA: Resolving the Conflict between Economic and Sovereignty Interests', *Stanford Journal of International Law*, 34(1): 39–73.

Cockfield, Arthur J. (1999) 'Balancing National Interests in the Taxation of Electronic Commerce Business Profits', *Tulane Law Review*, 74(1): 133–218.

Cockfield, A.J. (2000) 'Should We Really Tax Profits from Computer Servers? A Case Study in E-Commerce Taxation', *Tax Notes International*, 21(21): 2407–15.

Cockfield, A.J. (2001) 'Transforming the Internet into a Taxable Forum: A Case Study in E-Commerce Taxation', *Minnesota Law Review*, 85(5): 1171–266.

Cockfield, A.J. (2002a) 'Designing Tax Policy for the Digital Biosphere: How the Internet is Changing Tax Laws', *Connecticut Law Review*, 34: 333.

Cockfield, Arthur J. (2002b) 'The Law and Economics of Digital Taxation: Challenges to Traditional Tax Laws and Principles', Berkeley-Keio Seminar on International

Tax Law Concerning Digital Financial Innovation at Keio University in Tokyo, 6–7 June 2002.

Cockfield, Arthur J. (2002c) 'The Law and Economics of Digital Taxation: Challenges to Traditional Tax Laws and Principles', *Bulletin for International Fiscal Documentation*, 56: 606–19.

Cockfield, Arthur J. (2002d) 'The Real Digital Divide: Electronic Commerce, Developing Countries and Declining Tax Revenues', *UNESCO Encyclopedia of Life Support Systems*, manuscript section 6.31.3.6.

Cockfield, A.J. (2004a) 'Formulary Taxation Versus the Arm's Length Principle: The Battle among Doubting Thomases, Purists, and Pragmatists', *Canadian Tax Journal*, 52(1): 114–23.

Cockfield, A.J. (2004b) 'Reforming the Permanent Establishment Principle through a Quantitative Economic Presence Test', *Tax Notes International*, 33(7).

Cockfield, A.J. (2004c) 'Toward a Law and Technology Theory', Canadian Association of Law Teachers Annual Meeting, 2 June 2004, Law Forum Panel on 'What is Legal Knowledge?', University of Winnipeg.

Cockfield, Arthur J. (2004d) 'Towards a Law and Technology Theory', *Manitoba Law Journal*, 30: 383.

Cockfield, Arthur J. (2006) 'The Rise of the OECD as Informal "World Tax Organization" through the Shaping of National Responses to E-commerce Tax Challenges', *Yale Journal of Law and Technology*.

Collins, Charles (2003) 'The Streamlined Sales Tax Agreement: What it Means for Business', *Tax Executive*.

Colm G. (1955) *Essays in Public Finance and Fiscal Policy* (Oxford: Oxford University Press).

Comer, Douglas E. (2000) *The Internet Book* (3rd edn, London: Prentice Hall), pp. 207–22.

Commission of the European Community (CEC) (1998a) DG XXI, 'Interim Report on the Implications of Electronic Commerce for VAT and Customs', XXI/98/0359-EN, 3 April 1998.

CEC (1998b) 'E-Commerce and Indirect Taxation', Communication to the Council of Ministers, the European Parliament and to the Economic and Social Committee (COM (98) 374) June 1998, <http://europa.eu.int/comm/dgs/taxation_customs/>.

CEC (1998c) 'Financing the European Union: Commission Report on the Operation of the Own Resources System', DGXIX, October 1998, Brussels, <www.europa.eu.int/comm/dg19/agenda2000/ownresources/html/index.htm>.

Commission of the European Community (1999), 'Harmonization of Turnover Taxes', Working Paper of the Directorate General XXI, 8 June 1999.

Commission of the European Community (2000) 'Explanatory Memorandum to the Proposal for a Council Directive amending the Sixth Directive as regards the value added tax arrangements applicable to certain services supplied by electronic means' (COM (2000) 349 final) June 7, 2000

Cooper, Graeme S. (1994) 'The Benefit Theory of Taxation', *Australian Tax Forum*, 11: 397.

Coopers and Lybrand Belgium (1998) 'Does Cyber-Commerce Necessitate a Revision of International Tax Concepts?', ed. International Bureau of Fiscal Documentation.

Cordell, A. and J. Ide (1994) 'The New Wealth of Nations: Taxing Cyberspace', paper prepared for annual meeting of the Club of Rome, November (Buenos Aires: Between the Lines Publishers).

Davies, S. (1998) 'Computer Program Claims', *EIPR*, pp. 429–33.

Davis, Linda (1995) *Nest of Vipers* (London: Orion).

Desai, Ashok V. (2002) 'India's Market Shares', *Business Standard* (New Delhi).

Doernberg, R. (1998) 'Electronic Commerce and International Tax Sharing', *Tax Notes International*, 16: 1013–22.

Doernberg, Richard L. and Luc Hinnekens (1999) *Electronic Commerce and International Taxation* (The Hague: Kluwer Law International).

Doernberg, Richard L., et al. (2001) *Electronic Commerce and Multijurisdictional Taxation* (London: Kluwer Law International).

Dorgan, B. (2000) 'Global Shell Games', *Washington Monthly*, <http://www.alternet.org/story/9464>.

Drake, William J. and Kalypso Nicolaidis (2000) 'Global Electronic Commerce and GATS', in Pierre Sauve and Robert M. Stern (eds), *GATS 2000: New Directions in Services Trade Liberalization* (Washington, DC: Brookings Institution), pp. 411–14.

Dryden, John (2000) *The Work of the OECD on Electronic Commerce* (Paris: OECD).

Due, John F. and John L. Mikesell (1994) *Sales Taxation: State and Local Structure and Administration*, (2nd edn, Washington, DC: Urban Institute Press).

Duff, David G. (2005) 'Private Property and Tax Policy in a Libertarian World: A Critical Review', *The Canadian Journal of Law & Jurisprudence*, 18: 23–45.

Eggermont, Tino (1998) 'The Commission's Work Programme for the Gradual Introduction of the New Common VAT System', European Commission, available at <http://www.ecu-activities.be/1998_2/eggermont.html>.

Epstein, Richard A. (1985) *Takings: Private Property and the Power of Eminent Domain* (Cambridge, MA: Harvard University Press).

Eriksen, Nils and Kevin Hulsebos (2000) 'Electronic Commerce and VAT: An Odyssey towards 2001', *VAT Monitor*, July/August.

Fairpo, Anne (1999) 'Electronic Commerce: U.K. Policy Document', *Tax Planning International's E-commerce*, 1(5).

Ferrette, Chelsea P. (2000) 'E-Commerce and International Political Economics: The Legal and Political Ramifications of the Internet on World Economies', *ILSA Journal of International and Comparative Law*.

Fleming, J. Clifton (2000) 'Electronic Commerce and the State and Federal Tax Bases', *Brigham Young University Law Review*.

Forgione, Aldo (2004) 'Taxing Obscene Profits: Removing Government Incentives for Internet Porn', Centre for Innovation Law and Policy.

Forst, David L. (1997) 'The Continuing Vitality of Source-Based Taxation in the Electronic Age', *Tax Notes International*, 15(8): 1455–73.

Fox, William F. (1998) 'Current Conditions and Policy Options', in Philip Dearborn (ed.), *Taxing Simply, Taxing Fairly* (Greater Washington Research Centre).

Fox, William F. and LeAnn Luna (2000) 'Taxing E-Commerce: Neutral Taxation is Best for the Industry and the Economy', *Quarterly Journal of Electronic Commerce*, pp. 139–50.

Fox, William F., Matthew N. Murray and LeAnn Luna (2005) 'How Should a Subnational Corporate Income Tax on Multistate Businesses Be Structured?', *National Tax Journal*, 58(1).

Frankman, Myron J. (1996) 'International Taxation: The Trajectory of an Idea from Lorimer to Brandt', *World Development*, 24 (May).

Frieden, Karl and Michael Porter (1996) 'The Taxation of Cyberspace: State Tax Issues Related to the Internet and Electronic Commerce', part 5 (visited October 2005) <http://www.caltax.org/andersen/contents.htm>, or *State Tax Notes*, 14: 1363–94.

Fudenberg, D. and J. Tirole (1999) *Game Theory* (Cambridge, MA: MIT Press).

Furche, Andreas and Graham Wrightson (1996) *Computer Money: A Systematic Overview of Payment Systems*, (Heidelberg: Dpunk).

Garicano, L. and S.N. Kaplan (2001) 'The Effects of Business-to-Business E-Commerce on Transaction Costs', *The Journal of Industrial Economics*, 49(4): 463–85.

General Accounting Office US (2000) 'Sales Taxes: Electronic Commerce Growth Presents Challenges: Revenue Losses Are Uncertain', GAO/GGD/OCE-00-165.

Genschel, Philipp (2005) 'Globalization and the Transformation of the Tax State', *European Review*, 13(1): 53–71.

Genschel, Philipp and Thomas Rixen (2005) 'International Tax Cooperation and National Tax Sovereignty', paper prepared for the conference on 'Market Making and Market Shaping in the Global Political Economy', Open University, Hagen, December 2005.

Gilmore, James S., III (1999) 'No Internet Tax: A Proposal Submitted to the "Policies & Options" Paper of the Advisory Commission on Electronic Commerce', 8 November 1999, available at <www.ecommercecommission.org>.

Glasner, Joanna (2002) 'U.S. Not Happy about EU Tax', May 8, <http://www.wired.com/news/print/0,1294,52378,00.html>.

Global Information Infrastructure Commission (2000) 'E-Commerce Taxation Principles: A GIIC Perspective', *GIIC Focus*, <http://www.giic.org/focus/ecommerce/ectax.asp>.

Goldsmith, Jack and Tim Wu (2006) *Who Controls the Internet? Illusions of a Borderless World* (New York: Oxford University Press).

Goolsbee, A. (2000) 'In a World without Borders: The Impact of Taxes on Internet Commerce', National Bureau of Economic Research (NBER), Working Paper no. 6863, Cambridge, MA.

Goolsbee, A. (2001) 'The Implications of Electronic Commerce for Fiscal Policy', *Journal of Economic Perspectives*, 15(1): 13–23.

Gordon, Suzanne E. (2001) 'Changing Concepts of Sovereignty and Jurisdiction in the Global Economy: Is There a Territorial Connection?', Working Paper Series # 1, The Canadian Centre for German and European Studies.

Goulder, Robert (2001) 'American Bar Association Section of Taxation Panel Eyes OECD Conclusions on Taxation of E-Commerce', *Tax Notes International*, 22: 360.

Greve, Michael S. (2003) 'Sell Globally, Tax Locally: Sales Tax Reform for the New Economy', in Kevin A. Hassett (ed.), *AEI Studies On Tax Reform* (Washington, DC: The AEI Press).

Hammond, Ray (1996) *Digital Business: Surviving and Thriving in an On-Line World* (London: Hodder and Stoughton).

Hardesty, David (2000a) 'EU Proposes New Taxes on Non-EU Sellers', *E-Commerce Tax News*, 18 June 2000, <http://www.ecommercetax.com>.

Hardesty, David (2000b) 'EU Proposes Electronic VAT Invoices in E-Commerce', *E-Commerce Tax News*, 19 November 2000, <http://www.ecommercetax.com>.

Hardesty, David (2000c) 'EU Continues Efforts to Tax Digital Products', *E-Commerce Tax News*, 22 October 2000, <http://www.ecommercetax.com>.

Hardesty, David (2001a) *Sales Tax and E-Commerce* (EcommerceTax.com).

Hardesty, David (2001b) 'California to Assert Nexus against Online Bookseller', *EcommerceTax.com*, 22 July 2001, <http://ecommercetax.com/doc/072201.htm>.

Hardesty, David (2002a) 'European VAT on Digital Sales', *EcommerceTax.com*, 3 March 2002, <www.ecommercetax.com/doc/030302.htm>.

Hardesty, David (2002b) 'Streamlined Sales and Use Tax Agreement – Part 1', *EcommerceTax.com*, 1 December 2002, <www.ecommercetax.com/SSTP.htm>.

Harris, D., R. Morck, J. Slemrod and B. Yeung (1993) 'Income Shifting in U.S. Multinational Corporations', in A. Giovannini, R. Hubbard and J. Slemrod (eds), *Studies in International Taxation* (Chicago, IL: University of Chicago Press).

Haufler, Andreas (2001) *Taxation in a Global Economy* (Cambridge: Cambridge University Press).

Hellerstein, Walter (1997a) 'State Taxation of Electronic Commerce', Symposium on Taxation and Electronic Commerce, *Tax Law Review*, Spring: 431–505.

Hellerstein, Walter (1997b) 'Telecommunications and Electronic Commerce: Overview and Appraisal', *State Tax Notes*, 12: 525.

Hellerstein, Walter (2001) 'Electronic Commerce and the Challenge for Tax Administration', paper presented to the United Nations Ad Hoc Group of Experts on International Cooperation in Tax Matters in Geneva, Switzerland, 12 September.

Hellerstein, Walter (2002) 'Electronic Commerce and the Challenge for Tax Administration', *Seminar on Revenue Implications of E-commerce on Development* (Geneva: Committee on Trade and Development – WTO).

Hellerstein, Walter (2003) 'Jurisdiction to Tax Income and Consumption in the New Economy: A Theoretical and Comparative Perspective', *Georgia Law Review*, 38: 1–70.

Hellerstein, Jerome R. and Walter Hellerstein (1992) 'State Taxation: Sales and Use, Personal Income, and Death and Gift Taxes', *State Tax Notes*, 13.

Hellerstein, Jerome R. and Walter Hellerstein (1998) *State Taxation* (3rd edn, Boston, MA: Warren Gorham Lamont).

Hettich, Walter and Stanley L. Winer (2002) 'Rules, Politics and the Normative Analysis of Taxation', in Richard Wagner and Jurgen Backhouse (eds), *Handbook of Public Finance* (Boston: Kluwer Academic Publishers).

Hey, Friedrich E.F. (1999) 'German Authorities Rule That Server Does Not Constitute PE', *Tax Notes International*, 19: 635.

Hines, James R. Jr (1999) 'Lessons from Behavioural Responses to International Taxation', *National Tax Journal*, 52(2): 305–22.

Hinnekens, Luc (1998) 'The Challenges of Applying VAT and Income Tax', *Intertax*, 26: 52–70.

Hobbes, T. (1968 [1651]) *Leviathan* (New York: Penguin Books).

Hoffman, Philip T. and Kathryn Norberg (1994) *Fiscal Crises, Liberty and Representative Government* (Stanford, CA: Stanford University Press).

Holcombe, Randall G. (1999) *Public Finance Government Revenues and Expenditures in the United States Economy* (St Paul, MN: West).

Houtzager, Mark and Jeroen Tinholt (1998) 'E-Commerce and VAT', in E.D. Albarda et al., *Caught in the Web: The Tax and Legal Implications of Electronic Commerce* (Deventer), pp 99–102.

Ivinson, Jonathan (2003) 'Why the EU VAT and E-commerce Directive Does Not Work', *International Tax Review* (London).

Ivinson, Jonathan (2004) 'Overstepping The Boundary: How the EU Got It Wrong on E-Commerce', *Computer and Telecommunications Law Review*, 10(1): 1–4.

James, Simon (2001) 'Taxation Research as Economic Research', University of Exeter Research Discussion Paper, no. 01/07.

Jenkins, Peter (1999) 'VAT and Electronic Commerce: The Challenges and Opportunities', *VAT Monitor*, 10(1): 4.

Jenkins, Peter (2000) 'The Application of VAT to E-Commerce' (Ernst and Young).

Jenkins, Peter (2001) 'The Application of VAT to E-Commerce in the EU', *Tax Notes International*, 22 (22 January).

Johnson, Peter A. (2003) 'A Current Calculation of Uncollected Sales Tax Arising From Internet Growth', The Direct Marketing Association, March 11.

Jones, R. and S. Basu (2002) 'Taxation of Electronic Commerce: A Developing Problem', *International Review of Law Computers & Technology*, 16(1): 38–42.

Kabisch, Volker (2000) 'Tax Aspects of International Electronic Commerce', *Electronic Commerce Legal Issues Platform* (ECLIP – Esprit project 27028).

Kahn, Robert E. and Vinton G. Cerf (2004) 'What is the Internet (and What Makes It Work)', in Mark N. Cooper (ed.), *Open Architecture as Communications Policy: Preserving Internet Freedom in The Broadband Era* (Stanford, CA: Stanford Center for Internet and Society).

Kaldor, Nicolas (1955) *An Expenditure Tax* (London: George Allen and Unwin).

Kaufman, Nancy H. (1998) 'Fairness and the Taxation of International Income', *Law and Policy in Intentional Business*, 29: 145.

Keat, Khoo Chuan (2001) 'Towards a Global Tax System', available at <www.pwcglobal.com/servlet>, accessed 10 November 2001.

Kee, Charles, E. (2001) 'Taxing the Internet: The State's Next Frontier', *Journal of State Taxation*, pp. 1–14.

Kitchin, Rob (1998) *Cyberspace: The World in Wires* (Chichester: John Wiley & Sons).

Kobrin, Stephen J. (1997) 'Electronic Cash and the End of National Markets', *Foreign Policy*, 107 (summer): 65–77.

Kobrin, Stephen J. (2000) 'Taxing Internet Transactions', *University of Pennsylvania Journal of International Economic Law*, 21.

Kobrin, Stephen J. (2001) 'Territoriality and Governance of Cyberspace', *Journal of International Business Studies*, 32(4): 687–704.

Kogut, Bruce (2003) *The Global Internet Economy* (Cambridge, MA: MIT Press).

Köthenbürger, Marko and Bernd Rahmann (1999) 'Taxing E-commerce', in T. Gries and L. Suhl, *Economic Aspects of Digital Information Technologies* (Wiesbaden: Gabler Edition Wissenschaft).

Krever, R. (2000) 'Electronic Commerce and Taxation: A Summary of Emerging Issues', *Asia-Pacific Tax Bulletin*, 6(6): 151–63.

Krever, Richard (2001) 'Electronic Commerce and Taxation: An Overview of Key Issues', *Asia-Pacific Tax Bulletin*.

Lambert, Howard (1998) 'VAT and Electronic Commerce: European Union Insights into the Challenges Ahead', *Tax Notes International*, 17 (November 23).

Lau, Collin and Andrew Halkyard (2003) 'From E-Commerce to E-Business Taxation', *Asia-Pacific Tax Bulletin*, 9(1): 2–13.

Lebovitz, Michael S. and Theodore P. Seto (2001) 'The Fundamental Problem of International Taxation', *Loyola of Los Angeles International and Comparative Law Review*, 23(4): 529.

Lee, Boon-Chye and Olujoke Longe-Akindemowo (1998) 'Regulatory Issues in Electronic Money: A Legal-Economics Analysis', University of Wollongong Department of Economics, Working Paper Series.

Lee, Chang Hee (1999) 'Impact of E-Commerce on Allocation of Tax Revenue between Developed and Developing Countries', *Tax Notes International*, 18: 2569.

Leibfritz, W., J. Thornton and A. Bibbee (1997) 'Taxation and Economic Performance', OECD Economics Department Working Papers, no. 176.

Leiner, Barry M., et al. (2003) 'A Brief History of the Internet', <http://www.isoc. org/internet/history/brief.shtml>, last visited 26 August 2005.

Lejeune, Ine (1998) 'Does Cyber-Commerce Necessitate a Revision of International Tax Concepts?', *European Tax Notes*, 38: 50–58.

Lejeune, Ine, Bart Vanham, Isabelle Verlinden and Alain Verbeken (1998) 'Does Cyber-Commerce Necessitate a Revision of International Tax Concepts?', part I, *European Taxation*, 38: 4.

Lessig, Lawrence (1999) *Code and Other Laws of Cyberspace* (New York: Basic Books).

Levine, Howard J. and David A. Weintraub (2000) 'When Does E-Commerce Result in a Permanent Establishment? The OECD's initial response', *Tax Management International Journal*, 4 (14 April 2000): 219.

Li, Jinyan (1999) 'Rethinking Canada's Source Rules in the Age of Electronic Commerce: Part 2', *Canadian Tax Journal*, 47(6): 1411–78.

Li, Jinyan (2001) 'Slicing the Digital Pie with a Traditional Knife: Effectiveness of the Arm's Length Principle in the Age of E-Commerce', *Tax Notes International*, 24(8): 775–816.

Li, Jinyan (2002) 'Global Profit Split: An Evolutionary Approach to International Income Allocation', *Canadian Tax Journal*, 50(3): 823–83.

Li, Jinyan (2003) *International Taxation in the Age of Electronic Commerce: A Comparative Study* (Toronto: Canadian Tax Foundation).

Ligthart, Jenny E. (2004a) 'Consumption Taxation in a Digital World: A Primer', CentER Discussion Paper, no. 2004-12, Tilburg University.

Ligthart, J.E. (2004b) 'Consumption Taxation in a Digital World: A Primer', *Canadian Tax Journal*, 52(4): 1078.

Lockwood, B. (2001) 'Tax Competition and Tax Coordination under Destination and Origin Principles: A Synthesis', *Journal of Public Economics*, 81: 279–319.

Lodin, Sven-Olof (2001) 'International Tax Issues in a Rapidly Changing World', *Bulletin for International Fiscal Documentation*, 55(1): 2–7.

Lucking-Reiley, David and Daniel F. Spulber (2001) 'Business to Business Electronic Commerce', *Journal of Economic Perspectives*, 15(1): 55–68.

Lukas, Aaron (1999) 'Tax Bytes: A Primer on the Taxation of Electronic Commerce', Cato Institute, Trade Policy Analysis, no. 9, 17 December 1999 (028.2/C29).

Lyons, Susan M. (1997) 'An International Consensus Needed in Taxation of Electronic Commerce', *Tax Notes International*, 14: 1199.

McDaniel, Paul R. (1994) 'Formulary Taxation in the North American Free Trade Zone', *Tax Law Review*, 49(4): 691–744.

McKeown, Rich (2000) 'Questioning the Viability of the Sales Tax: Can It Be Simplified to Create a Level Playing Field?', Brigham Young University Law Review, Symposium Transcripts.

McLure, Charles E. Jr (1984) 'Defining a Unitary Business: An Economist's View', in Charles E. McLure (ed.), *The State Corporate Income Tax* (Stanford, CA: Hoover Institution Press).

McLure, Charles E. Jr (1986) 'Tax Competition: Is What's Good for the Private Goose Also Good for the Public Gander?', *National Tax Journal*, 39: 341–8.

McLure, Charles E. Jr (1997a) 'Taxation of Electronic Commerce: Economic Objectives, Technological Constraints, and Tax Laws', *Tax Law Review*, Symposium on Taxation and Electronic Commerce.

McLure, Charles E. Jr (1997b) 'Taxation of Electronic Commerce: Economic Objectives, Technological Constraints, and Tax Laws', *Tax Law Review*, 52(3): 269–423.

McLure, Charles E. Jr (1997c) 'Electronic Commerce, State Sales Taxation and Intergovernmental Fiscal Relations', *National Tax Journal*, 50(4): 731–49.

McLure, Charles (1998) 'Implementing State Corporate Income Taxes in the Digital Age', *National Tax Journal*, 53(4): 1287–306.

McLure, Charles E. Jr (1999a) 'The Taxation of Electronic Commerce: Background and Proposal', paper prepared for discussion at a Hoover Institution conference on 'Public Policy and the Internet: Taxation and Privacy', 12 October 1999; in Nicholas Imparato (ed.), *Public Policy and the Internet: Taxation and Privacy* (Stanford, CA: Hoover Press).

McLure, Charles E. Jr (1999b) *The Tax Assignment Problem: Conceptual and Administrative Considerations in Achieving Subnational Fiscal Autonomy* (Washington, DC: World Bank).

McLure, Charles E. Jr (2000) 'Alternatives to the Concept of Permanent Establishment', Report of the Proceedings of the World Tax Conference: Taxes Without Borders 61-15 (CTF 2000).

McLure, Charles E. (2001a) 'Globalization, Tax Rules and National Sovereignty', *Bulletin for International Fiscal Documentation*, 55(8): 328–41.

McLure, Charles E. (2001b) 'Taxation of Electronic Commerce in the European Union', paper prepared for the Hoover Institution, Stanford University.

Mann, Catherine L. (2000) 'Electronic Commerce in Developing Countries: Issues for Domestic Policy and WTO Negotiations', Working Paper, Institute for International Economics, March 2000.

Mann, Catherine L., Sue E. Eckert and Sarah C. Knight (2000) *Global Electronic Commerce: A Policy Primer* (Washington, DC: Institute for International Economics).

Mazerov, Michael and Iris J. Lav (1998) 'A Federal "Moratorium" on Internet Commerce Taxes Would Erode State and Local Revenues and Shift Burdens to Lower-Income Households', Centre on Budget and Policy Priorities, <http://www.cbpp.org/index.html>, 11 May 1998, <www.cbpp.org/512webtax.htm#III. A Moratorium on Taxation>.

Meijers, Huub (1998) 'Fiscal Impacts of the Growing Use of Advanced Communication Technologies and Services: A Quantitative Analysis', ACTS/FAIR working paper 34.

Metcalf, Gilbert E. (1999) 'Consumption Taxation', in *The Encyclopaedia of Taxation and Tax Policy*, ed. Joseph J. Cordes, Robert D. Ebel and Jane G. Gravelle (Washington, DC: Urban Institute Press).

Mitchell, Richard (1997) 'United States-Brazil Bilateral Income Tax Treaty Negotiations', *Hastings International & Computer Law Review*, 21: 209.

Morse, Geoffrey and David Williams (2004) *Davis: Principle of Tax Law* (5th edn, London: Sweet and Maxwell).

Mukherji, Rahul (2002) 'Governing the Taxation of Digitized Trade', Technical Report Working Paper no. 2002/05, ASARC, RSPAS, ANU.

Multistate Tax Commission (2003) 'Federalism at Risk', *State Tax Notes* 30(7).

Musgrave, Peggy B. (2006) 'Combining Fiscal Sovereignty and Coordination: National Taxation in a Globalizing World', in I. Kaul und P. Conceicao (eds), *The New Public Finance: Responding to Global Challenges* (New York: Oxford University Press).

Musgrave, Richard (1994) 'Fiscal Functions of the Public Sector', in *Defining the Role of Government: Economic Perspectives On The State*, 1, 3 (Queen's University School of Policy Studies).

Musgrave, R.A. and P.B. Musgrave (1973) *Public Finance in Theory and Practice* (New York: McGraw-Hill).

Myerson, Allen R. (1998) 'Ideas & Trends: Virtual Migrants: Need Programmers? Surf Abroad', *New York Times* (New York), 18 January 1998.

Neubig, Tom and Satya Poddar (2000) 'Blurred Tax Boundaries: The Economy's Implications for Tax Policy', *Tax Notes*, 28 August 2000.

Noord, Paul van den and Christopher Heady (2001) 'Surveillance of Tax Policies: A Synthesis of Findings in Economic Surveys', Economics Department Working Papers, no. 303, OECD, <http: www.oecd.org/eco/eco>.

OECD (1995) *Transfer Pricing Guidelines for Multinational Enterprises and Tax Administrations* (Paris: OECD).

OECD (1997a) 'Electronic Commerce: The Challenges to Tax Authorities and Taxpayers', An Informal Round Table Discussion between Business and Government, November 1997.

OECD (1997b) *Electronic Commerce: The Challenges to Tax Authorities and Taxpayers* (Paris: OECD).

OECD (1997c) 'Report on the Turku Conference', conference held on 19–21 November, Turku, Finland.

OECD (1998a) 'A Borderless World: Realising the Potential of Global Electronic Commerce', Report on the OECD Ministerial Conference, 7–9 October 1998, Ottawa, Canada.

OECD (1998b) 'Electronic Commerce: Taxation Framework Conditions', a report by the Committee on Fiscal Affairs of the OECD.

OECD (1998c) 'The Economic and Social Impact of Electronic Commerce: Preliminary Findings and Research Agenda', 24 August 1998, DSTI/ICCP (98) 15/PART5, available at <www.oecd.org/subject/e_commerce/summary.htm>.

OECD (1998d) 'Forces Shaping Tax Policy', *OECD Economic Outlook*, 1 June 1998.

OECD (1998e) *Model Tax Convention on Income and Capital* (Paris: OECD).

OECD (1998f) *Harmful Tax Competition: An Emerging Global Issue* (Paris: OECD).

OECD (1998g) 'Electronic Commerce: A Discussion Paper on Taxation Issues', Committee on Fiscal Affairs of the OECD.

OECD (1999) 'Electronic Commerce: Tax Collection Mechanisms', DAFFE/CFA/ WP9/EC/WD(99)4/REV2.

OECD (2000a) 'Report on Tax and e-Commerce', Technology Technical Advisory Group (TAG) (Paris: OECD).

OECD (2000b) 'Report by the Consumption Tax Technical Advisory Group (TAG)', December 2000.

OECD (2000c) 'The Application of the Permanent Establishment Definition in the Context of Electronic Commerce: Revised Draft', *Tax Notes International*, 20 (13 March): 1199.

OECD (2000d) 'E-Commerce: Implementing the Ottawa Taxation Framework Conditions', a report by the Committee on Fiscal Affairs.

OECD (2001a) 'Consumption Tax Aspects of Electronic Commerce', a report from Working Party No. 9 on Consumption Taxes to the Committee on Fiscal Affairs, 21 February.

OECD (2001b) 'Progresses towards Achieving an International Consensus on the Tax Treatment of E-commerce', news release, 12 February 2001, <http://www. oecde.org/media/release/nw01-15a.htm>.

OECD (2001c) 'The Impact of the Communications Revolution on the Application of "Place of Effective Management" as a Tie Breaker Rule', February 2001, <http:// w.w.w.oecd.org/daf/fa/e_com/ec_4_POEM_Eng.pdf>.

OECD (2001d) *Taxation and Electronic Commerce* (Paris: OECD).

OECD (2003a) *Model Tax Convention on Income and on Capital: Condensed Version* (Paris: OECD).

OECD (2003b) *Model Tax Convention on Income and on Capital* (Paris: OECD).

OECD (2005) 'The Application of Consumption Taxes to the International Trade in Services and Intangibles: Progress Report and Draft Principles, Informal Working Group of Working Party 9 of the Committee of Fiscal Affairs', OECD Centre for Tax Policy and Administration, 11 February 2005.

Ogley, Adrian (1993) *The Principles of International Tax* (London: Interfisc).

Ott, D.H. (1987) *Public International Law and the Modern World* (London: Pitman).

Owens, Jeffrey (1997a) 'Emerging Issues in Tax Reform: The Perspective of an International Bureaucrat', *Tax Notes International*, 22: 2035.

Owens, Jeffrey (1997b) 'The Tax Man Cometh to Cyberspace', paper presented at the Harvard Law School International Tax Program Symposium on Multi-jurisdictional Taxation of Electronic Commerce, 5 April 1997.

Owens, Jeffrey (1997c) 'The Tax Man Cometh to Cyberspace', *Tax Notes International*, 14: 1833.

Owens, Jeffrey (1998) 'Taxation within a Context of Economic Globalization', *Bulletin for International Fiscal Documentation*, 52: 290–96.

Owens, Jeffrey (1999) 'Electronic Commerce Answering the Emerging Taxation Challenges', paper presented to the US Advisory Commission on Electronic Commerce.

Palmer, Robert L. (1989) 'Toward Unilateral Coherence in Determining Jurisdiction to Tax Income', *Harvard International Law Journal*, 30: 6.

Panagariya, Arvind (2001) 'E-commerce, WTO and Developing Countries', *The World Economy*, 23(8): 959–78.

Paris, Roland (2001) 'Global Taxation and the Transformation of the State', Department of Political Science, University of Colorado at Boulder, paper presented at the 2001 Annual Convention of the American Political Science Association, San Francisco, 30 August – 2 September 2001.

Pérez-Esteve, Rosa and Ludger Schuknecht (1999) 'A Quantitative Assessment of Electronic Commerce', World Trade Organization, Economic Research and Analysis Division, Staff Working Paper ERAD-99-01, September 1999.

Peschcke-Koedt, Lisa (1998) 'A Practical Approach to Permanent Establishment Issues in a Multinational Enterprise', *Tax Notes International*, 16: 1601.

Peters, B. Guy (1991) *The Politics of Taxation: A Comparative Perspective* (Cambridge: Blackwell).

Picciotto, S. (1992) *International Business Taxation: A Study in the Internationalization of Business Regulation* (London: Weidenfeld and Nicoloson).

Picciotto, S. (2000) 'Lessons of the MAI: Towards a New Regulatory Framework for International Investment', *Law, Social Justice and Global Development (LGD)*, 2000(1), <http://elj.warwick.ac.uk/global/issue/2000-1/picciotto.html>.

Pinto, Dale (2002) 'E-Commerce and Source Based Income Taxation', Doctoral Series, vol. 6, International Bureau of Fiscal Documentation, Academic Council.

Pinto, Dale (2005a) 'A New Three-Tier Proposal for Determining Corporate Residence Based Principally on Individual Residence', *Asia-Pacific Tax Bulletin*, January/February.

Pinto, Dale (2005b) '"Conservative" and "Radical" Alternatives for Taxing E-Commerce (Part 1)', *Journal of International Taxation*.

Radler, Albert J. (2000) 'The Future of Exchange of Information', in Victor Uckmar (ed.), *L'evoluzione dell'ordinamento tributario italiano* (Milan: CEDAM).

Rasmussen, Sandemann (2004) 'On the Possibility and Desirability of Taxing E-Commerce', Working Paper no. 2004-08, Department of Economics, School Of Economics and Management, University of Aarhus.

Reese, J. Michael (2003) 'Does the Streamlined Agreement Signal the End of Quill in the Area of E-Commerce?', *State Tax Notes*, 1 September: 639.

Rixen, T. and I. Rohlfing (2004) 'Bilateralism and Multilaterlism: Institutional Choice in International Cooperation', paper presented at the American Political Science Association Meeting, Chicago, 3–7 September 2004.

Rosen, Harvey S. (1995) *Public Finance* (4th edn, Chicago, IL: Irwin).

Rosendorff, B. Peter and Helen V. Milner (2001) 'The Optimal Design of International Trade Institutions', *International Organization*, 55(4): 829–57.

Rowland, Diane and Elizabeth Macdonald (2005) *Information and Technology Law* (London: Cavendish).

Ryan, Terry and Eric Miethke (1998) 'The Seller-State Option: Solving the Electronic Commerce Dilemma', *State Tax Notes*, 5 October: 881–92.

Salter, Sarah W. (2002) 'E-Commerce and International Taxation', *New England Journal of International and Comparative Law*, 8(1): 6–17.

Schaefer, B. (1999) 'International Taxation of Electronic Commerce Income: A Proposal to Utilize Software Agents for Source-Based Taxation', *Santa Clara Computer and High Technology Law Journal*, 16: 111.

Schäfer, Anne and Christoph Spengel (2002) 'ICT and International Corporate Taxation: Tax Attributes and Scope of Taxation', ZEW Discussion Paper no. 02-81, Centre for European Economic Research (ZEW) and University of Mannheim.

Schenk, Alan and Oliver Oldman (2000) *Value Added Tax* (Ardsley, NY: Transnational).

Schenk, Alan and Oliver Oldman (2006) *Value Added Tax: A Comparative Approach* (Cambridge: Cambridge University Press).

Schuknecht, L. (1999) 'A Quantitative Assessment of Electronic Commerce', WTO Working Paper ERAD-99-01, September 1999, Geneva.

Sharma, Sushil K. (2005) 'Socio-Economic Impacts and Influences of E-Commerce in a Digital Economy', in H.S. Kehal, V.P. Singh (eds), *Digital Economy: Impacts, Influences and Challenges* (Hershey, PA: Idea).

Sher, Judd A. (1999) 'A Band-Aid or Surgery: It is Time to Evaluate the Health of the Permanent Establishment Concept', *Tax Management Journal*, 7: 415–26.

Silhan, Sidney S. (1999) 'If It Ain't Broke Don't Fix It: An Argument for the Codification of the Quill Standard for Taxing Internet Commerce', *Chicago-Kent Law Review*, 76.

Simon, Steven John (2002) 'Electronic Commerce: A Taxing Dilemma', *Informing Science*, 5(1): 29–41.

Skaar, Arvid A. (1991) *Permanent Establishment: Erosion of a Tax Treaty Principle* (Deventer: Kluwer Law and Taxation Publication).

Slemrod, Joel (1990) 'Optimal Taxation and Optimal Tax Systems', *Journal of Economic Perspectives*, 4(1): 157–78.

Smith, Adam (1937 [1776]) *The Wealth of Nations* (New York: Modern Library).

Smith, Adam (1977) *An Inquiry into the Nature and Causes of The Wealth of Nations* (1776), ed. Edwin Cannan (Chicago, IL: University of Chicago Press) vol. 2.

Smith, Brian W. and Paul S. Tufaro (1998) 'To Certify or Not to Certify? The OCC Opens the Door to Digital Signature Certification', *Ohio Northern University Law Review*, 24: 813.

Snel, Jan L.N. (2000) 'European Union Reaches out across Borders: EU Proposes to Tax US-based E-commerce Companies with Value Added Tax in the EU', Baker & McKenzie, Palo Alto, San Francisco.

Solomon, Elinor Harris (1997) *Virtual Money* (New York: Oxford University Press).

Sprague, Gary D. and Rachel Hersey (2003) 'Permanent Establishments and Internet-Enabled Enterprises: The Physical Presence and Contract Concluding Dependent Agent Tests', 27–28 February 2003, 1, available at <http://www.bmck.com/ecommerce/tax-art1.doc>.

Stiglitz, Joseph E. (1988) *Economics of the Public Sector* (2nd edn, New York and London: W.W. Norton & Co.).

Sweet, John K. (1998) 'Formulating International Tax Laws in the Age of Electronic Commerce: The Possible Ascendancy of Residence-Based Taxation in an Era of Eroding Traditional Income Tax Principles', *University of Pennsylvania Law Review*, 146: 1949.

Tadmore, Niv (2004) 'Further Discussion on Income Characterization', *Canadian Tax Journal*, 52(1): 124–40.

Tait, Alain A. (1998) *Value Added Tax*, 3 (Washington, DC: International Monetary Fund).

Tanzi, V. (1996) 'Globalization, Tax Competition and the Future of Tax Systems', International Monetary Fund Working Paper, Washington, DC.

Tanzi, V. (1999) 'Is There a Need for a World Tax Organization?', in A. Razin and E. Sadka (eds), *Economics of Globalization: Policy Perspectives from Public Economics* (Cambridge: Cambridge University Press), pp. 173–86.

Tanzi, Vito (2000) 'Globalization, Technological Developments, and the Work of Fiscal Termites', International Monetary Fund Working Paper 00/181, Washington, DC.

Tanzi, Vito and Howell Zee (2001) 'Tax Policy for Developing Countries', International Monetary Fund, Economic Issue no. 27, March 2001, <http://www.imf.org/external/index.htm>.

Tax Justice Briefing (2005) *Source and Residence Taxation* (Tax Justice Network).

Taylor, A. Scott (2000) 'An Ideal E-Commerce Consumption Tax in a Global Economy', *BILETA 2000: World Wide Law*, <www.bileta.ac.uk>.

Taylor, Dominic and Adrian Ogely (1997) 'VAT and Telecommunications in the European Union: An Update', *Tax Notes International*, 3 November 1997.

Teltscher, Susanne (2000) 'Tariffs, Taxes and Electronic Commerce: Revenue Implications for Developing Countries', UNCTAD Study Series on 'Policy Issues in International Trade and Commodities', no. 5 UNCTAD/ITCD/TAB/5, Geneva.

Teltscher, Susanne (2001) 'Measuring Electronic Commerce in Developing Countries', UNCTAD's Electronic Commerce and Development Report.

Terra, Ben (1998) *The Place of Supply in European VAT* (Boston, MA and The Hague: Kluwer Law International).

Terra, Ben and Julie Kajus (1992) *Value Added Tax in the EC after 1992* (Boston, MA and Deventer: Kluwer Law and Taxation Publishers).

Thomas, David (2001) 'Current Issues in US State and Federal Taxation of Electronic Commerce', paper presented at 16th Annual Conference, BILETA (2001), <www.bileta.ac.uk>.

Tillinghast, David R. (1996) 'The Impact of the Internet on the Taxation of Informational Transactions', *Bulletin for International Fiscal Documentation*, 50: 524–6.

Todd, Paul (2005) *E-Commerce Law* (London: Cavendish).

UNCTAD (1996) 'Incentives and Foreign Direct Investment', UNCTAD/DTCI/28, Current Studies, Series A, no. 30, Geneva.

UNCTAD (2000) *Taxation: On Issues in International Investment Agreements* (New York and Geneva: UN).

UNCTAD (2003) *E-commerce and Development Report, 2003* (New York and Geneva: UNCTAD)

UNCTAD (2004) *E-commerce and Development Report, 2004* (New York and Geneva: UNCTAD)

Vann, R.J. (1991) 'A Model Tax Treaty for the Asian-Pacific Region? (Part I)', *Bulletin for International Fiscal Documentation*, 45(3): 99–111.

Varian Hal R. (1996) 'Differential Pricing and Efficiency', *First Monday*, available at <http://www.firstmonday.dk/issues/issue2/different/>.

Vogel, Klaus (1997) *Double Taxation Conventions* (Boston, MA and The Hague: Kluwer Law International).

Vogel, Klaus (1998) 'Worldwide vs Source Taxation of Income: A Review and Re-evaluation of Arguments (Part III)', *Intertax*, 11: 394–5.

Wagner, Andrew and Wade Anderson (1999) 'Origin-Based Taxation of Internet Commerce', *State Tax Notes*, 19 July: 187–92.

Wagner, Elizabeth (2000) 'Advisory Commission on Electronic Commerce: Activities and Findings', *Journal of International Economic Law*, 21: 659.

Ward, Burke T. and Janice C. Sipior (2004) 'To Tax or Not To Tax E-Commerce: A United States Perspective', *Journal of Electronic Commerce Research*, 5(3): 172–80.

Warren, Alvin (1980) 'Would a Consumption Tax Be Fairer Than an Income Tax?', *Yale Law Journal*, 89: 1081–124.

Warren, Alvin C. Jr (2001) 'Income Tax Discrimination against International Commerce', *Tax Law Review*, 54: 131.

Weiner, Stuart E. (1999) 'Electronic Payments in the U.S. Economy: An Overview', *Federal Reserve Bank of Kansas City Economic Review*, 84(4) (Fourth Quarter, 1999): 53–64.

Westberg, Bjorn (2002) *Cross-border Taxation of E-Commerce* (Amsterdam: IBFD).

Wigand, R.T. (1997) 'Electronic Commerce: Definition, Theory and Context', *The Information Society*, 13: 1–16.

Wilson, J.D. (1999) 'Theories of Tax Competition', *National Tax Journal*, 52: 269–304.

WTO (1994) *The Results of the Uruguay Round of Multilateral Trade Negotiations, The Legal Texts* (Geneva: WTO, GATT Secretariat).

Yang, J.G.S., C. Chang and R. Xing (2005) 'Current Status of Internet Commerce Taxation', *Journal of State Taxation*, 23(3): 56–661.

Zapata, Sonia (1998) 'The Latin American Approach to the Concept of Permanent Establishment in Tax Treaties with Developed Countries', *Bulletin for International Fiscal Documentation*, 52(6): 252–61.

Zee, Howell H. (1998) 'Taxation of Financial Capital in a Globalized Environment: The Role of Withholding Taxes', *National Tax Journal*, 51(3) (September 1998): 587–99.

Index